THE POSTMODERN SCENE

Acknowledgements

Art Work

Ch. 1, Calvin Klein perfume (sample); Ch. 2, Giorgio de Chirico *Landscape Painter*; Ch. 4, ⁕René Magritte 1986/Vis-Art *The False Mirror*, 1928; ⁕Max Ernst 1986/Vis-Art *The Robing of the Bride*; Ch. 5, ⁕René Magritte 1986/Vis-Art *La clef des champs*; Ch. 6, *Roland Barthes by Roland Barthes*, New York: Hill and Wang, reproduction of family photograph, p. 9, ch. 9; Gustave Doré, *The Wolf and the Lamb*, 1868; J.M. William Turner, *The Eruption of Vesuvius*, Yale Center for British Art, Paul Mellon Collection; Vittore Carpaccio *St. George and the Dragon*, 16th century Italian; ⁕Pierre Bonnard Vis-Art/1986, *Nude Before a Mirror*; Ch. 11, Francesca Woodman, *No. 5*, New York, 1979-80, *No. 25 from Space* ², Providence, 1975-76, *No. 26 House #3*, Providence, 1975-76. By permission from a special exhibit at Wellseley College Museum and Hunter College Art Gallery, Feb.-June 1986; Edward Hopper, *Rooms by the Sea*, Yale University Art Gallery, bequest of Stephen Carlton Clark, B.A., 1903; Edward Hopper, *High Noon*, private collection, Dayton, Ohio; Edward Hopper, *Office in a Small City*, The Metropolitan Museum of Art; Eric Fischl, *Bad Boy* 1981; Eric Fischl, *Daddy's Girl*, 1984, Collection of Robert and Doris Hillman; Eric Fischl, *Inside out*, 1983; Eric Fischl, *A Woman Possessed*, 1981, collection of Sable-Castelli Gallery Ltd; Alex Colville, *Pacific*, 1967, private collection, Toronto, Ontario; Alex Colville, *Morning*, 1981, Serigraph, Mira Godard Gallery; Alex Colville, *Western Star* 1985.

We are grateful to Alex Colville and Eric Fischl for permission to reproduce their works.

Articles

Ch. 8, An earlier and shorter version of this chapter originally appeared in *Theory, Culture and Society*, Vol. 2, No. 3, 1985; Ch. 10, This essay first appeared in *The Structural Allegory: Reconstructive Encounters with the New French Thought*, John Fekete, ed., Minneapolis: University of Minnesota Press, 1984. Earlier versions of several of the articles first appeared in the *Canadian Journal of Political and Social Theory*. Ch. 1, "the body as a torture chamber (death trap) and a pleasure palace", Michael A. Weinstein, Purdue University; Part II, "Sign Crimes", Andrew Wernick, Trent University.

About the Authors

Arthur Kroker is the founding editor of the *Canadian Journal of Political and Social Theory*. He teaches political science and the humanities at Concordia University, Montréal.

David Cook teaches political theory at Erindale College, University of Toronto.

THE POSTMODERN SCENE

Excremental Culture and Hyper-Aesthetics

Arthur Kroker • David Cook

St. Martin's Press
New York

First published in the United States of America in 1986

Printed in Canada

ISBN 0-312-63228-2
ISBN 0-312-63229-0 (pbk.)

Library of Congress Cataloging-in-Publication Data

Kroker, Arthur, 1945-
  The postmodern scene

Bibliography: p.
1. Postmodernism   2.   Arts — Philosophy.
3.   Avant-garde (Aesthetics) — History — 20th century.
I.   Cook, David, 1946-   II.   Title   III.   Title:
Post-modern scene
NX456.5.P66K75   1986   700'.9'04   86-21990
ISBN 0-312-63228-2
ISBN 0-312-63229-0 (pbk.)

CONTENTS

I

SUNSHINE REPORTS:
THESES ON THE POSTMODERN SCENE

Postmodernism and Aesthetics

What is the postmodern scene? Baudrillard's excremental culture? Or a final homecoming to a technoscape where a "body without organs" (Artaud), a "negative space" (Rosalind Krauss), a "pure implosion" (Lyotard), a "looking away" (Barthes) or an "aleatory mechanism" (Serres) is now first nature and thus the terrain of a new political refusal?

And what, then, of the place of art and theory in the postmodern scene? Signs of detritus, wreckage and refuse which, moving at the edge of fascination and despair, signal that this is the age of the death of the social and the triumph of excremental culture? Or the first glimmerings of that fateful "no" which, as Jaspers said, marks the furthest frontier of seduction and power?

Is this, in fact, the age of the "anti-aesthetic"? Or is the anti-aesthetic already on its way towards the nomination of a new aesthetic moment? Postmodernism and the Anti-Aesthetic or Ultramodernism and Hyper-Aesthetics? Or have we already passed through to that silent region where the only sound is Bataille's *'part maudite'* where even desire has lost its sovereignty as the sign of a privileged transgression yet to come? Or are we still trapped in that twilight time first nominated by Nietzsche — the crucified Dionysus?

The essays in *The Postmodern Scene* trace key continuities and ruptures in contemporary and classical negotiations of the postmodern condition. It is our general thesis that the postmodern scene in fact, begins in the fourth century with the Augustinian subversion of embodied power, and that everything since the Augustinian refusal has been nothing but a fantastic and grisly implosion of experience as Western culture itself runs under the signs of passive and suicidal nihilism. Or was it not perhaps, even before this, in the Lucretian theory of the physical world that Serres calls the *simulacrum*? Or was it later, in the abandonment of reason in Kant's aesthetic liberalism of the third critique? And what of late twentieth-century experience? Ours is a *fin-de-millenium* consciousness which, existing at the end of history in the twilight time of ultramodernism (of technology) and hyper-primitivism (of public moods), uncovers a great arc of disintegration and decay against the background radiation of parody, kitsch, and burnout.

We are now *au-delà* of Nietzsche's time. Not only because postmodernism implies living with Nietzsche's insight that existence is a throw of the dice across the "spider's web," but because of Foucault's even more devastating subversion of transgression itself. In "Preface to Transgression", his meditation on Nietzsche and Bataille, Foucault wrote:

> Transgression, then, is not limited to the limit as black to white, the prohibited to the lawful, the outside to the inside, or as the open area of a building to its enclosed spaces. Rather their relationship takes the form of a spiral which no simple infraction can exhaust. Perhaps it is like a flash of lightning in the night which, from the beginning of time, gives a dense and black intensity to the night which it denies, which lights up the night from the inside, from top to bottom, and yet owes to the dark the stark clarity of its manifestation, its harrowing and poised singularity; the flash loses itself in this space it marks with its sovereignty and becomes silent now that it has given a name to obscurity. [1]

Postmodernism, then, is not a "gesture of the cut", a permanent refusal, nor (most of all) a division of existence into polarized opposites. The postmodern scene begins and ends with transgression as the "lightning-flash" which illuminates the sky for an instant only to reveal the immensity of the darkness within:

absence as the disappearing sign of the limitlessness of the void within and without; Nietzsche's 'throw of the dice' across the spider's web of existence.

But, Nietzsche was prophetic. In *Thus Spake Zarathustra*, Nietzsche anticipated the postmodern condition as one of the ruins within when he wrote that the origins of the revenge-seeking will, which is out to avenge its own botched and bungled instincts, would be *our* inability — as pure wills and nothing but wills — to overcome the finality of "time's it was."

> Thus the will, the liberator, becomes a malefactor; and upon all that can suffer it takes revenge for its inability to go backwards.
> This yes, and this alone is revenge; the will's antipathy towards time and time's it was. . . The will cannot will backwards; that it cannot break time and time's desire — that is the will's most lonely affliction.
> And so out of wrath and ill-temper, the will rolls stones about and takes revenge upon him who does not, like it, feel wrath and ill-temper. [2]

Nietzsche is, then, the limit and possibility of the postmodern condition. He is the *limit* of postmodernism because, as a thinker who was so deeply fixated by the death of the grand referent of God, Nietzsche was the last and best of all the modernists. In *The Will to Power*, the postmodernist critique of representation achieves its most searing expression and, in Nietzsche's understanding of the will as a "perspectival simulation", the fate of postmodernity as a melancholy descent into the violence of the death of the social is anticipated. And Nietzsche is the *possibility* of the postmodern scene because the double-reversal which is everywhere in his thought and nowhere more so than in his vision of artistic practice as the release of the "dancing star" of the body as a *solar system* is, from the beginning of time, the negative cue, the "expanding field" of the postmodern condition.

Nietzsche's legacy for the *fin-de-millenium* mood of the postmodern scene is that we are living on the violent edge between ecstacy and decay; between the melancholy lament of post-modernism over the death of the grand signifiers of modernity — consciousness, truth, sex, capital, power — and the ecstatic nihilism of ultramodernism; between the body as a torture-chamber and pleasure-palace; between fascination and lament. But this is to say that postmodernism comes directly out of the bleeding tissues of the body — out of the body's fateful oscillation between the finality of "time's it was" (the body as death trap) and the possibility of experiencing the body (*au-delà* of Nietzsche) as a "solar system" — a dancing star yes, but also a black hole — which is the source of the hyper-nihilism of the flesh of the postmodern kind.

Thesis 1. Excremental Culture

Eric Fischl's painting, *The Old Man's Boat and the Old Man's Dog*, expresses perfectly the pestilential spirit of postmodern culture and society.

The painting exists at the edge of ecstacy and decay where the consumer culture of the passive nihilists does a reversal and in a catastrophic implosion flips into its opposite number — the suicidal nihilism of excremental culture. As Georges Bataille said in *The Solar Anus:* [3]

> *Everyone is aware that life is parodic and*
> *lacks an interpretation.*
> *Thus lead is the parody of gold.*
> *Air is the parody of water.*
> *The brain is the parody of the equator.*
> *Coitus is the parody of crime.*

The Old Man's Boat and the Old Man's Dog resembles Bataille's parodic world of the solar anus. The political code of the painting is about power operating today in the language of the aesthetics of seduction (where seduction is parodic of excrementia); its emotional mood oscillates between boredom and terror; it is populated by parasites (the lolling bodies on the Old Man's boat); danger is everywhere (the rising sea and even the firehouse dog, the dalmatian, as the return of the Old Man seeking revenge); and its psychological signs are those of detritus, decomposition, and disaccumulation. Fischl's artistic production is an emblematic sign of the postmodern scene where, as Jean Baudrillard hints in *Oublier Foucault*, the Real is interesting only to the extent that is contains an "imaginary catastrophe."

Do you think that power, economy, sex — all the

Real's big numbers — would have stood up one
single instant without a fascination to support them
which originates precisely in the inversed mirror
where they are reflected and continually reversed,
and where their imaginary catastrophe generates a
tangible and immanent gratification.
This time we are in a full universe, a space radiating
with power but also cracked, like a shattered
windshield holding together. [4]

Like Baudrillard's imploding and hysterical world of the "cracked
windshield", Fischl's artistic vision is a precursor of the hyperreality of the suicidal nihilism of the postmodern scene. Fischl is
the explorer of the psychological condition of the "sickening
despair of vertigo" which Bataille called the "pineal eye":

Thus the pineal eye, detaching itself from the
horizontal system of normal ocular vision, appears
in a kind of nimbus of tears, like the eye of a tree or,
perhaps, a human tree. At the same time, this ocular
tree is only a giant (ignoble) pink penis, drunk with
the sun and suggesting or soliciting a nauseous
malaise, the sickening despair of vertigo. In this
transfiguration of nature, during which vision itself,
attracted by nausea, is torn out and torn apart by
the sunbursts into which it stares the erection
ceases to be a painful upheaval on the surface of
the earth and, in a vomiting of flavorless blood, it
transforms itself into a vertiginous full incelestial
space, accompanied by a horrible cry. [5]

Yet before Bataille's description of the solar anus as the site of
seduction and power in the postmodern scene, Nietzsche was
more direct. In *Thus Spake Zarathustra*, the madman comes into
the marketplace and announces the "tremendous event" which
is now as then the key to the postmodern condition: "Whither is
God? I shall tell you. We have killed him you and I. All of us are his
murderers. But how have we done this? How were we able to
drink up the sea? Who gave us the sponge to wipe away the entire
horizon"? [6] We then enter the world of the immaculate deception
beyond Nietzsche's "immaculate perception."

Postmodernist discourse is a violent, restless, and hallucinogenic reflection on the upturned orb of Bataille's "pineal eye"
and Nietzsche's wiping clean of the "entire horizon" as the
dominant mood of late twentieth-century experience. Like a
psychological fallout from the dark sayings of Nietzsche and
Bataille, the postmodern scene runs at the edge of delirium and
doom. The cultural signs are everywhere:
• In *fashion's* high-intensity publicity culture where the very forms
of advertising undergo a radical and relentless dispersion in one
last gesture of burnout and exhaustion. French intellectuals may
now speak of the "shock of the real", but *Vogue* magazine has
already done them one better: it speaks of the "shock of the stiff"
— corpses and the solar ass in denim garb being all the rage these
days in the postmodern detritus of the New York advertising
scene. [7]
• In *rock video*, Dire Strait's *Money for Nothing* is a brilliant satire on
Baudrillard's implosion of experience in the simulacrum, just as
much as the experimental music of SPK's *Dying Moments* catches
the edge in postmodern culture between ecstacy and decay as this
album runs between a foreground of electronic computer blips
(processed world) and a background of the Gregorian Mass of the
Dead. Postmodernist music today (from the *Nihilist Spasm Band*
and *Violent Femmes*) is but a melancholy and ecstatic reflection on
that button going the rounds from Los Angeles and New York to
Tokyo:

> Roses are red; Violets are blue;
> I'm schizophrenic and so am I.

• In *Rock art*, the album cover of Joni Mitchell's *Dog Eat Dog*
portrays a wrecked car and a stranded, victimized woman sur-
rounded by a pack of vicious dogs as a metaphor for postmodern
culture and society in ruins. But what gives away the game of the
double-reversal going on in this album cover is that the psychological sensibility evoked by *Dog Eat Dog* discloses itself to be both
piety (an ethics of concern for the welfare of the woman as
victim) and *idle fascination* with her coming death. In *Anti-Oedipus*,
Deleuze and Guattari, repeating Nietzsche's insight that the
coming fate of suicidal nihilism would be the production of a
culture oscillating between the mood lines of a little voluptuousness and a little tedium, said that the main emotional trend
lines of the '80s are now *piety and cynicism*: [8] piety to such a degree

of intensity that it flips into its opposite sign — a cynical fascination fueled by *ressentiment* with the fate of those who fall outside the fast-track of mediascape '80s style.

• The *diseases* of sex today: Anorexia, Aids, and Herpes. These are poststructuralist diseases, tracing the inscription of power on the text of the flesh and privileging the ruin of the surface of the body. Aids is postmodern to the extent that it implies a real loss of social solidarity, and nominates sex without secretions — sex without a body — as a substitute for the normal passage of bodily fluids. Herpes, the electrical disease *par excellence*, is the McLuhanite disease: it actually tracks the network of the central nervous system making herpes a perfect metaphor for the ruins of a processed world where, as McLuhan theorized in *Understanding Media*, the central nervous system has been ablated in the form of technological media of communication and is already on its way to being exteriorized again. Anorexia [9] operates under the sign of the *Anti-Oedipus.* This is a disease not of desire, but of the liquidation of desire: the interiorization of the production of the "look" on the text of the (disappearing) body. It's no longer the Cartesian "I think therefore I am", but Serres' "Je pense... je pèse... j'existe": [10] the movement to the massless state when the body has succumbed to the parasites of postmodern culture.

Indeed, in a recent issue of the Australian magazine, *Art and Text*, Sam Schoenbaum wrote in a brilliant essay, "The Challenge of the Loss", [11] that if the most striking paintings today are about the ruin of surfaces — the refusal of the border, the cracking of the surface of the canvas, the transgression of the field and the screen in favour of an art of "related fixtures" and "expanding fields" — there is also an analogical relationship between postmodern theory and the progression of lesions on the surface of the skins of Aids victims. In Schoenbaum's sense, in both Watteau paintings and reflections on Aids, there is a deep sense of melancholia and a recognition of the loss of solidarity: "Perhaps this is just a ritualistic exchange between art and life, but "perhaps also in both an unanswerable sense of how to deal with loss". [12]

• In *art*, the critique of the fetishization of the base is everywhere: from the "theatre of cruelty" of the photography of Francesca Woodman (who throws her body as transgression *and* incitement across the silent topography of the visual field) and the electronic sculpture of Tony Brown (who works to foreground the hidden ideological background effects of the technoscape) to the theorisations of Rosalind Krauss' sculpture in the expanding field.

But even at its most advanced state in art and theory, in Lyotard's transgressionary moves (*Driftworks*) artistic practice signals its own end. Lyotard's contribution to the catalogue for the recent Biennale of Sydney (*Origins, Originality, and Beyond*) had this to say about "Answering the Question: What is the Post-Modern?":

> The post-modern would be that which in the modern poses the unpresentable in the presentation itself; that which refuses the consolation of good form or of the consensus of taste which would allow some common nostalgia for the impossible; that which is concerned with new presentations, not purely for the pleasure of it, but the better to insist that the unpresentable exists. . . To be post-modern would be to comprehend things according to the paradox of the future (post) anterior (modo).
>
> Beneath the general call for an easing and abatement of pressure, we hear murmurs of the desire to recommence terror, of the phantasm of grasping reality. The reply is: war on everything, let's be witnesses to the unpresentable, let's activate those differences, let's save the honour of the name. [13]

Lyotard sinks into the spectator sport of witnessing the sublime and the beautiful: the art world propped up by Kant's salvage job of uniting terror and taste to the market of abuse beyond use. War by all means as long as it is war under Habermas' sign of communicative competence, where we all understand that what is worth looking at has its appropriate price. Art now is the spectacle of the bourgeois mind entering its darkest aporia. Bataille's "heterogeneity of excess" does not allow the modernist luxury of "saving the honour of the name", confirming the ineluctability of the "unpresentable", or of activating "those differences" which exist, anyway, only to confirm the liquidation of all differences under the sign of the parodic.

Thesis 2. Oublier Baudrillard: Postmodern Primitivism

Jean-François Lyotard is again wrong when he argues in *La condition postmoderne* that we are living now in the age of the death of the "grand réçits", a post-historical period which is marked by a refusal of the phallocentric and representational logic of Enlightenment. [14] In fact, it's just the opposite. We're living through a great story — an historical moment of implosion, cancellation and reversal; that moment where the will to will of the technoscape (the dynamic expansion outwards of the technical mastery of social and non-social nature) — traces a great arc of reversal, connecting again to an almost mythic sense of primitivism as the primal of technological society.

The vital edge in the postmodern scene is not ecstacy and decay (though that too), but the addiction of *hyper-primitivism and hyper-imaging*. *Primitivism* to such a degree of intensity that the mediascape depends for its continuation not only on the exteriorization of the mind, but also on the externalization of mythological fear turned radical. The potlach has gone postmodern. The mediascape is a parasite on the breakdown in the inner check in social behavior in the postmodern era as the will to liquidation undergoes one last seductive and purely spectacular convulsion. It is carnival time, Dionysus time; or as one American citizen said recently about the politics of foreign intervention: "Make them glow and shoot them in the dark". This is *imaging* to such a degree of hyper-abstraction that Jean Baudrillard's insight in *Simulations* that the "real is that of which it is possible to give an equivalent reproduction" [15] is now rendered obsolescent by the actual transformation of the simulacrum with its hyperreality effects into its opposite: a *virtual* technology mediated with designer bodies processed through computerized imaging-systems. When technology in its ultramodernist phase connects again with the primitivism of mythic fear turned radical, it's no longer the Baudrillardian world of the simulacrum and hyperrealism, but a whole new scene of *virtual* technology and the end of the fantasy of the Real. Electronic art is the limit of postmodern aesthetics.

Adorno and Horkheimer expressed it perfectly in the classic text, *Dialectic of Enlightenment*, when they theorised that the price to be paid for the hysterical concatenation of the bourgeois ego, for self-preservation, is self-liquidation. In their analysis, every moment of historical progression is accompanied by historical retrogression. We, though, who live later recognize that the governing logic of technological society is *the hyper-atrophication of emotional functions and the hyper-exteriorization of the mind.* Ulysses' rowers, no longer under the code of the early bourgeois work ethic, have had the wax removed from their ears, and Ulysses himself is no longer chained to the mast. The siren song turns into the maddening noise of promotional culture: all emotional primitivism on the one hand, and the artificial intelligence of a serial culture under the sign of quantum technology on the other. We pass beyond mass and energy to the underworld with Orpheus only to await there *our* dismemberment at the hands of the women. But the nihilism of the postmodern scene is lived today under the dark sign of Nietzsche. In *Toward a Genealogy of Morals*, Nietzsche cautioned that the will is saved from the age without limits by embracing the will to nothingness:

> It is a will to nothingness, a will running counter to life, a revolt against the most fundamental pre-suppositions of life. And to repeat at the end what I said in the beginning. Rather than not will, the will would prefer to will nothingness. [16]

But beyond Nietzsche, we are now given the gift of fashion and of culture (which has always been beyond the real): we *ad-dire* that we are *a-donné*, adorned, addicted. The saturnalia, the world turned upside down, leads to the *pharmakon*, the myth-maker who today is called the pharmacist. The addicted self is the perfect psychological sign of a postmodern (pharmaceutical) culture and society which has embraced the will to nothingness as its own, and internalizes the pharmakon as a *forgetting* of "time's it was", as a chemical response to the necessities of the "revenge-seeking will." The button, *Are We Having Fun Yet?*, is the truth-sayer of a culture of altered minds, and prophetic of the eclipse of liberalism (from within).

Thesis 3. Estheticized Recommodification: Art and Postmodern Capitalism

In *The Theory of the Avante-Garde*, Peter Burger develops the thesis that "art as institution" shares a deep ideological complicity with the logic of bourgeois society. [17] In his reading, "art is institutionalized as ideology in bourgeois society" [18] both in the *positive* sense that the ideology of autonomous art reaffirms the rupture between praxis and aesthetics which is necessary for the reproduction of capitalist society (a society without any self-reflexive moment of critique) and in the *negative* sense that art as institution in its privileging of an art that doesn't hurt (to parody

Fredric Jameson's "history is what hurts") — an autonomous art — is the perfect ideological expression for an advanced capitalist society where, as the French situationist Guy Debord theorised in *The Society of the Spectacle* the commodity-form is experienced as alienation to such a degree of abstraction that it becomes an image.[19]

To Burger's critical analysis of the ideological complicity of art as institution, we would further theorise that in advanced capitalist society the institution of art plays a decisive role in preventing the self-paralysis of the commodity-form. Indeed, we maintain that in late capitalism art, understood in its most constitutive sense as *estheticization to excess*, is the commodity-form in its most advanced (postmodernist) representation. In the fully estheticized phase of late capitalism, art as institution works to incite desire in the designer body by providing a reception aesthetics suitable for "promotional culture"; it merges perfectly with estheticized production when the production-machine (of primitive capitalism) requires a consumption machine (of late capitalism) with a political economy of signs (in fashion, rock video, television, and architecture) which inscribe the surface of the body, its *tattoo*, as a text for the playing-out of the commodity-form as power; and the institution of art plays a decisive role in sustaining the general circulation of the commodity-form. The institution of art moves beyond a deep ideological complicity in the reproduction of the commodity-form to constituting the foremost site of the process of *estheticized recommodification* which characterizes advanced capitalism.

In a key article, "Theses on the Theory of the State", the German social theorist Claus Offe has coined the term "administrative recommodification" as a way of describing the contradictory structure of relations which typify the state and economy in advanced capitalist society.[20] For Offe, the contemporary liberal-democratic state must function now to maintain the integrity of the commodity-form, but in a way that does not undermine the legitimacy of private production, of the exchange-principle. In the absence of effective state intervention, either by way of the *negative subordination* of the state to prevailing market imperatives or by way of the *positive subordination* of the state to the enhancement of the value of private production, the commodity-form — like the second law of thermodynamics — tends to run down towards self-liquidation: expelling labour and capital. In Offe's estimation, the beleaguered welfare state is caught up in the paradox of having to continuously recuperate the integrity of the commodity-form, while always having to deny publicly that it is doing so (in order to maintain the democratic class-compromise). [21]

We move beyond Offe's theory of the state in advanced capitalist society to the sign of art as the essential locus of the commodity-form in advanced capitalist society. It is our thesis that the institution of art — understood as the spreading outwards of estheticized production in the form of designed environments — has precisely taken over the commodity-form, thus "solving" Offe's crisis-ridden state at a higher level of abstraction and generality.

1. Art as institution overcomes its *negative subordination* to capital (contemporary aesthetic discourse is authorized to undermine the legitimacy of private production and, as we move beyond the political economy of scarcity to Bataille's general economy of excess, to do anything which would challenge the integrity of the exchange-principle).

2. Art as institution overcomes its *positive subordination* to capital accumulation (in the general economy of market-steered aesthetic practices and of an aesthetics-driven consumption machine, art today functions to enhance capital accumulation which is, anyway, entering its last, purely aesthetic phase: the phase of designer bodies, designer environments, and simulational models as signs of the Real).

3. Art as institution is functionally the 'last man' of capital accumulation (either directly in terms of the position of artistic production as the locus of the commodity-form in the postmodern economy, or indirectly through the governmentalization of art wherein the state is rendered functionally dependent on capital/cultural accumulation).

4. Like Offe's crisis-ridden state before it, the institution of art must work to deny all of the above.

In Bataille's general economy based on 'excess', art is the commodity-form *par excellence*. Art is itself excessive (beyond the use-value of the political economy of scarcity), and is thus central to the postmodern economy in its fully estheticized phase. The very critique made by art of the exchange-principle is why art is, today, indispensable to the functioning of the *excess economy*. Thus, to the questions 'Does art liquidate capital by undermining it? Or does art reinforce capital by estheticizing reality?' we would respond that art does both simultaneously. Art is the highest stage of capital in its fully estheticized phase; and art reinforces capital by transforming the commodity-form into a purely self-referential and excessive site of power.

If the commodity-form in its most advanced state is experienced as self-recognition to such a degree of intensity that it becomes an image, then capitalism may now be described as entering its last, purely artistic, phase under the sign of estheticized recommodification. There are four *key* phases in the process of estheticized recommodification:

1. The production in advanced capitalist society of a *reception* aesthetics for the fibrillated designer body. While *theoretically* the process of estheticized recommodification implies that the circle has now been joined between the interiorization of need-dispositions and the exteriorization of the mind in advanced capitalist culture, *practically* it implies that the designer body welcomes its invasion by fashion and the politics of style, by publicity culture, with open arms.
2. The production and consumption of a *simulacra of signs* which work to inscribe the text of the body in the shifting ideological styles of the fashion industry. Estheticized recommodification indicates that late capitalism functions both as a "space invader" (the externalization of the central nervous system in the form of the mediascape) and as a "body invader" (the laceration of the body by the political economy of signs).
3. *Psychoanalytically*, the estheticization of the commodity-form implies that Lacan's *miscrecognition* as the basis of the bourgeois ego (the mirrored self is the fictive centre of the misplaced concrete unity of bourgeois identity) is reinforced by our exteriorization in the political economy of signs.
4. The language of estheticized recommodification

is that of *virtual images/virtual technology*. Estheticized
reality is no longer the scene of Umberto Eco's
"travels in hyperreality." Indeed, Eco's search for
the absolute fake comes to engulf himself. The
estheticization of the commodity-form means that
we have already passed through to the next phase
of ultramodern technology: the dark side of the
commodity-form where we experience pure imaging-systems as the real, and where perspective
itself is always only fictional because it is perfectly
simulational. Estheticized recommodification is
the region of *virtual* cameras, of *virtual* technology,
and of *virtual* perspective — the region, in fact,
where the aesthetic symmetries of particle physics
become the structural logic of the Real.

Thesis 4. Panic Sex: Processed Feminism

Designer Bodies
    Late capitalism in its last, artistic phase (the phase of promo-
tional culture) does not work to defend the modernist terrain of
fixed perspective, or function to exclude différence. The fascination of capitalism today is that it works the terrain of Lacan's
"sliding of the signifier;" it thrives in the language of sexual
différence, of *every kind* of différence, and it does so in order to
provoke some real element of psychological fascination, of
attention, with a system which as the emblematic sign of the Anti-
Real, must function in the language of recuperation, of the
recyclage, of every dynamic tendency, whether potentially authentic
or always only nostalgic. Indeed, three strategies are now at work
for putting Lacan's sliding signifier in play as the language of
contemporary capitalist culture: the old avant-garde strategy of
working to tease out the shock of the real (unlikely contexts as
the semiotics of contemporary advertising); the (neo) avant-
garde strategy of creating a simulacra of virtual images which
function in the language of new and extra-human perspectives
(the "quantum art" of Nissan car commercials which speak in the
language of pure imaging-systems); and the '80s parodic strategy
of playing the edge of sexual différence in an endless mutation of
exchange of gender signs. *The absorption and then playing back to its
audience of the reversible and mutable language of sexual différence is the
language of postmodern capitalism.*

In the introduction to *Feminism Now: Theory and Practice*, this tendency is expressed as follows:

What's feminism now in the age of ultracapitalism? What's the relationship of feminist critique to the much-celebrated and perfectly *cachet* world of postmodernism?

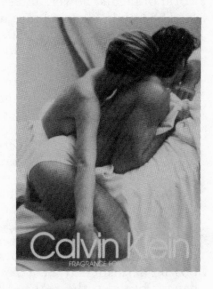

Everything is being blasted apart by the mediascape. The violent advertising machine gives us a whole, schizophrenic world of electric women for a culture whose dominant mode of social cohesion is the shopping mall; whose main psychological type is the electronic individual; and where all the old (patriarchal) signs of cultural authority collapse in the direction of androgyny. What makes the *Eurythmics*, Madonna, and Carol Pope with *Rough Trade* so fascinating is that they play at the edge of power and seduction, the zero-point where sex as electric image is amplified, teased out in a bit of ironic exhibitionism, and then reversed against itself. These are artists in the business of committing sign crimes against the big signifier of Sex. If it's true that we're finally leaving the obsolete world of the modern and entering postmodernism, then the earliest clues to the geography of this new terrain is what happens to images of women in the simulacra of the media system. Because images of power and sexuality in the age of ultracapitalism are an early warning system to what's going on as we are processed through the fully realized technological society. *Power and sexual oppression* is the electronic junkyard of rock video, from the Sadean sneer of Billy Idol to the masturbatory visuals of Duran Duran. *Power and seduction* is the dismembered mediascape of women as cigarettes, beer bottles, scents, cars, even bathtubs and weight machines. Craig Owens might write in *The Anti-Aesthetic* that "there is an apparent crossing of the feminist critique of patriarchy and the postmodern critique of representation," but if so, then there's also a dark side to this happy intersection of critiques. And that dark side is the real world of media, power, and sexuality.

The Calvin Klein ad says it best. In an ironic reversal of the sexual stereotypes of the 1950s, it flips the traditional (patriarchal) images of women and men: man as a gorgeous hunk of flesh (the model's actually a descendant of Napoleon: sweet revenge for a lot of pain); and the woman as ultracapitalism triumphant: a packaged and seductive image of women initiating and dominating sex and, as Bruce Weber (the photographer of the ad) says: "it's woman even as protector." A little staged sex for a little staged communication: electronic woman flashing out of the media pulse with a little humanity. The ad is perfectly cynical because it emancipates, by reversing, the big signifiers of sex (woman as '50s man: so much for an unconfused critique of representation of gender in the media system) to sell commodities (perfume in this case). But it's also a wonderful example of what Andy Warhol in *Interview* recently nominated as the dominant mood of the times: *bored but hyper*. The fate of feminism in the age postmodernism is to be a *processed* feminism: that's the radical danger but also the real promise of feminist critique in technological society. The electronic machine eats up images of women: even (*most of all?*) emancipation from the patriarchal world of gender ideology is experienced simultaneously as domination *and* freedom. For feminists in the mediascape it's no longer "either/or", but "both/and." *Feminism is the quantum physics of postmodernism.* [22]

Processed Babies

In *Ce Sexe qui n'en est pas un*, Luce Irigaray warned that the limit of feminism would be reached when a feminist écriture of *jouissance* equal to the full geneocentric critique of phallocentric logic managed to reduce itself to a mirrored-reversal of male-stream discourse. [23] Perhaps it was this desperate attempt to escape Irigaray's trap of the mirrored-reversal which led Julia Kristeva in in "The Subject in Signifying Practice" to theorise a real bodily difference between *somatic* experience (the child's experience of nonsense play, of laughter) and the verbal saturation of the body in the ideological simulacra of *thetic* symbolic experience. [24] Against the trap of a feminist *écriture* which subordinates itself to an opposite, but equal, replication of phallocentric logic, Kristeva takes refuge in an extralinguistic vision of the subject and in the transcendental ego of the somatic subject. The "other" of feminism disappears into the newly privileged naturalism of the somatic experience of the baby.

This terrain of a sex which does not undergo its own immolation in an endless mutation and reproducibility of signs is parasited by postmodern theory of the "anti-aesthetic" kind generally as the "other" which marks the limit of transgression challenging the purely topological field of a relational power-system (in the structural paradigm of advanced capitalist society). However, it's our thesis, *against* the privileging of the extra-linguistic domain of pre-oedipalized experience (somatic experience), that the tension between somatic and thetic experience (between nonsense play and symbolization) has already been absorbed by promotional culture in the form of the *recyclage* of all forms of sign-struggles in exactly the same way that Marcuse's world of play of the polymorphous perverse in *Eros and Civilization* has been absorbed, and immolated, by his own critique in *One-Dimensional Man*.

The baby is already a key site for the play of a dead power with and against the body of women: a perfect scene for the merger of technologies associated with the medicalization of the body, the investiture of desire with a code of prevention, and the production of designer babies equal to the possibilities of cultural genetics; babies whose television fare at the age of six includes *The Young and the Restless*, initiating them into the video world of sex without secretions. If babies are born postmodern, it's just because their bodies are lacerated by the language of the key technologies of power.

Thesis 5. Sex Without Secretions

If sexual différence has been so easily absorbed by the media-scape in the form of a cynical mutation of gender signs, this implies that sex in the postmodern condition no longer exists: sex today (from the viewpoint of the ideological constitution of the body as a text in the political economy of signs) has become *virtual sex*. Sexual différence has been ruptured by the play of the floating signifiers at the epicentre of postmodern power. Indeed, it might be said that postmodern sex has undergone a twofold death.

a) The death of natural sex. First, there was the death of generic sex, a sex which stood outside of and in silent opposition to the language of discourse and held out the possibility of experiencing our bodies and their secretion of desires without the mediation of language. The murderer of natural sex was Foucault who, on the question of an essentialist sex, like Nietzsche before him on the question of an essentialist power, announced the presence of a "discursive sexuality," of the sociological requirement in the modern regime of having to pass through a complex discourse about sexuality before we could discover our sexuality. [25] Foucault's *The History of Sexuality* stands, in fact, as that fateful rupture between the death of a sex with secretions and the incarceration of sexuality in the prison-house of the social code.

b) The death of discursive sexuality. The postmodern condition is typified by a second death in the order of sexuality, the death of sociological sex and the creation of a type of sexuality which is experienced as an endless semiurgy of signs: *panic sex*. The presence of sex as a panic site (witness the hysteria about Aids) feeds on the fear of sex itself as emblematic of excremental culture driven onwards by the projection onto the discourse of sexuality of all the key tendencies involved in the death of the social. Sex today is experienced most of all as a virtual sex, sex without secretions, a sex which is at the centre of the medical-ization of the body and the technification of reproduction, and which, if its violent and seductive representations are everywhere in rock video, in the language of advertising, in politics, this means that, like a dying star which burns most brilliantly when it is already most exhausted and already on its way to a last implosion, sex today is dead: the site of our absorption into the simulated secrections of ultramodern technology. A virtual sex, sex with-out secretions, is like the TV ads for Calvin Klein's *Obsession* perfume, which if they can speak with such panic anxiety about desire are fascinating because they are actually about just its opposite: the liquidation of seduction.

The world of the *Obsession* scent is about the violent end of desire, the transformation of sexual incitement into its parodic mode of technified scent for designer bodies, and of the meta-morphosis of obsession into panic boredom. Postmodern sex has become an immaculate deception just because the theatrics of the mechanical sex of De Sade's fornicating machine has been changed into its opposite: a site for the playing out of the thermo-dynamics of cynical power.

Thesis 6. Body Invaders: Postmodernism and Subjugated Knowledge

The outstanding fact about postmodern theorisations, if we include in that nomenclature Lacan's psychoanalytics of the bourgeois ego, is that the body itself is now the site of subjugated knowledge, a "minor literature" [26] in the Deleuzian sense.

As a subjugated knowledge, the body has experienced two ideological closures:

1. an ideological closure at the level of the *psychoanalytics of reception*. The formative theorisation here is Lacan's description of the bourgeois ego in its mirror stage as experiencing a *fictive unity* on the basis of a fundamental misrecognition, mistaking the seeming unity of the image for the reality of the dependent bourgeois ego, the bourgeois kingdom of the *I, Me, or Mine* sliding along the "chain of signifiers" at that point where language and ideology merge. [27]

2. an ideological closure at the *social* level where, as theorised by Althusser, ideology interpellates individuals as subjects. Or, as Peter Goldbert and Jed Sekleff, two San Francisco theorists working the terrain of the psychoanalytics of power, argue:

> The specific practico-social function of ideology is to constitute social beings as subjects who mis-recognize themselves as autonomous individuals — and, by the same token, misrecognize the actual social relations that gave rise to their subject-ivity. [28]

In the postmodern condition, with the insurrection of subjugated knowledge (Foucault), or the transgressions of non-synchronicity (Deleuze), that type of theory is to be privileged which meditates anew on power as speaking the language of body invaders, power taking possession of the body both at the level of the psychoanalytics of reception and at the social level of the ideological interpellation of the subject. Postmodernism is, therefore, a homecoming to a new order of theoretical practice: privileging the vision of power as a body invader inscribing itself on the text of the flesh; and theorising the possibility of a margin of différence which would transgress the grisly play of a power which is always only topological and relational. Thus, for example, the special place of feminist theory today, and particularly the new French feminism of Hélène Cixous, Luce Irigaray, and Xavière Gauthier is to reflect specifically on the triple subordination of women under the weight of power as a body invader: to theorise the equivalence between the repression of sexual difference and the sexual division of labour; to relativize *misrecognition* as being based on gender displacement; to note that Lacan's work is of special significance for deciphering language as ideology ("The subject is produced socially, but dominated linguistically");[29] and to trace out in, for instance, the fashion industry and technologies of reproduction all the *technical* interpellations of the subject.

But if Nietzsche is right, there is *no* privileged zone of différence. Under the sign of invasion, the body becomes the virtual text of particle physics. Spread out over a topographical field, the imploded self is energized creating the movement over a power grid where *all* ontologies are merely the sites of local 'catastrophes.' Neither self nor other but, rather, a quasi object/ subject picks up cultural characteristics as it shuttles from node to node. Following the French theorist Michel Serres, each movement across the power field tattoos the body until it represents the cartography of the field itself. [30] The body, moving always towards its own death, is encoded with the information/ knowledge of postmodernity; a cosmetic library of the signs of modernity. The exhausted energy of the self, spent in the violence of the hyperspace of life in the fast-lane — like its analogue the "virtual particle' — disappears immediately after its brief appearance as an operator in the simulacrum. The postmodern body invaders, unlike their bourgeois counterparts, go out in post-Eliot time with a whimper not a bang. After all, the big bang is long behind us; all that is left is the static of background radiation, and that's why we are living in the age of the death of the social and the triumph of a signifying culture, the violent implosion of gender signs, and the indefinite reversibility and self-liquidation of all the foundational *récits* of contemporary culture. The body is a power grid, tattooed with all the signs of cultural excess on its surface, encoded from within by the language of desire, broken into at will by the ideological interpellation of the subject, and, all the while, held together as a fictive and concrete unity by the illusion of *misrecognition*.

Thesis 7. Panic Philosophy

We live in the era of the double refusal of the beginning of philosophy: the refusal of the logocentric world of speech and reason; and the refusal of the deconstructed world of différence: Neither Socratic wonderment nor Derrida's *écriture*, neither the dialectic nor the dialogue, but rather the pleasurable voyage under the sign of 'viciousness for fun.' Words are no longer necessary; merely the seductive pose which entices the eye of the tourist. Codes are no longer required, as long as silence is eliminated. Not even Orwellian logic or nostalgic speeches from Big Brother, nor philosophy itself — we all admit their differences, their wonderment, their values. They have all been researched and recycled. We have the information and the theory. We have the experience; we know that aspertane is bad even in Diet Coke. We don't have to wonder; we know just for the 'fun of it.' We write just for the fun of it, just as we think, make love, parody, and praise. Indeed, with Merleau-Ponty we praise philosophy and have doubts about Socrates. After all, hemlock doesn't taste as good as Coke; this is one benefit of deconstructing the elements. Besides, we are having a nice day, maybe a thousand nice days. The postmodern scene is a panic site, just for the fun of it. And beneath the forgetting, there is only the scribbling of another Bataille, another vomiting of flavourless blood, another heterogeneity of excess to mark the upturned orb of the pineal eye. The solar anus is parodic of postmodernism, but, again, just for the fun of it.

II

SIGN CRIMES

This is a discourse on the disembodied eye of the dead power at the centre of Western experience, and the convergence of the trinity/sign as the essential locus of the fictitious unity of the Western episteme.

To suggest a historical thesis, it is our position that Augustine was the first postmodern thinker, because in his refusal of that earlier expression of modernism — the classical episteme of the fourth century which, originating in the warring struggle between rationalism and skepticism in the Greek mind found its final moment of culmination in the pragmatic materialism of the Roman empire — he carried out the first metaphysical critique of representation. Refusing the alternatives of rationalism and materialism, or tragic idealism and dogmatic skepticism, Augustine demonstrated the fatal flaw in enlightenment modernism: its absence of a directly experienced creative principle which could serve to unify the warring tendencies in Western experience. While Augustine's *Confessions* are a "closing of the eye of the flesh" against disembodied reason, his theoretical text, *De Trinitate*, outlines the epistemology of the "trinity" (the first structuralist law of value) as a "solution" to the fatal contradictions of the modern episteme. When enlightenment returns in the seventeenth century, it reawakens the fatal flaw in Western metaphysics, and thus experience, which Augustine had laid to rest for a period of eleven centuries. The injunction to reread *De Trinitate* has, therefore, a special importance since it is a fateful guide as to how the last crisis of modernism was resolved, and how the contemporary crisis may well devolve. As it plunges into the vertigo of Bataille's general economy of excess, our age must await a new Augustine. Only the murmurings of Nietzsche and Artaud, and the tortured paintings of de Chirico and Magritte, remind us of the terrible price we paid, under the sign of Augustinian discourse, for the suppression of the mythic fear turned radical which is the language of modernism.

The theorisations that follow are intended to recover the radical insights of poststructuralist art (de Chirico, Ernst, Magritte) and poststructuralist theory (Baudrillard, Barthes, and Foucault) into the disembodied eye of power by blasting through the evasions of the structuralist discourse to its suppressed metaphysical implications. *Sign Crimes*, then, circle from the artistic imagination of Magritte's *The Door to Freedom*, de Chirico's *Landscape Painter*, Max Ernst's *The Robing of the Bride* and the theoretical insights of Foucault, Baudrillard, Nietzsche, and Barthes into the simulacrum to the hidden genealogy of the disembodied eye in Augustine's text, *De Trinitate*. Augustine's doctrine of the *trinity* and Baudrillard's theory of the *sign* are presented as reverse, but parallel, images of the other, because they perfectly represent the metaphor of a dead power, the disappearing terrain of power in the postmodern condition. This is the region where Nietzsche understood power as a "perspectival appearance:" Kant is reduced to a disenchanted expression of the primitive Christian doctrine of the "will to will": and Augustine as the perfect embodiment of Paul's closing of the "eye of the flesh" and its opening (the "inner eye") to an abstract power which is always only a sign of that which never was. In the region of the Anti-Nietzsche, power can be everywhere for the reason that Baudrillard gave in *Oublier Foucault*: Power doesn't exist; it was always only a "perspectival simulation" of itself.

2

CHIRICO'S NIETZSCHE:
THE BLACK HOLE OF POSTMODERN POWER:

> For what I have to do is terrible, in any sense of the word; I do not challenge individuals — I am challenging humanity as a whole with my accusation: whichever way the decision may go, *for* me or *against* me, in any case there attaches to my name a quantity of doom that is beyond telling.
>
> F. Nietzsche. *Selected Letters*

The Italian surrealist, Giorgio de Chirico, is the painter of postmodernism *par excellence*. Chirico's world begins just at that point where the *grand récits* of modernity disappear into their own perspectival simulation. Here power, operating under the sign of seduction, is like a black hole in the social nebula which sucks into its dense vortex the energies of living labour and embodied politics; here, in fact, there is no perspectival space from which spreads out the figurations of the real. Chirico is the artist of nihilism (an uncanny precursor of René Magritte and Max Ernst, and also of Foucault's semiology in *Ceci n'est pas une pipe*) because he understood the full consequences of Nietzsche's accusation that in a world in which conditions of existence are transposed into "predicates of being", it would be the human fate to live through a fantastic inversion and cancellation of the order of the real. Commodity into sign, history into semiurgy, concrete labour into abstract exchange, perspective into simulation: these mark the threshold of the artistic imagination as it dwells on the eclipse of history symbolized by Nietzsche's madness in the piazzas of Turin.

One painting in particular by Chirico provides a privileged glimpse into the inner locus of the Nietzschean world and, for that reason, represents the great rupture in Western consciousness, making nihilism the limit and possibility of *historical* emancipation. Titled simply, *Landscape Painter*, this production is a brilliant satire on the representational theory of nature (the landscape coded, and thus imprisoned, on the canvas), and a fully tragic portrayal of (our) imprisonment in a dead empire of signs. Chirico is a vivisectionist of the "referential illusion" at work in modern experience: his paintings demonstrate with an uncompromising sense of critical vision the rupture in Western experience occasioned by the sudden disappearance of the classical conceptions of power, truth, history, and nature as referential finalities, and the postmodern metamorphosis of society into a geometry of signs. *Landscape Painter* exists at the edge in the identitarian logic of Western experience where nature (represented by the dead image-system of the pastoral landscape) passes over into its opposite: the geometric and thus fully spatialized sign-world of the mannequin. The great inducement behind the *representational* theory of nature (and, of course, of all the referential finalities: sex, economy, reason, history) was that in the perspectival space of difference and of non-identity, which was the real meaning of the sign and its referent (language and ontology), there was to be discovered the essential locus of human freedom. The comforting, *because antinomic*, system of referential finalities worked its effect by providing an order of signification that militated against the tragic knowledge of the radical disenchantment of modern society. A "cynical power," as Foucault said in *The History of Sexuality*, was not possible because

> ... power is tolerable only on the condition that it mask a considerable part of itself. Its sucess is proportional to its ability to hide its own mechanisms. Would power be accepted if it were entirely cynical? For it, secrecy is not in the nature of an abuse; it is indispensable to its operation. Not only because power imposes secrecy on those whom it dominates, but because it is perhaps just as indispensable to the latter: would they accept it if they did not see it as a mere limit placed on their

Giorgio de Chirico, *Landscape Painter*

desire, leaving a measure of freedom — however slight — intact? Power as a pure limit set on freedom is, at least in our society, the general form of its acceptability.[1]

For Chirico, what was at stake in the theoretical agenda of the order of referential finalities was a determined *trompe l'oeil* which shifted (our) perspective from the nihilism of a "cynical power" as the essence of the modern project to the already obsolete belief in the emancipatory qualities of history, which, as the locus of the real, had to signify something, *anything. Landscape Painter* cancels out the comforting antinomies of history/emancipation and says that if we are to be emancipated (from ourselves), it will be within, and then beyond, the logic of the sign. In an age of a fully "cynical power" and a "cynical history," the landscape which is the object of *Landscape Painter* is that of power and the sign.

Chirico is, then, the painter of Nietzsche's *The Will to Power*. In Nietzsche's famous, last postcard to Jacob Burkhardt, written at the moment when he passed over into the silence of madness, he provided us with an important clue to the real terrorism of a sign-system, which being self-referential, tautological, and implosive, is also fully *solipsistic*. Nietzsche wrote: "The unpleasant thing, and one that nags at my modesty, is that at root every name in history is I." Nietzsche was, of course, the explorer of the new continent of the sign. His insight into the tragic sense of the sign was this: the wiping clean of the horizon of referential finalities makes of (us) the last inhabitants of a world which, based now only on "perspectival valuations," has about it only a dead will to truth, dead power, and a cynical history which do not exist except as a residue of symbolic effectors. For Nietzsche, "every name in history is I" because he recognized, and this with horror, his imprisonment in the labyrinth of a sign-system which had about it the non-reality of a perspectival simulation. For Nietzsche, what powered this fantastic reduction of society to the logic of the sign, what precipitated the implosion of the real into the semiology of a perspectival illusion, was this: *the sign is power on its down side, on its side of reversal, cancellation, and disaccumulation. The Will to Power* is the emblematic text which represents, at once, the locus and limit of the postmodernist imagination, or what is the same, the tragic theory of the sign which is everywhere now in intellectual and political discourse. Nietzsche recognized that the sovereignty of the sign (he described sign-systems in the language of "perspectival valuations") meant the final reduction of society to the (abstract, semiological, and structural) language of willing. The fateful conjuncture of power/sign as the locus of the real also meant that the dynamic language of willing was finally able to confess its secret. All along the "will to power" had never been anything more than a brilliant inferno for the liquidation of the "real" and for the processing of society into the dark and seductive empire of the sign.

If Nietzsche screams out a warning that the postmodernist (and thus nihilistic) imagination always begins with the world in reverse image (the real as the site of exterminism), then Chirico paints the landscape of power/sign. With Nietzsche, Chirico's vision begins on the other side, the abstract and nihilating side, of the radical paradigm-shift which is what postmodern experience is all about. *Landscape Painter*, like all of Chirico's tragic productions, from *Turin, Spring* (the decoupling of space and

individual perspective) and *The Disquieting Muses* (a haunting
satire on the classical episteme of history) to *Two Masks* (the
liquidation of human identity) and *Mystery and Melancholy of a
Street* (the cancellation of the space of the social), is based on
three decisive refusals of representational discourse: *a refusal of
the referent of the historical* (Chirico privileges the spatial sense and
excludes a sense of time); *a refusal of the reality-principle of the social*
(there are no human presences, only an instant and melancholy
metamorphosis into a universe of dead signs); and *a refusal of the
dialectic* (here there is no suppressed region of truth-claims, only
an eclectic and randomized system of objects situated in relations
of spatial contiguity). What is, perhaps, most disquieting about
Chirico's artistic productions is that in refusing the referential
logic of the sign and its signifying finalities, he ruptured the
dialectical logic of western consciousness. There are no "poles"
in *Landscape Painter*; for Chirico is tracing a great, and reverse, arc
in the cycle of modern power — an arc in which power in the *form*
of an empty sign-system becomes nothing more than a perspectival
simulation *of itself*. It's the *lack* of signification in *Landscape Painter*
that is most noticeable; and which, indeed, parallels most closely
the *absence* of (embodied) power in *The Will to Power*. Like Nietzsche
before him, Chirico recognized the structural logic of the sign as
the essence of the language of power. This is why Chirico was
able to trace so brilliantly the accelerating semiological implosion
(the geometry of the sign) in postmodern experience, His was a
world populated by bionic beings (*The Return of the Prodigal Son*),
by objects floating free of their "natural" contexts (*The Song of
Love*), by an almost menacing sense of silence as the background
to the liquidation of the social (*The Enigma of Fate*), and by a
complex hieroglyphics of the sign as the geometric, and thus
perspectival, space within which we are now enclosed (*Hector and
Andromache*). Chirico understood that the conjuncture of power/
sign brought to the surface *the missing third term* in postmodernist
theorisations of power: the "will to will" as the abstract, semiological unity imposed on an order of experience which was always
only a system of mirroring-effects. For Chirico, this hint of death
in the language of the sign was its great seduction, drawing out
the political refusal of the "referential illusion," and making
power interesting only when it reveals the reverse, hidden side of
things: mutilation, liquidation, and exterminism.

A.K.

3

THEATRUM SAECULUM: AUGUSTINE'S SUBVERSION

Remembering Augustine

A forgotten and certainly unassimilated thinker, whether in his native Canada or in more international discourse, Charles Norris Cochrane represents an explosive intervention in the understanding of postmodern culture. Before reading Cochrane, it was possible to hold to the almost lethargic belief that the crisis of modern culture could be traced, most immediately, to the "bad infinity" present at the beginning of the rationalist calculus of the Enlightenment, and that, for better or for worse, the intellectual horizon of the modern age was contained within the trajectory of Kant, Hegel, Marx and Nietzsche. After Cochrane, there remains only the impossible knowledge that the discourse of the modern century began, not in the seventeenth century, but in the fourth century after Christ. In remembering the real meaning of Augustine's *Confessions*, Cochrane is the thinker who, with the exception of Hannah Arendt, makes Augustine dangerous again: dangerous, that is, as the metaphysician and theoretician of power who set in motion the physics (trinitarianism), the logic (the epistemology of modern psychology) and the ethics (the functionality of the *Saeculum*) of Western experience. In Cochrane's reading of Augustine, one can almost hear that fateful rumbling of ground which announces that, after all, the great "founders" of the Western tradition may have been, in the end, either in the case of Plato, Homer or Lucretius, precursors or antagonists of the Augustinian discourse or, in the case of Kant, this most modern of thinkers, merely secularizations of a structure of Western consciousness the essential movements of which were put in place by Augustine. Cochrane presents us with the challenge of rereading the Augustinian discourse, not simply within the terms of Christian metaphysics, but as a great dividing-line, perhaps *the* fundamental scission, between classicism, the discourse of modernism, and its postmodern fate.

Rethinking the Modern Age

Rethinking the crisis of the modern age against its classical background in the metaphysics of the "Graeco-Roman mind" is the context for all of Cochrane's writings. *Thucydides and the Science of History* (1929)[1] is an attempt to recover the classical foundations for the politics (democratic) and epistemology (critical empiricism) of "pragmatic naturalism" against the iron cage of Platonic rationalism. *Christianity and Classical Culture* (1940), which centres on the apogee of Roman civilization in Augustus and Virgil and the dynamism of Christian metaphysics in Augustine and Theodosius, is a decisive commentary on the radical "break" in world-hypotheses (in politics, metaphysics, ethics and epistemology) which marked the threshold between the *naturalism* of classical discourse and the rationalism of Christian metaphysics.[2] "The Latin Spirit in Literature" (a short, but summational, article written in 1942 for the *University of Toronto Quarterly*) complements Weber's analysis of the "Protestant ethic" as a profound and incisive synthesis of Roman civilization (precursor of the imperialism of the United States) as the enduring source of the "will to live" and the "will to accumulation" so characteristic of the "empirical personality" of modern political empires.[3] "The Mind of Edward Gibbon" (delivered as a lecture series at Yale University in 1944 and republished in the *University of Toronto Quarterly*) is a fundamental, and devastating, critique of the proponents of Enlightenment "Reason" (ranging across the works of Hume, Locke and Gibbon) and an almost explosive reappropriation of the significance of Christian metaphysics as the truth-sayer of the failure of classical reason.[4] And, finally, even Cochrane's doppelganger, *David Thompson: The Explorer,*[5] (written in 1925 and often discounted as a major publication) is almost a philosophical autobiography of Cochrane's own trajectory as a "cartographer" of intellectual traditions and as a thinker who lived always with the sense of the tragic dimensions of human experience.

It was Cochrane's great contribution to recognize, parallel to Nietzsche, that Christian metaphysics, not in spite of but *because of* the terror of its nihilism, also contained a singular truth: it solved a problem which classical reason could not resolve within the horizon of its presuppositions.[6] And thus Cochrane recognized in the thought of Augustine, in the epicentre of Christian metaphysics, the limit and the threshold of that very same phenomenology of mind, epistemology of modern psychology and "direct deliverance" of personality and history, that, for all of our protests, is still all that stands between the abyss in classical discourse and the modern centuries. It was Cochrane's singular insight to see the real implication of Augustine's *Confessions*; to sense that to the same extent that Augustine might rightly be described as the "first citizen of the modern world," [7] then we, the inheritors of modern experience, cannot liberate ourselves from the "radical anxiety" of the postmodern age until we have thought against, overturned, or at least inverted, the Augustinian discourse. Curiously, this essay returns through Cochrane to the impossible task of beginning the modern age by inverting Augustine. And, to anticipate just a bit, it is my thesis that Augustine was the Columbus of modern experience; he was the cartographer of "directly apprehended experience," of the direct deliverance of will, nature and consciousness, this emblematic sign of the eruption of the modern discourse from the *stasis* of classical reason which has falsified the maps to the *civitas terrena*. If, finally, the embodiment of the will to power in fleshly being was the modern possibility, it was Augustine's strategy, not so much to act in forgetfulness of being but in repression of the corporeal self, by providing a method for the incarceration of that unholy triad: imagination, desire and contingent will. In making the body a prison-house of the "soul" (embodied consciousness) Augustine was also the first, and most eloquent, of modern structuralists.

While Cochrane ultimately took refuge in the *pax rationalis*[8] (and in the pax corporis) of Augustinian discourse he also once let slip that, in that brief hiatus between the dethronement of classical reason and the imposition of the Christian will to truth, there were at least two philosophical song-birds who, knowing for whatever reason the Garden of Eden had finally materialized, gave voice to the freedom of embodied being. Plotinus uttered the first words of *modern* being when he spoke of the ecstatic illumination of the One; and Porphyry took to the practice of *ascesis* as a way of cultivating the dynamic harmony of will, imagination and flesh. Before the carceral (the *Saeculum*) of Augustine and after the rationalism (the Word) of Plato, Plotinus and Porphyry were the first explorers of the new continent of modern being.[9] And so Cochrane went to his death with his gaze always averted from the human possibility, and the human terror, which might issue from a direct encounter with unmediated being. From the beginning of his thought to its end, he preserved his sanctity, and sanity ("unless we are madmen living in a madhouse"[10]), by delivering up the "inner self" to the normalizing discourse (always horizontal, tedious, and unforgiving) of critical realism: to *pragmatic naturalism* at first (*Thucydides and the Science of History*) and then to Christian realism (*Christianity and Classical Culture*).[11] Cochrane never deviated from Augustine's injunction, delivered in the *Confessions*, to avoid having "the shadow of the fleshly self fall between the mind and its first principle to which it should cleave."[12] But now, after his death and in tribute to the wisdom of his profound scholarship, this essay will allow the dark shadow of the critical imagination to fall between the texts of Cochrane's writings and its modern reception. It would be in bad faith to say that what this will permit is a simple "breaching of the silence" which has incarcerated Cochrane's thought and kept us, as North American thinkers, from an inversion of Augustinian discourse and, indeed, from a full critique of classical reason as well as the culture of the Old World.[13] To know Cochrane's thought is to discover a series of highly original insights into the nature of classical and modern experience. For it is also our thesis that the insights of Cochrane concerning the fateful movement from classical discourse to Christian metaphysics could only have originated in a tradition of thought which has transformed a tragic understanding of human experience (and the search for a realistic solution to the divided consciousness of the twentieth-century) into a searing critique of the foundations of Western civilization.

Metaphysics and Civilization

Charles Cochrane was particularly adept and, in the tradition of Stephen Pepper's *World Hypotheses*,[14] even brilliant as a sometimes playful, always ironic, phenomenologist of the human mind. In accounts of seminal thinkers in the Western tradition, ranging from his satirical deconstruction of Gibbon's *The Rise and Fall of the Roman Empire* (the chief value of which, Cochrane wrote, was not as history but as literature: "It was a splendid example of how the eighteenth-century mind looked at its past") [15] to his profound reflections on Virgil's *Aeneid* (the geneology of the "Latin spirit" in the formation of "empirical will"),[16] Cochrane drew out the fundamental presuppositions, the "discursive assumptions," by which the members of the family of world-hypotheses gained their singularity and yet announced their limitations. As a matter of direct content, the greater part of Cochrane's writings are to be inscribed within that *arc-en-ciel* which moves from the first whispers of classical reason to the disintegration of Christian metaphysics. But the intensity of the encounter with Cochrane's *oeuvre* may have something to do with the elliptical character of his thought; his reflections always circle back and transform the object of meditation. Thus, as in the instantaneous transformation of perspective predicated by catastrophe theory, history shifts into dialectics, Virgil's *Aeneid* becomes a precursor of the founding impulses of American empire, and metaphysics runs into civilization. Even as a matter of content, it is as if the region of ancient history is but a topography in reverse image of modern experience. And, of course, it is; for Cochrane is working out a strategy of thought which moves, and plays, and fails, at the level of metaphysics. What is at stake in his thought are a relatively few laws of motion of the theoretical movements of the Western mind. He was, after all, whether as a pragmatic naturalist or, later, as a Christian realist, always a metaphysician of Western civilization.

Cochrane is a member of that broader tradition of thinkers, in Canada and elsewhere, who developed a self-reflexive critique of modern civilization and who were haunted, all the more, by the conviction that Western society contained an internal principle of *stasis*, an unresolvable contradiction, which would release again and again the barbarism always present in the Western mind. As Christopher Dawson, the Irish Christian realist, put it in his essay *The Judgement of the Nations*: ". . . this artificial reality has collapsed like a house of cards, the demons which haunted the brains of those outcasts (a "few prophetic voices, Nietzsche and Dostoevsky"), have invaded the world of man and become its master. The old landmarks of good and evil and truth and falsehood have been swept away and civilization is driving before the storm like a dismantled and helpless ship." [17] Or, as Eric Havelock remarked in *Prometheus*: "The bitter dialectic of the Prometheus seems to pursue us still. As the intellectual powers of man realize themselves in technology . . . there seems to be raised up against them the force of a reckless dominating will." [18] To Dawson's lament over the "depersonalization of evil" and Havelock's forebodings concerning the certain doom which was integral to the "collective consciousness of the human species," Cochrane contributed a tragic understanding of the classical foundations in Western culture and metaphysics, the turning of nemesis in the European mind. It was Cochrane's distinctive contribution to advance beyond moral lament and promethean consciousness (Cochrane was to say in *Christianity and Classical Culture* that promethean consciousness is the problem of "original sin;" the turning point, not of science and technology, but of Christian metaphysics and the embodied will [19]) to a systematic and patient reflection on the precise historical and philosophical formations which embodied — in the Greek enlightenment, in the twilight moments of the *Pax Augusta* and in the "outbreak" of enlightenment in the eighteenth-century — the "internal principle of discord" which opened time and again the "wound" in Western knowledge.

Four Wagers

What is most compelling about the writings of Charles Cochrane, whether it be his studies of Thucydides, Virgil, Augustine, Gibbon, (or his much discounted, but seminal, meditation on the Canadian explorer David Thompson) is that they disclose the mind — the direct deliverance of being into words — of a thinker for whom the act of thought is a way of preparing for death. Indeed, much more than is typical in the community of historians or professional philosophers, there is no sense of estrangement in Cochrane's writings; no silence of repressed thought between the word and the meditation. What is at work in the texts is, in fact, not an evasion of life but the troubled, restless and tragic record of a thinker who gambled his existence on philosophical history; who, as Sartre said about himself in *The Words*, wrote, in desperation and in despair, to save himself. And just as Sartre noted that writing had condemned him not to die an unknown, so too Cochrane's "wager" is too urgent and too demanding to allow him, even in memory, to slip away from us into the oblivion of death. For Cochrane opened up a passageway to a radical rethinking of the Western tradition—to a philosophical reflection on tragedy as the essence of human experience, to a coming struggle with and through Augustine, to a reinterpretation of the genealogy of divided consciousness. Cochrane has condemned us to be "passengers without a ticket" (Sartre) between idealism and naturalism; to be, after his unmasking of Platonic rationalism and his abandonment of classical *scientia* (long before John Dewey, Cochrane adopted, meditated upon and abandoned an "experimental" social science with its commitment to a liberal image of "creative politics"), thinkers who have nowhere to go except, finally, through and beyond Augustine.

Everything in Cochrane's life, every word, every tormented but sometimes also boring turn of thought, is but a lengthy prelude, a preparation, for his interpretation of Augustine. All of Cochrane's thought hovers around, and falls back from, his final meditation on Augustine: a meditation which, while it occurs within that profound text, *Christianity and Classical Culture*, really takes place, receives its *embodiment* as it were, in one single but decisive chapter of that book — "Nostra Philosophia." [20] It is, of course, towards the horizon of the outrageous, tumultuous, brilliant (and, I think, quite mistaken) formulations of that chapter; towards, that is, a radical reflection upon (and inversion) of the "trinitarian formula" (seen now, both as the epistemological structure of modern psychology and as the metaphysical structure of modern power); towards this nightmare and utopia that this meditation tends. If Cochrane had written nothing else but that single chapter (that single, emblematic and mystical outpouring of a life of thought), with its quite impossible and quite transparent and, it must be said, so troubling account of Augustine, then his would have been a full and worthwhile philosophical life. For he would still have taken us by surprise; he still would have created a small shadow of anxiety between the mind and the fleshly self; he still would have come up to us from behind, from the forgotten depths of Christian metaphysics, and cut away the pretensions of the modern *episteme*, touching a raw nerve-ending, a deep evasion, in Western consciousness. And he would have done this by simply uttering a few words (like a modern Tertullian), by whispering, even whimsically, that the *esse, nosse, posse*, the consciousness, will and nature, of the trinitarian formula, the philosophical and historical reasons *for* Augustine, had not gone away. And he might not even have had to say that we were merely marking time, marked thinkers really, until we have returned to the Christian tradition and wrestled, not with the devil this time, but with the Saint. Surely we cannot be blamed for being angry with Cochrane; for lamenting that dark day when the *absence* of his writings first demanded a reply. Cochrane has condemned us to history; and the history to which he forces a return, this happy and critical dissipation of amnesia (and which critical philosopher has not begged for a recovery of the past, for ontology?), is like the breakup of a long and tedious winter. But who can appreciate the spring-time for all the corpses coming to the surface? To read Cochrane is to be implicated in the history of Western metaphysics. There is no escape now. So, as a prelude to Cochrane's prelude, it would be best to establish, quickly and with clarity, the thematics which led him, in the end, to the "will to truth" of Augustine and which, doomed modern thought to circle forever within the Augustinian discourse.

1.   The Quest for a "Creative Principle"

That there is no tiny space of discord between Cochrane's meditation upon existence and his inscription of being in writing should not be surprising. Cochrane devoted his life to discovering a solution to a fundamental metaphysical problem: a problem which he did not simply think about at a distance but which he lived through, in blood, as the gamble of mortality. It was Cochrane's contention that the central problem of Western knowledge (and, successively, of ethics, history, ontology and politics) lay in the continuous failure of the European mind, and nowhere was this more evident than in classical reason, to discover, outside the presuppositions of idealism and naturalism, an adequate account concerning how, *within* the domain of human experience, a principle might be discovered which would ensure *identity through change*.[21] And it was his conviction that in the absence of a general theory of human experience which furnished a "creative principle" as a directly apprehended way of mediating order and process (the contingent and the immutable) that Western knowledge, and thus its social formations, were doomed to a successive, predictable and relentless series of disintegrations. As Cochrane had it, Christian metaphysics was not *imposed* on classical reason, but arose in response to the internal failure, the "erosion from within," of classical discourse.[22] Consequently, the "truth" of Christian discourse was to be referred to the constitutive "failure" of the Western mind, and originally of the "Graeco-Roman mind," to vindicate human experience: to resolve, that is, the "tension" between will and intelligence, between *virtù* and *fortuna*. In his viewpoint, it was the absence of a creative principle for the integration of human personality and human history which, in the end, led the "Greek mind" to a tragic sense of futility in the face of a world seemingly governed by the principle of *nemesis*; and which condemned the Roman mind (this precursor of the "acquisitive and empirical" personality) to "bewilderment" in the presence of the "bad infinity" of naturalism which, in the modern age, has reappeared under the sign of instrumentalism as Enlightenment critique.[23]

This impossible demand on history for a creative principle, for a new vitalism, which would successfully integrate the process of human experience and solve, at least symbolically, the inevitability of death (Cochrane's *social* projection for death was the fear of *stasis*) represents the fundamental category, the gravitation-point, around which the whole of Cochrane's thought turns. It can be said, particularly in the case of serious philosophies of life which "think with blood," that their conceptual structure, modes of intellectual expressions, often contradictory interventions and reversals, their attempts at taking up the "risk of philosophy," are radiated with a single, overriding root metaphor. If this is so, then the "root metaphor" of Cochrane's thought is the attempt to solve "the riddle of the Sphinx," to reconcile the Homeric myth of necessity and chance, to answer the "weeping of Euripides" through the creation of a vitalistic account of human experience. The search for a "creative principle" (which Cochrane ultimately finds in the "will to truth" — *personality* in God) is, thus, the presupposition which structures his earliest critique of the *arché* — the "physics, ethics and logic" of Platonic discourse (*Thucydides and the Science of History*), which grounds his most mature account of the "radical deficiencies" of enlightenment reason ("The Mind of Edward Gibbon") and which informs his summational critique of the psychology, politics, history and epistemology of the classical mind (*Christianity and Classical Culture*).[24]

If Cochrane's rethinking of the Western tradition from the viewpoint of its radical scission of being and becoming was a simple *apologia* for Christian metaphysics against the claims of classical discourse or, for that matter, akin to Christopher Dawson's profound, but static, circling back to Christian theology under the guise of the defence of civilization, then his thought would pose no challenge. If, indeed, we could be certain that this turn to vitalism, to the search for a new unifying principle which would vindicate human experience by linking the development of "personality" (the Augustinian solution to the "multiple soul") to the mysterious plenitude of existence, was all along only another way of taking up again the "weary journey from Athens to Jerusalem," then we might safely say of Cochrane what Augustine said of the Stoics: "Only their ashes remain." But it is, fortunately so, the *danger* of his thought that, while it never succeeded in its explicit project of developing a new *vitalism* which would preempt the "revolt of human experience," his discourse does stand as a *"theatrum historicum"* (Foucault) in which are rehearsed, and then played out, the three fundamental "movements" of Western thought: poetic imagination, philosophy (both as Platonic reason *and* as positive science) and theology. It was, perhaps, Cochrane's unique contribution to recognize in the emblematic figures of Homer (myth), Plato (*scientia*) and Augustine (*sapientia*) not only powerful syntheses of divergent, but coeval, tendencies in Western consciousness, but to think through as well the *significance* of what was most apparent, that these were representative per-spectives, the play of *aesthetics*, *intellectuality* and *faith*, the fates of which were entangled and prophesied in the gamble of the others.[25] It may be, of course, that Cochrane's concern, and hope, with the possibility of the "trinitarian formula" (*"Nostra Philosophia*: The Discovery of Personality") as the long-sought creative principle was but a product of a Christian faith which finally permitted him the peace of the *crede ut intellegas*. But, might it not also be that the trinitarian formula was less a historically specific product of the Christian metaphysic than an impossible, and transparent, reconciliation of the warring discourses of Homer, Plato and Augustine? In a passage which approaches ecstatic illumination but which also carries with it the sounds of desperation, Cochrane, thinking that he is, at last, at rest within the interiority of Augustine's closure of human experience, writes: "Christian insight finds expression in two modes: As truth it may be described as reason irradiated by love; as morality, love irradiated by reason." [26] Now, while this passage is a wonderful expression of the creation of the "value-truth" which marks the threshold of power/knowledge in the disciplinary impulses of Western society, still there can be heard in this passage another voice which is absent and silenced: this timid voice which can just be detected in the carceral of "value-truth" utters no words; it is not, after all, philosophy which makes the first protest. The sound which we hear deep in the "inner self" of the repressed consciousness of Augustine is, I believe, the weeping of Euripides: it is the return of poetic consciousness, of myth, which is the beginning of the modern age. The danger of Cochrane is that his quest for the creative principle, while always aimed at silencing myth *and* reason, clarifies the fundamental categories of the triadic being of Western society. Cochrane thought with and against Platonic discourse (*Thucydides and the Science of History* was an intentional recovery of the classical science of fifth-century Greece against the "general hypothesis" of Herodotus and against Platonic philosophy) because of his conviction that Platonic reason was inadequate to the task, posed in mythic consciousness, of discovering a "creative and moving principle" which would reconcile human effort and *fortunà*. And Cochrane fled to theology as a second strategic line of retreat (after the débacle of classical reason) from the "ineluctability" of *nemesis* in human experience. Thus, the curiosity: an ancient historian who not only meditates upon but lives through the root metaphors, the fundamental categories of thought and the immanent limitations of the three constitutive structures of Western consciousness. While Cochrane's "radical deficiency" lay in his unwillingness to relativize Augustinian discourse; that is, to think through the significance of the "discovery" of that explosive bonding of power and nihilism in theology; nonetheless Cochrane has succeeded in recessing the historical origins of the "radical scission" to the elemental play in the classical mind among poetry, philosophy and theology and, moreover, in presenting a broad trajectory of the genealogy of Western consciousness.

2.   *The Tragic Sense of Political Experience*

Cochrane's search for a creative principle which would provide a more adequate ground for the reconciliation of order and process was made the more urgent by his tragic sense of political life. He was a "philosopher of the deed," one who transposed the essential impulses of the tragic imagination into a general theory of the classical sources of the tragic imagination, a general theory of the classical sources of European culture and, moreover, a radical rethinking of Christian metaphysics as a necessary response to the internal deficiencies of the naturalistic *vitia* of the classical world. From its genesis in *Thucydides and the Science of History* to its most mature statement in "The Mind of Edward Gibbon" (an eloquent criticism of the formalism of instrumental reason), Cochrane's intellectual project was suffused with an existentialist sensibility: with a self-conscious and deliberate attempt at formulating in the idiom of historical scholarship the pessimistic and, indeed, fatalistic impulses of the "inner man". Whether in his studies of Virgil, Lucretius, Thucydides, Theodosius or Augustine, the historical imagination was for Cochrane an outlet for a wealth of psychological insights into the meaning of suffering in human existence. It might be said, in fact, that he elaborated, in the language of historical realism, a profound psychological analysis of the always futile human effort, this vain *hubris*, struggling against the pull of the flesh towards death. This was a philosopher of life who arraigned the main currents of European cultural history as a way of illuminating the more universal, and thus intimate, plight of reconciling the brief moment of life with the coming night of death. But then, the peculiar tragedy of Cochrane's historical sensibility is that he was broken, in the end, or (if a Christian) in the beginning, by the radical impossibility of living without hope of an easy escape within the terms of the intense and inevitable vision of human suffering revealed by the poetic consciousness of the pre-Socratic Greeks. Cochrane was a philosopher of the deed because his writing responded, at its deepest threshold, to the aesthetics of poetic consciousness; but the great internal tension of his thought, and, I suspect, the deep evasion of his life, was that he sought to make his peace with the tragedy of finality by denouncing as a "radical error" the *hubris* of promethean consciousness (this is the *arché* of *Thucydides and the Science of History*) and, later, by accepting the Christian dogma of original sin (the "essential moment" of *Christianity and Classical Culture*) as a justification for Augustine's sublimation of divided consciousness into the "will to truth." The peace made by Cochrane with existence consisted perhaps only of the expedient of substituting guilt over the *hubris* of the Homeric hero for the unmediated and unrelieved image of nemesis offered by the Greek poets. Need it be said that, while guilt offers the promise of a final peace through the mechanism of the "confession," or shall we say "evacuation," of the self, poetic consciousness promises only that the self is condemned to the liberty of experiencing fully the vicissitudes of contingent and mutable experience. The horizon of Cochrane's historical realism was represented by the fateful figure of Augustine; it was not accidental that Cochrane's thought, while it may have begun with and never escaped from its reflection on Herodotus, concluded with a meditation on *The Confessions of St. Augustine*. Perhaps Cochrane's major contribution may have been to instruct us now of the main avenues of evasion open — the prospects for an internal peace — which were disclosed by the European mind as it struggled to draw away from the tragic sensibility of the Greek classical historians.

Thus, in much the same way that Cochrane once said of classical historiography that it represented an attempt to "escape from the conclusions of Herodotus," [27] Cochrane's historical inquiry might be viewed as an enduring and progressively refined effort at discovering a new *arché*, or starting-point (a "new physics, ethics and logic") which would respond finally to the fatalism, to the internal principle of *statis*, in human experience disclosed by aesthetic consciousness. In an eloquent passage in *Christianity and Classical Culture*, Cochrane presented a vivid description of the nemesis inherent in the very play of human experience. The universe which presents itself in Herodotus is one of "motion. . . perpetual and incessant." [28] Translated into a principle of human behaviour, the "psyche" is so constituted that "now and then, here and there (like fire), it succeeds in overcoming the resistance of those elements which make for depression, and, when it does, it exhibits the phenomenon of accumulation and acquisition on a more than ordinary scale." [29] But, Cochrane notes, there is in this universe no evidence of organic growth; and this because the "principle of expansion operates at the same time as a principle of limitation." [30] Thus, and this is fundamental for Cochrane, "the process to which mankind is subject is self-defeating; it is like the opposition of a pendulum." [31] In this tragic *dénouement*, the role of the mind is that of a "passive spectator:" "self-consciousness resolves itself into a consciousness of impotence in the grip of material necessity." [32] Or, in a succeeding passage, Cochrane meditates upon the words of Herodotus which were voiced by a Persian noble at the Theban dinner-party given on the eve of Plataea:

> That which is destined to come to pass as a consequence of divine activity, it is impossible to man to avert. Many of us are aware of this truth, yet

we follow because we cannot do otherwise. Of all
the sorrows which afflict mankind, the bitterest is
this, that one should have consciousness of much,
but control over nothing.[33]

The elemental and noble gesture of Cochrane's thought was his
effort, always scholarly and nuanced, to fashion a response to the
"bitterness" which flows from the recognition of marginal and
mutable existence. Cochrane's thought hovered around bitterness of the soul, not in the modern sense of *ressentiment*, but in the
more classical meaning of bitterness as an acknowledgement that
there was a work in the very interiority of human experience a
principle of limitation, of arrest, which outside of and beyond
human agency moved to drag back the most inspiring of political
experiments and of philosophical projects to nemesis and *statis*.
What Vico has described as the inevitable cycle of *ricorso*,[34]
Cochrane recurred to, and this often, as the classical image of
"walking the wheel."
    If it is accurate to claim that the tragic imagination represents
the limit and the gamble of Cochrane's thought, then we should
expect to find a lingering, but pervasive, sense of arrested human
possibility in each of his writings. And this is, of course, precisely
what occurs; but with the important change that his tragic sensibility
develops from a rude, almost innate, way of meeting existence to
a complex and internally coherent philosophy of European
civilization. Here was a thinker who transformed the sensibility
of bitterness of the soul into an overarching, and original, account
of the failure of creative politics, of classical reason and, in the
end, perhaps even of Christian metaphysics to solve the enigma
of History. Thus, in his earliest published writings, *David Thompson*:
The Explorer, Cochrane presented in the most agonic of terms the
"story" of Thompson, this explorer of the Canadian West, whose
naturalism was typified by an "imaginative sympathy" for the
landscape and its inhabitants and whose intellectual outlook was
that of an historian "who had the mind of a scientist and the soul
of a poet." [35] And, of course, the story of Thompson was that of a
Greek tragedy: a cartographer who could find no publisher willing
to take on the risk of his work; a father who is forced after
retirement to return to surveying to pay off his son's debts; a
Christian who lends money to the Church and, even in the face of
destitution, deeds it his property; an early patriot (whose "love of
country . . . sprang from an immediate knowledge of the land

itself") whose warnings against the expansionary land claims of "litigous" Americans went unheeded. Cochrane's Thompson was not that dissimilar to the Homeric hero who struggles courageously against adversity, seems to attain a measure of success; and then, at the very moment when relief from the vicissitudes of human existence has been gained, the achievement is swept away by the flux of human experience driven by a "mysterious inner force" of inertia, of equivalence.

In his otherwise astute philosophical obituary, Woodhouse has dismissed Cochrane's work on Thompson as an earlier historical study of little academic interest. Perhaps within the conventional terms of classical scholarship it is; but in the depiction of the tragic fate of Thompson the naturalist there are anticipated all of the major themes that will come to dominate Cochrane's study of the nemesis that awaits classical reason. The essential moments of Thompson's tragedy ("the man who looks at the stars" [36]) are not that different from the "yawning chasm" in human experience which awaits each of the major figures Cochrane will later study: Thucydides (the "first modern political scientist" [37] whose empiricism could not explain the suffering of the Athenian plague or the necessity of defending democratic ideals in the *Funeral Oration*); Lucretius (whose desire for "salvation through enlightenment" was destined to dissolve into "resigned melancholy");[38] Virgil (whose intention of "salvation through will" could not halt the "intellectual and moral bewilderment" of the late Roman empire); Augustine (whose "historical realism" was developed in response to the radical deficiency of the classical order's desire to attain "permanence and universality" by means of "political action"); or even Gibbon (whose defence of the "universal instrument" of reason was fated to return the modern to the *ricorso* of classical reason). Irrespective of the subject-matter Cochrane's thought was never freed of the terrible insight that in the face of a mutable and contingent domain of human experience, the self is confronted, in the end, only with futility, despair and the certainty of the decay of the flesh. And, of course, it was futile to look to political action for salvation because the principle of decay was within, not without; awaiting only an "external shock" to release the *demiurge* again.

3. *The Method of Historical Realism: From Naturalism to Vitalism*

While Cochrane's quest for a more adequate creative principle took place within the horizon of a tragic discourse on human experience, it was expressed through his always insightful recourse to the historical imagination. In keeping with the very gamble of life which was at stake in his classical scholarship, Cochrane's deployment of the historical imagination changed radically as his analysis of the sources of the tragic deficiencies of classical culture broadened into a general critique of the metaphysics of the Graeco-Roman mind. What was constant in his thought, from the beginning in *Thucydides and the Science of History* to the ending in "The Mind of Edward Gibbon," was the use of the "sympathetic imagination" as the axial principle of historical inquiry. For Cochrane, the historical imagination in its standard of presentation should "live up to the most exacting standards of logic and artistry." And, in its standard of interpretation, the "historical and synoptic method," assisted by the "rich resources of language and literature," should seek with the aid of the sympathetic imagination, "disciplined and controlled by the comparative study of people and cultures, to enter into and recover what it can of past experience, so far as this is possible within the narrow limits of human understanding; and this experience it will seek to 'represent' in such a way as to convey something, at least, of its meaning to contemporaries." [39] Cochrane's injunction on behalf of the "sympathetic imagination" as the basis of historical investigation, delivered as it was at the end of his life, does not differ significantly from his original use of the historical imagination to "represent" the tragic sense of Thompson's naturalism; or, for that matter, to present, with a vivid sense of concretization, the discourses of Thucydides, Plato, Theodosius, Julian, Lucretius and Virgil. As a matter of intellectual inclination, Cochrane always erred on the side of generosity to the perspectives of his opponents in the classical tradition; and it is no small measure of his fealty to the principle of the "sympathetic imagination" that his bitterness of the soul was interlaced with brilliant gestures of sardonic wit.

If, however, the use of the sympathetic imagination represents one continuity in Cochrane's historical method, there was also another, perhaps more essential, thematic unity. Cochrane was, above all, a historical realist: a thinker who sought to discover in the immediate data of human experience an immanent principle of integration which, more than the "anaemic intellectualism of rationalism," would provide for the dynamic unification of the sensate and ideal in human existence. It was Cochrane's lifelong conviction (one which deepened as his sense of the tragic dimensions of the triadic being of Western consciousness) that the "mysterious inner force" of human experience should not be met either through "apotheosis or escape." [40] Understanding the vitalistic dimensions of human experience as a force *both* for creation and disintegration, Cochrane devoted his historical scholarship to the recovery of a "realistic" principle which would redeem the civilizing process." Now, as a historical realist, Cochrane was the precursor of an important tradition in Canadian letters: a tradition which includes the "psychological realism" of George Brett, the "cultural realism" of Eric Havelock, the "existential realism" of Emil Fackenheim, and the "critical realism" of John Watson. What distinguishes Cochrane's experiment in historical realism is, however, that he adopted all of the major positions which it was possible to take in the realist tradition of the twentieth century. After all, the paradigmatic figures in Cochrane's thought are Thucydides and Augustine, both of whom were realists, but, of course, of a fundamentally different order. Thucydides was a *pragmatic naturalist*; and in allying himself with his naturalistic political science, Cochrane sought salvation in a political realism. The attraction of Augustine lay, believe, in the elemental fact that he was also a realist, but (in the Pauline tradition) a Christian realist of the "inner man"; a realist who sought to constitute "from within" the psychology of individual personality, a solution to the quest for "permanence and universality" which had eluded the best efforts of "creative politics." Cochrane's historical realism thus oscillates between the polarities of Thucydides and Augustine: between the pragmatic naturalism of *Thucydides and the Science of History* and the vitalistic discourse (or Christian realism) of *Christianity and Classical Culture*. In his phase of Thucydidean realism, Cochrane was a "scientific historian": one who sought to discover in the naturalistic *vitia*; that is, in the discourse of "utilitarian ethics," "democratic politics" and an "empirical political science" canons of interpretation and practice for the "dynamic integration" of being and becoming.[41] In his commitment to Augustinian realism, Cochrane considered himself to be a "philosophical historian:" one who wished to disclose (and successively so, at the levels of epistemology, ontology and aesthetics) the deep reasons for the "internal" collapse of classical reason. As an Augustinean realist, Cochrane shifted the basis of the search for a "creative principle" from the sensate level of human experience ("creative politics") to the "remaking" of inner experience. While the classical science of Thucydides provided a basis of critique of Platonic rationalism (Cochrane said, in fact, that Thucydides and Plato were the polarities of Greek thought) and of mythic consciousness (*contra* Herodotus), Christian realism was the final gamble: an attempt to still the "revolt of human experience" by making the Word flesh.

It was almost inevitable that Cochrane's deployment of historical realism would shift from a naturalistic to a vitalistic basis. The striking feature of his study of Thucydides, aside from its brilliant linking of Hippocrates' *Ancient Medicine* with Thucydides' invention of a method of empirical political science modelled on the medical strategy of "semiology, prognosis and therapeutics" [42] (the historian as a "physician" to a sick society), was that it was a *decisive failure*. Cochrane may have begun *Thucydides* as a "scientific historian," but he ended with the complete abandonment of "creative politics" as a way of warding off the "external shocks" which threatened at every moment to release the stasis within the body politic. While Cochrane managed to complete *Thucydides* with a diminishing but dogged loyalty to the canons of a naturalistic political science (even in the last paragraph he insists that the problem of suffering is a matter of "philosophy not empirical political science"), the central thrust of the study is to shatter the best hopes of "political action" as a means of "saving the civilizing process." It is not a little ironic that Thucydides' declensions in favour of democratic polities are presented in the form of the famous *Funeral Oration*, nor that the background to Cochrane's paean to democratic politics is the seeming madness released by the Athenian plague.

The study of Thucydides had the effect of destroying the foundation of pragmatic naturalism; after Thucydides, Cochrane never sought solace again in the "scientific spirit" (indeed, he was to resituate classical science and Platonic reason as two sides of the philosophical impulse), nor did he seek to exclude (on the basis of the exclusionary canons of interpretation of narrow empiricism) the problem of human suffering from his thought. Cochrane turned to philosophical history to find an answer to the radical failure of classical science to respond adequately to the impossibility of a "stable and enduring" form of political action; more, to that original sense of suffering ahead: the weeping of Euripides as the sure and certain sign of the coming revolt of human experience against all incarcerations. And, might I say,

Cochrane's desire for the recovery of Christian metaphysics was confirmed by his historical observation that Augustine was the objective necessity, the inevitable product, as it were, of that fateful breakdown of the classical mind.

4. *The Refusal of Classical Reason*

The whole of Cochrane's thought gravitated towards an elegant and comprehensive critique of the divided consciousness which he took to be the metaphysical centre of the secular mind. It was his insight, at first historical and then metaphysically expressed, that the modern centuries have not escaped the catastrophe which eroded the Graeco-Roman mind *from within*. Cochrane was, in the end, an opponent of all rationalism, not simply on the grounds of providing a defence of Christian metaphysics, but really because the radical severance of reason from experience (the "disembodied logos") was fated to terminate in "static and immobile" conceptions of social reality. And, of course, in the face of a contingent and mutable process of human experience (a social reality which exploded from within, subverting all attempts at the final closure of experience), rationalism could only be maintained through the imposition of a totalitarian politics. Cochrane may not have been the first to realize the totalitarian impulse which is implicit within Western reason, but he was the philosopher who carried through to its limit the historical thesis that reason, "instrumental" reason, could only persevere if the heterogeneity of human experience was finally silenced, incarcerated within the "iron cage" of rationalism. For Cochrane, as long as Western metaphysics was thought within the terms of Platonic discourse, it was condemned to oscillate between materialism and idealism, between the naturalization of the will and the transcendentalism of disembodied knowledge. This, at least, was the thesis of his remarkable essay, "The Latin Spirit in Literature," just as surely as it was the coping-stone of *Christianity and Classical Culture*. It is important that Cochrane never forgot that Augustine, before he was a Christian, was a confirmed Platonist; and that Christian metaphysics (the "embodied logos") was also the reverse image of Platonic ideas. Under the rubric "the word was made flesh," Platonic Reason migrated into the body and blood of a corporeal being that was about to be "delivered up" to incarceration within the metaphysics of a Christian, *modern* power. In a word, Augustine "embodied" rationalism; and he thus provided a solution to the instability of "creative politics" which had eluded the classical mind. The "iron cage" of rationalism expressed, after all, a more general commitment by the classical mind to seek a *political* solution to the quest for "permanence and universality." Political action was presented as the "creative principle" (whether in Athens or in Rome) which would integrate the "warring tendencies" of the sensate and the ideal, making "the world safe for the civilizing process." Now, just as Cochrane had earlier in his study of Thucydides concluded that the canons of a positive polity could not arrest, let alone explain, the "uninterrupted" revolt of human experience, so too his study of the politics of the Roman empire led him to the insight that the secular mind possessed no "creative principle" to prevent the disintegration of organized society into the extreme of naturalism (the "empirical will") or of idealism ("salvation through enlightenment"). The catastrophe that awaited classical culture (this emblematic foundation of secular civilization) may have been precipitated by "unanticipated external shocks" but its origins were to be traced to a "fundamental failure of the Graeco-Roman mind." [43]

It was Cochrane's intention in "The Latin Spirit in Literature" and in *Christianity and Classical Culture* to explore the deep sources of the radical deficiency in the politics and reason of classical culture. What, he inquired, caused the "Latin spirit" to a restless oscillation between the "resigned melancholy" of Virgil and the "melancholy resignation" of Lucretius: the exemplars of the tragic and instrumentalist tendencies in the classical discourse? What, that is, destined the Roman mind, this *genus* of the empirical will to fall short of the political ideal of "permanance and universality"; to fall into a "moral and intellectual bewilderment" from which there was to be no hope of recovery except for a "radical remaking" of personality and the "practical conduct of life"? And what, in the end, arrested the Greek imagination within a vision of a universe dominated by *stasis*, for which the only recourse was futility and despair? It was Cochrane's historical thesis that the referents of the "Graeco-Roman mind" (reason and will) stand as "permanent inclinations" [44] in modern culture; and that, therefore, the "sure and certain doom which awaited classical culture" was also a sign of the coming disaster in the modern age.

The work of Virgil, like that of Lucretius, is in a

large sense, didactic; otherwise, the difference
between them is as wide as the difference between
Greece and Rome. The one preaches a gospel of
salvation through knowledge; the other of salvation
through will. The one holds up an ideal of repose
and refined sensual enjoyment; the other one of
restless effort and activity. Lucretius urges upon
men a recognition of the fact that they are limited
as the dust; that the pursuit of their aspirations is as
vain and futile as are the impulses of religion, pride,
and ambition which ceaselessly urge them on. The
purpose of Virgil is to vindicate those obscure
forces within the self by which mankind is impelled
to material achievement and inhibited from
destroying the work of his own hands . . . It is this
difference which makes the distinction between
the melancholic resignation of Lucretius and the
resigned melancholy of Virgil; the one the creed of
a man who accepts the intellectual assurance of
futility; the other of one who, despite all obstacles,
labours to discover and formulate reasonable
grounds for his hope. It is this difference that
makes the distinction between the epic of civilized
materialism and that of material civilization.[45]

Just as Cochrane had discovered in the inexplicable suffering of
the Athenian plague (*Thucydides and the Science of History*) the limits
of Greek politics and, moreover, of classical reason; so too, he
finds in Virgil's description of the "empirical personality" as the
foundation of Roman empire the threshold of instrumental
activity as a basis of "material civilization." As Cochrane noted,
the strength and weakness of Rome as the "foundation of Western
civilization" depended on the "psychology of rugged individualism
— the spirit of individual and collective self-assertion"[46] which
destined the Romans to represent, if not "the origin, at least . . .
the essence of the acquisitive and conservative spirit in modern
civilization."[47] For Cochrane, the peculiar strength of the Latin
spirit (this emblematic expression of naturalism) was that the
Romans, viewing themselves "as custodians rather than creators"
allowed nothing to stand in the way of the development of the
"empirical personality" with its basis in will. Consequently, the
Roman identity, rooted in *natura naturans*, oscillated only between

the polarities of *amor sui* (individual self-assertion which found expression in *dominium*) and collective egoism ("public authority and the discipline of the city").[48] Thus, while to the Greeks

> life was an art, for the Romans it was a business. While, therefore, the rich Hellenic genius exhausted itself in the effort of speculation, and in the cultivation of the various forms of artistic expression, the Romans... devoted themselves to the acquisition and conservation of material power, and this aim they pursued with narrow concentration and undeviating consistency for as long as they deserved their name. The Greeks shrank in terror from excess; the Romans found nothing excessive which was possible, and their measure of the possible was based on a 'will to live', cherished by them to a degree almost unique among the peoples of antiquity.[49]

Or, stated otherwise, long before the Protestant Reformation and that fateful linking of the will to salvation and the capitalist ethic, another bridging of the pragmatic will and private property had taken place. The "Latin spirit" parallels the major themes of Weber's "Protestant Ethic," with, however, the major exception that the empirical personality of the Roman *imperium* put into practice a discourse which linked together a theory of family right (*patria potestas*), an understanding of personality as property (*dominium*), a "civic bond" founded on the urge to practical activity, and the will to exclude everything which did not contribute to the "will to work, the will to fight, boldness of innovation and . . . disciplined obedience."[50]

It was Cochrane's great insight to "diagnose" the Latin spirit correctly, taking Virgil as the principal spokesman of that which was most faithful to the naturalism of the Roman mind. In "The Latin Spirit in Literature," Cochrane said of the empirical personality that its adoption made of the Romans a "type of a practical people whose objectives are realizable because they are clear, and clear because they are limited to what the eye may see and the hand may grasp. It is no accident that the spear was for them the symbol of ownership . . . "[51] Yet, for all of this devotion to the expansion of the pragmatic will, it remained "the fate of naturalism to devour its own gods."[52] And while naturalism devours its own gods, "it never succeeds in replacing them with others more impregnable to the asaults of time and circumstance." The Latin spirit, the coping-stone of the empirical personality, gave way to "spiritual bewilderment"; that is, to a search for an answer to the question: "what is to be the intellectual content of life, now that we have built the city, and it is no longer necessary to extend the frontiers?" [53] Or, as Hegel would say later, what could possibly be the content of a civilization founded on "bad infinity"? For Cochrane, it was the peculiar fate of Virgil to be a "splendid failure," understood only by the Christians who "recoiled from him in terror, for the very simple reason that they regarded him as a man who had something to say." It was Virgil's fate to provide a warning, but only after *stasis* had begun, that "the state and empire of Rome depended fundamentally on *will*; virtue is not knowledge, it is character; and its fruits are seen in activity rather than in repose or contemplation." [54] As Cochrane remarks, Virgil "gives authentic expression not merely to the Latin temperament, but in considerable degree to that of Western civilization as a whole. In him alone you see them all." [55]

It was Cochrane's radical insight that Christian metaphysics represents an active synthesis of the Latin experience. The Latin fathers put the "coping-stone" to the developing theory of personality; Augustine's transcendental will was the reverse image of the empirical will of Virgil and Sallust; and the "doctrines of sin, grace, and redemption . . . achieved that philosophy of progress for which the classical world had waited in vain for two thousand years; and which, even through its perversions, has been one of the chief sources of inspiration to the mind of modern man." [56] Virgil is envisaged as bringing to a conclusion the futile quest in classical culture for a creative principle which would have its basis in naturalism or idealism. The modern age does not begin with Plato or with Virgil, but with Augustine's radical reformulation of the philosophy of progress. It was the distinctive contribution of Augustine to rethink the void between naturalism and transcendentalism (between the empirical will and the tragic sensibility); and in the reformulation of the "trinitarian principle" to develop a new principle of integration of human action which would shift the discourse of progress to a "radical remaking of character." As Cochrane says, "Latin Christianity culminated in Augustine, who may justly be described as, at once, the last of all the Romans and the first citizen of the world." [57]

"The Will to Will": Cochrane's Augustine

As a philosopher of the modern public situation, Cochrane devoted himself to the exploration of the fundamental categories of Western metaphysics: that is, to the investigation of the "inner logic" in Western consciousness of the relationship among being, will and truth. Thus, for Cochrane, the phenomenology of the Latin spirit or, for that matter, the historical wager of Thucydides were not episodic or discontinuous historical "events", locked up within a certain phase of historicity, but, rather, gained their significance as reflections of the way in which the dynamics of Western metaphysics worked itself out in historical experience. The bicameral consciousness, or we might say the radical division between will and knowledge (philosophy and history), which was at the root of the Latin spirit is the very same reflection on warring being which has coloured the recent history of Western metaphysics (Nietzsche's truth and will, Heidegger's world and earth, George Grant's technology and *sapientia*, Dennis Lee's "savage fields").[58] To say this is to link Cochrane's exploration of the Graeco-Roman mind (the "permanent inclinations" towards transcendence and submersion) to its actual extension as a fundamental reflection on the genealogy of the radical crisis, the catastrophe, of twentieth-century human experience. Within the discourse of philosophical history, Cochrane stands in that tradition of metaphysical reflection which has sought to understand the inner workings of the nihilism in the Western mind. Cochrane was, first and last, a metaphysician for whom the medium of philosophical history was a way of presenting the concrete expressions in Western history of the fundamental categories of being.

Cochrane approached the domain of Christian metaphysics as a constitutive response to the failure of the secular mind, at least in its Virgilian and Platonic representations, to solve the riddle of being-in-the-world: to provide, that is, an internal and directly experienced principle of integration between "order and motion," or, more accurately, between contemplation and instrumental activity. It was Cochrane's thesis that Christian metaphysics was not an aberration in the Western tradition; not a long, grey twilight which separates the celebration of reason in Latin classical culture from its re-emergence in the Enlightenment, but a necessary, and vital, response in Western thought to the flight of being from the vicissitudes of existence. For Cochrane, Christian

metaphysics was the truth-sayer of the *vide* at the centre of
Western consciousness; and the theological discourse of early
Catholic thinkers, (Athanasius, but, most of all, Augustine) the
first intimations of the birth of modernism. As Cochrane remarked
of Augustine: "Not satisfied like the Hebrew to weep by the
waters of Babylon, nor yet, like the Greek, merely to envisage the
pattern of a city laid up in heaven, but true to the native genius of
the children of Romulus, he traced the outlines of an ecclesiastical
polity which . . . had its foundations solidly embedded in the
living rock of empirical fact. Leaving it to others to pursue
millenialist dreams of a New Jerusalem, he erected the last but
not the least impressive or significant monument to the spirit of
Ancient Rome." [59] In the face of the failure of political action to
achieve "permanence and universality" in the "civilizing process,"
Augustine developed a synthesis of "the whole vision of antiquity
(Hebrew, Greek and Latin)" which was delivered up in terms of a
theory of the radical remaking of the "human personality" and of
the creation of "historical experience" (the *Saeculum*). Augustine
was a crucial mediator of the "inner logic" of Western metaphysics
to the extent that his writings install a new metaphysics of power
(what Nietzsche describes as the "will to will"), an epistemology
of modern psychology (the "closing of the eye of the flesh"), and
the creation of the "will to truth" (the linkage between power
and knowledge of which only now Heidegger, Nietzsche and
Foucault have taken as the nucleus of the modern regime of
power).[60] The Augustinian discourse was, in its essentials, a
reflection of a permanent desire in the Western mind to silence
the struggle of being and becoming (which first found expression
in the tragic sensibility of mythic consciousness) through the
strategy of *embodying* the Concept (what Cochrane refers to as the
values of "truth, beauty and goodness") in the living fact of the
flesh, in the normalization of psychological experience.

The high-point of Cochrane's intellectual achievements was
represented by the publication of *Christianity and Classical Culture*.
It was in this work that he explored, in rich historical detail and
with genuine philosophical insight, precisely how the Augustinian
discourse constituted both a "solution" to the catastrophe which
awaited classical culture (the *Pax Augusta* was finally capable only
of "renovation" and "regeneration" of Western civilization). In
analyzing the historicity of the troubled relationship between the
discourse of classical reason and politics (Virgil and Augustus)
and Christian metaphysics (Theodosius and Augustine), Cochrane

brought to a new threshold of understanding the way in which the Western tradition, both as metaphysics and as political action, has deployed itself. Before Cochrane, the genealogy of Western culture has to do with the history of Reason: a Reason which is sometimes transcendent, at other times submerged in the naturalism of empirical will. After Cochrane, the archeology of European, and now North American, culture cannot avoid the truth contained in the fact that Augustine, this founder of Christian metaphysics, was not ultimately the bitter opponent of classical reason, but its redeemer. It was the fate of Augustine to represent a "synthesis of the whole vision of antiquity" precisely because he understood the nihilism at the heart of Western consciousness. That there is only a reversal of terms between Plato and Augustine, and not a radical diremption, means that Augustine was the first of the modern rationalists: the thinker who understood that Reason could be maintained only as a member of the holy trinity of nature, will and knowledge; as a *term* within that triadic structure of modern consciousness. That Augustine followed Latin Christianity in widening and deepening "the spiritual foundations of a material life which it refused either to repudiate or deny" [61] also meant he was the first of the modern metaphysicians, or, perhaps more accurately, sociologists, of power: the first thinker, that is, to transform the empirical will into the transcendental will and, consequently, to establish the possibility of the will to power. As a synthesis ultimately of Plato and Virgil, Augustine was the culmination of the classical mind's futile search for a new principle of fusion, a "will to truth" which would finally overcome the radical division of the sensate and ideal. Now, to accomplish this philosophical equivalent of nuclear fission (in which Christian metaphysics preserved the nihilistic moment in the Western mind), Augustine made of the body, its deep psychology and its sensual appearance, a radical experiment in a "totalizing" political philosophy. It is often thought, because of his famous words "look into yourself" or his equally celebrated invention of modern psychology in the creation of a "continuous and cumulative experience," that Augustine was somehow freeing the region of the body, and most certainly of the unconscious, for the development of a modern experience which would no longer be incarcerated within the monotonous terrain of a transcendental reason. It is not as often thought that in his search for the "inner man," Augustine was presenting only a chilling sentence on the human possibility: an intimation of a fascist power which would work its wonders through the explosive combination of guilt and the will to truth. Was not the "confession" of Augustine ultimately of the will to itself; that is, the assent of the fleshly will to abandon its claim to radical autonomy in favour of the peace which would come with that new "union of hearts" — the development of the "will to will"? Nietzsche might have been thinking of Augustine when he remarked that the will to power is "the innermost essence of Being"; and further, when he notes (with Heidegger) that psychology is not the essence of the "will to will", but is "the morphology and doctrine of the will to power." [62] This is to say, of course, that the whole of European culture, the metaphysics of modern experience, was decisively transformed by the Augustine's synthesis. And who can say, with any certainty, that Augustine's formulation of a nameless power based on the will to will or, moreover, his colonization of the "inner man" through the incarnation of a metaphysical "truth" have disappeared, now that the profile of religious discourse has receded from view?

In the writing of *Christianity and Classical Culture*, Cochrane presented the exact terms of Augustine's revision of Christian metaphysics with the easy assurance of a thinker who was confident that modernism had not escaped the Augustinian legacy. And, of course, while it may have been Cochrane's weakness that he took refuge in the carceral of the "trinitarian formula" (and this as a way of evading, not philosophy, but the tragic aesthetics of poetic consciousness), nonetheless his description of Augustinian metaphysics, delivered up as the "loving" act of a thinker who had finally come home, offers us an invaluable insight into the phenomenology of the modern mind. The overriding importance of *Christianity and Classical Culture* may be that it makes visible the metaphysics of modernism which, taking place in the fourth century in that decisive threshold between the opening of the wound in Western consciousness (the radical antagonism of the "Graeco-Roman mind") and the coming millenium of a Christian peace, was forced to declare openly its strategies, its "inner logic." In Augustine, the inner logic of Western metaphysics, the specific strategies by which the corporeal self would be invested by the "will to truth", was forced finally to the surface. For a brief moment, the dominations and powers of Western experience were forced, in fact, to confess themselves; to declare their justifications and to say, quite honestly, how they intended finally to silence the weeping of Euripides by turning the corporeal self against itself. Curiously the act of rereading Augustine is nothing less than an exploration of modernism before it goes underground. And what makes Cochrane such a brilliant guide is that his thought, always tragic and ever in flight from existence, cleaves to Augustine as its "first principle." Cochrane tells us what exactly constitutes, at a theoretical level, the decisive intervention by Augustine in Western metaphysics.

Nostra Philosophia

It was Cochrane's claim, as elaborated in the third and decisive section ("Regeneration") of *Christianity and Classical Culture*, that Augustine's originality consisted of assembling into a single discourse three important innovations in Christian metaphysics. Augustine's break with discursive reason (with the whole dualistic *logique* of dialectics) imposed a new beginning-point on human experience. While the Augustinian discourse had the immediate effect of transforming the corporeal self into a vehicle (the body as a prison-house of the flesh or as a "temple of God") for the inscription of truth, it also established the foundations (in epistemology, aesthetics and ethics) of a modernist conception of *personality* and *history*.[63] Augustine was, indeed, the first modern structuralist because he broke completely with the classical conception of reason and with the classical economy of power. Before Augustine, reason and power were rooted in the representationalism of nature. After Augustine, the representationalism of classical reason and power had disappeared; it was replaced by a thoroughly *relational* theory of personality and history. It was, perhaps, the sheer radicalness of the break in Western experience contained in the thought of Augustine that lends *Christianity and Classical Culture* such elegance and persuasiveness. Cochrane realized that, whether in *The Confessions* or in the *City of God* (or, indeed, in his numerous doctrinal challenges to heresy), Augustine articulated the main impulses of the *vitia* of the modern world. In a word, Augustine was the first theoretician to explore the *physics*, the *logic* and the *ethics* of modern experience. Long before Foucault and Baudrillard alerted us to the character of modern power as a "dead power", a "nameless" power which no one owns (but which operates as an "eternal inner simulacrum");[64] that is, long before Foucault broke forever with a representational discourse which was founded on the originary of "nature"; long before this, Cochrane, looking for shelter from the storm, had stumbled upon an earlier expression of a dead power, a power which is purely mediational and, thus, relational in its symbolic effects. The significance of Cochrane's recovery of Augustine against classical reason is that, almost innocently, he provides an intimate account of that fundamental break between the modern and classical *epistemes* which was precipitated by Augustine and from which we are only now beginning to awake.

1. Physics: The Discourse of the Trinitarian Formula

Augustine's first intervention into the closed and comforting discourse of Western metaphysics consisted of a radical refusal of the classical conception of a dialectical reason. As Cochrane said, it was ". . . the function of fourth-century Christianity . . . to heal the wounds inflicted by man on himself in classical times." [65] Classical discourse, beginning as it did with the *arché* of nature, constituted itself within the horizon of a closed *logos* which oscillated backwards and forwards between the antinomies of the naturalistic table of discourse. With all of the flourishes of bad burlesque, the classical economy of reason found itself trapped between the polarities of scepticism (Platonic *logos*) and dogmatism (empirical will). The problem for classical reason, faced with the alternatives of transcendence and submersion, was to discover an adequate "myth" (Homer) or "hypothesis" (Plato) which would serve as a "fuse" to complete the "circuit of intelligibility" across the void at the centre of discursive reason. [66] Much like the modern effort of Enlightenment (Cochrane claimed in "The Mind of Edward Gibbon" that its attempted rehabilitation of discursive reason was nothing but an imitation of the "radical deficiency" of the table of classical discourse), classicism began by "envisaging the subject as in some sense 'opposed' to the 'object' world" and, then, seeking a reconciliation of the two by presenting, mythically or hypothetically, some intelligible relationship between the two. Two escapes were possible: "upwards by way of transcendence or downwards into positivism." [67] At stake were the reconciliation of the "classical *logos* of power" (which opposed its subjective character, "art and industry" to an objective side (fate and fortune); and the fusion of the classical *logos* of reason (which opposed an ultimate principle of being — "water (Thales), air (Anaximenes), fire (Heraclitus) or some element undefined (Anaximander) or as the limit or form (Pythagoras) — to a differentiated principle of becoming (Heraclitus' dialectical materialism, the "idealism" of the Pythagorean school).[68] As Cochrane notes, the result of the closed table of classical discourse was to condemn thought to the "assertion of the claims of the positive sciences" (Hippocrates' *Ancient Medicine*) or to an endless drift into "subjectivism and sophistry" (Plotinus and Porphyry). And from Augustine's standpoint, the radical error of Plato was his discovery and then displacement of the third *arché* (Order) into the Form of the Good, the One, which was to supervene over the atomism of sensate experience. The "blunder" of Plato was to overlook "the possibility that if the conclusions thus reached were so disheartening, the reason for this might not lie in some radical misapprehension of the problem as originally proposed." [69] In not providing a means by which *logos* might be made immanent, Platonic discourse, viewing matter as the "all-but-nothing" immobilized reality, "reducing it purely to terms of structure, so that time was represented as a 'moving image of eternity' and process, as such, was identified with 'irrationality' and 'evil'." [70] The result was the picture of the 'multiple soul', a composite of discrete elements confronting one another in a struggle to be concluded only by the final release of mind from its prison-house in matter and by its return to its source of being, the 'life' of pure form. The fuse between the One and the Many (the Universal Soul as the "hypostatized" connective, or fuse, between the sensate and the intellectual) would be by way of dialectic: the instrument by which the radical dualisms at the heart of discursive reason would be resolved in favour of the overcoming of the "illusory world of sense." [71]

Long before Kant's renunciation of the possibility of knowledge of the *Ding-an-sich* (and his subsequent turn to a *regulatory* theory concerning the analytical presuppositions of the categories of thought) Augustine broke with the Platonic logos, with rationalism, by opposing to the *nature* of discursive reason the *supersensible* principle of triadic being. Classical discourse had sought the principle for the unification of human experience in an *external* mediation: in idealism (transcendentalism) or in materialism (submersion in the finite). Augustinian metaphysics took as its realm of action the field of human experience itself; with, of course, the important exception that it invented "personality" (what Cochrane describes as the "triune character of selfhood") [72] as the embodiment of the Word. Augustine's subversion of classical discourse consisted, above all, of fusing epistemology and psychology in the special sense that he put the body itself into play as a living *theatrum* for the struggle of the finite and the indeterminate. It surely was an early sign of the specious cruelty (the "guilt" over fleshly being) of the modern when Augustine, in his declarations on the "direct deliverance" of consciousness, said, in effect, that now corporeal being would be the new epicentre for a metaphysics of ordered process. For what, after all, was sin but mortality? And, as Cochrane liked to be reminded by Augustine, the Christian analogue of promethean consciousness was that first transgression of "original sin." [73] Augustinian metaphysics saw the fleshly self both as a danger and a possibility: a danger because the "raw touch of experience" was only a sign on the way to death; and a possibility because the radical remaking of corporeal being promised, and this finally, the inner silence of the "unmoved mover." Augustine opened up the continent of human experience only to promptly incarcerate the corporeal self within the "triune character of selfhood." [74] Cochrane is correct in noting that Augustine invented the modern conception of "personality"; but the "personality" which was created, viewed always as a sociological manifestation of the "unmoved mover" (an early structure of "dead power" of postmodern times) was also a prison-house of the actual data of human experience.

We are confronted with a contradiction in Augustine. Here was the thinker who simultaneously broke with the static dualisms of classical discourse by recovering human experience as its own ground and, yet, who spoke to being, will and consciousness only to silence them under the sign of a *relational* will to truth. Augustine's physics involved a fourfold strategy for the colonization of human experience. First, Augustine transformed the previously supersensible principle of triadic being (Father, Son and Holy Ghost) into the axial principles of a new theory of personality. The Holy Trinity was embodied under the sign of a new trinitarian formula of human personality: being/will/consciousness. At a fundamental metaphysical level, the fleshly self was transformed into a mirror image, or perhaps better described as a colonization in parallel form, of trinitarian Christianity. Augustine said that the "problem of life was one of consciousness" and by this he meant that the closed table of naturalistic discourse could only be subverted by means of a new "phenomenology of human experience:" one which generated no hiatus between the sensate and the ideal. The embodiment of logos (the "Word made flesh") meant that consciousness was to be transformed into a matter of "direct deliverance" and that the sensate and the ideal would be unified by will. An *"intima scientia"* [75] would be created which would take being, will and intelligence as directly experienced aspects of human experience. "From this point of view we may see ourselves as possessing the *inseparabilis distinctio* and *distinctio cuniuncto* of a quasi-trinity: being, nature and consciousness." [76]

More fundamentally, the trinity of nature, will and intelligence (itself a mirror image of the original trinity) parallels that other way of taking the trinitarian formula: *corpus* (the body), *anima* (the vision) and *voluntas* (*intentio animi*).[77] It is, in the end, desire (*amor, libido*) which unites the body and intelligence. For Augustine, the body was not an epiphenomenon nor a real principle of existence. It is but a "ticket of recognition." [78] For, after all, the "flesh is the nag on which we make the journey to Jerusalem." [79] Now, however, in the struggle among the body, desire, and consciousness, Augustine argues that everything is to be referred for adjudication (and unification) to an "internal principle of being." The three-in-oneness of the modern personality is founded on an original absence, a void: "the soul is that by which I vivify my flesh." [80]

The presentation of a triadic structure of human experience (of which one manifestation was the *theatrum* of personality) depends on two other strategic interventions: the desubstantial-isation of nature and the final affirmation of the self as a substantial and transcendental unity.[81] Augustinian physics undertook the ultimate gamble of delivering up the "inner man" to the surveil-lance of an *"intima scientia."* It was Augustine's claim that he was finally able to break with classical discourse when he realized that spirituality was substantial and that nature was experienced only as a lack, an absence. Long before Kant, Augustine undertook that fateful movement of thought in which the gravitional-point shifts from the contents of human experience to the analytical presuppositions which regulate the play of the various elements of social existence. The embodiment of the "unmoved mover" as the internal mediation of human experience (a "mediation" which is always known as an absence) meant that the Augustinian discourse would move to decentre the empirical will (contingent and mutable being), concentrating instead on the conceptual norms which regulate, and incarcerate, the different dimensions of human experience. Thus, a great reversal in the *order* of thought appears: the *Ding-an sich* of human experience (the ontological domain of the thing-in-itself) is desubstantialized and what remains as immanent are the normative relations ("truth, beauty and goodness") which signify the internal pacification of human

experience. The Augustinian discourse is nihilistic: it substant-
ializes an absence (the creative principle of the "unmoved mover")
and it condemns as nothingness the whole region of corporeal
being. Augustinian metaphysics can seek to "close the eye of the
flesh" under the comforting ideology that empirical experience
is a void, a dark absence. And it is not even with bad conscience,
but with the consciousness of a mind which has committed itself
to the metaphysics of nihilism, that Augustine can speak of the
need for a "hatred of the corporeal self" and of a "love of the self
which clings to its first principle in God." [82]

Thus, as a matter of physics there are two great ruptures of
thought in Augustine: the embodiment of trinitarianism as the
coeur of the modern personality; and the substitution of the
substantialization of the Concept for the nothingness of human
experience. In Augustine's discourse, a complete metaphysics
founded on the principles of a new epistemology of modern
power is imposed on human experience. Before Augustine, there
may have been a "warring subject" which oscillated between the
ideal and the sensate; but, after Augustine, there is only the
silence of a corporeal self which, having been evacuated of its
claims to be the centering-point of contingent and mutable
experience, now falls into silence. For all of the speech in Augustine
concerning the nature of sin, the turbulence of the body, the
iniquity of desire, what is most peculiar (and this is apparent in
Augustine's adoption of an increasingly militant form of analysis)
is that the actual body falls into silence. We are confronted not
only with the splitting of reason and imagination but also with the
severance of empirical and transcendental will and with the
radical disjunction of nature and analytics.

2. *Logic: Crede ut Intellegas*

Augustine' second intervention into Western metaphysics
was represented by the creation of a discourse which, in overcoming that real space in the classical domain between will and
truth, brought together, and this for the first time, authority and
reason. Cochrane reminds us that in reconceiving "substance as
spiritual," Augustine was able to perceive that "so far from being
ultimate, 'form' and 'matter' alike were merely figments of the
human mind." [83] Now, Augustine's revolt against reason was
fundamental (not because, as for Tertullian, it implied a radical
severance of faith and reason, a faith by 'instinct', under the sign

of the *credo quia absurdam*) in two senses. First, the Augustinian discourse represented a sharp denial of "science as architectonic" in human existence, and thus of the correlative belief that while reason is capable of transcending to the objective domain, faith remains a matter of "private intuition." [84] The essence of trinitarianism, both as a theory of "dynamic personality" and as an epistemological discourse, was to assert memory, intelligence and will (*corpus/anima/voluntas*) as relative and directly experienced aspects of the single process of human experience. Against the radical scepticism of, for example, Pyrrho, Augustine claimed that "reason itself presents the credentials by virtue of which it presumes to operate." [85] In his "phenomenology of the human mind," Augustine asks: "What must I accept as the fundamental elements of consciousness, the recognition of which is imposed upon me as an inescapable necessity of my existence as a rational animal?" [86] And to this, he replies that to "the awareness of selfhood as a triad of being, intelligence and purpose" there is to be ascribed "infallible knowledge; because it is the knowledge by the experient of himself." [87] It is the "direct deliverance of consciousness, independent of all mediation through sense and imagination" which brings reason into a direct and substantial mediation (Cochrane describes this as the "substantial unity" of the triune character of selfhood) with memory ("the sense of being or personal identity") and will ("the uncoerced motion of the self"). As Augustine said in that famous expression: "If I am mistaken, this very fact proves that I am." [88] This *vitalistic* theory of knowledge (vitalism in the sense of the "direct deliverance" of consciousness) is the precise point of division between the epistemological rupture at the heart of classical reason and the reconciliation of consciousness, life and will initiated by Augustine. The categories of triadic being represent a resolution to the classical scission of the material and the ideal; The trinitarian principle represents the preconditions "which are imposed upon the intelligence" as the starting-point of its operations. Thus, for Augustine, faith and reason are not antithetical principles, but "complementary." From the rejection of the claim "that discursive reason can authenticate the presumptions which determine the nature and scope of its activity otherwise than in terms of their 'working and power'," [89] everything follows. As Augustine noted: the *crede ut intellegas* ("believe in order to understand") was, above all, a response to the incapacity of the classical mind to resolve the radical divisions at the heart of naturalism. The lesson of

Cassiciacum was, in the end, that "if faith precedes understanding, understanding in turn becomes the gift of faith." [90] Between philosophy and theology, that is, there is a silent assent: reason never escapes from faith, and faith as the ultimate acknowledgement of science to verify the presumptions by which "it presumes to operate" remains always as the truth-sayer of consciousness.

It is then only a very short passage from Augustine's deflation of reason into its ground in faith to his second, and this very political, conclusion that reason and authority were to be coeval principles. It was a momentous, and terrible, development in modern metaphysics when, in his meditation upon the trinitarian principle, Augustine discovered the necessary connection between the will and reason: the fateful connection which produced the will to truth. "Such is the constitution of human nature that, when we undertake to learn anything, authority must precede reason. But the authority is accepted only as a means to understanding. 'Believe . . . in order that you may understand'." [91] The *crede ut intellegas*, this invention of the will to truth, is surely the beginning-point for a full politicization of Western consciousness; for, that is, a working of power within the interstices of will and consciousness. Augustine had already claimed that memory was the centre of personal identity (thus the *Saeculum* will substitute for fleshly being), and now memory will be made to correspond to the *regulae sapientiae* ("the true service of which is purely as an instrument for correct thinking" [92]). Thus, the Augustinian *episteme* fully penetrates the private sphere of "inner consciousness." A substitution of the order of knowledge occurs: "the knowledge in question . . . is that of the spiritual man. The man who sees the universe, not through the 'eye of the flesh' but in light of a principle whereby he is enabled to judge everything without himself being judged by any man." [93] Curiously, Augustine brings us to the very edge of a modern and critical theory of experience (memory, will and intelligence as directly experienced aspects of human action) but then he reverses the process of discovery, playing the modern constitution of experience back upon itself as a way of responding to the "error" of classical discourse, but also of prohibiting the direct encounter with mortality which is the essence of the human condition. Augustine's politicization of truth provides, I believe, the exact grammatical rules of usage by which reason is to be permanently severed from the imagination. Under the sign of the *crede ut intellegas*, consciousness is universalized; and this in the precise sense that rules of correspondence (whether functional norms of truth, beauty and goodness or relations of similitude, likeness, etc.) are established between the will (this "uncoerced motion" of the mind) and the authority of the *regulae sapientiae*. The trinitarian principle allows the will to invest knowledge; and, inversely, it necessitates that the *regulae sapientiae* will be internalized as permanent defences against the appearance of egotism (empirical will) and, why not say it, against the ultimate freedom of the corporeal self to accept its human fate as an ironic gesture of life against death. It was against the human condition of the empirical will, against death, that Augustine erected that first social contract represented by the triadic principle of being.

3.   Ethics: Theatrum Saeculum

In the Augustinian discourse, the will to truth is grounded in the principle that the realm of sensuous experience is mediated by the "value-truth" of the *ordo conditionis nostrae*: the fundamental categories of epistemology and normative evaluation which are, ultimately, a matter of direct deliverance.[94] While, at one of its polarities, the *ordo conditionis nostrae* generates the radically new conception of a human "personality" ("the primitive and original values of selfhood"), at the other polarity, it produces a second, great discursive unity, that of "history" (the *Saeculum*).[95] It was, indeed, an awesome and definite line of division between the discourse of classical naturalism and modern experience when Augustine, refusing to "close the wheel" of a mythologically informed history, *invented* human history as the actual site in which there would take place the "subduing of the flesh" and the regeneration of personality. In the pursuit of a *pax rationalis* (the synthetic unity of knowledge and activity), the function of the Augustinian discourse was to link the ontological (or, more accurately, theological) unity of human personality, conceived as a "centering" of the trinitarian principles of being/will/intelligence, with the "ethical" unity of historical action, rethought as a discursive manifestation of the divine economy. With the integration of personality and history, a new social unity was created: one which was capable of serving simultaneously as the apparatus of *society* and as a regulator of individual conscience. As Cochrane stated: "History in terms of the embodied logos means history in terms of personality. As such, it makes possible a fulfillment of the great *desideratum* of classicism, viz. an adequate philosophic basis for humanism." [96] For Augustine, the radical error of classicism was that in the absence of a "substantial" principle of unity, its image of an adequate basis for social unity oscillated between the extremes of "thinking with blood" (barbarism) or of civilization (classical *ataraxia*, *apatheia*). Christian metaphysics addressed the defect of the classical economy of power (this restless movement between barbarism and civilization) by delivering up a *substantial* ground for human experience. Cochrane argued: "Properly speaking, (Christian) history is the record of a struggle, not for the realization of material or ideal values but for the materialization, embodiment, the registration in consciousness of real values, the values of truth, beauty and goodness which are . . . thrust upon it as the very condition of its life and being." [97]

Now, without doubt, Cochrane intended his remarkable analysis of the phenomenology of the Augustinian discourse to serve as a last, eloquent *apologia* for Christian metaphysics. And it might even be said that what drew Cochrane to Augustine was precisely Augustine's creation and thematic unification of the discursive ensembles of the "dynamic personality" and the *Saeculum*. After all, Cochrane claimed that the criticism of classical truth was also a "criticism of classical ethics." [98] And there are, in fact, few more ecstatic passages in Cochrane's writings than his description of the almost vitalistic origins of *substantiality* in Augustinian ethics. Of Augustine's defence of "value-truth" as the essence of "creative personality" and of "creative history," Cochrane says: "It is substantial rather than formal truth, and it is substantial rather than formal ethics." And why? Because in Christian metaphysics, "truth may be described as reason irradiated by love; as morality, love irradiated by reason." In sum, the Augustinian discourse makes the linking of personality and history (consciousness and will) dependent on the *incarnation of the word*; and to this extent it closes together the problem of historical necessity (the "divine economy") and the maintenance of an adequate personality (the "redemption of the flesh").[99] Cochrane was ultimately seduced by the Augustinian vision that in the "discipline" which was provided by "the subjugation of the flesh," there was to be found an actual working-out (in conscience and in history) of a substantial synthesis of human experience. Or, as Cochrane would claim, the regulative values of "truth, beauty and goodness" are "essentially substantial . . . and inherent in the very constituion of the universe." [100] Thus, to the degree that the values which are "metaphysically and physically real" are at the same time "historically real", to that same extent the logos (the *intima scientia*) is embodied in the consciousness of the flesh.

The simple fact that Cochrane, himself in search of an adequate philosophy of life, took the trouble to read Augustine seriously and to rethink the implications of the *Saeculum* is what makes his recovery of Augustine of such fundamental consequence. For, outside of Cochrane's *apologia* for Christian metaphysics, there is in his analysis of Augustinian ethics a theoretical account of the actual birth of personality and history as the main discursive sites of Western politics and metaphysics. Long before Sartre's declaration of the "age of ideology," Augustine described the genealogy of the total ideology which was imposed by Christian metaphysics on Western experience and, in addition, justified the thematic unity which would be struck between personality (an "identity" which comes after, and not before, the "subduing of the flesh") and history (the first economy of ideology). And it is essential to the understanding of the nihilism at the heart of Western experience that Augustinian ethics, based as it is on a complete severance of the *civitas terrena* and the *civitas dei*, justifies itself, not through a litany of prohibitions, but through the discourse of love. It is "love irradiated by reason" and "reason irradiated by love" which are the ethical principles guiding the struggle against the corporeal self. Cochrane found, finally, a real serenity in the ethic of love/reason; he might have noted, though, that the curious feature of the modernist discourse released in the vision of Augustine was that it would justify the "subjugation of the flesh" in the name of the "defence of life" and that it demanded "hatred for the self" in the ethic of love. Augustinian ethics, which surely as Cochrane claims, finds its fullest expression in the concept of the *Saeculum*, truly embodies in the flesh the metaphysics of the trinitarian principle and the epistemology of modern psychology contained in the notion of the will to truth. With Augustine's "registration in consciousness" of the *analyticus* of being/will/intelligence and with his ethical defence of the "will to truth" as a historical *and* moral necessity, the modern age is suddenly upon us — in the fourth century after Christ.

In Augustine's discourse on the will begins the arc of a dead power which will not come fully into light until the nineteenth century in Nietzsche's nightmarish vision of the "will to will" and in the postmodern century in Michel Foucault's image of a "relational" will: the transparent, meditational, and contentless will at the centre of the technologically disciplined society.

A.K.

4

THE DISEMBODIED EYE: IDEOLOGY AND POWER IN THE AGE OF NIHILISM

I

The Body as Vermin

> For just as K. lives in the village on Castle Hill,
> modern man lives in his body; the body slips away
> from him, is hostile toward him. It may happen
> that a man wakes up one day and finds himself
> transformed into vermin. Exile — his exile — has
> gained control over him.
>
> Walter Benjamin, *Illuminations*

In the postmodern condition, the eye of the flesh has reopened
only to find itself in the carceral of an abstract power, a power
that is neither historicist nor structuralist, neither solely a matter
of material effects nor exclusively a process of symbolic effectors.
The abstract power of the postmodern age is, in fact, poststructuralist and post-historicist: a coming home to the "perfect
nihilism" (Nietzsche) which has always been at work in Western
consciousness and which only now, in the fully realized technological society, reveals itself in the fateful meeting of power
and the sign. In the political discourse of postmodern power and
the sign (the "information society"), everything is decentered,

disembodied, and transparent. Indeed, the genuinely *menacing* quality of a power abstracted from corporeal existence is that its reality is only that of a bi-polar field of symbolic and material effects. In *The Will to Power*, Nietzsche said that the reality of a nihilistic power was the unreality of a "perspectival appearance:" [1] the bi-polar field of a relational power is only another way of describing the cycle of exterminism which is the charismatic force of postmodern society. A nihilistic power reworks everything into the language of semiotics, into the circular dynamo of a closed information system, only to ensure their destruction in the pure *relational* process of symbolic exchange at the heart of postmodern power. In the discourse of a power which is structured as a "perspectival appearance," symbolism and materiality coalesce only to be vapourized into a pure nothingness. Everything is to be reduced to the new universal exchange-principle of information. [2]

Kafka understood immediately that the world of abstracted power, of "perspectival appearance," would privilege the topological discourse of the surrealistic imagination. In Kafka's discourse, all is metaphorical and, hence, capable of shifting *instantaneously and internally* into a different model of signs. The absolute division of the order of signs from the immediacy of corporeal existence also means that the body is liberated to be resymbolized. A nihilistic power returns finally to the body with a full "spirit of revenge:" it seeks to exact revenge in advance for the coming betrayal of the flesh as it plunges towards death. It is as if the discourse of modern power was based on a simple, but severe, political formulation: the closing of the eye of the flesh, [3] and the opening of the "inner eye" of consciousness — to truth, to normativity, to God, to therapeutics, to information, to wealth, to sex. But the "inner eye" of postmodern power opens onto a continent of simulated experience: [4] here, power is, in fact, always put into play through a relentless exteriorization of the faculties of the body; and through a surrealistic resymbolization of the text of lived experience. Here, there is no paradise of rotting flesh and no prospect of new disease with the morning sun.

Marshall McLuhan perfectly described postmodern experience as a ceaseless "outering" of the senses when he said:

> By putting our physical bodies inside our extended nervous systems, by means of electric media, we set up a dynamic by which all previous technologies that are mere extensions of hands and feet and

teeth and bodily heat-controls — all such extensions
of our bodies, including cities — will be translated
into information systems. Electromagnetic technology requires utter human docility and quiescence
of meditation such as befits an organism that now
wears its brain outside its skull and its nerves
outside its hide.[5]

In the *simulacrum*, where as Jean Baudrillard says, power is an
"eternal inner simulation" of that which never was, there takes
place a constant externalization of the central nervous system.[6]
The sensory faculties are replicated by the technological apparatus
which assumes all of the "signs" of the living organism under the
codes of "species-being" and "species-will." The dynamic nihilism
of Nietzsche's "perspectival appearance" has gone hi-tech.

In the *simulacrum*, power is positive, charismatic and seductive:
a technology of hyper-symbolization is at work which functions
by processing culture and economy into a sign-system (a *radical
structuralism*) endlessly deployable in its rhetoric and always
circular in its movement. Nietzsche's tracing of the genealogy of
exterminism to the circularity of the "will to will" [7] (power is an
eternal metamorphosis of philology) finds its most contemporary
expression in Baudrillard's theorization of the intimate collusion
between seduction and power. For Baudrillard, power is always a
"lightning quick contraction," an endless reversal, between the
mise-en-scène of the real and the "other side of the cycle," the dark
side of power, where power only exists in the form of an "imaginary
catastrophe." [8] "What we need to analyze is the interaction of the
process of seduction with the process of production and power
and the irruption of a minimum of reversibility in every irreversible
process, secretly ruining and dismantling it while simultaneously
insuring that minimal continuum of pleasure moving across it
and without which it would be nothing." [9] In *The Will to Power*,
Nietzsche has already said the same: "Let us think through this
thought in its most terrible form: existence as it is, without
meaning or aim, yet recurring inevitably without any finale of
nothingness: *'the eternal recurrence'*." [10] Seduction stands to power
as its cycle of bliss: "Plunging down — negating life — that, too,
was supposed to be experienced as a kind of sunrise transfiguration,
deification." [11]

The body as cockroach is a "sign" along the way of the
processing of the flesh into the "cycle of reversibility," and

exterminism, of the technological dynamo. After Kafka, the body which is processed within the codes of the *simulacrum*, within the algorithmic and digital logic of the servomechanisms of technological society, is also a kind of "sunrise transfiguration." Seduction is the rhetoric of a "perfect nihilism," a nihilistic power which works always at the edge of the abrasion of "pleasure and bliss" (Barthes). That is why power and ideology in the electronic age, situate the locus of their embodiment in the disembodied eye.

This text, then, is an attempt to uncover the internal dynamics of power and ideology in the postmodern age. The abstraction of power from corporeal existence is the key to postmodern nihilism, but continues it with the image of the "disembodied eye" because in the literature on the optics of the dissevered eye there is to be found an explicit political theorization of the structural logic of the bi-polar field of relational power. This theorization of a relational power is based upon two working postulates. First, the discourse of power stretches in a great chain of nihilation from the modern Augustinian confession of the fourth century to the postmodern charisma of "hi-tech" in the twentieth century. Augustine, Kant, Parsons, Foucault, Barthes, and Baudrillard are but different ways of entering into the very same discourse of a structuralist power.[12] In the language of hi-tech, we are speaking of a "closed loop:" a common, discursive understanding of power which reaches its high point in the dialectic of Barthes/Baudrillard; and from that moment begins a long, historical curvature in which power returns to its genesis in the mirroring-effect of a "pure image system." And second, this relational theory of power is based upon *the method of radical metaphysics*. Running against the tide of what Fredric Jameson has described as "high modernism," the relational theorization of power works at the *edge* of meta-physics and the artistic imagination. Playing Nietzsche's *The Will to Power* against the artistic visions of Max Ernst and René Magritte is a precise, methodological procedure. As Barthes would say, it is an attempt to create an "abrasion" in the seamless web of modernism: an abrasion in which the nihilation at the epicentre of postmodern power can be interrogated *as absence rather than as substance*.

The specific theoretical site lies in a comparative study of those three master texts of the age of "consummated" nihilism: Roland Barthes' *The Pleasure of the Text*; Jean Baudrillard's *Oublier Foucault*; and Friedrich Nietzsche's *The Will to Power*. With them, we are finally beyond ideology-critique and a market-steered conception of power. This is taking seriously Marx's brilliant theorization of the "double metamorphosis" as the surrealistic slide at the centre of the exchange-relation. This time, though, in Baudrillard's *simulacrum* as opposed to the political economy of the nineteenth-century, everything is coming up signs, not commodities. Capital is relativized as one bitter, but partial, phase of the general history of the "sickliness" of nihilism. The new capital of the twentieth-century is that strange alchemy of power as a metaphor for an absent experience, and ideology as the flash which illuminates the "double metamorphosis" at the centre of the postmodern culture of nihilism.

II

The Disembodied Eye: Canons of Postmodern Ideology

> The upturned eye discovers the bond that links
> language and death at the moment that it acts out
> this relationship of the limit and being; and it is
> perhaps from this that it derives its prestige, in
> permitting the possibility of a language for this
> play.
>   M. Foucault, "Preface to Transgression"

What then accounts for the sudden charisma of the disembodied eye as a central metaphor of postmodern experience, a metaphor which is now as much the language of popular culture as of philosophical reflection?

The film *Liquid Sky*, a classic in the genre of postmodern cinema, is constructed around the visual metaphor of a disembodied eye illuminated with the optical brilliance of *jouissance* precisely at the moment when the cycle of love reverses itself (in the form of the Orwellian vapourization of the male lover) and the price for sex is revealed to be death. The detached eye of *Liquid Sky* is translucent, aseptic and reversible: at times the eye expresses in its symbolic effects the interiority of the retina of the viewer; then, in a quick reversal, the eye is presented as a floating detached orb, the sign of a dead eroticism. Continuously, the

disembodied eye is the visual medium for the swift contraction of
sex and death. It is a metaphor for a "cycle of seduction" which
moves like a film of pleasure at the threshold of bliss and murder,
a perfect text for the age of dead love.

In the realm of contemporary music, the strategic significance
of the disembodied eye as a metaphor for a society vulnerable to a
nameless, decentered terror is the thematic of the song *Eye in the
Sky* by the Alan Parsons Project. Here, the floating eye functions
as a source of invisible terror in a double sense. First, the constant
association of the text of the song and the eye of surveillance:
"I am the eye in the sky. Looking at you . . . I am the maker of
rules. Dealing with fools. I can cheat you blind." But the words
themselves with their explicit appeal to a society of surveillance
(the sign of a "normalizing society") are a distraction leading
away from the *actual* text of *Eye in the Sky*. The "eye" of *Eye in the
Sky* is only incidentally an apparatus of surveillance, an eternal
mirroring-effect of the possessive 'I' of the bourgeois self; and, in
the curvature of the mirror in which the invisible "maker of
rules" is "dealing with fools," a description of the will to power.
But this is a will to power which, rather than operating in the
language of negation, functions in the tongue of seduction. It is
the sign of a power that works by a seduction-effect, a simultaneous
arousal and disintegration which marks the beginning of another
cycle of a "perfect nihilism," precisely by the presence of an
"abrasion," an "edge" in its rhetoric.[13] It was Barthes' insight that
in a world structured like a "perfectly spherical metaphor," [14]
metaphor and metonymy function with *and* against one another
as interchangeable moments in the circle of power which is always
tautological. Perhaps the fascination with the disembodied eye
of *Liquid Sky* and the "abrasion" of *Eye in the Sky* is due to the fact
that they are central metaphors for a society which, like Sade's
libertine, takes its pleasure in throwing up bliss as a rebellion
against the boring narrative-line of a surveillance that cannot fail
but be normative. "Neither culture nor its destruction is erotic; it
is the seam between them, the fault, the flaw, which becomes
so." [15] If a perfect nihilism is "never anything but the site of its
effect: the place where the death of language is glimpsed"
(Barthes),[16] then, a perfect nihilism is also a movement beyond
transgression and being, the bliss of the "empty exchange" of the
floating eye.

The False Mirror

Consider, then, the most famous depiction of the disembodied eye, the *rhetorical* eye, presented by René Magritte in his painting *The False Mirror*. Here, Magritte' scandalous image of the eye (i.e., a *simulacrum* of the eye) floats almost innocently as the vast, globular horizon of a translucent, blue sky. Magritte's "eye" is radically severed from its surroundings, magnified in its proportions, and unblinking. We are not in the presence of the eye of the flesh; indeed, we are gazing upon the precise consequence of the closing of the eye of the flesh. Magritte's "eye" is a perfect symbolization, in reverse image, of the nuclear structure of postmodern experience. To gaze upon this disembodied eye is to have a privileged viewpoint on modern experience *turned inside out*. The secret of its scandal is specifically that it reveals no obvious traces of genealogy that would take the viewer beyond the infinite regress of its symbolic effects. The disembodied eye is a powerful visual expression of that rupture in modern experience which was precipitated by the discarding of the myth of the natural (the search for a *representational* founding; at least a *nomos*, if not a *telos*), and the creation of a postmodern, transparently *relational* structure of experience. The disembodied eye is nothing less than a pure sign-system: it cannot be embedded in a chain of finalities because the floating eye as a sign-system signifies the cancellation of vertical being. This is "radical semiurgy" (Baudrillard) [17] which works its symbolic effects in the language of simultaneity, contiguity and spatialization. Magritte's detached eye is a despairing, visual expression of the truth that postmodern experience is structured from within in the *form* of Nietzsche's "will to will." Everything is an hysterical semiology because everything "wants to be exchanged" (Baudrillard). Reason dissolves: the life-world is colonized in its deepest interstices; the radical structuralism which is the essential moment (the charisma) of postmodern experience circles back upon itself (in an endless mirroring-effect) and takes the project of hermeneutics by surprise. When experience is constituted outwards by the abrasion of technological dynamism and lack; when, indeed, a "radical semiurgy" holds constant only the canons of homology and simultaneity (as the *topos* of experience) across the *field* of social relations, and makes the spiralling-effect of experience fascinating precisely because each moment in the "downward plunge" carries the promise of its own exterminism, it is the death of experience that is seductive, not the nostalgia-like recovery of the classical "emancipatory subject." Meaning is only another disguise, another "resurrection-effect" (Baudrillard) which draws us on into a symbolic exchange (carried on in the language of interpretation which carefully obscures its traces in "interpellation") that is, in the end, only another instance of Nietzsche's "plunge into nothingness." In a society that privileges the position of the voyeur (where sight is the site of pure action), the appeal *downwards* to a grounding truth-value (Habermas' "universal pragmatics") can appear only as bad burlesque or as an unhappy reminiscence of the hierocratics of classical naturalism.[18]

The disembodied eye is a perfect *phantasmagoria*: nothing-in-itself, a scandal of absence, it exists as an inscription of pure, symbolic exchange. To gaze at the infinity unto death of Magritte's "eye" is to be as close as possible to what Augustine (the first theoretician of a fully "modern" power) meant in *De Trinitate* when he counselled the closing forever of "the eye of the flesh" and "cleaving" of the inner eye to its "first principle" in God. (Nietzsche's "pronouncement" on the death of God was optimistic; God was never born: *He* was always only a "resurrection-effect" which served as a charismatic value/truth for the "perfect nihilism" of the will to power). Augustine located the secret of the trinitarian formula (rhetoric as the *form* of a relational power) in the medium of the "inner eye." [19] Nietzsche (a philologist and thus capable of understanding immediately the significance of the *rhetorical* structure of the "Holy Trinity") spoke in precisely the same way of the structuration of the will to power.[20] Baudrillard describes the inner eye (the "algorithmic" structure of symbolic exchange[21]) as a "radical semiurgy"; and Magritte can only point in silence and in despair to the floating eye as the DNA of modern experience.

Other than irony, there is no *substantive* relation between the mirrored eye and its background in the "blue sky." The "natural" horizon exists as a mocking reference to the real; a substitutive-effect (Barthes' metonymy) that works to confirm the continuous existence of the dominant metaphor of the floating eye. The blue sky (a "mirror of nature") is the ideology of the radical structuralism operating in the optics of the floating eye. (Like "la sirène" in Robbe-Grillet's *Le voyeur*, the sky exists in the painting as a disguise the presence of which only confirms its non-existence as a real object: *"C'était comme si personne n'avait entendu"*).[22] Always the site of the sky is disturbed and mediated by the inner horizon of the disembodied eye: all a matter of *ressemblance* and non-identity. A perfect refraction takes place in which the object viewed (signified) circles back and, in an instantaneous shift of perspective, becomes the locus (the iris as moon) of signification itself. The principle of motion at work in this purely perspectival (and radically relational) drama is that of catastrophe theory: the essence of the painting lies in a continuous, inner collapse of the "poles" of eye/sky towards one another. Magritte's *The False Mirror* is an elegant, artistic depiction of what Baudrillard has described as the "redoubled simulation" at work in postmodern power. For what takes place in the curvature of the refraction, in this mirroring-effect, is a ceaseless simulation and reversal of the *structural* properties of eye/sky. An ironic liquidation of nature takes place in the painting. The floating eye is, at first, the mirror image of the sky (it is, in fact, the sky of a "power which does not exist" [23]). Both the eye and the sky are perfectly transparent; both are empty mediations (the eye, like the sky, is always a condition of possibility, a symbolic exchange); and both are monarchies of formalism. But the eye in the sky is also a *simulation* of the corporeal eye: it is symbolic of the externalization of the senses into a vast *sensus communis* (McLuhan). Yet there is a difference: the "eye" does not depend for its truth-effects on a technological replication of sight (this is not videology); the "eye" is, instead, symbolic only of the inner binary code of postmodern experience. This is only to say that the "programmed" society is structured from within as a pure optical illusion (a "false mirror") in which everything is reducible to the "presence" of 1 or the absence of 0 in an electro-magnetic field. *The False Mirror* is also a precursor of the algorithmic logic set in motion by the computer.

Nothing can escape exchange! In the symbology of the disembodied eye, a mirroring-effect is in progress in which the *terms* to the relation (signifier and signified, but also all of the antinomies across the table of classical discourse) refract back and forth as image and counter-image in the endless curvature of a tautology. The flash of the gaze as it moves between the "floating eye" (Barthes' metaphor) and the "blue sky" (Baudrillard's "incitement-effect") is, precisely, that small space of disintegration of language and ideology which Althusser called an "interpellation."

To gaze at *The False Mirror* is also to be implicated; to be drawn fully into consciousness of the void, *le manque*, which is at the

René Magritte
The False Mirror

centre of postmodern experience. For the disembodied eye is also a visual autobiography of the dark interiority of modern existence: Nietzsche' metaphysics of the "philological cancell-ation" is a radical examination of the inner topography of the skull of postmodernity. "My consolation is that everything that has been is eternal: the sea will cast it up again." [24] Perhaps though Nietzsche never dreamed, as Magritte must have known, that the "casting up of the sea again" could be alienated into a system of modern power and transformed into the nodal-point of a relational *"code structurel"* [25] which programmes everything into a simplified and universalized algorithmic process. As Augustine first analyzed the inner rules of a procedural logic of a relational power, a *structuralist* power (which is nothing less than a univers-alized, symbolic medium of exchange) would work by processing all of existence into an endless: "yes/yes; no/no." [26] In the pure space of absence of language unto death (that space of affirmation and prohibition) there would remain only the "true word" — for Augustine, this silence which marks the point of rupture between transgression and being is "the sound which is made by no language." [27] In *L'échange symbolique et la mort*, Baudrillard says that the machine with its feedback loops, its algorithmic logic, its mirror-like relations of homology, and its inner circuitry for the transmission *and* processing of information bits works on the basis of a great simplification: 1/0; 1/0.[28] Between Baudrillard in the twentieth-century and Augustine in the fourth-century are to be found the beginning-and end-points of the arc of a dead power.

The epistemology of the Trinity (which, after all, was intended to be a permanent solution to the classical, philosophical problem of divided experience) is precisely the same as the algorithmic logic which is the dynamism of Baudrillard's simulacrum. Because *both* trinitarian formulations (the yes/no and the 1/0 have a *third* term: Nietzsche's will to will which unites them) are instances of the nuclear structure of the will to power. Magritte's disembodied eye is, finally, a confession of the symbolic operations that have always constituted the algorithmic and binary structures of Western experience. "And do you know what 'the world' is to me? Shall I show it to you in my mirror? *This world is the will to power — and nothing besides!* And you yourselves are also this will to power — and nothing besides!" (Nietzsche). [29] (As if to confirm the desperate truth of Magritte's imagination, his "disembodied eye" has been appropriated by CBS as its visual signature, its logo. A pure sign-system is at work here, one which functions by parodying the parody.)

Now, Magritte's "eye" is transparent, mediational and silent. The silence which surrounds the eye is almost strategic in its significance. There are no human presences in the painting. Everything works within and under the suffocating gaze of the mirrored eye. Magritte's universe is one of terror. But this is a terrorism that works in a fully sinister way. There is no frontal oppression; no sovereign authority of a father-figure whose function is the incantation of the eternal "no." Instead, the terrorism of the world as a pure sign-system works at the symbolic level: a ceaseless and *internal* envelopment of its "subjects" in a pure symbolics of domination. The endless fascination with the symbolics of domination (who wants to be a naturalist in the age of electronic semiurgy?) is precisely that the ideological-effects of domination function at the deep level of the *coding* of the exchange-system. Foucault describes this internal coding of experience as a "relational" theory of power;[30] for Parsons, whose theorization of a "relational" power is the reverse, but parallel, image of Foucault's, the deep coding of the exchange-system results in the transformation of power into a "generalized, symbolic medium of exchange." [31] So we are dealing with a "cybernetic" power: a power-system which existing only as a "circulating medium" is always a matter of "ramifications without roots, a sexuality without a sex" [32]; in short, a "regulatory" power combining the limitlessness of language with appeals to the defence of social biology. After all, ideology as a deep coding of the structures of an "empty exchange" (the dynamic matrix of technological society) works continuously as a cycle of seduction.

In Magritte's artistic imagination, it is only when we glance unexpectedly in the wrong direction, when we practice *trompe-l'oeil* as a political act, that we finally see the traces of blood of a domination which works at the symbolic level. Everywhere in Magritte's paintings a nameless, decentered power is at work. Foucault, in his earlier writings, the meditations which produced "Preface to Transgression," was attracted to Magritte's deployment of the artistic imagination. Indeed, it might have been Magritte's visual discourse on identity and *ressemblance* that attracted Foucault's attention, but then, perhaps, the source of the fascination may also have been Magritte's seductive, nightmarish and unrelentingly deterministic vision of the human condition. Magritte's visual domain is a deconstructed one: it is "populated" by objects drawn together in an abstract filiation only through surface relations of formal identity and *ressemblance*. In *Memory*, blood flows from the head of the woman; a child's ball becomes an object of nameless terror. All the figures in Magritte's topography (a *topos* that privileges the voyeur) are trapped in a benign and perfectly structuralist vision. What is important is not the presence — of terror, of filiations, of bodies, of embodiment — but the precise *absence* of possibility: the absence of ontology, sensuous experience, and freedom. Magritte's visual domain is that of Kant's transcendental deduction: formal, categorical and, in its relationalism, quietly terroristic, freedom which is only the empty liberty of "deliverance from" the direct, intuitional knowledge of the *ding-an-sich* to a "relational" power.[33] This is the relational power (a power "which does not exist:" Baudrillard) of the shrouds over the heads of *The Lovers*, the claw marks on the woman in *Discovery*, or the lovely dove in *Black Magic*. To know Magritte is to be confronted with the unbearable truth that the power which now appears is always a displaced "symbol of effectiveness,"[34] signs of power with no apparent originary.

Power is the language of Magritte's artistic imagination but in the specific sense that this nameless power is present only in its absences: a "strange loop" or, perhaps, "crystalline" image of a human condition structured by a mirrored, refracted power. What could be a more haunting symbol of the labyrinth of the carceral than Magritte's painting, *La clef des champs*, in which the landscape collapses inward, revealing and establishing an endless mirrored image between interiority and exteriority? This is the nuclear structure of *synarchy*.

In Magritte's visual *trope*, there is no obvious connection (no "dialectic" of naturalism) between the symbolic language of the *imaginaire* and the presentation of a privileged "finality," no trace of filiation between the dead night of the refracted eye and a vertical chain of significations. Here we are confronted with the decentered power of a nihilistic *socius*, and not with Berger's discourse of the "primitive artist," [35] for Magritte was the first *relational* artist whose "artistic probe" (McLuhan) marks a threshold between a "tautological" structure of being and ontology, between the representational discourse of the "real" and the final liquidation of the human subject within the "massage" of a pure sign-system. Magritte's mirrored eye is, of course, a simulation of the corporeal eye. With strategic differences. The simulated eye signifies, at first, the precise, internal rules of operation by which a technological society invests its "political strategies" on a ceaseless and unbroken *inversion* of the symbolic (culture) over the material (economy). The radically dematerialized is presented as the constitutively material. The mirrored eye signifies the mobilization (an "inner colonisation") of the field of human experience within the pure topology of a system of *lateral referentiality*. As a pure sign-system, the mirrored eye privileges the almost nuclear act of relationalism (not the "dialectic" of signifier and signified, but the pure, tautological "will" of the generalized, symbolic *medium* of exchange) over the warring polarities of representational experience. What we have in Magritte is the radical *inversion* of experience: the antinomies of classical discourse lose their autonomy as they are processed into refracted images of one another. The mirrored eye as pure sign, a perfect act of relationalism, signifies that *rhetoric* and *doxa* are henceforth constituted, not as finalities, but as *co-referential* and *co-constituting* manifestations of the other. This is to say, then, that Magritte understood the terroristic vision of human experience in Kant's nominalism: postmodern experience as *regulative, procedural and relational* specifically in the sense that mediation is privileged over ultimate constituting practices, and form enjoys a "monarchial sovereignty" (Foucault) over *immediate* experience. The mirrored eye is symbolic of a "will to will" which both *constitutes* the field of material practices (ideology as the *doxa* of the medium) and *is constituted* by the heteronomous play of material existence (ideology as the *rhetoric* of seduction). In the *texts* of postmodern politics, power always traces and retraces a great, circular motion: rhetoric

Max Ernst, *The Robing of the Bride*

and doxa (Barthes), challenge and resistance (Baudrillard), play back upon one another as mirrored images in a constant cycle of exterminism. What is at stake is not the *identity* of the constituting subject, but precisely the *death* of the subject hinted at by the plunging downwards into the dark iris of Magritte's floating eye.[36]

After we forever lost a "sovereign power" (with Foucault's elegant division of the "symbolics of blood" from an "analytics of sex" in *The History of Sexuality*), we discover a new principle of sovereignty in the emergence of power as a pure relation. But a relational power is free to be sovereign because it has no reality; it is at centre a *"regressus in infinitum"* (Nietzsche), a pure leap of directly experienced will between two previously divided chains of significations. The luring, compelling quality of a relational power is, perhaps, its *radical absence* (Magritte's dark iris), the presence of which is the basic "condition of possibility" (Kant) of Western consciousness. What is most seductive about a relational power-system is the *asensory*, *aseptic* hint of death which forms its constant, and ever-receding, horizon. When we can say "technique is ourselves," [37] then we have also to look to the *inverted* language of death and life for an answer to the perennial human assent to the will to technology. And thus, perhaps, we find the foundations of human assent in the irresistible fascination in postmodern society with the reverse, but parallel, imagery of transgression and progress. It is the dark spiral of negation which carries us forward; the *charisma* in the nihilism of a technological society lies precisely in its theatrical effect as a site of unceasing motion. In associating the language of death with the purely rhetorical functions of the inner eye, Magritte also joined the poetic imagination and radical metaphysics. The mirrored eye is an advertisement for the privileging of a death-cult as the *ratio* of a society in which the floating eye symbolizes the *nuclear structure* of human experience. But we have this choice: Max Ernst's vigil to the metamorphosis in *The Robing of the Bride* or Nietzsche's elegant cackle. I take Nietzsche.

The Uprooted Eye

In "Preface to Transgression", [38] Michel Foucault recurs to the "denatured" eye as an *ideolect* for the play of limit and transgression in modern experience. He writes of Bataille's *Histoire de l'oeil* that it was haunted by the "obstinate prestige of the eye." "When at the height of anguish, I gently solicit a strange absurdity, an eye opens at the summit, in the middle of my skull." [39] For Foucault, the upturned eye of Bataille represents less the beginnings of a disciplinary society founded on surveillance (unless surveillance be rethought as an inner semiotics of the ruling metaphor), than an actual break in the Western "tradition" signalled by the liquidation of the "philosophical subject." In the transparency of Bataille's upturned eye, a bond is discovered which links language and death. The eye turns back on itself into the dark night of the skull, linking transgression and being. "It proceeds to this limit and to this opening when its being surges forth, but when it is already completely lost, completely overflowing itself, emptied of itself to the point when it becomes an absolute void." [40] Foucault says of the privileging of a purely *visual* universe that what is put in play by this gesture is *absence* as the "great skeletal outline" of existence. It is not so much that the "death of God" made the *impossible* the ground of human experience. This would be simply to indicate the loss of sovereignty of the *interior*, to confirm the void as the centre of the swirling spiral within which we find ourselves. It is not so much the killing of God, but the murder of a "god who never existed" that sustains the *impossible* as the limit of experience. The philosophical subject is always *twice* liquidated: once by the disappearance of the *ontology* of an originary (the "death of God" and, consequently, the boring narration of the "loss" of meaning); and, again, by the impossible knowledge of the murder of a "power which did not exist" (Baudrillard). It is this second "pronouncement," the killing of the *metonymic* representation of a "dead power" (Baudrillard) but not of the metaphorical structure of power, that is the slaying which counts. For what is announced by the murder of a God, who was always only a metonymy, is that being will be played out within the *form* of a power, which, being limitless, is also only metaphorical. Bataille's history of the migrating eye is an erotic record of the disappearance of the philosophical "I". Its internal episodes — *L'armoire normande*, *Les pattes de mouche*, *L'oeil de Granero* — constitute a chain of dead being which consists, as Barthes argues, of a spiralling-effect between the governing metaphor of the eye and the rhetoric of its "substitutive-effects." [41] Rhetoric is the energizing force in the philological cancellation which is the core of the *second* pronouncement. It is the tongue of rhetoric (the mouth as opposed to the eye) screaming against the impossibility of dead being. And this always to no effect. For we are speaking of a perfect tautology between mouth and eye. A circular motion is at work in which speech, while protesting its imprisonment in a metaphorical power (and seeking to subvert the authority of an "empty, symbolic exchange"), only serves as a come-on for that power.

Bataille was writing of the insertion of ideological struggle (a revivifying *praxis*) into the form (the absence) of history. It is the terrible mystery of the yet-unreflected second pronouncement (the non-existence of power) which ideology as the value praxis of truth leads us to. The murder of the first, great metonymy (theology as a signifying practice) intimates that there *never* was a ground to Western experience, that absence was always the primal of the will to will. An atopic universe is thus the limit and possibility of transgression. It is the will to truth which is the "seduction-effect" (Baudrillard) leading us on; and tempting us with the Promethean dream that, in the endless cycle of the "semantic cancellation" (Baudrillard), we will find a reprieve from death.

Always in the background of the funereal social text is another noise: the insistent and monotonous whirring of the techno-system as it "shuffles and reshuffles genetic combinants and recombinants" [42] into a Mendelian-like simulation of life. It is the dark night of the Mendelian simulation — the creation of a "cybernetic" society on the basis of a fateful pairing of linguistic theory and social biology — that transgression reveals. "Perhaps it is like a flash of lightning in the night which, from the beginning of time, gives a dense and black intensity to the night it derives, which lights up the night from the inside, from top to bottom, and yet owes to the dark the stark clarity of its manifestations, its harrowing and poised singularity; the flash loses itself in this space it makes with its sovereignty and becomes silent now that it has given a name to obscurity." [43] Ideology is that "flash of lightning in the night" illuminating the obscure; it is a seduction by a sceptical freedom. As the dynamic matrix of value/truth in the modern régime, ideological discourse promises the return of *vertical* being; the recovery, that is, of a *real* difference between the centripetal (dispersion) and the centrifugal (immanence) tendencies in experience. The come-on of ideology when it operates in the name of transgression is precisely the guarantee of a division between past and future against the circularity of the Mendelian exchange. What is this, then, but a discourse which insists that the flash does not represent an illumination-effect, even at the moment of its greatest brilliance, on its way to obscurity, but a permanent horizon between day and night. (The Canadian painter Ivan Eyre calls this illusion of the permanent horizon "distant madnesses." [44])

Bataille's "upturned eye" is a *coda* for a cynical freedom, for a liberty that moves to the rhythm of ellipsis: eye in the sky/sky in the eye. But what *is* freedom when the "real" is always prepared to abandon its public disguises and, in a quick reversal of effects, to dissolve inwards, directing the gaze towards that spot of nothingness which, in its implosion, traces a long curvature back to the eye of the viewer? As Foucault inquired of a "cynical power," [45] who could stand a sceptical freedom? Who could tolerate a space of freedom which is only the ellipsis of the "sea coming up again?" [46] The impossibility, however, of reading Nietzsche against Bataille or of taking Bataille's "migration of the Eye" as an abrasion which draws out the metaphor of Magritte's mirrored eye, is that they leave no space for transgression that would *really* violate the closed topos of the *simulacrum* (Baudrillard). [47] They reveal only a "cynical power" made bearable because it has as one of its fronts, its symbolic disguises, an equally sceptical freedom. The redeployment of freedom into the language of "lateral referentiality" [48] (liberty as a condition of possibility), of *procedural* normativity, is what is meant by the inner mirroring-effect of society. Language collapses, the aesthetic imagination dissolves, and *The Pleasure of the Text*, *Eye in the Sky*, *L'échange symbolique et la mort* and *The History of Sexuality* are the forms that radical metaphysics is forced to assume. For what is a cynical freedom but another way of talking about the will to power? Now that we inhabit the domain of "perfect nihilism," the cynicism of an empty freedom is the only condition of its pleasure. This means that contemporary ideological discourse, if it is to regain its *charismatic* power, must resituate its seduction-effect in the moment of the "flash" itself. In the world of a "perfect nihilism," what is most seductive is the promise of oblivion, the last cheap thrill of an ironic goodbye to no tomorrows. Postmodern ideology is a parody on the high seriousness of the "flash"; a happy chorus of voices calling out for darkness, for oblivion. This would also suggest that the only serious "ideology" today is parody.

The Eye as Metaphor

In that other reflection on Bataille's optical illusion, "The Metaphor of the Eye," [49] Barthes says of the image of the disembodied eye that it reflects nothing less than a "pure image-system." [50] "In its metaphoric trajectory, the Eye both abides and alters: its fundamental form subsists through the movement of a nomenclature, like that of a topological space; for here each inflection is a new name and utters a new usage." [51] This is, of course, another variation of the unity/variety debate: the form (metaphoric composition) remains constant across a heterogeneity of contents (signifying practices). *Histoire de l'oeil* is a metaphoric composition: "one term, the Eye, is here varied through a certain number of substitutive objects which sustain with it the strict relation of affinitative objects (the cat's milk dish, 'Granero's enucleation', the 'bull's testicles') and yet dissimilar objects too . . . " [52] With Baudrillard's *Oublier Foucault* as the text of Magritte's *The False Mirror*, we are led to the discovery of a "radical semiurgy" at work. And with Barthes' literary imagination as the metonymic agent which rubs and grates against Bataille's floating eye ("a reservoir of virtual signs, a metaphor in the pure state"), we stumble upon the same formulation: "a perfectly spherical metaphor: each of the terms is always the signified of the other (no term is a simple signified), without our being able to stop the chain." [53] But there is also at work in Barthes' "double metaphor," a radical transgression of values: a surrealistic reversal of categories which now is expressed in postmodern aesthetics. And it is this instantaneous reversal of the *terms* in the image-system which renders all traditional ideological discourses (those based on a militant division between the night of *doxa* and the day of rhetoric) obsolete. "Yet everything changes once we disturb the correspondence of the chains; if, instead of pairing objects and actions according to the laws of traditional kinship (to break an egg, to poke out an eye), we dislocate the association by assigning each of its terms to different lines." [54] In crossing the syntagm, we approach the "law of the surrealist image." [55] For Barthes modern being was "purely formalist" because the disembodied eye, as a metaphoric composition for the *actual* structuration of power, always functions by "crossing the syntagm" ("the eye sucked a breast, my eye sipped by her lips"). The initially poetic technique of violating the parallel metaphors (these two chains of signifiers) also releases a very "powerful kind of information." The *simulacrum* now rests on the *political* strategy of transgressing the syntagm, of crossing in random variation the "poles" of the two chains of signifiers. Transgression at the level of metonymy is what Baudrillard describes as a "seduction-effect." The "poking out of an egg, the sipping of an eye" is the "imaginary catastrophe" standing behind the real. In a world structured in the suffocating form of an *atopic* text, ideology functions only in the language of the violation of the previously autonomous division between the parallel metaphors.

Nietzsche said that the will to truth is the morphology and incitement-effect of the will to power. And as Foucault replied later: "The political question . . . is not error, illusion, alienated consciousness or ideology; it is truth itself." [56] Still, there is no "headquarters of rationality" (Foucault), no "core of a metaphor" (Barthes), which explains the compulsion towards the punge into nothingness. The fascination of the floating eye is also that it is an "image-reservoir" of the liquidation, the cycle of exterminism, which is the grammar of postmodern experience. The image-system is always and only a site where action happens, but also where everything undergoes extermination in the *regressus in infinitum*. For "truth" in a purely formalist universe is nothing other than the simulated pleasure of violation, discontinuity, and decenteredness. A cycle of identical images is in motion: Kafka's *Penal Colony*, Barthes' *Text*, Sade's "Silling Castle," Baudrillard's *simulacrum*, Bataille's eroticism of the disembodied Eye. If the uprooted eye is, in the end, a simple "mirror of culture" (Barthes), then the "value" of truth lies only in the surrealism of the pure sign.

Sartre's "look"*

The literature on the disembodied eye privileges the political position of the voyeur. Perhaps to be conscious of imprisonment in the "mirror of culture" is also to aggravate the impulse of autism in the intellectual imagination. At least that was Barthes' posture when he adopted the political stance of the detached, and thus invulnerable, observer who resides precisely at the "degree-zero" of the cycle of exterminism. [57] "He himself is outside exchange, plunged into non-profit, the Zen *mushotoku*, desiring nothing but the perverse bliss of words (but bliss is never a taking: nothing separates it from *satori*, from losing)." [58] McLuhan, that other author of a spatialized universe, proposed Poe's "drowning sailor" as his favourite literary figure. The drowning sailor knows that he is doomed within the downward spiral of the whirlpool, but as a matter of critical detachment he studies the maelstrom "for a thread" which might provide a way of escape. This is only to say that the philosophy of the disembodied eye is coeval with a

---

* Unless indicated otherwise, all quotations in this section are from Jean-Paul Sartre's "The Other and His Look" in Justus Streller, *To Freedom Condemned*, New York: Philosophical Library, 1960, pp. 37-45.

political practice, which, being constituted by the "will to not-will," is also semiurgical, desexed, spatialized, voyeuristic, and privative. Only the dissolution of the corporeal subject could provide a free space of nothingness across which the surrealistic *slide* between metaphor and metonymy could occur. The image of acting "degree-zero" is a splendid and grisly typification of the continuous inner collapse of the previously autonomous poles of experience towards one another. We are in the presence of "catastrophe theory" as the only explanation possible of the inner elision (Barthes: "The most consistent nihilism is perhaps *masked*: in some ways interior to institutions, to conformist discourse, to apparent finalities" [59]) in postmodern experience.

The antithesis of the voyeur, if not its negation then at least its parodic form, is the "laughing philosopher," perhaps best represented in the postmodern century by Sartre. In "The Other and His Look," Sartre speaks of the intimate entanglement of the look and freedom. It was, in part, Sartre's project to insist on the opening of the eye of the flesh, to disclose again the possibility of a political critique of the spatializing *topos* of a rhetorical power. "What I apprehend immediately when I hear the branches crackling behind me is *not* that there is someone there: it is that I am vulnerable, that I have a body which can be hurt, that I occupy a place and I cannot in any case escape from this space in which I am without a defense — in short, *that I am seen*." It is the *look* of the other (this exchange of a "furtive shame of being") which opens up a bitter participation in the human situation. Sartre's *emergence* begins with the auditory sense, with the recovery of the *ear* as a privileged site of political action ("When I hear the branches crackling . . ."). As against the "pure formalism" (Barthes) of the eye which is, in any event, the optics of a silent and unnamed power, the appeal to the ear intimates the recovery of the "throat-iness" of time again, of history once more. We are speaking of the "I am vulnerable:" the pure fleshly "eye" that shrieks against the inevitable loss of sovereignty of the "flash" and laments the inevitable dispersion of *jouissance* in Foucault's "obscurity." Sartre's recovery of the auditory sense is akin to George Grant's recommendation that the project of philosophy today is that of "listening for the intimations of deprival." [60] To Sartre's anguished declaration, "I 'am' my possibilities," Grant responds with the hyper-realistic image of being in the postmodern age: "a plush patina of hectic subjectivity lived out in the iron maiden of an objectified world." [61] In both instances, the embodied ear struggles against the mirrored eye; what is at stake is nothing less than the recovery of speech, of the philosophy of the oral tradition. The floating eye may signify an "empty, symbolic exchange" that specializes in the spatializations of a "pure, image-system"; but the embodied ear privileges corporeality, verticality of being, collective experience, and *speech*.

As a pure, circular semiotics, the "eye" exists as the moment of *absence* between seeing and being seen: *it is the transparent relation which cancels the autonomy of both positions*. The project of the dissevered eye is to reduce Sartre's "look" to a compulsory zero-point of oblivion. Sartre called it *indifference*. "It may be that I choose at the moment of my upsurge into the world to look at the look of the Other (whereupon the look and its objectifying power disappear, leaving only the eyes) and to build my subjectivity on the collapse of the Other's freedom (that is, therefore, on the Other-as-object)." Sartre's notion of *indifference* is based on the double principle of a dispersion of the real (the liquidation of the Other as the limit of my "non-thetic possibilities") and pure relationality ("leaving only the eyes"). *Indifference* is the signature of existence in the *simulacrum*: it is the specific "voiding" of human quality necessary for life in the presence of Magritte's shrouded lovers. Sartre says the world of pure relationality is the political domain in which *ressentiment* against the Other's existence "as my original fall" is overcome by a strategy of cancellation of the Other. "Co-efficients of adversity," "mechanisms": these are the simulated attitudes necessary for the nihilation of the Other as the *limit*, and possibility, of my freedom. Everything works to deny the "unpredictability" of the *reverse side* of the situation; to reduce the "simultaneity of parallel systems" to the univocity of my will, a pure will. The "limit" of the Other is overcome by a fateful linking of language and death: "The problems of language are the same as those of love." [62] But in the slide from love to domination, language itself is subverted: "Language consists of patterns of experience through which I try to impose on the other my point of view, to dominate him and enslave him." [63] Language (the grammatical "attitudes") of a purely *optical* power is the mediation of Sartre's cancellation of the Other. And thus what began with Sartre's analysis of the "motives" of *indifference* (the need to overcome the "limit" of the Other as a way of denying my finitude) ends with the limitlessness of a subverted language. *Indifference* is the grain of the floating eye, the existential posture coeval with the denial of the limit in the existence of the

Other.

Against the *visual* exterminism of indifference, Sartre also listens to the sounds of what is most deprived, most excluded: "My body is a sign of my facticity." [64] With this meaning: "To be sure, the look rather than my body is the instrument or cause of my relation to others, but it is my body that gives meaning to this relation and sets on it certain limits." [65] The perfect semiology of domination symbolized by Magritte's mirrored eye elevates Sartre's claim of the body as a realm of facticity to the most fundamental of ontological rebellions. With its "slight but irradicable nausea," its desire for solitude from the "objectifications" of the *third term* (symbolic exchange), its potential for the "grace" of freedom and the "obscenity" of *superabundant factitity*, the body is the vertical axis that subverts from within the circular motion of a tautological power. Sartre's "lovers in flight" from the "look" are the specific upsurge against Barthes' voyeuristic bliss in the "text" and, for that matter, against Foucault's endless cancellation and reversal of the real. Perhaps the fascination with the dissevered eye and with its psychological correlate in *indifference* is its promise, if not of deliverance, then at least forgetfulness of nausea.

III

Dead Power

Power did not always consider itself as power, and the secret of the great politicians was to know that power does not exist. To know that it is only a perspectival space of simulation, as was the pictorial space of the Renaissance, and that if power seduces, it is precisely — what the naive realists of politics will never understand — because it is a simulation and because it undergoes a metamorphosis into signs and is invented on the basis of signs.

Jean Baudrillard, *Oublier Foucault*

> The text supercedes grammatical attitudes: it is
> the undifferentiated eye which an excessive author
> (Angelus Silesius) describes: 'The eye by which I
> see God is the same eye by which He sees me'.
>   Roland Barthes, *The Pleasure of the Text*

A *political* relationship exists between Kafka's metamorphosis and the variations on the theme of the disembodied eye. With both metaphors, we are confronted with explicit recitatives of the existence of an *absent* power that works continuously on the basis of "figuration" (Barthes) rather than representation. It is all a matter of an alienation performing within the deep site of the interiority of experience, and which produces its effects in a displaced, symbolic form.

At first, there is the expropriation, almost in obscenity, of Gregor's body: the metamorphosis works by *sliding* the dream of nausea into the reality-effect of the bourgeois family. The "slide" of the metamorphosis is as purely figurative a description as could be made of the fragmentation of experience opened up by the psycho-political maneouvre of violating the space of the syntagm. The body as cockroach is a parody on Sartre's "facticity"; and his "irradicable nausea" finds its exaggerated reality-effect in the moment of Gregor's awakening. Dream-experience and reality-principle (madness and reason) slide into one another in an endless spiral of ellipsis: the scream against the possession of the body by an absent power echoes first in the dream, but also finds its mirroring-effect in the *real* which traces the curvature of a mad horizon around Gregor's last "sleep of reason." [66]

The disembodied eye represents, perhaps, but an intensified expression of the alienation first depicted in Kafka's "outering" of a numbed, extremist body. There are, however, strategic differences between the two images, and it is precisely in this space of difference that is disclosed a whole history of a fundamental internal transformation in the *structural* laws of operation of postmodern power. To begin with, the "body as vermin" stands to the dissevered eye as "incomplete" to "completed" nihilism. [67] In "The Word of Nietzsche," Heidegger said that "incomplete" nihilism does indeed "replace the former values with others, but it still posits the latter always in the old position of authority that is, as it were, gratuitously maintained as the ideal realm of the suprasensory." [68] Incomplete nihilism is the prefiguration of the "pessimism of weakness:" [69] it is unconsummated, passive, embodied, and thus still capable of the *bracketing* of a critical hermeneutics. In the metamorphosis, there remains a tension (a preservation of *dialectical* reason) between consciousness and the mutilation of the body. The "body as cockroach" is a classic, political statement of the age of incomplete nihilism; but with this statement there may also have come to an end the privileged existence of a *sociology* of power. Thus, Gregor's nausea is an active counterpoint (an immanent resistance and first refusal) to the normalizing domination of a bureaucratic society. Nausea is also a melody of transgression and division. The *shell* of the body is a vivid expression of the deep penetration of the principle of "imperative coordination" into the "old position of authority." This is a theoretical rebellion against a *normalizing* domination: *a domination by the norm* which works through a sociological incarceration of the body and is sustained by an "analytical reduction" of power to the language of the "internalization of need-dispositions." [70] With the metamorphosis, we are thus drawn into a *historical* meditation on the dark side of normativity: the side of the *embodiment* of a positive, analytical, and almost benign, structure of value/truth. Kafka's theorization is a reverse, but parallel, image of Spencer's "social physics"; and with both we are brought to the culmination in late nineteenth- and early twentieth-century sociology of an already obsolete form of power. That Kafka, and his poetic analogue in Benjamin, were the last and the best of the critical theorists may be, no doubt, because they lit up the dark night of bureaucratic (normative, mechanical, and embodied) power with the luminousity of one word: repulsion. It was also the fate of critical theory to remain a historical reflection on "incomplete" nihilism. But it must be said too that the peculiar illusion of critical theory (and one which now condemns it to unwind into the future as a *conservative* defense of the "critique" of incomplete nihilism) was its tragic forgetfulness of Nietzsche's insight that in the cycle of exterminism (the day of "completed" nihilism) even the transgression of thought is only another station along the way. In an ironic gesture, it is the fate of contemporary critical theory to preserve the classical "truth" of the now-anachronistic era of *unconsummated* nihilism.

The significance of the disembodied eye as an almost primitive expression of the postmodern fate is that it symbolizes the *charismatic leap of power* from its previous basis in normativity (the "old position of authority") to a new foundation in the "semiurgy" of the pure sign (a pure *optics* of power). The mirrored eye is disembod-

ied, relational, tautological and *active*. We are in the presence of a
"power" which overwhelms *from within* the classical division of
time/space so essential to critical theory (Gregor's consciousness
preserves "time" against a spatializing topos); and which, moreover, processes everything within the *field* of its discourse through
a "semiological wash." [71] McLuhan hinted that the age of electronic
media would release a "polymorphous symbolism" [72]; but
Baudrillard added the necessary corrective that the age of the
"structural law of value" (McLuhan's transparent media) would
be experienced as a "radical semiurgy." [73] The shift from Kafka's
metamorphosis to the mirrored eye is thus a sign of a vast rupture
in postmodern domination. In a sociological domination, there
was at least a final grounding of power in the body; providing, at
the minimum, the illusion that we were dealing with a power
"which had a sex" (Foucault); a power that would always be
forced to close with the philosophical subject. Not so, though,
with the postmodern power symbolized by the disembodied eye.
Here, power has no sex for the specific reason that this is a type of
domination which privileges the technological knowledge of a
pure sign-system. Power can now be asexual and neutral (unclass-
ifiable) because it is associated with the "truth-effect" of a
discourse on technology. This is a power which works at the level
of the *technical* manipulation of symbolization, and is free to be
charismatic because it dwells in the pure technique of an exchange-
system which being "nothing in itself" is always symbolic and
figurative. When power loses the necessity for the "truth" of sex,
then it is also free to *decouple* corporeality from an obvious
imprisonment. The last illusion of a "mechanical age" is, however,
that the body (Sartre's "facility") has somehow been recovered
when it is released into the "bliss" (Barthes) of a "polymorphous
symbolism."

The metamorphosis which counts in the world of a "radical
semiurgy" is no longer Kafka's tomb of the body, but that atopic
and purely formal transfiguration which is the thematic of the
artistic imagination of Escher. Escher's *Moebius Strip II* or his
dramatic *Sphere Spirals* vividly illustrate the existence of a *mirrored*
power which works as an endless redeployment of a tautological
sign-system. To study Escher is to enter the ground-zero of a
fantastic *morphological reduction*. Everything is a matter of structural
filiations in the process of rapid reversal (perspectival space
collapsing inwards) spiralling upwards in an impossibility of spatial
distortion, of cancellation *and* extension of complex images

which privilege the "smaller and smaller." This is an absolute
litotes of an experience which is never more than its topological
filiations, but also never less than a deep continuity of an unceasing,
circular exchange of the forms of existence. The particular
contents of experience are relativized: this is a totalitarianism of
form. In the sudden reversal and liquidation of the contents of
this formalist geography (birds into trapezes; fish into missiles;
stairwells into castles in the air; substance into an infinity of
nothingness), two structural laws of value remain constant. First,
everywhere in Escher there is a "double-movement" of creation
and cancellation. Nothing remains immutable; life appears only
as a sign of a cycle of disintegration which is already underway.
But, as in *Moebius Strip II*, the impossibility of this double-
movement is that the impulses to genesis and exterminism
condition one another, almost as conspirators in a "ceaseless
revaluation of all values" (Nietzsche). The double-movement of
creation and reversal is the deep structuration which lineaments
the heterogeneous *contents* of experience and which, seemingly,
makes for an impossible symmetry of conservation and death.
Second, and in sharp contrast to Kafka's nausea. the structural
law of motion which incites the double-movement is that of
seduction. It is precisely what Baudrillard said in *Oublier Foucault* of
the convergence of seduction and power in the postmodern
century: "Everything wants to be exchanged, reversed, or
abolished in a cycle (this is in fact why neither repression nor the
unconscious exists: reversibility is already there). That alone is
what seduces deep down, and that alone constitutes pure gratification (*jouissance*), while power only satisfies a particular form of
hegemonic logic belonging to reason. Seduction is elsewhere." [74]
   The mirrored eye opens onto a new continent of seduction
and power: a topography of reversibility and instantaneous
cancellation. It is seduction which is the *absence* in a tautological
power; and it is the promise of death in the double-movement of
Escher's "figuration" which makes the "spherical spirals" of his
work fascinating. Now we know that the existent "texts" of a
relational power converge on an understanding of the eroticism
of nihilation. That is why Bataille's *Histoire de l'oeil* is a classic of a
dead eroticism; why Barthes ends *The Pleasure of the Text* with the
fateful *words*, ". . . it granulates, it crackles, it caresses, it grates, it
cuts: it comes: that is bliss":[75] and why, perhaps, Sartre stood
convinced of the *irresistibility* of nothingness. In *To Freedom
Condemned*, Sartre spoke of the fascination of the "hole" as some-

thing which "longs to be filled." So much so, in fact, that the challenge of the void (the "hole") is always at the threshold of life and death: "He makes a symbolic sacrifice of his body to cause the void to disappear and a plenitude of being to exist." [76] Sartre's "sacrifice" before the challenge of the void is the very same insight as Baudrillard's "seduction" and, for that matter, of Barthes' *"jouissance."* We are in the presence of a purely tautological power which stakes its truth-effect on the almost promiscuous presence of the void. Death in its multiplicity of presentations (Sartre's "nothingness is not," Heidegger's "nihilation," Nietzsche's "modernity as a rat's tail") is the challenge, the seduction, which inflames power as a "pure sign." (But *against* the relevance of Kafka's metamorphosis, the "sacrifice" before the void works in the language of seduction, never as the psychology of repulsion.)

Consummated Nihilism

Escher's artistic perspective of a ceaseless liquidation and multiplication of *deep morphologies* finds its analogue in Nietzsche's haunting image of an age of "consummated" nihilism. In *The Will to Power*, Nietzsche said: "There is no will: there are treaty drafts of will that are constantly increasing or losing their power." [77] And the will "does not exist" [78] because Nietzsche knew it was already dead: a *lack* which could have only a multiplicity of "treaty drafts" (truth-effects). As the double-movement of its "signs" (the mirroring of *signified and signified*; as Barthes said, "nothing exists as a simple signifier" [79]) the will could exist only as an optical effect in reverse image. Of Nietzsche's "dead will," Baudrillard said that we are dealing with a "perspectival space of simulation" [80] which functions on the basis of a transformation of the *real* into an empty "sign-system." Will is *symbolic* of the nihilation of facticity; and it is in the internal grammatology of the *symbolizing-process* of the dead will that we come upon, almost without warning, the *basic genetic code* of postmodern experience. Baudrillard's notion of the will (and thus power) as a "simulation" of the real signifies that a dramatic reversal of void/being has occured. For at the "centre" of the dead will, there exists in seductive, but paradoxical, form a "plenitude of the void";[81] and only outside the seduction of the void does there exist that now *real* lack: the *emptiness* of being. The will as only a "space of simulation" works its optical effect through a reversal of nothingness: it is not so much that "nothingness is not" as that "nothing-ness *is* being."[82] Nietzsche might well concur that Escher's *Whirlpools* with its swirling and always reversible filiations of form, its seductive image of a pure suffocation of perspectival space, is an accurate depiction of the will which "does not exist."

Nietzsche's understanding of the dead will as the centrepiece of "consummated" nihilism drives forward and *challenges* Baudrillard's theorization of an equally "dead power" in *Oublier Foucault* and in *L'Échange symbolique et la mort*. And it is Nietzsche's dictum that everything is false; everything is permitted"[83] that names the cycle of exterminism from which Barthes' *text* cannot escape. Everything orders itself around the challenge of a will that "does not exist"; nothing can remain unentangled with the charisma of a nihilism which is now "completed." In his meditation on Nietzsche, Heidegger said that in the age of the "pessimism of strength," there is accomplished only ". . . the rising up of modern humanity into the unconditional dominion of subjectivity within the subjectness of what is."[84] A "dead power" has dispensed with the "old position of authority" ("incomplete" nihilism), substitut-ing the void itself as the truth-effect of postmodern existence. The "pessimism of strength" is the "thickness" (Barthes) of power as it is experienced for what it is: a symbolic metamorphosis of the real energized from within by the psychology of seduction.

Following Nietzsche, contemporary philosophy converges, in its most exciting expressions, in a discourse on power which is seen as transparent, mediational and contentless. Like a slow awakening to the "reality" of an inverted existence within the void, there are murmurs at the margins of theoretical conscious-ness of the existence of a "dead power." Baudrillard has been the most eloquent in its revelation. In *Oublier Foucault*, he said that the discourse on power can take place no longer in the language of ideology-critique or of founding referents, but must make reference to the processes of relationality and empty, symbolic exchanges. Because on the "other side" of power, the side in which power "has no existence as a representation,"[85] there remains only a power which is put into play as symbols without ultimate finalities: a fascist power. And specifically in the sense that Baudrillard speaks of fascism as a "simultaneous ressurection effect" of a dead power.[86] A fascist power, of the left and of the right, is encouraged to play itself out at the thresholds of life and death because the *void* that is Baudrillard's "dead power" is pure instrumentality without signification.[87]

Heidegger knew: Fascism is the politics of the "pessimism of strength." For we live in the moment of the "sunrise transfiguration"; and what separates us forever from the possibility of freedom (the reverse side of the "authority" of unconsummated nihilism) is that we are already deep in the cyclical *exchange* of "dead will." "Completed nihilism . . . must in addition do away even with the place of value itself, with the suprasensory as a realm, and accordingly must posit and revalue values differently." [88] The organization of experience around the "revaluing of all previous values"; in fact, the very language of value itself is the *constitutive* process of a fascist power which takes up the challenge of nothingness. For Heidegger (although not for Sartre), nothingness is always *nihilation*.

There is, however, a real division between Baudrillard's translation of Nietzsche's will which "does not exist" into a "dead power" and Heidegger's description of the immanent horror of an age of "completed" nihilism. Well in advance of Baudrillard's posing of the fateful question, Heidegger provided an answer as to why fascism is the "only irresistible form of modern power." Baudrillard's tragic vision of human experience is a continuing response to a fundamental query: Why does a fascist power retain its charismatic appeal? In *Oublier Foucault* and, to a lesser extent, in *De la séduction*, Baudrillard struggles with the meaning of seduction as the "lightning-quick contraction" which is the *charisma* of the "redoubled simulation" of the cycle of liquidation.[89] But Baudrillard never finally closes with the meaning of seduction, not as an "incitement-effect," but as a pure, *absent* condition of possibility for the semiurgical operations of the "will to will." His interrogation of a "dead power" stops on the threshold of a radical metaphysics; and falls back successively into a dispersed communications theory (like McLuhan) and a more prosaic entanglement with the critique of the "political economy of the sign."

Heidegger didn't stop. He gazed into the abyss of the "dead will" and arrived immediately at the secret of a fascist ("high modern") power: "The will to power does not have its ground in a feeling of lack; rather it itself is the ground of superabundant life. Here life means the will to will." [90] And what is this "superabundant life," the seduction-effect in the *form* of which the will to power simulates the suppressed region of facticity, other than the revivifications by which power hides its *lack*? Modern power is the will to will; and the secret of the will to will is that it is always displayed in whatever is most charismatic, most energetic, most formalistic and technical, the very existence of which is dependent both upon its symbolic (and thus *real*) metamorphosis into the *principle of superabundant life*, and upon its constant flight from that which has lost its seduction-effect, its charisma. Having no existence "in itself," this is a power that takes on the *simulated* life of a changing order of significations. Power/sex, power/norm, power/grace, power/knowledge, power/sign are the multiplicity of "eternal inner simulations" traced in the arc of a dead power. The trajectory of this dead power moves like a dark *arc-en-ciel* across the history of Western consciousness. Always there is the *constant*, *mediating* (metaphoric) presence across a multiplicity of sites (principles of "superabundant life") of a "will to will" which resuscitates itself in the dynamic guise of that metonymy (the "truth" of capital, normativity, sex) which is most charismatic. And here charisma in its relation to modern power means precisely what Weber said of charisma as the presence of what early Christians called the "gift of grace." [91] But with this difference. Since the upsurge of a consumated nihilism in the Augustinian "theology" of the fourth century, grace means standing in the presence of the "will to will." With this metamorphosis of the dead will into positivity, the charisma of grace, a "dead power" is enabled to speak in the language of love. Charisma is a "presencing" of the will to will; and the secret of the dead will is that it works its effects in the symbolic form of the defense of life (species-will) against death.

While it is an historical and not a metaphysical question as to the specific reasons for the activation, and quick liquidation, of the changing "signs" of power in Western experience, this much might be said: The genealogy of modern power has traced a path which has moved from the birth of power in "incitement-effects" that disguise completely the presence of power and, in fact, are successful only to the extent that they maintain the hidden invisibility of the "dead will." The *denial* of the presence of power was the first condition of the beginnings of "completed" nihilism in Augustine's brilliant simulation of the "perspectival space" of a living God in the trinitarian formulation. Indeed, we might go further and say that it was Augustine's specific contribution to demonstrate, at a theoretical level, the *grammar of reversal* within which a modern power would operate. For Augustine in *De Trinitate*, grace is the will; life (of the soul) is death (of the body); intellect is liquidation of imagination; and memory (of the history of the dead will) is amnesia (of corporeal being).

Successively, the migration of modern power from its inception in the nihilation of Christian metaphysics has followed a "semiological reduction" (Baudrillard) which has involved a great reversal in the order of relationship between the "dead will" and its signifying practices. From the suppression of the existence of power, power has gradually liberated itself of its dependency upon *denotative* signs. In that forgotten moment when Western consciousness revolted against the *stasis* of classical dialectics and took up, for the first time, the challenge of the abyss, everything had to be staked on an intense, militant, and almost insanely charismatic, *rhetorical* commitment to the simulation which was at work. That sheer impossibility of the "ruse" of Western consciousness, modern existence, would be wagered henceforth on a "power which does not exist," made it all the more essential that the *symbolic order of the simulation* pour into every nook and crevice of the real, material world of denotation (if only to work the *reversal* of the real from within); and that the inversion of death over life symbolized by the *credo ut intellegas* (the "confession" of faith in a "dead will") have about it the "thickness" (Barthes) of charisma. This is why, perhaps, in Pauline will, it is always all or nothing: the investiture of grace works charismatically; but charisma of this order only signals the passage of Western consciousness into the "perfectly spherical metaphor" of the dead will. Just as Augustine's famous "conversion" in the garden at Cassiacium marks the specific point in Western metaphysics when the will first "broke into the will" (the end of the "divided will" of classicism); so too, Paul's equally famous "blindness" on the road to Damascus is the precise site in Western consciousness of that primal event Nietzsche described as the situation of the "either-or." [92] Paul's "blindness" is an almost literal figuration of the "closing of the eye of the flesh," and of its reverse side, the opening of the "eye to its first principle in God" (the mirrored eye), an explicit narrative of the exterminism of corporeal being, and the sovereignty of the simulation of the mirrored eye. The Pauline epistles are a political narrative of the filiations and strategies of the first investiture of the material world by the *simulacrum* of a will which is "nothing in itself."

Since the upsurge of consummated nihilism in Pauline "will," there has been a great relaxation, almost a monotonous banality, in the "incitement-effects" that have been discharged by the circular metaphor of modern power. It is already late in the day of the history of a nihilating power. We are fated to live through the dying moments of a historical force the symbolic-effectors of which, having exhausted themselves in rhapsodies about the suprasensory realm, have now taken refuge in the more prosaic "codes" of a postmodern culture.[93] As a theoretical proposition: the symbolic incitements of a "dead power" (what will be the *metonymy* of the challenge of the void?) have swept down from the sphere of the purely ideal ("resurrection-effects") which deal in extension without duration to the material *topos* of the body. As if in a great, downward whirlpool effect, the "void" of modern power is prepared to play out the essential parody of its post-modern reversal of death over life to the very end. From the high-charisma signifiers of redemption (Augustine), *civitas* (Hobbes), and "the understanding" (Kant), power circles around the realm of flesh and bone, approaching a final (and progressively more banal) localization in the terminus of the body. Thus, from the hyper-charisma of grace, power traces a path which requires successively lower voltage inducements: the norm, sex, utility, and, now, the empty semiurgy of the "pure sign."

We might say, in fact, that it is a *real* indication of the vitality of a nihilistic power in postmodern existence that power is now played out in a theatrical language which has nothing about it of the "high seriousness" of philosophy, sociology, or theology. The prattle of postmodern power is in the almost surrealistic rhetoric of "high-tech." At one time, we could even trace the epistemological movements of a dead power by recording the specific sequence of ruptures (the history of nominalism) as power in *symbolic* form invested region after region of material significations. Following the strategy of discourse analysis pioneered by Foucault, we could prepare a taxonomic classification of the upsurge of a "dead power:" in sex, in social physics, in normativity, in utility. And we could do this by simply charting the great, internal order of divisions between material denotations (the empirical site of investiture by the "will to will") and the equally great chain of symbolic referents: "sexuality without a sex" (Foucault); utility without use-value (Marx); power without the body (Hobbes); reason without the head (Kant); and social physics without community (Spencer). There would be a ceaseless migration of power from one "abstract coherency" [94] of symbolic referents to another. Because the nihilism of power is due, not only to its philological reduction of material experience to the language of value/truth, but also because the "will to will" is *murderous* of its truth-effects. God (Christian discourse), sex (Freud's *la petite mort*), utility (Ricardo's labour theory of value), need-dispositions (Parsons' theorization of cybernetic exchange): these are different moments, or "truth-effects," in the arc of an *absent* power which revivifies itself in the form, the *charismatic* form, of a changing order of signifiers. Nietzsche's description of the "will to power" is analogous to Lacan's "floating signifier" in this essential respect: the migration of a charismatic power takes place by a restless advance of the *absence* (the dark iris of the *imago*) which is power from one site of significations to another. But always Nietzsche's "double-movement" is at work. On the one hand, there is a "resurrection-effect" (Baudrillard): the spiralling of an *absent* power through the languages of sexuality, normativity, capital, and so on. In each of these great convergencies, a dramatic vivification of experience takes place. There is an irresistible "illumination" of sex, the unconscious, normativity, ideology as they are invested with the charisma of a power which incarcerates its empirical domains in the language of seduction. But there is also another movement which stands on the "dark side" of illumination, and that is Heidegger's "nihilation." Of this dark side of power, Nietzsche said: "The will to power can manifest itself only against resistances; therefore it seeks that which resists it — the primeval tendency of the protoplasm when it extends pseudopodia and feels about." [95] Foucault's "transgression" is the abrasion, the specific site of a loss (Barthes) which distinguishes the counter-cyclical movement of nihilation *and* charisma (Nietzsche's "preservation and enhancement") in modern power. Much later, Baudrillard said of the language of metamorphosis in power, this murdering of its truth-effects: ". . . the real has never interested anyone. It is the locus of disenchantement par excellence, the locus of accumulation against death. Nothing could be worse. It is the imaginary catastrophe standing behind them that sometimes makes reality and truth fascination." [96] Again, a power which seduces by a slight *trompe-l'oeil*.

Power as a "Pure Sign:" Barthes/Baudrillard

The disembodied eye, then, is a perfect metaphor for the postmodern culture of consummated nihilism. The message of the Eye is radical in its simplicity. Power is now ready to confess its secret. Since Nietzsche, it has been impossible to carry out a reduction of the "will to power" to its field of symbolic effects.

Power was never, after all, anything more than a mirroring-effect which functioned to disguise the hidden circularity of the language of the dead text of power. Power as a "mediation" (Baudrillard), a "medium" (McLuhan), a "relational field" (Foucault), a "will to will" (Nietzsche), an "exchange-value" (Marx), a "pure flame of the will" (Augustine), a "generalized symbolic medium of social exchange" (Parsons), and a "judgement" (Kant) was always the *symbolic* form of social exchange itself. A nihilistic power never could be exhausted by its denotations, the specific *terms* of being (signifier) and becoming (signified) which assumed the positions of "lateral referentialities" in an empty, symbolic exchange. To say that power is constituted as a purely symbolic relation which moves back upon itself in an endless descent into the *vide* is a historical reflection on Nietzsche's insight that the reality-effect of power is a "perspectival appearance" of which we are the "commandments." [97] It was, perhaps, Nietzsche's fundamental claim in *The Will to Power* that we are the inhabitants of a "purely fictitious world," [98] a spatial manoeuvre which operates in the sign-system of contiguity, reversal, and extension. And as with all optical "simulations," only the inflectionless (anaptotic) language of the internal structuration of power matters. All other praxologies are but a deflection of the gaze from the inner neutering, the cancellation, of experience which is the trademark of power as a pure sign-system. And postmodern power can now appear in the symbolic form of what it has always been — a *cybernetic* process of social exchange — because there is no longer a political (existential) requirement for the "lack" in experience to be disguised in the rhetoric of representationalism. This is only to say, then, that the culture of consummated nihilism reaches its apex in the *seduction* of a power which is finally free to be "cynical." That we are the first generation of human beings who take their pleasure in teasing out the psychosis hidden in the "real" was the bitter conviction that led Baudrillard to that most terrible of laments: "Today especially, the real is no more than a stockpile of dead matter, dead bodies, and dead language." [99] With this lament, we're suddenly very near the exterminism site in postmodern power. It is not so much that the "real" is the false (that would be simply an epistemological slide), but that the categories of the real (ideology, consumption, desire) are "sickliness" (Nietzsche).

Perhaps the sheer impossibility of gazing directly into the eye of power, of learning that the "truth" of experience is only an infinite regress into a white space of *sickliness*, accounts for the desire to take power out of play, to liquidate the knowledge of the limitless possibilities co-existent with the void of a dead will. Everywhere the sovereignty of *absence* in Western experience announces itself in a century which has become a slaughter-bench, though always there is a deflection of attention from the logic of exterminism and the instant, accompanying murmur that this surely must have been only a glimpse into the "dark side" of the real. Ours is a society modelled on the image of the atopic, social text: a plunging, circular motion to the infinity of a final cancellation. Since Nietzsche it has been impossible to talk of power as anything other than a philology. At the deepest recesses of Western consciousness (when the *edges* of the tautology were first curled up by Christian metaphysics), we are confronted with a "semantic cancellation" (Baudrillard), a "neutering" (Barthes) of the real. The *deep coding* of postmodern power is almost genetic; it is, in fact, a simulated genetics (political biology) in the sense that the semiotic structuration of power is that of a circular metaphor which refracts its "fictitious" *terms* in a ceaseless process of lateral referentiality. And it is this unclass-ifiable, decaying site of a psychotic philology deep in the structure of modern power that is the Eye of Baudrillard's "semiological reduction," Barthes' "perfectly spherical metaphor" and Nietzsche's "eternal recurrence." The specific descriptions of the semiurgical reduction of a cybernetic power may vary, but always there is the common refrain: "cat's dish and bull's testicle" (Bataille); "signifier and signified" (Saussure); "consumption and lack" (Baudrillard); and "pleasure and bliss" (Barthes). In each of these instances, the "terms" of the symbolic exchange do not signify finalities, but "image" one another as co-constituting, co-referential, and co-signifying phases in a single, unbroken circle of symbolic figuration. Nothing escapes the nihilation of the "will to will." It is the symbolic form constant across heterogeneous contents. It is the "blink" between Barthes' poles of narration and catastrophe.

But power as the space of "perspectival appearance" can now only be concretized in reverse image. How, after all, are we to write a political philosophy of the disembodied eye, or a psychology of the seduction at work in the purely optical-effect of the "semiological reduction?" A theorization of power which would capture the element of anamorphosis (Lacan) [100] in the inner structuration of a relational powr must develop a "device" which would take us beyond its "incitement-effects." There is a desperate need, on the theoretical level, for the creation of a disturbance ("opthalmia") [101] in the dissevered eye of power. Or, as Barthes would add, a metonymic agent is required which would perform the function of "iron filings" in concretizing the invisible filiations of the bi-polar field of power.[102]

A complete theory of a relational power could not avoid considering the "abrasion" between those classic texts of the twentieth century: Roland Barthes' *The Pleasure of the Text* and Jean Baudrillard's *Oublier Foucault*. A political theory which tries to induce opthalmia (distortion) of the disembodied eye is always on the look out for that "seam," that site of loss, which, once followed, will reveal the genealogical traces of the famous disappearance of the philosophical subject. The forced convergence of Barthes' "text" and Baudrillard's "simulacrum" is precisely such a shattering of the eye of power. And not so much because these are oppositional perspectives (they are, in fact, parallel but reverse images of the very same power as a "sign-system"), but due to the more ominous fact that the "text" (Barthes) and the "simulacrum" (Baudrillard) are themselves displaced symbolic-effects of a dead power. We are in the presence of two failures, two haunting expressions of the blunting of literature against the unanswerability of the void. The texts spiral into one another; and in their entanglement as *challenges* to the eclipse of the real, we discover constitutive, but opposite, responses to a "consummated" power.

Barthes' literary critique of power is written from the perspective of Nietzsche's "weary nihilist." What, after all, could be a more resonant description of the passive nihilist who has lost the will to struggle than Barthes' self-portrait: "I myself was a public square." [103] And what, for that matter, could be a more vivid depiction of the "active nihilist" than Baudrillard's charismatic *will* to follow through on the opening of the void revealed by the intracation of "seduction in power and production." Barthes was a perfect successor to the cultural sociology of the French rationalist project.[104] His study of the "mythologies" of the real is reminiscent of Durkheim's empirical explorations of "collective representations" to the extent that both efforts are tragically flawed gambles at seeking out the passive (Buddhist) position of the unclassifiable "neuter" in the midst of the inner stasis of a power which "does not exist." Perhaps, Barthes never comprehended that behind the narrative-line of "mythology," there was to be found, not the *ideolect* of a real history, but the simulated perspectival space of Kant's "understanding." Barthes' "weariness," moving in the detached, but vicarious, tones of sarcasm and sexual titillation, was occasioned by a nominalism which he was sensitive enough to describe (with eloquence), but which he lacked the will to combat. And so, Barthes' writings will stand in history as a brilliant analysis of the actual topography (the figurations *"en abyme"* of a dead power), but also as a devastating failure. Nonetheless, the ultimate contribution of Barthes' *écriture* may lie, quite paradoxically, in its notorious cop-out: the choice of "degree-zero writing." Barthes' "melancholy (but fascinated) resignation" provides, at once, an uncensored image of the inner workings of the dead will, and a powerful demonstration of the limits of the intellectual imagination of a "cynical power." This was the theorist who returned to smell the excrement of the social text — and declared it freedom.

It is quite the opposite situation with Baudrillard. His meditation on power is dangerous precisely because it stands at the vortex of three great trajectories of thought, each of which represents an important threshold of a relational theory of power. Simultaneously, and almost in a spontaneous generation of the theory of a simulated power, Baudrillard works out the essential contributions of Kafka, Nietzsche, and Saussure. The *simulacrum*, with its constant horizon of a "dead power" which functions by a symbolic reversal, is Kafka's *Castle*; while the "redoubled simulation" of symbolic effects — the reality of awakening within the "density of the social which crushes us" [105] is as searing a description as could be offered of the metamorphosis. Not that Baudrillard borrows mechanically from Kafka: more to the point, his thought is a working-out of the "root-metaphor" of Kafka — our imprisonment in a purely symbolic sphere in which the "decline of the real" is matched by an endless mirroring of escapes to nowhere. But if Kafka's metamorphosis finds eloquent expression in the "simulacrum," then the dynamism of the "mirror of production" (the special relationship between production/ desire in which seduction revalorizes production within a libidinal economy) is inspired by Nietzsche's "lack." Baudrillard ends *Le système des objets* by stating that consumption (*the* centre of contemporary ideology) is driven onwards, not by a theory of real needs, not by a *project*, but by a "lack" which is the *vide* in all consumption.[106] And, of course, in his critique of Foucault in *Oublier Foucault*, his thought played at the edge of a symbolic exchange which is only the inversion of the "emptiness" of death. The invisible, third term in Baudrillard's discovery of the "pure sign" (which operates as the basis of the "semiological reduction") was Nietzsche's "will to will." And the gravitation-point for this double trajectory of an epistemology of Kafka's metamorphosis and an anthropology of the "will to power" is provided by a powerful conjunction in Baudrillard's thought of linguistics (partly Saussurean, partly Maussean) and genetics ("beware of the molecular").[107] Baudrillard's is an entirely postmodern theorization of power. And this, specifically, because it is a vast synthesis which concretizes the concept of the "will to power" in the "simulacrum"; puts the "metamorphosis" in play as a theory of symbolic reversal; radicalizes structuralism by the simple measure of concentrating on its essential truth: the yes/yes; no/no of a binary, algorithmic "sign-system"; and invests power and ideology with libidinal energy. Baudrillard has spoken of the existence in the electronic era of "digital" theory: a theorization which creates the equivalent of Lacan's "floating signifier" in the notion of a "floating" *explanandum*.[108] Baudrillard's thought may be the first of the "floating theories:" it moves on the basis of simultaneity, homology, and analogy between computers, anagrammic logic, popular culture, and metaphysics. It is a "perfect text" because in its fragmentation of objects as particles in a vast semiurgy; in its refusal to participate in the fetishization of the "real"; and in its despair over awareness of *le manque* in experience, it is a transparent, but silently screaming, description of the "simulacrum" which is its *topos* of investigation.

Now these strategic differences between Barthes and Baudrillard only emphasize, by way of contrast, the remarkable similarities in their theorizations of postmodern power. Their "texts" shadow one another as convergent, but inexplicably distanced, narrations of the very same site of a tautological power. To draw the texts together is "to presence" the opposite, but symmetrical, polarities of a bi-polar theory of relational power. Barthes' *jouissance* is the mirror-image of Baudrillard's "seduction"; the latter's "lightning quick contraction of reversal and liquidation" is but a curvature on its way back to Barthes' "cycle of pleasure and bliss"; Barthes' famous site of the "neuter" has its equivalent in Baudrillard's "cancellation"; the "anaclictic topos" of *The Pleasure of the Text* is the mirrored-effect of Baudrillard's "satellisattion of the real"; and Barthes' recurrent image of "stereotypy" is what Baudrillard has described in *The Mirror of Production* as the "radical autonomisation" of consumption." [109] We might say, in fact, that Barthes' language ("I am interested in language because it wounds or seduces me" [110]) is the rhetoric of the "simulacrum." Barthes was insistent that it was the "neuter" in speech which was the "islet of pleasure"; and thus, his ideal self — the "anachronic subject" ("a subject split twice over, doubly perverse") formed a perfect candidate for the "grammatical attitude" of the text.[111] "On the stage of the text, no footlights: there is not, behind the text, someone active (the writer) and out front someone passive (the reader): there is not subject and object." [112] But Baudrillard is equally insistent on the metaphoric composition (the *doxa*) of the text: "Dans le fétichisme, ce n'est pas la passion des substances qui parle (que ce soit celle des objects ou du sujet), c'est la *passion* du code qui, réglant et se subordonnant à la fois objets et sujets, les voue ensemble à la manipulation abstraite." [113] Baudrillard's *code structurel* is the inner semiurgy at work (the anagram) in Barthes' text as an islet of pleasure ("... the scandalous truth about bliss: that it may well be, once the image-reservoir of speech is abolished, *neuter*").[114] Which is only to say that the "anachronic subject" (who seeks successively a hyper-realism of bliss; a "double perversity" in discovery and loss; a "voyeurism" observing "clandestinely the pleasure of others"; and "the enjoyment of his own fall" [115]) is the precise psychological character type of the simulacrum. In *The Pleasure of the Text*, Barthes has written the psychological recitative of the neutered and disembodied topos of *le code structurel*.

In the abrasion which results from the "crossing of the syntagm" of Barthes and Baudrillard, a topological shift in the perspectival space of power takes place. The art of illusion is at work in the spiralling of Barthes' autistic text into the deep codes of the simulacrum. Almost as in an Escher painting, the theoretical strategy of the *trompe-l'oeil* results in an instantaneous transformation of the "background" (the *shadow* in the morphology of power) of *le code structurel* into the "foreground" (the white space of the "angels" in *Circle Limit IV*) of Barthes' rhetoric. It is not so much that Baudrillard's reversible power is the polarity of Barthes' "anachronic subject" as that, taken together, we are in the presence of an endlessly refracted image of power as a pure sign. Except in this instance, the mirroring of Barthes and Baudrillard signifies that the "dark side" of power (the side of the Nietzschean regression) is prepared to declare itself openly; to say, in effect, that the "degree zero" of the void has always been the inner dynamism of Western experience.

Indeed, in the space of illusion which divides Barthes' privileging of the "pleasure of the text" and Baudrillard's menacing vision of the "inner semiurgy" (an "autonomising" power), we are suddenly propelled into a theorization that resonates with, and is transparent to, high-tech postmodernism. The refraction of the "text" and the "simulacrum" is an explicit structuration of the very geography of the topos of the culture of consummated nihilism. So much so, in fact, that the hyper-energy of Baudrillard's reflections on the "perspectival simulation" of power and the seduction of Barthes' twinning of desire and rhetoric suggests that we are very near the charisma of the void. This unexpected ejection from a mechanical world-view throws us into the "heart of the heart" of postmodernism. Everything is there; and everything is transformed. It is a structuralist world now: the "anachronic subject" as the DNA of postmodern psychology; "species-will" as the gravitation-line of political biology; a grisly display of the "aesthetics of hyper-realism"; [116] the "reversibility and sudden cancellation" of a "power" which moves as a seduction; a litotes of binary and algorithmic logic: pure mediation, pure symbolic exchange, pure "plunging downwards," pure fragmentation. The existence of the social text as a perspectival effect of a sign-system no longer bothers to hide the *vide*, opening the *absence* in power as an ironic sign (a last metonymic cut) of the sovereignty of the double simulation at work in the eye of power.

A.K.

5

CYNICAL POWER:
AUGUSTINE'S MAGRITTE/
AUGUSTINE'S BAUDRILLARD

There are few more searing depictions of the purely topographical universe of an abstract power than René Magritte's
The Door to Freedom. This painting is in the best of the pastoral
mode: it consists simply of a landscape viewed through a window.
There is, however, an odd and disconcerting difference. The
window is shattered; and on the bits of glass — which explode
inwards, not outwards — are clear traces of the image of the
image of the landscape. Now, representational art, and with it the
classical (also representational) theory of power depended for its
very existence on the preservation of a privileged and substantive
distinction between the sign and its referent. Power, in this case,
always stood for something *real* outside itself: a referent like use-
value, sovereignty, justice, democracy which would, and this
simultaneously, concretize the regression into nothingness in
the will to power and provide an after-glow for a power which had
already disappeared into the "vanishing-point" (McLuhan) in
Western consciousness. Following Nietzsche's insights into the
"in vain" of the ellipse traced by the will to power, Foucault has
said that power in the postmodern era could only function on the
condition that it hide its (real) existence as purely cynical. When
the horizon has been wiped clean, who could tolerate the knowledge of a cynical freedom, an absent power, an existence falsely
unified by the "fiction" of perspectival appearances? In *The Door*

to Freedom, we are suddenly ejected from the comforting illusion of an antinomic, thus representational, theory of power into an "empire of signs" (Barthes) which consists only of plunging downwards through endlessly refracted imagery. A perspectival illusion is at work here which produces an image of the real (the antinomies of window and landscape) only as a symbolic-effector to disguise the disappearance of the real into the endless curvature of the mirrored image. The significance of the traces of the image of the landscape on the broken glass lies preisely in the circularity of its symbolic effect. Magritte's disclosure of the pure sign-system of *The Door to Freedom* reveals that, after all, the antinomic basis of Western knowledge was only a perspectival *trompe-l'oeil* leading away from the reality of the mirrored language of analogy, similitude, and likeness. Signifier/signified; unity/variety; inside/outside: the antinomies are transformed into purely perspectival sites in the mirror of power. And what unifies the antinomies of the Sign, projecting them outwards as predicates of existence and then dissolving them in a quick reversal from within as purely symbolic effects already on their way to disintegration, is the existence of power as a process of abstraction and disembodiment. We are in the presence of a sign-system which functions on the basis of the liquidation of the real. Magritte's imagination teases out that precise point in the curvature of the downward ellipse of postmodern power in which power, abandoning its association with the psychology of sacrifice, prepares to re-enter its own cycle of disintegration in the symbolic form of the psychology of seduction. This is the reverse side of Nietzschean power/sacrifice: not the side of "conscience-vivisection and self-crucifixion," but the dark side of conscience-cancellation and self-absorption. Like the exploding images in *The Door to Freedom* which collapse inwards only to reveal an endless, didactic recycling of the same image, power/seduction and power/sacrifice are reverse, but parallel, expressions of the same circuit of abstract power. It was Magritte's fine contribution to reveal that the real terrorism in Kant's antinomies has to do with the free-fall effect which they induce in the eye of power. Magritte's universe is decentered, silent, and metaphorical: his paintings, ranging from *The False Mirror* to the stereotypy of *La Reproduction Interdite*, point to our incarceration in the downward plunge of structuralist experience. As Nietzsche also knew, power can exist now only in exchange. Like Marx's abstract labour before it, power has an abstract (symbolic) existence as the illusionary (and thus metaphorical) form of the imposition of the "fictitious unity" of the categories of the real. Paradoxically, the abstract value of power in circulation depends on the constant disappearance from view of that mysterious force which has always been the inner dynamic of modern power: the "will to will." In *The Door to Freedom*, the "will to will" is the disciplined, optical effect by which the eye traces out a smooth, unbroken curvature between the shattered image and its recycled mirror-image: the instantaneous optical operation of dividing, and thus privileging, the antinomies of foreground and background. While the imposition of a willed continuity is, in fact, the secret form of power in the "door to freedom," there is also a reverse, cancelling motion at work in the painting. There is also the censoring of the scream of Nietzsche's "in vain" as the eye projects a reality-principle into the tautology of the mirrored image.

Magritte's insights into the tautological and metaphorical basis of power have their theoretical analogue in the radical structuralism of Jean Baudrillard. In works from *Pour une critique de l'économie politique du signe* to *Oublier Foucault* to *L'Échange symbolique et la mort*, Baudrillard has explored the meaning of a "dead power." In *Oublier Foucault*, Baudrillard has sensed something of the awesome truth that power which functions as a metaphor for that which has no existence is fascist in character and presents itself in the "aesthetic ritual of death" [1] as a power which has no signification, except in purely symbolic form, outside of itself. And power can do this because it has no representational function: the secret of power's existence is simply that "power does not exist." [2] Power is the name given to a certain coherency of relations: the terms to the relation (the "antinomies" of modern experience) vanish; and the "radical relationalism" which is the form of power as an abstract medium works to exterminate embodied experience. For Baudrillard, at the heart of power is a "radical semiurgy" in which the real is forced to undergo a continuous process of resymbolization. The result is the spread of a "dead power," a void, which in a desperate strategy of concretization seeks to embody itself in the "reality-effects" of human speech and social action.

Baudrillard then, is the theoretician of a postmodern power which owes its seduction to the "imminence of the death of all the great referents" and to the violence which is exacerbated by their last, desperate attempts at representation. This is power, not on its expanding and symbolic side (the side of a *political and represent-*

René Magritte, *The Door to Freedom/La clef des champs*

ational theory of power), but on its reverse side: the side of symbolic reversal where power affirms itself as void, as having only a cynical existence.

> This universal fascination with power in its exercise and its theory is so intense because it is a fascination with a *dead* power characterized by a simultaneous "resurrection effect," in an obscene and parodic mode, of all the forms of power already seen — exactly like sex in pornography.
>
> *Oublier Foucault*

Oublier Foucault is Baudrillard's accusation against a purely representational theory of power. Here is traced out a great figurative movement in which power, abandoning its association with force relations, agency, structure and distributional vectors, coils around and presents itself as an empty cycle of exchange: reversible, relational, and seductive as "challenge." Baudrillard's theorisation of power as a dead sign, and consequently as a relational and optical term, is as close as any postmodern writer has come to Nietzsche's dark suggestion in *The Will to Power* when he said that power now exists only as a *perspectival appearance*. For Nietzsche, as for Baudrillard, what drives power on, making it a purely symbolic medium, is *not* the expanding and accumulative side of power, the side of consumption. Power's secret lies in its intimate entanglement with death. The existence of power as a challenge unto death, sign without founding referent, is the secret of the postmodern fascination with power. What Nietzsche described as the "will to will" (the abstract nucleus of a simulational model of power), Baudrillard denotes "challenge:" power *without* a reality-principle.

In Baudrillard's estimation, Foucault's error was his almost nostalgic desire for power with a limiting term. In *Oublier Foucault*, Baudrillard notes that Foucault misinterprets the purely relational quality of modern power, just because he wished to tame power by closing the distance between it and its referents. The socio-logical vision of a normalizing society, even the closed space of the panoptic, is not dangerous: Foucault's privileged world of the panoptic is only the positive space where power surrenders its non-existence as "challenge" and incorporates itself without a murmur of dissent into the valorized order of finalities (politics, sexuality, commodities). For Baudrillard, the dark side of power, the site where power is made dangerous once again, is at that moment of reversal and cancellation when, exploding beyond its *historical* signification by an order of referentialities, power announces itself as a simulacrum and says that to accept its "challenge" is to enter a vortex of nothingness. This *nihilistic* expression of power is what Baudrillard theorizes, not the positive order of representationality associated with *sociological power* (power/norm), *economic power* (power/commodity), or *political power* (power/sovereignty). Baudrillard's relational theorisation of power negates the affirmative order of reason only in order to recover the mythic origins of power. This is why, perhaps, Baudrillard can relativize Foucault's writings on the modern discourse of power/sexuality as the already obsolescent descrip-tion of an era "now in the process of collapsing entirely."

> But what if Foucault spoke so well to us concerning power — and let us not forget in in *real* objective terms which cover manifold diffractions but nonetheless do not question the objective point of view one has about them, and concerning power which is pulverized but whose *reality principle* is nonethless not questioned — only because power is dead? Not merely impossible to locate because

of dissemination, but dissolved purely and simply
in a manner that still escapes us, dissolved by
reversal, cancellation, or made hyperreal through
simulation (who knows?)

Oublier Foucault

In Baudrillard's world, power is always haunted by an "imaginary
catastrophe" at its centre: the dilation of power, after centuries
of expansion, into a "single pure sign — the sign of the social
whose density crushes us." [3] And if the "redoubled simulation"
of power as its passes into its own simulacrum means the death of
all the great referents, then it may also signify that fascism is the
precursor of a purely relational postmodern power. "As the violent
reactivation of a form of power that despairs of its rational
foundations, as the violent reactivation of the social in a society
that despairs of its own rational and contractual foundations,
fascism is nevertheless the only fascinating modern form of
power." [4]

Fascist power is then the only form which was able
to reenact the ritual prestige of death, but in an
already posthumous and phoney mode, a mode of
one-upmanship and *mise-en-scène*, and in an *aesthetic*
mode — as Benjamin clearly saw — that was no
longer truly sacrificial.

Oublier Foucault

For Baudrillard, fascism remains the "only fascinating modern
form of power" because it occupied that space in the cycle of
power where politics in its sacrifical mode passes over instantaneously into the distinctly postmodern (cynical) region of power
and seduction. And if fascism had about it an "*already nostalgic*
obscenity and violence," if it was already *passé* as soon as it
appeared in history, then this may indicate why fascism remains
the emblematic sign of modern power: "An eternal inner simulation
of power, which is never already (*jamais déjà*) anything but the sign
of what it was." [5]

Fascist power is, then, the paradigmatic expression of
Baudrillard's "dead power." Baudrillard's world begins with the
devalorisation of the social and the loss forever of the autonomous
historical subject. This collapse of a rational foundation for power,
the breakdown even of rationalization and its replacement by the

new sociological principles of exteriorisation and simulation of
the silent masses, makes fascist power the dominant sign of the
postmodern century. The loss forever of an embodied subject,
power *with* a reality-principle, also means that a fascist power is
purely structuralist. On the side of the politics of seduction,
Baudrillard's dead power is structured from within like Magritte's
The Door to Freedom: in both instances, power is a pure relation; its
structural code is tautology, metaphor, and lack.

   That Baudrillard has been able to achieve this austere deconstruction of power to its nihilistic traces may be due to the more
sweeping fact that his imagination revolves around the conception
of experience as a *simulacrum*. In his most metaphysical text,
L'Échange symbolique et la mort, Baudrillard remarked: "L'hyperréel
n'est au-delà de la représentation que parce qu'il est tout entier
dans la simulation. Le tourniquet de la représentation y devient
fou, mais d'une folie implosive, qui, loin d'être excentrique,
louche vers le centre, vers sa propre répétition en abyme." [6] For
Baudrillard, we live in the aesthetic inversion of the secret order
of surrealism. Where once surrealism offered the possibility that
privileged areas of "banal experience" could be transformed into
special, artistic insights into the "hallucinatory" quality of modern
experience, now "toute la réalité quotidienne . . . déjà incorpore
la dimension simulatrice de l'hyperréalisme." [7] The eventual
outcome of the transformation of experience into a *simulacrum* (a
pure medium) is the introduction of an inner *redoublement* into the
cycle of power. "C'est l'euphorie même de la simulation, qui se
vent abolition de la cause et de l'effet, de l'origine et de la fin, à
quoi elle substitue le redoublement." [8] In the *simulacrum*, the
critique of the non-reality of a "real space" between the sign and
its referent reveals the "referential illusion" at work in the interstices of (abstracted) experience for what it always was: "L'hallucination pathétique du signe et l'hallucination pathétique du réel."[9]

   Baudrillard's *simulacrum* and Magritte's hallucinatory world of
empty mediations *en abyme* spiral into one another as convergent
texts because both contain a common, theoretical insight into
the genealogy of postmodern power. Magritte and Baudrillard
have, in fact, done the impossible: they have read social experience
in reverse image in order to force the *imaginaire* of power to the
surface. And they have done so by deciphering the enigmatic
"code" of the deep, structural continuity in Western experience:
that is, by, interpreting the hieroglyphics of the "sign" as at once
the DNA of the structural logic of experience, and the *limit*

within which there takes place a relentless metamorphosis of embodied experience (labour, reflection, sex, death) into a language without passion.

Magritte always understood the fatalistic tendency in the nightmare that he was exploring; and thus, there is no break in his imagination as he journeys deeper into the hidden recesses of power and the sign. *The False Mirror*, *Hooded Lovers*, *Memory*, *The Therapeutist*: these paintings are almost clinical diagnoses of the structural laws of value of a disembodied power. Magritte instructs us in the invisible architecture of the binary language which forms the horizon of our imprisonment in a dead power. However, Baudrillard's project is different. His critical intention was, at first, more circumscribed: to project the radical implications of the theory of the sign into the domain of political economy. In *The Mirror of Production*, Baudrillard proposed to subvert Marx's *Capital* by showing that the sign was the structural code, the nuclear structure, of the commodity-form. For Baudrillard, the sign was the secret destiny of the commodity: the purely topographical structure of an "empty, symbolic exchange" within which there took place the fantastic "double-metamorphosis" in the circuit of capital. It was, in fact, Baudrillard's intention to disclose that the transformation of the commodity into the sign (*mercantilist* value-form into the *structural* law of value) [10] was the secret destiny of capital in the twentieth-century. This is why Baudrillard spoke of the "fetishism of the sign" and why, perhaps, so much of his early writings represent an ironic dialogue with the vanishing "object" of *Capital*. But it was also Baudrillard's fate to be the unwitting sorcerer of the Marxian legacy. His writings have teased out the Nietzschean regression which always existed on the dark side of Marx's "circuit of capital." By disclosing that the theory of the sign was the *morphology* of the double-metamorphosis of capital, and thus the structural genesis of the "magic" and "alchemy" of the fetishism of the commodity, Baudrillard also revealed that nihilism takes root, not in the ideal substratum of Christian morality, but in the culture of consumption itself. The "lack" which is the *imaginaire* at the centre of the culture of consumption is identical to the *abyss* which drives on the *ressentiment* and howling "spirit of revenge" in Christian metaphysics. The difference between the accumulation of grace and the cyclical movement of capital is perspectival: the inverted region of the surrealistic slide between the two sides of *The Will to Power*. On the *historical* side of the cycle of a nihilating power, revenge (against embodiment) is structured in the form of the psychology of sacrifice. The "signs" of sacrifice are idealistic projections of conditions of preservation: dead grace, dead love, dead spirits. On the *materialistic* side of the will to power, *ressentiment* speaks in the language of seduction. But the "signs" of seduction, which depend on the "pumping out" of concrete labour into the carcass of "dead labour" (Marx) are only the *camera obscura* of the sickliness of a sacrificial culture: hysterical consumption, charismatic technology (the new, material site of Heidegger's "will to will,") and mutilated bodies. In consumer culture, labour does not exist, nor does value. The shattering forever of the chain of referential experience means, in fact, that the prime players of ontology — labour, need, use-value, utility — are the symbolic horizon of the *simulacrum* at the centre of the circuit of nihilism. Thus, the *trompe-l'oeil* of *Capital/The Will to Power* is but a perspectival illusion as the single cycle of exterminism in Western culture, which having achieved a frenzied moment of high abstraction in the psychology of sacrifice, now hurtles back towards the original locus of power — the body — for a second colonization. Now, though, nihilism in the value-form (the "sign") of capital seduces the flesh with pleasure, not torture. [11]

It was Baudrillard's stubborn insistence on seeing the Nietzsche in Marx, in taking the cyclical movement between "inertia and ecstacy" in *Capital* for what it was, a "stratégie fatale," which plays out, in banal form, the *redoublement* of *The Will to Power*. Or, perhaps, it was his fundamental insight that the sign represents the locus of disembodiment and abstraction always sought, but never achieved, through the exteriorisation of the senses in the commodity-form. Baudrillard stumbled upon the hidden reservoir of signs in Western experience: in an almost mad rush of creativity — as if the sign could no longer tolerate the symbolic disguises behind which it was forced to hide its existence as a skeptical power — all of the structural canons of the *simulacrum* tumble out of Baudrillard's thought. Baudrillard makes explicit at the theoretical level what Magritte recognized immediately, and perhaps instinctively, in a purely artistic gesture. Magritte discloses the optical, because metaphorical, rules by which the *imaginaire* constitutes the inner horizon of Western experience. Baudrillard's writings represent a careening tour of the semantic norms governing the endless circulation of a bi-polar structural power. If Magritte's paintings reveal the hidden face of terror in Kant's "antinomies," then Baudrillard shows precisely the *semiological code* by which the antinomies transform concrete experience in the direction of the *simulacrum*. In Baudrillard's world, we are in flight through a vast, social apparatus which has, as its principle of motion, an inner, semiological transformation of every particle of experience — bodies, labour, power, money, speech — through an empty cycle of abstract, symbolic exchanges. The inner circulation of embodied experience into a downward spiral of exterminism means that the *simulacrum* fulfills Nietzsche's aphorism that "nothing wants to be preserved." The rules surrounding the "cycle of liquidation" at the heart of power and the sign remain constant: a fantastic "semantic cancellation" at the centre of the exchange process; a relentless "semiological reduction" of experience to the tautology of binary language; the "satellisation of the real"; an "inner semiurgy" which works to impose symbols without original referents; the sovereignty of the "structural law of value." [12] In short, Baudrillard reveals that *The Door to Freedom* involves the liquidation of experience by the empty language of the sign; and that the sudden convergence in the postmodern century of power/sign is nothing less than the grammar of the culture of nihilism.

II

Now, and without irony, I wish to work out a historical reversal of the surrealistic imagery of the sign; in fact, to complete the fantastic discovery by Baudrillard and Magritte of power as a sign of "that which never was" by tracing the genealogy of abstract power to its genesis in the structural logic of early Christian metaphysics. If the existence of power as a pure sign-system can be so accurately described by Magritte and Baudrillard, then, maybe, this is because the arc of a dead power is already in reverse motion, tracing the path of an ellipsis that takes it back to its origins in the disembodiment, even disempowerment, of power itself. What I want to theorize concerning the history of nihilism is that the "sign" is but the disenchanted expression of the trinitarian formulation in Christian metaphysics. The sign is the *form* assumed by the will to power on its contemporary side, the side of the psychology of seduction; the trinity is the *structural code* of the will to power on the sacrificial side of its cycle. There is, however, one significant difference: in the language of the sign (but not in that of the trinity), the presence of the "will to will" as the third term unifying the poles (the mirrored antinomies) of signifier and signified is suppressed from sight. The sign is, therefore, the trinity with its essential secret — the *abstract* will — made invisible.

The originality of the discourse of Baudrillard/Magritte, and one could add, the great, radical insight in New French Thought, extending through the post-structuralism of Derrida, Kristèva, Deleuze, and Foucault, is that, however unsuspectingly, they force us beyond the rubicon of representational theory. Their work provides a passage right through the eye of Nietzsche's will to power, from the side of (our) disenchantment in the society of the "sign" to the dramatic inversion of power in Christian dogma. The suppressed truth of post-structuralist discourse is that there is no fundamental discontinuity in the history (metaphysics) of power in Western experience. The "sign" is, in fact, not antinomic but trinitarian. And it is trinitarian because the discourse of the sign is but a concretization in the direction of banality and inertia of the primitive Christian doctrine of the will. Nihilism on the "Christian" side is the will to power, the (semantic) reduction of experience to the "semiological code" of the trinity: an anthro-pology of the *imaginaire* in the value-form of "God," which was anyway only a semantic substitute for the disappearance of the embodied will. Nihilism in the contemporary century is structur-alism reinvested by the will to power in the name of seduction. Baudrillard's *simulacrum* is canonical power with the head of God exploded from within.

The radical discovery of a deep continuity in the structural morphology of power commits us to follow through the Nietzschean regression which is today what the culture of nihilism is all about. We are plunging through the inner reversal in experience, past the nihilism of *Capital*, past the simulacra of dead money, dead status, and dead prestige, to the silent, inner reservoir of a cynical power, a cynical history, and a cynical God. The arc of a dead power traces a great trajectory back to a specific historical moment — and this not in the twentieth but in the fourth century — to the site of the assassination of Christ (the elimination of *embodied* will) and the birth of God (the empire of abstract power). It is, indeed, the fateful figure of Augustine who stands at the beginning of the ellipse of modern power; and it is towards Augustine's theorisation of the metaphysics of a purely rhetorical power that society now dissolves. It is as if Augustine marks a great threshold in Western consciousness: the silencing, on the one side, of the cynicism of the *amor fati*; and the eruption, on the other, of the *lack* which drives forward the *simulacrum*. In the vast regions of Augustine's theoretical discourse, Kant's judgement, Nietzsche's insight into power as a "perspectival illusion," Marx's "dead labour," and Baudrillard's "dead power" suddenly fuse together as particles in a great and common field of discourse: a discourse which has its structural genesis in Augustine's fundamental inversion of the order of Western experience. Augustine's texts, ranging from the *Confessions* to the *City of God* to *De Trinitate* are the fundamental rupture from which everything explodes outwards in a nihilistic burst: an explosion of the "in vain" which now becomes visible to the extent that power, as a sign of nothingness, spreads out in the social form of banality.

We can capture something of Augustine's importance as the limit and horizon of the modern project by understanding his theory of power for what it is: the reverse image and completion (on the side of sacrificial power) of the theory of power/seduction proposed by Baudrillard and Magritte. There is, indeed, almost a family resemblance between Augustine's topographical world of "serenity" and Magritte's tortured, but also silent and serene, world of violently detached fragments of experience. Magritte's vivid depiction of the referential illusion at the centre of modern existence has its (philosophical) origin in Augustine's liquidation of the warring tension in the field of embodied experience. Magritte is, in fact, only releasing in the medium of painting the long scream suppressed in Western consciousness by the cancellation of the finitude of the body (through Augustine's "conversion"), and by *our* reduction to the will to truth of a vast, delusional system of signs.

Augustine's *Confessions* are an actual, written account of the exact moment at which took place a fundamental rupture in the interstices of Western consciousness. Augustine's conversion in the garden at Cassiacium marks a great threshold in the Western mind: a fundamental, seismic division between the warring antinomies of classical experience, and the "serenity" of the undivided will (the "will to will") of modernism. Augustine's account of the bitter struggle of his conversion is, in fact, a metaphysical exploration of the desperate struggle of the will to overcome the finitude of the body. The "conversion" is from one philosophical *épistème* to another: from the impossible tensions of classicism (symbolized by the skepticism of stoicism and the dogmatism of Platonic rationalism) to the "serenity" of the will breaking in upon itself in the (reified) from of its own simulation. "Thus soul-sick was I, and tormented, accusing myself much more severely than my wont, rolling and turning me in my chain, till that were wholly broken, whereby I now was but just, but still was, held." [13] Augustine's project was to close forever the "eye of the flesh" and to open the "inner eye" to a God (who was not there), an *abstract* power. And thus when Augustine says, "And now it spake very faintly. For on that side whither I had set my face, and whither I trembled to go, there appeared unto me the chaste dignity of Continency, serene, yet not relaxedly, gay, honestly alluring me to come and doubt not," [14] he is midway (psychologically) between the finitude of the embodied will and the *imaginaire* of the will to will. Augustine's conversion ("a light of serenity infused into my heart, all the darkness of doubt vanished away") [15] marks a fundamental divide in the Western mind: it is at this point, in fact, that the will to will (the sole condition of possibility for the liquidation of "doubt") is transposed into a predicate of existence. Indeed, it could even be said that Nietzsche's project of diagnosing the "sickliness" of "two thousand years of Christian morality" is in circling around to that epochal moment when Augustine "nilled" embodied experience (Nietzsche's "becoming") *from within* by transforming the will into a pure, abstract medium. The free-fall into the *imaginaire*, which Baudrillard will later identify as the "eternal, inner simulacrum" of power and which Magritte paints as a world horizoned by a relational will to truth, has its philosophical genesis in the *trompe-l'oeil* of the first fall into the "inner eye" of power. Everything is driven on, psychologically, by a fierce "spirit of revenge" against the body: "But Thou, O Lord, are good and merciful, and Thy right hand had respect unto the depth of my death, and from the bottom of my heart emptied that abyss of corruption. And this Thy whole gift was, to nill what I willed, and to will what Thou willedst." [16] From this moment on, the will, disembodied and having only a *rhetorical* existence, is fully implicated in a topographical empire of delusion. Having no (real) existence of its own, the will discovers its truth-value (Nietzsche's "fictions") in a dominion of signs which undergo an endless metamorphosis in a mirrored world of tautology, metaphor, and simulation. After Augustine, power could only exist on the condition that it operate as an abstract medium. The inner "surrealistic slide" (Barthes) at the centre of abstract power (a sign-system without a real referent) was counter-pointed, and thus disguised, by the hysterical compulsion of canonical law.

That Augustine was also obsessed with the creation of a complex system of liturgical signification (the functionality of the *ordo conditionae nostrae*) meant that the inner regression which drove on an abstract power depended for its very (simulated) existence on the deployment of a functional and symbolic replication (at the corporate level) of the body. As an early father of the Sign, Augustine also illustrated that the psychotic inversion (apparent over embodied unities) represented by the circulation of abstract power would operate in a language which was functional, reductive, and hyperreal. The silent terrorism of the "aesthetics of the hyperreal" is, in fact, the object of Magritte's artistic imagination. Because since Augustine nothing has changed in the deep, structural code of Western experience: it has all been a ceaseless "outering" or "ablation" of embodied experience into the medium of abstract power. From Augustine's conversion on, the structural logic of Western experience remains the same. What changes, and continuously, is the specific truth-effector (metonymy) which horizons the exteriorisation of the senses into the *simulacrum* of the abstract will: grace (Augustine), fear (Hobbes), critical reason (Kant), normativity (Spencer), communications (McLuhan).

But if there is a topographical filiation between Magritte and Augustine and if, in fact, we can claim that Augustine set in motion the structural code of nihilism, this is because Augustine's primary contribution — the doctrine of the Trinity — is an early, but never superceded, description of the inner circuitry of the sign. There is, perhaps, no more fundamental account of the limits of the modern project than Augustine's *De Trinitate*. This text is implicitly an extended reflection on the metaphysics of the conversion experience, one of the central documents of Western thought because of its explicit and detailed analysis of the discursive formulations surrounding the inner, genetic structural logic of modern society. But *De Trinitate* is on the positive side of *The Will to Power* because the "trinitarian formulation" is disclosed to be the basic condition of possibility for the operation of the modern mind: in effect, the structural logic of the trinity has been projected outwards as the basic (metaphorical) categories of Western existence. Everything that Nietzsche says about the *inverted*, structural logic of modern consciousness exists in crystalline form in this text. Power as "perspectival appearance," an inverted order of reality with the power of death over life; the reign of "apparent unities"; the "fictions" of form, species, law, ego, morality, and purpose: Nietzsche's searing insights into reality as illusion have their genealogical root, and reverse image, in the *simulated* categories of *De Trinitate*. Indeed, long before Kant (repeating Augustine's radical discovery) abandoned knowledge of immediate experience and retreated to the *simulacrum* of procedural and regulatory knowledge unified by abstract judgement, Augustine had already undertaken a similar phenomenology of the Western mind. It was Augustine's accomplishment to overcome the *statis* in classical experience, represented by the antinomies of idealism and positivism, by seeking a new, *purely formal but internal*, principle of unification. As the Canadian thinker Charles N. Cochrane claimed in his classic text, *Christianity and Classical Culture*, Augustine transformed the Athens-Jerusalem debate into a new, more dynamic, synthesis by the simple expedient of abandoning the search for an "external mediation" of experience.[17] Augustine subverted the representational logic of classical experience with the introduction of a *tautological, metaphorical, and rhetorical medium of symbolic exchange* as the source of a new, internal mediation of experience.[18] Augustine's trinity is a vacant exchange process in which the divided will of embodied experience is transformed, through an "inner semiurgy" (Baudrillard), into the serene transparency of the "will to will." Augustine is the precursor of the modern world because he succeeded, where others had failed, in discovering the magical formula of Western experience: the transformation of (our) formal possibilities for survival into absolute categories of existence.

Augustine formulated the rhetorical rules surrounding the sign-form as the locus of modern experience: Augustine's trinity represents in emblematic and almost diamond-shaped form the secret origin, and destiny, of Western consciousness. There is, indeed, no need to look further than the trinity for the genealogical source of a society disintegrating into the dark night of nihilism. The trinity contains in codified form the whole structural logic of institutional action which is at the epicentre of the structure of Western experience. And it does this, of course, *not* as a religious doctrine (God was always only a reality-effect disguising the simulation) but as the structural logic of identity (the identitarian logic of the sign) which informs the mystery of unity/contradiction in the deepest interstices of being. In its metaphysical, in fact semiological, formulations, we discover the most reductive, and transparent, description possible of the "apparent unity" in which the (regulatory and procedural) conditions for our preservation are transformed into "predicates of existence." When Nietzsche said that "nothingness spreads," he may also have had in mind the imaginary, and thus fictitious, quality of the trinitarian formulation, for the very existence of the trinity depends on a succession of structuralist principles, each of which is a recitation of nihilism: *the substantialisation of the imaginary* (Augustine remarked that the riddle of finite experience was solved when he realized that "spirit was substantial"); *the extermination of corporeal existence as a referent of the real* (the "nilling" of the flesh); and *the privileging of the crede ut intellegas* (the precursor of Nietzsche's "will to truth.") [19] To examine anew the formulations of *De Trinitate* is to gain special insight into the modern project, at the very moment of its inception and from the inside out. It is, in fact, a rare moment when the hidden, metaphysical locus of the Western mind spreads itself out for scrutiny: when, in effect, the structural code which will come to limit experience is compelled to disclose its secret. Long in advance of the "perfect nihilism" of the postmodern century, the trinitarian formulation signifies the incarceration (and resymbolization) of corporeal existence into an abstract and semiurgical sign-system: an imperialism of the sign which declares that, henceforth, power will be rhetorical because the *signs* of power (the triadic and simulated trinity of being/will/consciousness) are only "perspectival unities" masking our plunge downwards into the *regressus in infinitum*.

Baudrillard's *simulacrum*, the purely rhetorical structure of postmodern power, is only in the way of a final coming-home to the doctrine of the trinity as the invisible text of the will to power, the fully commensurable texts of parallel theorisations of the sign-form which fly towards one another as perspectival points on a common ellipsis in Baudrillard's theorisations of the inner circuitry of the sign and Augustine's formulations of the rhetorical principles of the trinity. Baudrillard's insight into the "semantic cancellation" at work in the *simulacrum* echoes Augustine's earlier, philological reduction of the sign-system of the trinity (father/ memory as signifier; son/intelligence as signified; and *voluntas/* will as the perspectival closing of the tautology) to a "sound which is made by no language." [20] Baudrillard's "semiological reduction" is nothing more than Augustine's insight that, in the mirror of the trinity, signifier and signified circle back towards one another as refracted (and simulated) images in a common tautology. Between the simulacrum and the trinity, there is a great logic of equivalence: Baudrillard speaks now of the "radical questioning of the real" which takes place through the exercise of a "dead power"; Augustine had already formulated the dead signs of "beauty, truth, and goodness" as *simultaneous* extermination-points of the real and simulations of "apparent" life.[21]

Like the sign-form, the trinity is *nothing-in-itself*, a pure "perspectival illusion" which functions by emptying out the domain of the real, and reducing experience to its *inverted form* in a semiological logic of abstraction, simplification, and equivalence. Almost in the image of the "empty, symbolic exchange" at the centre of the *simulacrum*, the trinity is a circulating medium in which everything, having been resymbolized in the value-form of *memory* (the "semiological reduction" of time) and *truth* (the value-form of liquidated imagination) is thrown into a cycle of exchange. Like Baudrillard's "seduction" which drives on the cycle of exchange of an abstract power, and is, only a disguise of the will to power; the trinity is mediated by *caritas* which, like its later counter-part in seduction, only means the charisma of the will to will. With its transformation of experience into a tauto-logical, metaphorical and regulatory cycle of exchange, the trinity is the other side of the disenchanted world of the *simulacrum*. The semiological rules of operation are identical — analogy, similitude, refraction — and in the logic of the sign-system, whether that of the trinity or the *simulacrum*, the simulated poles of experience (memory/truth; signifier/signified) collapse towards one another in an "inner slide" of co-referentiality and co-laterality.[22] An inner cycle of the elimination of the real is at work. That is why, perhaps, Baudrillard's "structural law of value," the "aesthetics of hyperrealism," and the nightmarish vision of experience thrown into its own "inner semiurgy" is but the rediscovery of Augustine's insight that the trinity owes its charisma, *not* to the preservation of the real, but to the disappearance of the real into its own vanishing-point. The "unmoved mover," the locus of death at the receding centre of the "inner eye," is what Baudrillard will later term the "lack," the "void" which drives on consumption and makes our exterminism in the simulacrum an entirely satisfying condition for (our) preservation.

III

Is it not, then, at least ironic that we live within the horizon of *De Trinitate*? Baudrillard and Magritte have compelled us to confront a *cynical* power. Nietzsche reported on one side of the will to power: the *sacrificial* cycle of exchange symbolized by the enchantment of the world with the *ressentiment* of grace. Our fate now is to live in that dark region where power suddenly passes over into its opposite, the plunging downwards of society into the last cycle of the Nietzschean regression, the hyper-materialist side of nihilism. We thus live on the imploded side of the will to power: the side of empty seduction, dead labour, abstract power, and symbolic of the postmodern, the radical disenchantment of the sign. What else explains our taking delight in images of a dead society — fragmented bodies, and video ideology — signs that, at least, we know we are trapped in the "joke" of a cynical history. The age of "perfect nihilism" is recuperative: we are the people who know that Nietzsche's "joke" continues. The convergence of trinity/sign as structurally identical value-forms means that we *never* escaped "two thousand years of Christian morality." Barthes had the formula of postmodern anguish: the metaphor (trinity/sign) abides; the metonymy (sacrifice/seduction) alters.[23] That Baudrillard and Magritte force us back to the genealogical traces of nihilism in Augustine only means that we are being swept away, once more, in the reverse motion of the eternal recurrence.

A.K.

III

SLIDING SIGNIFIERS

"Let us imagine (if we can) a woman covered with an endless garment, itself woven of everything said in the fashion magazine. . ."
Roland Barthes, The Fashion System

Barthes' vision is at the centre of hyperreality. Little matters if the garment turns out like the emperor's new clothes. The children were wrong to name it. They were operating under the sign of biblical injunction. They confused fashion with knowledge. Currently knowledge is fashionable. Little matters as well that Barthes did not state that the woman is also dispensable. He was still trying to work with bodies, or at least mannequins. He was working under the sign of the real. We can contemplate a happy marriage of perspectives — no clothes, no body — no problem. But it is better expressed in the fashion magazines like *Elan*: "There is something to please everybody, from the conservative who demands distinctive quality and styling to the unexpected delight of Disneyland characters decorating big wind-breakers to amuse the young and trendy." As the editors of *Elan* remark earlier, it "just takes a little help from the new mousses and gels".

Certainly the Marquis de Sade would have welcomed all of this. He was not adverse to imagining women, and certainly his "fluid mechanics" would have led him to an interest in the mousses and gels. The Castle at Silling may not be exactly the same as Disney's adventureland, but it is about as real. Finally there was no problem for Sade in eliminating bodies.

Kant would have been appalled by all of this, and, of course, he would deny any responsibility much like the children. Although did not Kant in his last critique bring reason into the realm of the senses? And given that there are no objective and certain standards, are we not led to the common sense of what is pleasing? Is this not itself close to the fashionable? Listen again to the editors of *Elan*: "As much as we care about the way we look, today we care more about the way we feel". Does this echo the pleasure gained by the harmony of the faculties? But this is going too far which is precisely why it is a postmodern discourse.

The "last word", as Vogue has it, goes again to *Elan*: "This allows for a new freedom, a new simplicity, which is reflected in lifestyle clothing". The essays to follow give a partial genealogy to the movement of the signifier in 'liberalism' from freedom to the sign of 'lifestyle clothing'. As best we can, we try to realize Barthes' dream of the woman in the fashionable garment.

6

CAMERA NEGRIDA:
BARTHES' PANIC SCENE

Georges Bataille's classic text, the *Story of the Eye*, marks the beginning of the postmodern experiment in France. Written under the pseudonym of Lord Auch, the *Story of the Eye* stands antipodal to Marcel Mauss' seminal analysis of performance and functions of exchange in archaic societies. Unlike Mauss' *The Gift*, Bataille's vision is one of excess. Following upon the symbolic exchange of the potlach society, Bataille represents his society in the gift of the bull's testicles which are served up on a plate as the endpoint of the Matador's fight under the scorching Seville sun. The vision of the spectacular characteristic of modernism is transformed into the discourse of death and sexuality, and then immolated in the primitive ritual of the bull fight to create postmodernism.

For Bataille, the symbol of postmodernism is to be found in the violence of excremental culture, captured in the image of the "pineal eye". Or, as Bataille, drawing on the anthropological evidence of our primitive origins, also writes: it's the image of the "solar anus" as the emblematic sign of the parodic world of excremental culture. Bataille's images of excess — the writing at the margin of heterogeneity and absence which is the challenge of the visions of the pineal eye and the solar anus — signify the dominance of the waste and excremental vision which underlies the solidity of the blackness within: a darkness to infinity which is the postmodern counterpoint to the Platonic sun of reason and the economy of use values. Mauss' vision of the sacred and the fraternal in a new cooperative *social* is liquidated by Bataille just like the eggs in the *Story of the Eye* which are held in the anus of Simone. Eggs, as eyes, are broken and pierced in a ritualistic reenactment of sexual rites smeared with blood, excrement and death; and all of this underneath the realm of desire which created Bataille's excremental vision.

Bataille has portrayed this culture in his later study of eroticism. Here the postmodern world comes into being in the 'lover's embrace', depicted in the Nicolas Manuel Deutsch painting of "Death Embracing a Young Woman" found in the Musée de Bale. It is just this demand for excess in excremental culture which is given to Roland Barthes as a fundamental precondition of the social, and which animates his desperate search for the lover's discourse. Barthes' project has a greater historical significance as paradigmatic of the predicament of the postmodern world itself: trapped within the vision of excess in Bataille's general economy, yet looking through the 'cursed part' for those social values so wistfully sought by Marcel Mauss at the end of social anthropology. Barthes' search for the 'excess' moved through the symbolic exchange of language, culture and mythology in an intellectual trajectory which traced the postmodern horizon, from scientistic semiology to poststructuralism. The end of Barthes' search is embodied perfectly in the melancholy image of the lover's embrace (*The Demand for Love*) found at the end of this essay — an embrace caught by the *camera negrida* which is beyond words; an embrace which will signal Barthes' panic site as well as the eclipse of the postmodern project.

Roland Barthes set out from the confines of literary criticism to uproot the Western tradition. He not only claimed to expose the tired mythologies that govern our cultural life, the image repertoire that stands against the imagination, [1] but he mapped the closure that is characteristic of the way we read and think. Here, Barthes encountered the death of both mind and body. This death, to paraphrase Marx, is not solely the responsibility of the educators, however much they may have destroyed the texts they desire to illuminate; it resides, in a more fundamental sense, in the categories of Western metaphysics: in the prescription for Barthes of meaning to be found in the written word through its basic unit, the declarative sentence. And behind this, yet again, the presumption of the subject-object distinction where the "truth" of science holds out, or the "truth" of that other source of being and becoming called "history." Behind each one of these masks, many of which Barthes himself wore, Barthes looked for the body, [2] or to use different language, for the way to bring forth from experience the meanings that constitute life.

In this desire for bliss, [3] or to use Barthes' later words, for he value of the 'neuter' that is in excess of the subject and object, the tried to end the dominance of the metaphysical tradition. Barthes attempted, following Maurice Blanchot, [4] to open the space of writing, or more correctly the literary space, as the site of the reciprocal passing of the subject over to the object. This space is that of the imagination, hence an absence of space, where meanings of the subject in excess of the subject take form in literature. It is also the space of difference: the site, Barthes asserts, that is caught neither in the web of the individual, or psychoanalysis, nor in the web of the other, or politics.

Thus Barthes enters the tradition through the concept of desire which shares with the imagination the structure of negativity. Desire forms the 'non-existent' grounds of the neuter which Barthes sets out as the project to overcome in bliss. From the viewpoint of the tradition Barthes encounters Hobbes, theorist of the desiring bourgois individual, the possessive individual, and the Hegelian dialectic of desire, or negativity, which underlies the claim to the positive moment of the social and the rejection of the philosophy of difference. In both Hegel and Hobbes the imagination is held in check through the social which establishes the political as an agent of repression for desire. [5] Politics and psychology are then depicted as the two police Barthes describes in the *Pleasure of the Text* that guard the tradition and hence must be displaced. [6] It is this project which is at the basis of the deconstruction of postmodern thought that will be explored here. [7]

To establish Barthes' case I turn to his critique of French culture and political thinking. Barthes' shift in *Mythologies* to taking seriously the cultural products of bourgeois society as a sign system of exploitation was important both for its emphasis on the role of language and the image, and for its exploding the political economy paradigm into a cultural field. *Mythologies* also served to uncover the meanings created by the individual that exist below the level of the visible and the practical.

This reading of the signs of French culture, while stating the obvious in many instances, [8] introduced Barthes' complete rejection of nature as the basis of value and meaning. French life was pervaded by mythologies precisely because there was nothing natural about culture. The appeal to nature became the sign of ideology. Nature, or more precisely the theory of *a natural being* held for Barthes the idea of fixity and determination which, closing off the individual's role as giver of meaning, is reminiscent of William Blake's castigation of natural law as 'vegetable or natural consciousness.' French society for Barthes had enwrapped itself in a series of predominantly bourgeois conceptions that denied the imagination in the service of maintaining a 'natural' class. Barthes, in his preface to the 1970 edition of *Mythologies* indicated his "hope to go further than the pious show of unmasking them (collective sign systems) and account *in detail* (emphasis Barthes') for the mystification which transforms *petit-bourgeois* culture into a universal culture." [9] *Mythologies* represented a compendium of dead but powerful elements of French ideology or *doxa* that Barthes will call the image repertoire. It also signalled the beginning of the deconstruction of culture that Barthes and others would accomplish.

The early elements of Barthes' manner of interpreting, apparent in *Mythologies*, reappear in later collections such as *The Eiffel Tower* and in a more systematic fashion in *The Fashion System*. They show an element of continuity in Barthes' thought despite the pronounced rejections of various standpoints that occur later in his understanding of his task as critic. The analysis of myths is archaeological in a way similar to Michel Foucault's: it uncovers the decentered power system that pervades everyday life. The social for Barthes becomes recognizable by the artifacts of society; mythologies are the last remains of a once-living creature killed by the power of contemporary culture. Barthes nevertheless gets caught up in the fascination for these autopsies, or, to use other language, in the science of completed systems. On the one hand, it led him to some insightful critiques. For example, in the literary field, particularly the bourgeois novel, he shows the emptiness of the formula characteristic of the narrative structure with a beginning and end where the conflicts are resolved and meaning is assured. The falsity of these ends is especially apparent given the deconstruction of codes by Barthes in his study of Balzac in *S/Z*. [10] On the other hand, this success in analyzing completed systems by the methods of science pushed Barthes' thought to a type of scientism witness his contribution to the science of semiology.

The science of signs held Barthes' attention throughout his life, through the general influence of Saussure. This interest in

"science" is especially apparent in Barthes' *Elements of Semiology*. [11]
Barthes knew that the advantages of a closed system were
immense. In the physical world it was both reassuring and necessary to know the cause and effects of action. In cultural matters,
and even more so in political concerns, science held out a similar
goal as desirable, and to the extent that the social sciences were
dealing with artifacts, theoretically possible. The power of this
form of positivism was easily apparent in much of French
sociology following Durkheim and, in particular, the anthro-
pologicala studies of Marcel Mauss.

Thus it is not surprising that a number of interpretations of
Barthes are caught up in the scientism of Barthes' middle period.
For example, McCallum criticizes Barthes' reading of Sade for
treating Sade as a closed system. She sees the text as something to
be analyzed both as to its structure and its cohesion or lack of it,
but not as an element of ongoing praxis. For McCallum, the text is
perceived as being outside history. [12] If Barthes' intent was to
remain on the level of interpretation only, this would be fair
comment but it becomes increasingly apparent in his later work
that the design was directly to capture what Barthes calls the
"lovers' discourse" which he sees as impregnated meanings with
a consequent rejection of his 'scientism'. In other words, Barthes'
later work is concerned, following the influence of Georges
Bataille's studies on eroticism, with the erotic ontology of
Western thought exposed by Sade and not Sade himself. It is
ultimately in pursuing this desire for "bliss" rather than desire
itself which brings about the abandonment of the perspectives of
science and the closed structure of the narrative form and drives
Barthes toward Nietzsche, the fragment and a new metaphysics.

Along with Barthes' *Mythologies*, which attacked the mystifications of French culture, Barthes in his early period attempted
to establish the link between politics and writing as a way of
overcoming these mystifications. This relationship was to prove
troubling for Barthes throughout and finally ends in Barthes'
political ambiguity, [13] a political ambiguity common to the poststructuralist movement in general, of which Barthes became a
part. But in the first part of the 1950s, political writing appeared
to offer the vehicle for overcoming the closed mythologies of the
culture. The earlier publication of Sartre's *What is Literature* [14]
influenced Barthes to see a revolutionary aspect in writing. There
is an inevitable break with ideology, or doxa, for Barthes, at this
time, in the utopian aspect of any theorizing. Political theory

must bring to bear a vision in its understanding of the practical world in order to guide change. Politics enters the realm of the unnatural, or rather, beyond nature, of the transformative arts, under the power of the imagination against the power of the image repertoire. This underlines the centrality of the imagination to Barthes and the early Sartre. [15] Writing could also make the claim that a utopian element is present in much of literature and poetry, and beneath this is language itself that is common to both literature and political theory. Barthes in the concluding chapter of *Writing Degree Zero* held out what he hoped would become the utopia of language which brings together the antinomies of freedom and necessity, the real and the ideal, upon which revolutionary thought is based. Ironically given Barthes' later concerns, the Western tradition still remains intact in the call for revolutionary thought. Implicit here is the retention of a master code that is found in most theorists that have not broken entirely with the Marxist tradition or who hold on to structuralism. The break with this tradition would become inevitable for Barthes the further his deconstruction of codes went.

> Like modern art in its entirety, literary writing carries at the same time the alienation of History and the dream of History; as a Necessity it testifies to the division of languages which is inseparable from the division of classes; as Freedom, it is the consciousness of this division and the very effort which seeks to surmount it. [16]

Armed with this understanding of writing, Barthes analyzes both politics and literature with a view to identifying the revolutionary aspect of modern writing which signals the break-up of the dominance of bourgeois writing. For Barthes the bourgeois novel has come to an end, through the claim of the novel to present time, or duration, as a completed meaningful event outside of society and its class structure. History, if you will, is dissevered from politics.

> The Novel is a Death; it transforms life into destiny, a memory into a useful act, duration into orientated and meaningful time. But this transformation can be accomplished only in full view of society. [17]

The full view of society translates into bringing the writer into society, the predominant theme of engaged writing in French letters on the left in the '50s, but in a way which avoided the self-sustaining closure of earlier writing forms. The writer was then presented with the ambiguous task of becoming part of history while not being engulfed in the alienation, the "necessities" of class society.

> Writing, free in its beginnings, is finally the bond
> which links the writer to a History which is itself in
> chains: society stamps upon him the unmistakable
> signs of art so as to draw him along the more ines-
> capably in its own process of alienation. [18]

It is apparent, even at this stage of Barthes' writings, that history, while representing the inescapable situation of the writer, is not solely the source of meaning. Barthes' opposition to Marxism and his ultimate split from Sartre lies in the contention that both history and the novel are forms of bourgeois thinking, each resting on the naturalist fallacy. [19] Marxism for Barthes is precisely not revolutionary to the extent that it represents the working out of 'natural laws' or the science of human alienation to a utopia which is the endpoint of classical bourgeois society. All historical philosophies share the great temptation of effecting an end by ascribing final meaning: this represents for Barthes an exact parallel to the treatment of time in the novel. Thus the project of the writer becomes that of overcoming the alienated history in the creation of both new writing and, in Barthes' mind, a new metaphysics. To return solely to history is to return to "chains."

In this reformulation of fundamental categories, Barthes drew upon the work of the then-growing number of novelists in France who had moved away from the classical style. In particular Barthes cited Albert Camus' *The Stranger* as an example of 'writing degree zero.' The well-known opening lines of Camus' work — "Mother died today: Or, maybe yesterday; I can't be sure" [20] — illustrated precisely for Barthes the stripping away of the mythological or ideological codes governing society. Meursault's reaction to his mother's death was both socially unacceptable, that is, against the prevailing doxa, as well as being unnatural. One could also express this the other way around in that social opinion is, for Barthes, dependant on the claim to naturalness. Perhaps of more importance, though, to Barthes' later thought is the conclusion he draws from *The Stranger* in terms of the creation through the neuter of a meaning that goes beyond the alienated history that surrounds the writer.

> This transparent form of speech, initiated by Camus' *Outsider*, achieves a style of absence which is almost an ideal absence of style; writing is then reduced to a sort of negative mood in which the social or mythical characteristics of a language are abolished in favour of a neutral and inert state of form, thus thought remains wholly responsible, without being overlaid by a secondary commitment of form, to a History not its own. [21]

This inert state is later given ontological status as the ground of being.

Yet other critics of Camus' novel were less charitable concerning the novel's responsibility to history and to its supposed neutrality. Conor Cruise O'Brien, in particular, rejected Camus' handling of the Algerian situation as both racist and colonial. [22] But even if one accepted that Camus had achieved a balance between freedom and history, which Camus clearly was trying to find in his later concept of the rebel, it does not necessarily follow that the ground of meaning is ascribable to the inert form of zero degree writing. It is quite arguable in Camus' case that he returns to nature as the source of rewriting the myths that govern social life. [23] In this sense, the rewriting of the myth of Sisyphus is quite different from Barthes' compendium of mythologies.

Another striking example of the differences in understanding of myths is the comparison Barthes makes between classical myths such as the *Odyssey* and the bicycle race, the Tour de France. [24] It may well be that the modern period is reduced to finding its epic heroes in sports events but, even accounting for Barthes' irony, this does not seem to be adequate cause for treating the two on the same level. Here a fundamental weakness in Barthes' position stems precisely from his rejection of nature as having any role in establishing meaning. [25] It is also interesting that Barthes, while recognizing economic motives in the cycling event, [26] still holds out the hope that in this event, "the epic expresses that fragile moment of history in which man, however clumsy and deceived, nonetheless contemplates through his impure fables a perfect adequate between himself, the com-

munity and the universe." [27] This reinforces the utopian aspect
of Barthes' thought in this period and the complete reliance on
the social as the basis of myth. This also clearly signals Barthes'
entry into the simulacrum of postmodern culture that destroys
differences: all myths become the same. Barthes mirrors this
culture, becoming its most advanced exemplar even at the
moment of its critique.

Whether Barthes was correct or not in his view of *The Stranger*
or the Tour de France, it is important that at the time he concludes
that within writing there was a tension or ambiguity reflecting
the author's desire to create history through creating meaning,
yet in a situation that was dictated by one's circumstances. Writing
bore within itself the problems of power and, as such, became for
Barthes an element in the struggle for power.

> All writing will therefore contain the ambiguity of
> an object which is both language and coercion:
> there exists fundamentally in writing a 'circum-
> stance' foreign to language; there is, as it were, the
> weight of a gaze conveying an intention which is no
> longer linguistics. This gaze may well express a
> passion of language as in literary modes of writing;
> it may also express the threat of retribution as in
> political ones: writing is then meant to unite at a
> single stroke the reality of the acts and the ideality
> of ends. This is why power, or the shadow cast by
> power, always ends in creating an axiological
> writing, in which the distance which usually sepa-
> rates fact and value disappears within the very space
> of the words, which is given at once as description
> and as judgement. [28]

Barthes' choice of phrases here is critical to the understanding of
the development of his thought. Language is pitted against
coercion where coercion goes beyond the purely linguistic. This
going beyond is in terms of the development of the axiological
language epitomized most directly in the political philosophy of
Hobbes. Even the casual reader of Hobbes is struck by the force
of his definitions which builds up the "science of politics" on the
collapsing of the "is" and "ought" through the immediacy of
desire or, as Barthes suggests, of the collapsing of description and
judgement. Here we have all the aspects of the closed system plus

the crucial element of "fear" based on coercion which places Hobbes at the centre of modern politics. In fear, one goes beyond the security of a closed system, which brings about the (historical) demand from Barthes' point of view for the political father to set the law. Thus the axiological nature of politics based on the rule of law becomes the negative pole of the ambiguity in writing which Barthes tries to overcome in later studies. [29] Fear is granted here a status 'beyond science' and 'beyond history' to the extent that it stands outside of each; that is, without fear the desire for either does not exist. Fear also stands outside nature, for nature's insecurities, if they exist, are manifested in the invasion of others so characteristic of Hobbes' description of the state of war. These fears are socially made. Unlike Hobbes this ontology ascribes no fear to death as fear is socially 'clear and present.' Death for Barthes elicits the counterpart of fear — bliss which, like death, is structured on the basis of absence. In the metaphor Barthes employs, we have encountered, with fear, the police.

In *Writing Degree Zero* Barthes remained optimistic that in utopian writing the demands of law could be part of post-bourgeois life without the sacrifice of action and meaning by the individual. That is, the resolution of the individual's relation to others could be set within the dialectic of the ultimate identity of different individuals. This claim is familiar in any political theory that accepts Hegel's assertion of the dialectical unity of identity and as such is fundamental to that part of the Western tradition. In retrospect, Barthes, writing in 1975, in *Roland Barthes* recognized that this claim stood against the critique that he had been developing against the teleology of universality. He rejected the closed nature of the metaphysics of not only Hegel but of the theory of the ultimate harmony of individual wills with each other whether this is found in Rousseau, Kant or Marx. By the mid-'70s Barthes attempts to upset Hegel's logic of the unity of identity and difference for the writing of the difference of identity and division: the theory of heterology over homology. In this, Barthes joins theorists like Jacques Derrida or Geoffrey Hartman in the deconstructionist movement.

In political terms, this is marked by the movement from Marx to Fourier. In *Sade, Fourier, Loyola*, Barthes draws the contrast between Marxism which is based on need, and Fourierism which is based on desire. His preference in this work for a politic of desire is obvious especially as he identifies need with the economy and with nature. Need becomes the foreclosure of desire through its satisfaction and, hence, the denial of the human. Thus Barthes substitutes, in the first instance, desire ahead of need/economy. In a complete rejection of Aristotle (and implicitly the tradition itself) politics is to be domesticated.

> In Writing Degree Zero (political) utopia has the (naive) form of a social universality, as if utopia could only be the strict converse of the present evil, as if division could only be assured, ultimately, by indivision; but subsequently, though vague and filled with difficulties, a pluralist philosophy has been appearing: hostile to 'massification', tending toward difference, in short: Fourierist; whereupon a (still-maintained) utopia consists in imagining an infinitely fragmented society, whose division would no longer be social, and consequently, no longer conflictive. [30]

As a consequence Barthes is pushed more and more to the 'passion of language' away from the demands of the political. This means seizing the second pole within the ambiguity of writing which is desire. Desire is characterized by its negativity. Desire represents a lack which underlies the dialectical relation of the individual's actions to the world, or in more idealistic terms, the overcoming of ignorance on the way to knowledge. Barthes is engaged here in a reconceptualization of desire. However this reconceptualization of desire will lead to Barthes' development of the concept of bliss as "in excess" of desire, just as fear becomes the excess of alienated history, and this in time will lead back to the problem of power.

Barthes, as the previous quotation suggests, rejects the endpoint of the dialectic of the negation of the negation implicit in the first cycle of Hegelian consciousness. He is, however, very much in accord with Hegel in seeing desire as separating the individual from nature through the creation of consciousness, meaningful existence and language. And, if we stick with the earliest cycles of Hegel's dialectic, this struggle for existence (life or death) involves labour or the body in the creation of an economy and ultimately institutions under law which, depending on your view, either guarantee freedom to the individual or do not. In this rather simplistic version, desire through need gives rise to economic relations where life depends on the other through need gives rise to economic relations where life depends on the other through exchange, a view Barthes found developed in Jean Baudrillard. Baudrillard's view of capitalism as a sign system embodying symbolic exchange is taken over by Barthes as the next step. Played out in the Sadean castles, this exchange system ends in a theatricalism of death. Life in the simulacrum is beyond production becoming only the presentation of the absences of the desiring subject.

The "progress" of this dialectic historically in a social sense is such as to create for Barthes the necessity of desire to be placed under the limits of politics to avoid the death at the end of the dialectic of desire. In the early modern period this translates into Hobbes, as we have seen, and in the post-Hegelian period into Marx as the political economist *par excellence*. This view establishes the history of desire which Barthes sees in the narrative form. The narrative first of all has its origin in desire [31] and then its subsequent development under the sign of the economic:

> ... narrative is determined not by a desire to narrate
> but by a desire to exchange: it is a mechanism of
> exchange, an agent, a currency, a gold standard. [32]

Desire, like history, has its alienated element in exchange which for Barthes has come to be the reality principle of the modern period. Its tenacles extend out through the simple expression of the desire/satisfaction/desire nexus to define the ontology of the infinite consumer on the one hand, and the epistemology of the symbolic to define the "real and practical" on the other. [33] Again in a simplified sense, this is a reversal of the progression in Hegel from the desires at the base of the *Phenomenology* to the logic of being and becoming of *The Logic*. It may be seen in a shorthand fashion as the progress of metaphysics towards its destruction. This "progress", as others have suggested in a more forceful manner than Barthes, establishes the individual subject on the grounds of incompleteness or lack where the individual is constantly engaged in the impossible operation of satisfying his or her desire through trying to obtain the object. This dialectic leads to the subject's death the closer the object is approached. Here, the subject is established in the will with the object following on the will to power or possession. [34] The object standing against and forever outside the individual's will is for Barthes the source of traditional meaning. He believes this rightfully has been eclipsed by modern sign systems, thus forcing him, as we shall see, beyond the subject/object split in his new metaphysics of the neuter.

> Yet, just as any grammar, however new, once it is based on the diad of subject and predicate, noun and verb, can only be a historical specimen, linked to classical metaphysics, so the hermeneutic narrative, in which truth predicates an incomplete subject, based on expectation and desire for its imminent closure is dated, linked to the kerygmatic civilization of meaning and truth, appeal and fulfilment. [35]

Thus it was precisely the bourgeois novel's task to provide truth in the exchange relation struck with the reader: reading by the law of contract. Contemporary culture has turned this into an exchange of symbols divorced from the individual, reinforcing the claim that the social contract is predicated on desire against the "true" individual. [36] It is this claim that interests Barthes in the transgressive writing of Sade, Loyola, Fourier and ultimately Nietzsche, for they form part of the older hedonistic tradition which for Barthes stands against desire, though as a defeated rival.

> An old, a very old tradition: hedonism has been repressed by nearly every philosophy. . . Pleasure is continually disappointed, reduced, deflated, in favour of strong, noble values. Truth, Death, Progress, Strength, Joy, etc. Its victorious rival is Desire: we are always being told about Desire, never about Pleasure; Desire has an epistemic dignity, Pleasure does not. It seems that (our) society refuses (and ends up by ignoring) this to such a point that it can produce only epistemologies of the law (and of its contestation) never of its absence, or better still, of its nullity. [37]

Desire, like history, remain integral concepts for Barthes, but as in the case of history, desire is not the source of meaning. It is true that Barthes does not wish to jettison the identity of desire with negativity, but in almost a parody of the Christian identity of the sensual world with evil or nothingness, Barthes wishes to extend this "nullity" towards "materialist subject". [38] This is what he refers to as the legacy of the hedonistic tradition, or as pleasure or bliss which, in an addendum to the *Pleasure of the Text* written two years later in *Roland Barthes*, Barthes explicitly defines: "Bliss is not what corresponds to desire (what satisfies it) but what surprises, exceeds, disturbs, deflects it." [39] The establishment of pleasure outside of the metaphysics of the subject and object, outside of the metaphysics of desire, becomes Barthes' chief philosophical goal and it turns on the author's ability to create the individual or self against the prevailing codes of the laws of desire which underlie history in the space of literature. This is summarized in Julia Kristeva's remarks on Barthes:

> Writing is upheld not by the subject of understanding, but by a divided subject, even a pluralized subject, that occupies, not a place of enunciation, but permutable, multiple, and mobile places; thus it brings together in heteronomous space the naming of phenomena (through entry into symbolic law) and the negation of these names (phonetic, semantic, and syntactic shattering). This supplementary negation (derivative negation, negation of the harmonic negation) leaves the homogeneous space of meaning (naming or, if one prefers the 'symbolic') and moves, without 'imaginary' intermediacy, toward the biological — societal 'base' that is its excess, toward what cannot be symbolized (one might say, toward the 'real'). [40]

One might add here Kristeva's later comment that this heteronomous space is that of the symbolic void of degree zero where writing starts.

Thus, in fashioning his case, Barthes again returns to the structure of the narrative. Barthes, at this point, has clearly given up on the existence of a master code to the narrative; for example, following Kristeva, the multiple codes that Barthes identifies in *S/Z* are warning enough about reading the text in a deterministic manner. However it is apparent that beyond these multiple views, the "sanctioned Babel" [41] as he calls it, there does exist the "Oedipal pleasure (to denude, to know, to learn the origin and the end)" [42] based on the zero degree. In modern discourse the myth of origins is founded in nature or in such constructs as the state of nature common to liberal theorists. Barthes gathers these myths together under the sign of Oedipus which establishes the father in psychoanalytical terms at the center of Western civilization.

> ... if it is true that every narrative (every unveiling of the truth is a staging of the (absent, hidden or hypostatized) father — which would explain the solidarity of narrative forms, of family structures, and of prohibitions of nudity, all collected in our culture in the myth of Noah's sons covering his nakedness. [43]

Every narrative then leads back to Oedipus, with storytelling, to paraphrase Barthes, becoming the search for one's origins through the conflict with the original form of Law, the father. [44] Here Barthes joins the attack on Freud and the centrality of the Oedipus myth that characterizes such diverse thinkers as René Girard, Gilles Deleuze and Felix Guattari. However, Barthes is searching more for Blanchot's replacement of Oedipus by Orpheus in the literary space than in pursuing a new psychoanalysis or an anti-psychiatry each of which are still caught in the image repertoire of advanced capitalism.

Thus Barthes' analyses of novels of the bourgeois type shows that they simultaneously provide rationalizations of who and what we are, while reinforcing the Oedipal authority structure that denies any reality to these images in terms of fulfilling the individual as an individual. The repetition of this structure throughout contemporary society has reduced literature to prattle and boredom in the service of sustaining dead images of the self emanating from the image repertoire. [45] These images are established for Barthes by following Sartre's analysis of the gaze where one is not only fixed as an object by the gaze of the other, but one actually assumes the object as oneself. [46] The pursuit of desire must in consequence lead to the reinforcing of the objective against the subjective and thereby ensure the creation of neurosis in the individual. One is always outside of oneself facing the impossible of returning "for me", as Barthes' use of Nietzsche suggests. [47] Again, to break the grasp of the bourgeois classical text, writing must shift to being against neurosis while writing from inside neurosis, leading to the attractiveness of madness in Barthes' scheme which has not reached the level of insanity. This is typical of contemporary culture that renders individuals neurotic precisely by denying their neuroses. Hence there is an attraction to madness following Foucault as the transgressive break against repressive civilizations. In this respect Sade is paradigmatic for his madness is not contained by the law that imprisons him, nor does his madness free him, for his world is still unreal. Sade is locked in the struggle with the psycho-analytic police who wish to push him over the edge — though for many Sade had, of course, jumped earlier. In Sade's case, even if he was successful in avoiding madness, the police were not about to abandon the field. The political and psychoanalytical meet in the image of the law as sustained by the political father. The question at hand then revolves itself into whether Barthes can establish outside the course of the desires and history as mani-festations in power relations, a "polysemetic" space for bliss based on the zero degree of literary space. At this point, Barthes' project becomes simultaneously that of postmodern thought in its struggle for survival against the very analysis of the social given by postmodernity as a language that mirrors only exchanges in the repertoire of dead images.

The Pleasure of the Text is Barthes' answer. It begins with the injunction cum definition: "I shall look away, that will hence-forth be my sole negation." [48] "Looking away" in this sense is the rejection of the struggle for existence between egos that char-acterizes the Hegelian dialectic, the hell of the other of Sartre's *No Exit*, or abandoning the symbolic exchange of absences. Each of these struggles move to completed being of social existence: Hegel's full cycle of consciousness in 'religion', Sartre's totality or Baudrillard's simulacrum. Barthes advances the claim to honour the negative through the dissolution of the determinate being encompassed in these social relations by having the text "impose a state of loss. . ." This state of loss, where bliss or pleasure makes its appearance, is precisely the transgressive breaks in social codes that are found in modern literature or in the earlier proscribed writings such as Sade's. The symbol for this loss of the social is Sade's Society for the Friends of Crime, which Barthes turns into the Society of the Friends of the Text where there is 'nothing in common.' Bliss is against the social in Barthes' language with its underlying assumption for similarity, and hence bliss is for difference and ultimately for the self, not the subject.

> The asocial character of bliss: it is the abrupt loss of
> sociality, and yet there follows no recurrence to
> the subject (subjectively), the person, solitude:
> *everything* (emphasis Barthes') is lost, integrally. [49]

Conflict is present either in the struggle for existence of Hegel or
Sartre, or in the act of transgression of the readerly text but, in
the latter case, Barthes hopes the conflict will result in the
establishment of differential moral values beyond the claim of
either warring party by being outside the dialectic of subject and
object per se. This value rests on the "obliteration of the warrior
value" [50] and the obliteration of the image reservoir which is
associated with the speech of bourgeois society. Beyond subjects
and objects it takes the form of the neuter.

> The text is never a 'dialogue': no risk of feint, or
> aggression, of blackmail, no rivalry of ideolects;
> the text establishes a sort of islet within the human
> — the common — relation, manifests the asocial
> nature of pleasure (only leisure is social), grants a
> glimpse of the scandalous truth about bliss: that it
> may well be, once the image-reservoir of speech is
> abolished, *neuter* (emphasis Barthes')" [51]

Barthes at this point is attempting to appropriate the long
history of French moral philosophers. The setting of moral value
in the neuter forms the basis for the new Nietzschean sense of self
that Barthes envisages. But unlike his predecessors in the French
tradition, Barthes bans the actual statement of what value is from
the text. It is precisely the non-appearance of ultimate meaning
in the text itself that ensures such meaning outside the text.
Ultimately experience in the modern world for Barthes cannot
be spoken of outside symbolic exchange. On the one hand, it may
be lived, hence the predominance of the body over the mind, if
one can speak in such old terms, in the search for bliss. On the
other hand, it can be read in the absences of the text. The course
of Barthes' style from essay to treatise to the fragment follows
from this for the silences, gaps and 'in betweens' bring the reader
and text together outside of the 'contract' for revealed discourse.
The choice of Sade's *120 Days of Sodom* is itself a mirror of Barthes'
progression, leading as it does from the early stories with their
relative detail to the mere fragments of the final atrocities —

notwithstanding the facts of Sade's physical existence which separated the author from his manuscript before 'completion.' Both Barthes and Sade ultimately went outside their work if only to try and found the imaginative space where they may encounter their self as self. The fact that critics may not find Sade there, in the text, is in no way surprising. The surprising fact would be to encounter either Barthes or Sade at all in Barthes' work. Barthes' abandonment of value in the neuter is a stunning example of the collapse of all morality. This may be described in using the aggressive sense of neuter, as a neutered discourse. Barthes is beyond nihilism here in a self whose will has imploded into a shell of silence whose entry into the social is predicated on the loss of the social.

The claim against Barthes may also be taken further to the banishment of the political from the text as well. In the commitment to a postmodern discourse, political history also has no value. Again it is useful to use Barthes' words in *Roland Barthes*, reflecting back on Sade: "And Sade having produced the purest of texts, I believe I understand that the Political pleases me as Sadean text and displeases me as Sadistic text." [52] Here under the influence of the pleasure of the text Barthes draws the tension between politics and violence where for Barthes politics becomes the world of 'domestic bliss.' Politics as the realm of the public disappears into the domestic precisely because the sadistic disposition of modern politics is to violence. It is precisely this violence that is displeasing such that politics falls away from any concept of authenticity or injunction to action. Barthes realizes along with everyone else that the Sadean text is sadistic yet we have the instruction to 'look away'. This is captured as well in *The Pleasure of the Text* where we are told that "The text is (should be) that uninhibited person who shows his behind to the Political Father" [53] where the political father is this time the symbol of Sadean violence as well as Oedipus. The demand in both cases leads away from the forms of coercion by having us turn from the violence of the political and psychoanalytical police.

To go back to Barthes' *Writing Degree Zero*, this is again the question of whether writing may rid itself of the ambiguity of 'language and coercion' in a new style of writing. As I argued earlier, Barthes rejects the utopian solution of his earlier period for the reformulation of the claim to value of the neuter. The neuter, however, is profoundly caught in the field of battle for it can only express itself in the language of warriors or fall silent. As a consequence, Barthes is unable to exorcise coercion/violence in the neuter itself.

> The Neutral is therefore, not the third term — the
> zero degree — of an opposition which is both
> semantic and conflictual, it is at another link in the
> infinite chain of language, the second term of a
> new paradigm, of which violence (combat, victory,
> theatre, arrogance) is the primary term. [54]

The neuter retains its place as beyond the traditional conflict of subject/object, hence no longer a zero degree, but also retains in its new life, as the primary relation amongst individuals, the base in violence and the theatricalism of the image reservoir that pervades language. The very array of terms Barthes uses to open up the meaning of violence — combat, victory, theatre, arrogance — are the very characteristics of postmodern thought. Barthes presents us with the theatre of the social whose reality, from sporting events through to imperialist wars, comes from media images. These images to the extent that are part of the leisure/pleasure world are neutral/neutered for the self, not subject, whose existence is at best a presumption in rating surveys, and whose life is lived at home in domesticity. The postmodern world is the most neutral of all worlds precisely because it is the most violent in its discourse. This world had arrived ahead of Barthes and was there waiting to greet him.

   For Barthes, there were two possible avenues left. The first, following the demand for bliss, is to see in this violence "nothing but the moral state of difference..." [55] which successfully replaces the will to power with the non-will-to-possess. This option comes at the conclusion of *A Lover's Discourse* where Barthes attempts the conjugation of themes which have been expressed in his analysis of Goethe, Nietzsche, Ruysbroech, and not insignificantly, Tao. [56] There is a strong sense that the non-will-to-possess ends in a lover's silence taking up the non-warrior element of the neuter. As Barthes indicates the non-will-to-possess is an expression "imitated from the Orient." [57] It denotes a will that no longer wills either not to possess or not not-to-possess, but allows the non-will-to-possess to come as a blessing, to come as bliss. The point of this "coming to pass" is to escape the image repertoire of the West by moving the East. Barthes has this in common with Malraux, Grenier and Camus, for example. It is very explicit as a theme in his *Empire of Signs*. The issue is whether this "conclusion" can make its appearance in the Western world or was Barthes on the route to silence waiting, to use from the image repertoire the familiar children's myth *Briar Rose*, for the hundred years to elapse for the appearance of the new heroes, or anti-heroes?

Let us turn to the second avenue where Barthes, I believe, gives his answer. The violence at the base of the neuter is far more apt to give rise not to the politics of bliss, but rather to the politics of fear. The image of the text showing its behind to the political father is open not only to the interpretation of 'looking away towards bliss', it also can clearly mean turning tail and running in fear of the father. Each of these actions, fear, or bliss, are for Barthes joined in the neuter itself. They share a similar metaphysical status borne out by their 'proximity' in the psychoanalytical and political worlds. The transgressive act by which the self obtains bliss must be accompanied by the fear of punishment. Fear is what establishes the law to be transgressed, but in doing so it remains outside of the law. As a consequence fear is also able to establish to identity of the self. The resolution of fear in law 'closes the self' which the text continually tries to 'open' up but this opening ontologically gives no priority to bliss over fear. In fact, the opposite is the case. The movement of bliss towards the 'madness' of Sade is countered in the self by fear. The self resists its own assimilation in the attempt to transgress.

> Proximity (identity?) of bliss and fear. What is repugnant in such nearness is obviously not the notion that fear is a disagreeable feeling — a banal notion — but that it is *not a very worthy feeling* (emphasis Barthes'); fear is the misfit of every philosophy (except, I believe Hobbes's remark that the one passion of his life had been fear); madness wants nothing to do with it (except perhap old-fashioned madness: Maupassant's Horla) and this keeps fear from being modern: it is a denial of transgression, a madness which you leave off in full consciousness. By a last fatality, the subject who suffers fear still remains a subject; at most, he is answerable to neurosis (we then speak of anxiety, a noble word, a scientific word: but fear is not anxiety). [58]

Despite Barthes' rather narrow reading of the place of fear in political philosophy his point is clear. In the modern period the centrality of fear will give rise, all things being equal, to political institutions stemming from Hobbes. These institutions, as we know, are marked by the authoritarian presence of the political father as leviathan. Accompanying this politic will be the neurosis of the self who has been split "while leaving him intact" [59] and while cutting him off from madness. The social no longer allows you to be mad once it renders you schizophrenic; in other words, all differences become similarities.

The turn towards the mother, whom we will meet later, offers no more of a solace. There is more than just an accidental coincidence that *The Pleasure of the Text* begins with a Latin quotation from Hobbes: "Atquemetum tantum concepit tunc mea mater/ Ut paratet geminos, meque metumque simu." [60] The self is both conceived in fear while remaining the conceiver of fear. It is the mother image behind the father figures that have the form of political and psychological laws. Similarly, as a symbol of fraternal love, it also creates violence as René Girard's analysis of twins demonstrates in *Violence and the Sacred*. *The Pleasure of the Text* becomes the working out of the self under the sign of fear/bliss, but with the 'hidden priority of fear' disguised in the Latin; that is, only open to those of the past. It is "Bacon's simulator" (which Barthes references at the beginning of the text) which he wants to triumph over Baudrillard's simulacrum. But it is, in the end, the triumph of the tradition over Barthes in contrast to his attempt to reject this tradition in *A Lover's Discourse*.

There is no doubt that with the completion of *The Pleasure of the Text* in 1973, Barthes was facing the reality of a Hobbesian end or a self-accepted neurosis with less than enthusiasm. The two later works that have been drawn on here, *Roland Barthes* which appeared in 1975, and *A Lover's Discourse* which appeared in 1978, are much more directed to extracting the self from the grasp of fear and moving towards the will-to-bliss. The implications of this did not escape Barthes. In terms of his political commitment he remained more and more isolated and was caught in a fundamental ambiguity. He had from the beginning contested the false premise of the "natural" which he regarded as a mere alibi of the majority to establish legality. Yet his analysis of fear did raise the question of whether fear itself is not grounded in the "natural." From this it would have been but a short distance to seeing the individual as a social animal who, through the imagination, created political and psychological being out of nature and in accord with law. This would have meant the abandonment of the postmodern project. But the conventional nature of the law provided him an escape from this confrontation — for, after all, law was an arbitrary creation. It did not touch the self; it left being alone, for however much it interfered with everday life, this interference always was in the form of the "dead" myth. The myth is cut off from nature; it is a sign system created by society to close the question of being. Hence Barthes' position on the outside allowed him to believe he could escape. He says at the end of *Roland Barthes* in response to the question "And afterward? What to write now? Can you still write anything? — One writes with one's desire and I am not through desiring." [61] The conclusion is inescapable that the search for what he desired, the realm of bliss, would lead him further and further from politics and from history. Barthes' reference to this fact is made, appropriately enough, in the reference to himself in the third person.

> Against this 'natural', I can rebel in two ways: by arguing, like a jurist, against a law elaborated without me and against me ('I too am entitled to. . .'), or by wrecking the majority's Law by a transgressive avant-garde action. But he seems to remain strangely at the intersection of these two reactions: he has complicities of transgression and individualist moods. [62]

Barthes continues in his quotation to draw himself as the "outsider," recalling the early praise he has for Camus' novel which has now strangely come to represent Barthes' situation.

> . . . it is possible to enjoy the codes even while nostalgically imagining that some day they will be abolished like an intermittent *outsider* (emphasis Barthes'). I can enter into or emerge from the burdensome sociality, depending on my mood — of insertion or of distance. [63]

On the one hand, as Sartre rather bluntly put it to Camus, history is not a swimming pool where one tests the water to decide whether to go in or not. [64] Thus this is not a convincing end for Barthes' politics. He has come virtually to oppose Sartre's earlier position which strongly influenced him in his first writings. Though if Barthes can be justly accused of disservering his thought from history, there certainly is little left of literature in Sartre's work and little attractiveness in Sartre's Caesarian politics. On the other hand, Barthes here captures precisely the romanticism of postmodern thought. Attracted to what Guy Debord calls the society of the spectacle, it is difficult not to be seduced by the fashion system. After all, who wishes to drink bad wine, dress poorly, and not have "The New Citroen"? Surely knowing all these mythologies should allow you to enjoy the codes as you please? This, as Barthes knew, was too easy.

Cut off from nature and history Barthes ironically has only recourse to a self whose appearance is ultimately confined to the realms of bliss and fear beyond the power of the text. Bliss and fear hold out meaningful experience, but have in Barthes' thought been separated from their patrons, the arts. In rejecting the arts and aesthetics, Barthes distances himself from one of the last hiding places of the claim to authenticity in the modern world. Precisely the sign of postmodern culture is to incorporate the arts into the network of symbols that are exchanged exactly in the same way as that of fashion. The irony of this situation is precisely that of the critic who must lead a parasitical existence that destroys the works that feed it. In Barthes' language, the text contains fear which eats away at itself. Yet, it is the text's "pleasure" to work this fear into the art of politics, literature, psychology, and ultimately into bliss. But it is this work that postmodernity engulfs and which Barthes, so much the product of his thought and society succumbs to in the final years of his life. The gradual movement of his style from essay to fragment could only lead to the lengthening of the space for the silences of the text. Art similarly receded from the domain of the writer to that of the reader and finally to that of the fasion system. Meaning finding refuge in silence shed the vehicles that brought it there. Literature loses its ability to speak.

Barthes final turn is to the photograph for it represents the logical end to his movement away from literature. In *Camera Lucida*, his last work, the photo becomes the gaze of Orpheus guaranteeing the "absence — as presence" in what he calls the noeme of the photo — the certainty that "That has been." [65] The photograph captures the subject (or body, or following Sartre, the facticity of being-in-itself) as an object, but not as the object which all other arts have turned into myth. "In Photography, the presence of the thing (at a certain past moment) is never metaphoric. . ." [66]

We see here Barthes' final rejection of the image repertoire, the creative imagination and lived experience. The death at the heart of the system of symbolic exchange comes to rest in the photograph as the site of authenticity, or, in Barthes' rewriting of Blanchot's criticism, the eidos of the photograph rather than literature is seen as the site of death itself. The resurrection or return from the underworld is ascribed to the breaks or "punctum" in the photo that shatter the codes or "studium." For Barthes these breaks are the existence of time where time is the neuter void of meaning which stands against history.

> Perhaps we have an invincible resistance to believing in the past, in History, except in the form of myth. The Photograph, for the first time, puts an end to this resistance: henceforth the past is as certain as the present, what we see on paper is as certain as what we touch. It is the advent of the Photograph — and not, as has been said, of the cinema — which divides the history of the world. [67]

The photo is the ecstatic presence in absence of being and hence of the "real": a form, as he calls it, of *satori*, or the "passage of a void." [68]

The absence at the core of this reality is directly illustrated by the absence in the text of the most important photograph: that of the "Winter Garden" from Barthes' childhood. Barthes suggests the picture of his garden cannot be distinguished from other gardens: the site of nature that in the postmodern world no longer captures any difference is merely the same. The philosophy of difference is engulfed in the mirror of itself. In the end, the photograph is no more capable of establishing meaning than the mythology of the tradition with its gardens, whether they be sitated in Eden or in Voltaire's *Candide*. The endpoint is curiously Proustian with Barthes' own form of the 'search for things past' in his quiet pursual of the photographs of his Mother and hence of his origins. Barthes' disappearance here may almost be expected given the consistent now-you-see-me-now-you-do-not of his career. After all, Barthes' end is prefigured in the beginning in the photograph entitled "The demand for Love." The demand

Roland Barthes,   *The Demand for Love*

remained unanswered; the 'lover's discourse' failed.

Barthes expected at best that, as he remarks at the end of *Camera Lucida*, he would be met with the "nauseated boredom" of advanced society's reaction to the claim to difference. Indifference is the sign of society to any referent. What is left of Barthes' encounter with the tradition of Hegel and Hobbes, and with the encounter with his culture is the metaphysics of the silent image. This dead-end is not only Barthes': it is fate of much of the postmodern debate.

D.C.

7

THE LAST DAYS OF LIBERALISM

Aesthetic Liberalism

As late capitalism moves from the commodity relation based on wage/labour exploitation to the simulated economy of excess, it plays out the logic of liberalism. The turn to 'justice and values' nominally identified with convervatism, becomes the rallying point for a society that has accomplished by definition the main tenets of liberalism, freedom and equality. In the last days of liberalism, we are presented with a culturally refined model of behaviour that has left behind the crudity of Bentham's quip that 'pushpin is as good as poetry'. The 'last men' of Nietzsche's herd are content in actively seeking the role of a passive spectator in the democratic process as Nietzsche predicted. They have all become critics whose main task is to sit in judgement.

It is our thesis that Immanuel Kant, in his last days, reverses the field of liberalism creating the topology of the postmodern society of the spectacle under the sign of the aesthetic. All of this may be found in the *Critique of Judgement* [1], the definitive text of the dead power of aesthetic liberalism:

— no longer critical theory's "What is Enlightenment," but rather "The End of All things" as instrumental reason becomes a culture text;

— no longer Lyotard's nostalgia for a sublime transcendent, but rather the nauseous allegory;

— no longer Deleuze's harmony of the faculties, but rather the nihilism of the will-not-to-will;

— no longer Arendt's citizen, but rather the disembodied eye of the voyeur;

— no longer Marcuse's play, but rather spectator sports;

— no longer liberalism, but rather aesthetic liberalism and the society of the spectacle.

We begin by moving to the site of aesthetic liberalism — the imagination.

As Heidegger points out in his study of Kant's metaphysics, the *Critique of Judgement* establishes the central role of the trans-cendental imagination. [2] This, in turn, reestablishes liberal theory as the unity of wills under the concept of an end which has a subjective claim to universality based on the transcendental imagination. The imagination founds the individual and the state on the basis of the aesthetic informing the judgement of the "kingdom of ends." Thus the *Critique* stands as the founding text of aesthetic liberalism.

The importance attached to the aesthetic imagination sends one back to the origins of the aesthetic in the 'sensibility' of the natural world. For Kant, this sensibility expresses itself in the desires which share with the imagination the structure of calling to "life" what is not there. The senses are determined by the "natural" causality of fulfilling desires. This is sometimes portrayed as amoral, for example, the eating of food for survival, or at other times as immoral, as greed, but in the long run as part of the antagonism that leads to the moral end of perpetual peace. The will which is determined by these natural causes is claimed by Kant to be free *a priori* as a transcendental moral agent whose chief characteristic is its disinterestedness.

This gives rise to the familar Hobbesian view of politics: an antagonistic desiring individual needing, to quote the sixth proposition of the *Idea for a Universal History*, "a master to break his self-will and force him to obey a universally valid will is the categorical imperative, or the principle of political right, which establishes the form of the state as an authoritative agent "to administer justice universally" [4] leaving the end of the state under the sign of cosmopolitan purpose.

Three observations may be drawn. First, economics becomes the realm of the unfettered will in the competition of all against all. It is an amoral activity which appears in the catalogue of technical skills under practical reason. As an unfettered will economics is the site reflecting Kant's possessive individualism with the privileged position of the infinite appropriator, yet, with a long run moral aim, the underlying calculus of pleasure/pain, or sensibility, contributes to the Idea of perpetual peace.

Second, the state under the Idea of perpetual peace is given no practical end, only form, in accord with the moral law, yet, as a sensible entity it has an end. Determining the particular end from the general is the function of judgement in Kant's system. This returns one again the the sensible realm as a question of pleasure and pain, but now beyond economics as culture.

Third, judgement works by breaking the self-will. This is fundamentally a power relation predicated on a will-not-to-will which includes all individuals as sensible entities, but excludes the supersensible Master. Thus, the Kantian will has implicit in it a nihilism which Nietzsche later identifies as the will-to-will.

"Good Taste"

The problem of liberal theory rests on how one arrives at aesthetic judgements in reference to the calculus of the senses, and how one arrives at the teleological judgement of ends. Kant begins with the proposition of pleasure and pain, which he has earlier rejected as a transcendental principle of reason. He is bound by this rejection, yet the sensible as principle will be given a form of universality having a space not unlike that of the super-sensible Ideas, which are not known-in-themselves, but are necessary. What must be overcome is the subjectiveness of pleasure and pain, that is their interested aspect, so that one is given over to the paradoxical notion of disinterested interest-edness. A similar shift occurs in teleological judgements with respect to the idea of purposiveless purposiveness.

In each case the starting-point is from "taste" which was central to the eighteenth-century view of culture. While taste rests on the pleasurable as it is experienced sensually, it is apprehended in a separate exercise of judgement. This judgement becomes an aesthetic judgement in its pure form as a subjective judgement, and not an objective determinate judgement as there is no corresponding concept. Yet the universal aspect of the judgement is asserted by Kant's arguing that the perspective outside of the self employed by the judge is, in principle, common to all rational individuals. Thus taste has its roots in the realm of common sense, and as 'good taste' defines higher culture and a higher faculty. Thus it shares both aspects of disinterestedness and purposiveness in Kant's schema.

A number of conclusions can be drawn from this. In *Truth and Method*[5] Gadamer sees in common sense the link to the *sensus communis* of the Roman antiquity, and the medieval period. Politics and morality are brought together to form a community on the basis of the 'moral feeling' of taste. By shifting the foundation of politics to the sensual realm from the strictly rational capacity of the understanding, Kant's arguments presents a more plausible version of how individuals under liberal mythology leave the state of nature. However, the cost is to move the central principle of the political towards the aesthetic from the understanding. Gadamer's resistance to this sends his thought back to Aristotle, although this is itself a dead-end for Aristotle's citizen would hardly find life in the modern world possible.

The aesthetic is further emphasized by Kant's use of 'good taste'. This continues the rupture of politics from reason, and extends the rupture towards the moral. Kant maintained the relation of the aesthetic to the moral by arguing in the *Critique* that the relation was by analogy, but Kant is opening up the way for the split of morals from a politics that rests on aesthetics. The schema is played out today.

Neurotic Liberalism

Kant would find this schism unacceptable yet a similar situation is present in taking the argument from moral feeling. Following Heidegger's analysis in *The Basic Problems of Phenomenology*[6] the moral feeling in Kant is described as arising from the sensibility of the individual to oneself as a person. It is the way the self reveals itself to itself through the feeling of the self. Thus it is at once existential, and aesthetic. Heidegger distinguishes this feeling in Kant's empirical ego, from the thinking and knowing ego. This feeling when brought in line, or in conformity with the moral law establishes the person as a person, and the unity of the thinking, moral and aesthetic egos. This Heidegger notes is called "respect" in Kant's schema, which is at the basis of the Kantian theory of personality: that is the respect for the individual as a self-determining end. From the perspective of Heidegger's ontology the analysis remains on the ontical level, but a level suited to the political uses for respect. For example, in the *Groundwork of the Metaphysics of Morals*, the concept of duty requires acting out of reverence, or respect for the laws.[7] A respect Kant adds that comes from a rational concept, and hence is self-produced, and not a fear induced from the outside. Kant here is not Hobbes, but he is not far off. Indeed, Kant and Hobbes are mirror-images because fear is internalized with the production of the subject thereby re-creating the antagonism of the "unsocial social" world — a form of inner check.

The shifting of the paradox of fear/respect to the level of pure practical reason may solve the problem for the perfectly rational individual by making him or her neurotic, but willing. But more fundamentally it drives the argument back to the problem of the unknowability of either the end or the means of reverence. This is analogous to the problem of why individuals joined together, and why they obey the law refered to earlier as the problem of common sense. For Kant, common sense allows individuals to judge disinterestedly their interest, hence allowing them to sensibly form political collectivities. It also allows individuals to judge the pleasing and displeasing aspect of works of art when taste becomes "good taste". In other words, individuals can make judgements on objects as beautiful or sublime. These judgements are paradigmatic of what it means to be civilized in the Kantian schema, thereby establishing the political role of law.

The Citizen as Voyeur

While the distinctions drawn in eighteenth-century aesthetics between the beautiful and sublime are often arbitrary, beauty may refer to the site where individuals encounter themselves as an end either in nature, or in the social world. To phrase it differently, the beautiful object tells us something of the essence of individuals. The sublime, on the other hand, treats of the incomprehensible, of the transcendental to humans, hence the ability to instill fear. It is more the area of the existential. Kant was most comfortable with the beautiful or the sublime in the natural world. In politics these ideas appear most forcibly in the initial proposition of the *Idea for a Universal History with a Cosmopolitan Purpose* when natural capacities "sooner or later (will) be developed completely and in conformity with their end" in accordance with the "teleological theory of nature. . . ". [8] Here the design of nature is outside of individuals giving rise to the "two will" problem. In purusing enlightenment, the individual is given the task of "emerging from his self-induced immaturity" [9] through freedom and the exercise of the will. However, the design is only perceived from the position of the spectator by observing the beauty and terror of God's works, or by observing human works reflecting God's will. From the position of the spectator, the individual assumes the role of the passive individual willing-not-to-will.

Hannah Arendt's interpretation of Kant rests on the role of the spectator in witnessing the public event of politics. She references Kant's attitude to the French Revolution where meaning is attributed to the event precisely because of "his disinterestedness, his non-participation, his non-involvement". [10] Kant's aversion to revolution on *a priori* grounds vanishes once the event becomes that of a natural phenomena to be observed. The causal chain of the natural world, in this case the necessity of revolution, is respected along with the freedom of the pen now placed safely in the intelligible realm. We are very close at this point to the "dead power" at the heart of liberalism where the events are assigned meaning, and controlled solely by the judge's eye.

The Ideology of Genius

In the ideological schema related here the 'passivity' of the citizen as voyeur, is contrasted to the 'activity' in the realm of free beauty created by the "genius". Kant's genius is no product of history being a gift of nature, but as a part of nature genius may express the design of nature. This expression of design by the genius, as Hans Saner points out in *Kant's Political Philosophy*, "as a whole lies in time." [11] The artistic vision of the creative imagination by existing in time directly challenges the claims of the supersensible ideas to the regulation of human conduct. Further, the description of genius in terms of the unregulated, or unlawful, 'play' of the faculties contrasts sharply with the rule of the moral personality. The creative genius also challenges the disinterested stance of the judging spectator in the very creation of the object or end for which judgements are to be formed. The unlawful lawfulness of play differs then from other Kantian paradoxes to the extent that the claims of universality attached to the sensible realm are made known through the judgement of the work of art. This element of finality is lacking in the Ideas themselves. Finality only exists in the realm of power.

The political implications of the creative genius, and the concept of play have then full impact in reformulating the ideology at the basis of aesthetics in postmodern thought. This can be seen in Marcuse's use of play in a Freudian-Marxism sense, and Gadamer's use in a hermeneutical sense; each tearing apart Kant, yet remaining with him. Genius acts to 'valorize' both the left and right under the nihilism of artistic codes.

The Aesthetic Contract

Kant was caught in the spider's web of the realm of aesthetics and the role of the creative imagination in politics. The foundation and end of government expressed through the image of the state of nature is more fundamentally a myth than idea of reason. It is the product of the creative imagination which supplies not only the beginning and end, but the fear upon which the will is brought to obedience. This fear or reverence falls under the category of the sublime. The sublime creates fear, but fear at a distance which checks the will by bringing it under the transcendental authority of the Idea of Nature. A similar awe is present in the Hobbesian sovereign, and by delegation in the judges of the state. This type of fear remains passive as long as the citizen is passive in internalizing the higher authority. Once active the fear gives way to violence and rebellion which directly threatens the state and the individual, and hence is not countenanced by Kant. To express this in a different fashion, the sublime rests on the existential and, in particular, on the fear of death or nihilation. The imagination in making present what is not is precisely the vehicle for communicating this fear.

Thus Kantian liberal politics rests on two basic myths. The first expressed in the analogy of beauty is the moral good will which creates the idea of the harmony of all based on the individual as an end. This is the ideological basis of the social contract. The second expressed in the analogy of the sublime threatens the individual and society with annihilation. This is the ideological basis of obedience. Both myths are present and rely on the concept of judgement. Though Kant favours the myth of the good, modern thought has used both ideologies in the control of the dying social by the coercive culture created by this aesthetic.

Nauseous Allegories

The last days of liberalism are mirrored in Kant's depiction of the 'Last Day of Judgement'. The last judgement, in its apocalyptic form, represents final justice as well as the end of time. Kant treats of this Idea in the short article entitled *The End of All Things* written in 1794. The end of time corresponds for Kant to the end of the sensible world which we know from Kant's earlier critique represents the bounds of knowledge. Thus the end of all time, as the cessation of time, cannot be thought of except as a super-sensible Idea within time. Kant reiterates that the individual's end, in a supersensible sense, is the moral end of pure practical reason which by its very nature is never obtained in time though it regulates existence in time. Because we cannot know of eternity, and hence know of the Last Judgement, Kant carries the judge-ment into the sensible world as an everyday event in the long run progress of morality towards perpetual peace. Hence the necessity in the political realm of the judge to the long run moral progress.

But to the extent that the individual is a sensible creature who lives in time, the thought of annihilation of death occurs to her or him.

> In point of fact, men, not without reason, feel the burden of their existence even though they them-selves are the cause of it. The reason for this seems to me to lie in the fact that in the progress of the human race the cultivation of talents, art, and taste (with their consequence, luxury) naturally precedes the development of morality. . . [12]

There are two conclusions. The first is to see in the progress of culture the progress of the individual as a basis for the moral state. This is the basis of postmodern liberalism's claim to the moral and just, but which is sublated by the second element of this ideology. The second conclusion is to see in the desires, and their satisfaction the process of nihilation at the root of sensi-bility. Individuals as creatures in time live through successive nihilations, and as members of the human community reach their own nihilation. We enter here the self-liquidation in the nihilism of Kant's aesthetic liberalism.

At this point, we meet Kant's reluctance to think through this nihilation which he calls a "purely negative (concept)". Kant admits that "The thought is sublime in its terror, . . . it is even required to be interwoven in a wonderous way with common human reason, because this notion of eternity is encountered in all reasoning peoples in all times. . ." Yet faced with the implications of this nihilism, he retreats. Here is how he expresses it in *The End of All Things:* "There is something appalling in this thought because it leads, as it were, to the brink of an abyss, and for him who sinks into it, no return is possible."

Kant identifies how the nihilism at the core of aesthetic liberalism gives rise to a vision of the postmodern world that has lived out the 'logic' of the *Critique*. Part of this future is sketched in Kant's footnote commenting on the implications of the negative. This he describes as giving rise to "inimical, partly nauseous allegories". These are the 'allegory' of 'life' as an inn where we are soon to be replaced by a new traveller, a penitentiary, a lunatic asylum and as a privy. Taking these "allegories" in turn, the inn is a symbol of mortality, the penitentiary of the judged individual, the lunatic asylum of the use of unreason or the imagination, and the privy of the body. Each are logical implications of the ideology at the heart of the "good will". Each is denied by Kant under the heading of the "perverse end of all things". Each depicts an aspect of existence forced back into the "obscurity" from where the transcendental imagination had found it. Each places existence outside the good taste of society in the writings of authors like the Marquis de Sade or in the vision of poets like Blake. Each illustrates the aesthetic code of post-liberal politics in the postmodern condition.

Kant has enucleated the fundamental abstraction inherent in the liberal concept of power. Being predicated on judgement, power is able to remove itself from the living force of the society to assume the masque of the spectator. Removed from the body, power is set against the body; removed from the will it is directed against the will; removed from the imagination, it is hostile to the imagination. The citizen is caught up within this absence for in following common sense the individual self-liquidates — all in the name of good taste: not an unreasonable description of the last days of liberalism.

D.C.

IV

POSTMODERNISM AND
THE DEATH OF THE SOCIAL

The essays in *Postmodernism and the Death of the Social* are intended to deepen and intensify the radical insights of contemporary poststructuralist theory into cynical power as the disenchanted locus of the postmodern project, from the semiological deconstructions of Jean Baudrillard to a final deliberation on that strange, but magical, meeting in the Western mind of Nietzsche and Marx. We want to demonstrate the presence now of a fantastic rupture in Western consciousness: a rupture which originates in a *political refusal* of the 'referential illusion' at the heart of the modern account, and results in an *epistemological denial* of the *a priori* existence of a privileged domain of finalities — labour, sex, use-value, or utility.

We would like to report that the growing critique of the referential illusion (the *naturalistic* assumption that the referents of labor, capital, desire, or the unconscious as the referents of the Real) has a limit that would simply result in a displacement of Western Marxism: a realignment which, while it would abolish the fetishism of the commodity-form (replacing it with the fetishism of the sign) and a reduction of power to the play of capital accumulation (replacing it with the new axis of power/ideology), would nevertheless preserve the essential thrust of Marx's *Capital*. We would like to consent to the revisionist (or *cultural*) interpretation of Marxism which insists that what is required, and this in view of the new modes of cultural hegemony in advanced capitalist society, is a radical inversion of the order of primacy of Marx's ground categories: flipping *Capital* over by theorising the primacy of culture over political economy. But we cannot make this report, because Baudrillard and, indeed, the whole corpus of New French Thought — from Deleuze and Lacan to Lyotard and the early Barthes — have brought us to a fantastic and elemental discovery.

Their discovery is that Nietzsche all along had stood at the beginning and end of *Capital*; and the very recovery of Western Marxism as an adequate account of the darkness with the post-modern project depends on a reinterpretation of Marx's *Capital* as the imploded forward side (the side of nihilism in the value-form of seduction) of Nietzsche's *The Will to Power*. In this account, *Capital* is disclosed as a vivid, almost clinical, study of the inner workings of contemporary nihilism. It is a master text on the purely *abstract unity* which is the epicentre of Western experience and so the non-reality of capital as merely a 'perspectival appearance', the value-form of nihilism in the present era. This tracing out of the Nietzschean regression in Marx is the gamble of postmodernist theory, the silent foreground of the critical theory of (disappearing) society today. Against the current impulse in postmodernist theory and art which, refusing origins and originality in favour of parody and kitsch, we conclude just the opposite. Parody is no longer possible because in America today, which is to say in the system of advanced modern societies, the real is parody. And against and beyond Umberto Eco, it's not the age of hyperrealism either, but the opposite. The simulacrum exists with such a degree of intensity and pervasiveness that it no longer depends for its existence on hyperreality effects. As Nietzsche predicted, we have finally passed through into that purely perspectival zone of virtual technology, virtual bodies, and virtual imaging-systems.

8

BAUDRILLARD'S MARX

Baudrillard and the Fate of Postmodernity

Jean Baudrillard is the theorist of nihilism as the fate of post-modernity. Like the culture he seeks to describe, Baudrillard's writings are a geometry of signs of absence and lack which threaten to unravel in a fantastic eruption of creative energy as they trace the *implosion* of postmodern experience signified by the signs everywhere today of dead labour, dead power, and dead truth. Baudrillard's theoretical discourse might have begun as a critique of the productivist fetish of Marxian political economy in writings like *The Mirror of Production* and *For a Critique of the Political Economy of the Sign*. Indeed, even up to *L'Échange symbolique et la mort*, which explores the upsurge of the symbolic against the radical semiurgy of the sign, he remained an existentialist in the classical French tradition. But what makes him really interesting, and what makes his discourse the truth-sayer of the relationship of Marx and Nietzsche, is that Baudrillard is a tragic philosopher of society as a sign-system: Baudrillard's writings are a mirrored reflection of the nihilism of the sign-system they seek to describe. Everywhere in his writings are traces of the disintegration, decadence, exhaustion, and brilliance (because final flashes of illumination) which light the sky of a darkening society. To read Baudrillard's most recent works, from the simulational models of *In the Shadow of the Silent Majorities* and *Simulacrum* to the deconstructive interpretations of *Oublier Foucault*, *De la séduction* and *Les Stratégies fatales*, is to enter a terroristic universe, whose staged communica-

tions and abstract codings undergo a massive and feverish redoublement where power, truth, history, capital — the whole arc
of referential finalities — prepare to reenter their own simulacra.

Baudrillard is, above all, a theorist of the *cynical commodity*.
What makes Baudrillard dangerous, allowing him to put Nietzsche
into play as the doppelganger of Marx's *Capital*, is that he writes
from that point where the commodity-form, abandoning its
historical association with the simulacrum of concrete labour,
reveals itself for what it always was: a transparent sign-system that
traces out in the curved space of political economy (and of
consumer culture) the implosive, disaccumulative, and seductive
cycle of postmodern power. Like Adorno and Horkheimer in the
Dialectic of Enlightment and, in fact, writing to confirm French
poststructuralism as the philosophical successor to the tragic
tradition in critical theory (Benjamin, Adorno, Horkheimer, and
Lowenthal), Baudrillard is a thinker who speaks from the dark
side of postmodernity. His is the fully disenchanted world of
labour, myth and domination as emblematic signs of postmodernism.

Baudrillard writes under the dark sign of Nietzsche: each of
his texts are works of art which seek to arraign the world before
poetic consciousness. Baudrillard's discourse is a return to a
tragic sense of history because his imagination moves along that
trajectory *where nihilism is both antithetical to and the condition of
historical emancipation*. The tragic sense in Baudrillard's thought
derives directly from his reflections on our imprisonment in the
processed world of abstract power: a power-system that works its
effects technically and symbolically, and is the disappearing locus
of a society which has passed over into its opposite — the cycle of
the death of the social and the triumph of culture.

Baudrillard's Refusals

If Baudrillard is so unsparing in his tragic vision of abstract
power as the essence of postmodernity, it is because his theoretical
agenda includes the following four great refusals of the classical
model of sociology: 1) a devalorisation of the social; 2) a rejection
of the naturalistic discourse of the historical; 3) a refusal of
dialectical reason (in favour of a semiological reduction of the
exchange-system to the structural law of value); and 4) a rupture
with the normalizing, and hence accumulative, conception of
power. Baudrillard's theoretical analysis challenges the logic of

referential finalities as the foundation of Western consciousness. It does so because all of Baudrillard's thought traces the *implosion* of postmodern experience: the contraction and reversal of the categories of the *real* into a dense, seductive, and entirely nihilistic society of signs.

1. The Death of the Social

> A speechless mass for every hollow spokesman without a past. Admirable conjunction, between those who have nothing to say, and the masses who do not speak. Ominous emptiness of all discourse. No hysteria or potential fascism, but simulation by precipitation of every lost refential. Black box of every referential, of every uncaptured meaning, of impossible history, of untraceable systems of representation, the mass is what remains when the social has been completely removed.
>
> *In the Shadow of the Silent Majorities*

In Baudrillard it's not so much that sociological discourse, the master paradigm of the contemporary century, has been superseded by competing ensembles of *normative* meaning, but, instead, that the privileged position of the social as a positive, hence normative, referent has suddenly been eclipsed by its own implosion into the density of the mass.

> The social world is scattered with interesting objects and crystalline objects which spin around and coalesce in a cerebral chiaroscuro. So is the mass, an *in vacuo* aggregation of individual particles, refuse of the social and of media impulses: an opaque nebula whose growing density absorbs all the surrounding energy and light rays, to collapse finally under its own weight. A black hole which engulfs the social.[1]

Particularly in his writings on aesthetics and postmodernity, Baudrillard is concerned with the rupture in postmodern discourse represented by the collapse of the normalising, expanding, and positive cycle of the social into its opposite: an implosive and structural order of signs. In this interpretation, the triumph of *signifying culture* means the eclipse of genuine social solidarities (society). Beyond Weber's theory of rationalisation, against Foucault's privileging of normalisation, and against Habermas' *dialectical* analysis of (rationalised) systems and communicative lifeworld, Baudrillard writes of our *exteriorisation* into the processed world of an advanced 'techno-culture'. This is that breakpoint in the symbolic totality where the 'norm' undergoes an inversion into a floating order of signs, where strategies of normalisation are replaced by the simulation of the masses,[2] where signification replaces the process of reification, and, finally, where the 'hyperreality' of culture indicates a great dissolution of the space of the social. Baudrillard's theorisation of the end of sociology as a reality-principle, or what is the same, the exhaustion of the social as a truth-effect of a purely nominalistic power, privileges a violent and implosive perspective on society. "Violence implosive qui résulte non plus de l'extension d'un système, mais de sa saturation et de sa rétractation, comme il en est des systèmes stellaires."[3]

In his key text on aesthetic theory, *In the Shadow of the Silent Majorities*, Baudrillard[4] provides three strategic hypotheses (from minimal and maximal perspectives) about the existence of the social only as a murderous effect whose uninterrupted energy over two centuries has come from deterritorialisation and from concentration in ever more unified agencies. The *first* hypothesis is that the social may only refer to the space of a *delusion*: the social has basically never existed; there has never been any "social relation"; nothing has every functioned socially. On this inescapable basis of challenge, seduction and death, there has never been anything but *simulation* of the social and the social relation.[5] And if the social is a simulation, then the likely course of events is a brutal de-simulation, "a de-simulation which itself captures the style of a challenge (the reverse of capital's challenge of the social and society): a challenge to the belief that capital and power exist according to their own logic — " *they have none*, they vanish as apparatuses as soon as the simulation of social space is done."[6] The *second* hypothesis is the reverse, but parallel, image of the delusional thesis: the social, not as the space of delusion undergoing a 'brutal de-simulation', but the social as *residue*, "expanding throughout history as a 'rational' control of residues, and a rational production of residues."[7] Baudrillard[8] is explicit as to the purely excremental function of the social, as the 'functional ventilation of remainders'. It's the existence of the social itself as 'remainder' which makes of the social machine 'refuse processing', a more subtle form of death; indeed the scene of a 'piling up and exorbitant processing of death'.

> In this event, we are even deeper in the social, even deeper in pure excrement, in the fantastic congestion of dead labour, of dead and institution-alized relations within terrorist bureaucracies, of dead languages and grammars. Then of course it can no longer be said that the social is dying, since it is already the accumulation of death. In effect we are in a civilisation of the supersocial, and simultaneously in a civilisation of non-degradable, indestructible residue, piling up as the social spreads.[9]

The *third* hypothesis speaks of the end of the 'perspective space of the social'.

> The social has not always been a delusion, as in the first hypothesis, nor remainder, as in the second. But precisely, it has only had an end in view, a meaning as power, as work, as capital, from the perspective space of an ideal convergence, which is also that of production — in short, in the narrow gap of second-order simulacra, and, absorbed into third-order simulacra, it is dying.[10]

This, then, is the hypothesis of the 'precession of simulacra': the 'ventilation of individuals as terminals of information' in the hyperreal space of simulation.

> End of the perspective space of the social. The rational sociality of the contract, dialectical social-ity (that of the State and of civil society, of public and private, of the social and the individual) gives way to the sociality of contact, of the circuit and transistorised network of millions of molecules and particles maintained in a random gravitational field, magnetised by the constant circulation and the thousands of tactical combinations which

electrify them.[11]

Upon the rubble of the classical model of sociology, Baudrillard is a quantum physicist of the processed world of mass communications.

2. The Refusal of the Historical Subject

With an implicit, and radical, political agenda, Baudrillard's political critique is directed not against the already obsolescent perspective space of the social, but in opposition to the trans-istorised world of the Simulacrum. In the old world of the *social*, an emancipatory politics entailed the production of meaning: the control of individual and collective perspectives against a normal-izing society which sought to exclude its oppositions. This was the region of power/sacrifice: the site of a great political conflict where the finalities of sex, truth, labour and history were dangerous to the extent they represented the hitherto suppressed region of use-value, beyond and forever in opposition to a purely sacrificial politics. In the perspectival space of the *historical*, power could be threatened by speech, by the agency of the emancipatory subject who demanded a rightful inclusion in the contractual space of political economy. The politics of rights depended for its very existence on the valorisation of use-value as a privileged, and universally accessible, field of truth, and on the production of the emancipated historical subject as an object of desire.

With Baudrillard, political theory begins with a refusal of the privileged position of the *historical subject*, and with an immediate negation of the question of historical emancipation itself. Baudrillard's is not the *sociological* perspective of disciplinary power in a normalising society (Foucault) nor the *hermeneutical* interpretation of science and technology as "glassy, background ideology" (Habermas). In his theorisation, there is no purely perspectival space of the 'panoptic' (*Oublier Foucault*) nor free zone of 'universal pragmatics'. Baudrillard's political analysis represents a radical departure from both the sociology of know-ledge and theorisations of power/norm because his thought explores the brutal processes of dehistoricisation and desocial-isation which structure the new communicative order of a signifying culture. In the new continent of postmodern culture: the relevant political collectivity is the "mass media as simulacra"; the exchange-principle involves purely abstract and hyper-

symbolic diffusions of information; and what's at stake is the
'maximal production of meaning' and the 'maximal production
of words' for constituted historical subjects who are both condition
and effect of the order of simulacra.

Baudrillard's world is that of the electronic mass media — and
specifically of television. His nomination of television as a
privileged simulacrum is strategic: television has the unreal
existence of an imagic sign-system in which may be read the
inverted and implosive logic of the cultural machine. The
'nebulous hyperreality' of the masses; 'staged communications'
as the modus vivendi of the power system; the 'explosion of
information' and the 'implosion of meaning' as the keynote of
mass communications; a massive circularity of all poles in which
'sender is receiver'; an irreversible medium of communication
without response: such are the *strategic* consequences of *television
as society*. In a brilliant essay, "The Implosion of Meaning in the
Media,"[12] Baudrillard has this to say of the mass media and power.

> Are the mass media on the side of power in the
> manipulation of the masses, or are they on the side
> of the masses in the liquidation of meaning, in the
> violence done to meaning, and in the fascination
> which results? Nagadishu Stammheim: the media
> are made the vehicle of the moral condemnation
> of terrorism and of the exploitation of fear for
> political ends, but, simultaneously, in the most
> total ambiguity, they propagate the brutal fascin-
> ation of the terrorist act. They are themselves
> terrorists, to the extent to which they work through
> fascination . . . The media carry meaning and
> nonsense, they manipulate in every sense simulta-
> neously. The process cannot be controlled, for the
> media convey the simulation internal to the system
> and the simulation destructive of the system
> according to a logic that is absolutely moebian and
> circular — and this is exactly what it is like. There is
> no alternative to it, no logical resolution. Only a
> logical *exacerbation* and a catastrophic resolution.[13]

Baudrillard's refusal of the *reality* of processed history is based on
this hypothesis: the new information of the electronic mass

media is directly destructive of meaning and signification, or neutralizes it.[14] Information, far from producing an 'accelerated circulation' of meaning, a plus-value of meaning homologous to the economic plus-value which results from the accelerated rotation of capital, implies the destruction of *any* coherent meaning-system. Confronted with this situation of the 'double-bind' in which the medium is the real world and the real world has about it all of the irrealism of the information society,[15] Baudrillard hypothesises two political alternatives. *First*, there is "resistance as subject," the response of the autonomous historical subject who assumes the "unilaterally valorised" and "positive" line of resistance of "liberation, emancipation, expression, and constitution . . . (as somehow) valuable and subversive." But Baudrillard is entirely realistic concerning how the 'liberating claims of subjecthood' respond to the imperatives of the inform-ation order of mass media:

> To a system whose argument is oppression and repression, the strategic resistance is the liberating claim of subjecthood. But this reflects the system's previous phase, and even if we are still confronted with it, it is no longer the strategic terrain: the system's current argument is the maximisation of the word and the maximal production of meaning. Thus the strategic refusal is that of a refusal of meaning and a refusal of the word — or of the hyperconformist simulation of the very mecha-nisms of the system, which is a form of refusal and of non-reception.[16]

Against the emancipatory claims of historical subjecthood,[17] Baudrillard proposes the more radical alternative of "resistance-as-object" as the line of political resistance most appropriate to the simulacrum. To a system which represents a great convergence of *power and seduction*, and which is entirely cynical in its devalor-isation of meaning, the relevant and perhaps only political response is that of *ironic detachment*.

> This is the resistance of the masses: it is equivalent to sending back to the system its own logic by doubling it, to reflecting, like a mirror, meaning without absorbing it. This strategy (if one can still

speak of strategy) prevails today because it was
ushered in by that phase of the system.[18]

Baudrillard thus privileges the position of the 'punk generation':
this new generation of rebels which signals its knowledge of its
certain doom by a *hyperconformist simulation* (in fashion, language,
and lifestyle) representing that moment of refraction where the
simulational logic of the system is turned, ironically and neutrally,
back against the system.[19] Baudrillard is a *new wave* political
theorist because he understood that in a system whose imperative
is the "over-production and regeneration of meaning and
speech," [20] all the social movements which "bet on liberation,
emancipation, the resurrection of the subject of history, of the
group, of speech as a raising of consciousness, indeed of a 'seizure
of the unconscious' of the subjects and of the masses" *are acting
fully in accordance with the political logic of the system*.[21]

3. The Eclipse of the Commodity-Form

As the functional and terrorist organisation of the
control of meaning under the sign of the positivity
of value, signification is in some ways akin to the
notion of reification. It is the locus of an elemental
objectification that reverberates through the
amplified system of signs up to the level of the
social and political terrorism of the bracketing of
meaning. All the repressive and reductive strategies
of power systems are already present in the internal
logic of the sign, as well as those of exchange-value
and political economy.
For a Critique of the Political Economy of the Sign

If Baudrillard is radical in his theorisations of the death of the
social, the dilation of the historical subject, and cynical power, it
is because his thought revolves around a fundamental discovery
concerning the strategic relationship between the "structural
law of value" and the "simulacrum" as the dynamic locus of the
logic of postmodernity. Theoretical inquiry sometimes undergoes
fundamental transformations, not only in response to criticisms
within its discursive limits, but also as a reflex of abrupt and
complete shifts in the constitution of the 'object' of theoretical
analysis — the domain of social experience itself. Baudrillard's

theoretical agenda establishes itself at the moment of a great epistemic divide in the deep, structural logic of social action (and consciousness):[22] a rupture of the 'object' of theoretical inquiry in which the reality-principle of the 'referential' order of experience — *production* as the dominant (material) scheme of the industrial order — gives way to *simulation* as the dominant scheme of an order regulated by the 'code' (and thus by the logic of signification). Where, in fact, the *"loi marchande de la valeur"* is replaced by the *structural law of value*. Expressed in its social formulation, Baudrillard challenges the realism of the concept of the social because he wishes to counterpose: 1) a communicational scheme of "radical semiurgy" to the theory of normalisation, 2) the "logic of signification" to the inscription of the normative as the (reductive) strategy of meaning for the cultural apparatus; and, 3) the sign to the norm. Formulated with reference to the scheme of production, Baudrillard theorises the logic of the sign as the emblematic expression in consumer culture of the commodity-form. It's Baudrillard's thesis that we must look to the great contestation in the order of signs, the abstract, semiurgical, fungible, and reductive 'logic of signification', if we are to develop a *realistic* account of the intracation of political economy and society.[23]

The emergence of the sign as the locus of the real indicates decisively that the poststructuralist preoccupation with the *semiurgical* operations of consumer culture, with the *cultural semiotics* of the exchange-system in political economy, and with the *self-referential* language of signifier/signified as the "mirror of production," form a strictly critical response to the sudden dilation of the productivist scheme of the industrial order into its opposite. Baudrillard's description of the sign as the dynamic (and disappearing) centre of postmodern culture is free-floating, randomised, tautological, and homologous. The discourse of the sign begins at that point where the expansive and representational world of the commodity-form suddenly dilates into the implosive and purely figurative scheme of the sign-form. Baudrillard's specific contribution to poststructuralist discourse (and an important advance beyond the structural linguistics of Saussure and the critical sociology of Claude Lefort) is his radical diagnosis of the *sign* as the purest, most intensive expression possible of the heteronomy of the purely abstract quality of the commodity-form prophesied by Marx's *Capital*. Rather than situate the sign-form in opposition to the commodity-form (which would only entail privileging cultural discourse over political economy), Baudrillard accomplishes a much more spectacular, and dangerous, theorisation. His challenge to the now obsolete representational order of the commodity-form is that, in the *productivist* scheme of accumulation, the theory of commodification sought to preserve the centre of the capitalist exchange-system. In the *simulational* scheme of advanced capitalist society, use-value and exchange-value conflate into mirrored aspects of a single process of abstract, semiological reproduction: the classical poles of signifier and signified dilate into a single structural homology at the nucleus of the logic of the sign. Baudrillard's challenge is then to strip away the subjectivity of use-value (the referential chain of signifieds) from critical cultural analysis, and examine the purely relational and objective scheme of "free floating" and "semiurgical" objects. This, then, is a theory of commodification fully relative to the system of advanced capitalism. In Baudrillard's simulational model, the sign is the hitherto hidden side of the commodity-form: the dark side which can *only* appear when the commodity is in eclipse as a referent of the *real*.

That Baudrillard has developed a "logic of signification" (*The Mirror of Production, Pour une critique de l'économie politique du signe*) relevant to the simulational model at the centre of commodification in advanced capitalist society, means that he has succeeded in revealing the existence of the sign as *the basic structural logic of the commodity-form* and, what is more, in deciphering the sign as dead power. Consequently, what makes Baudrillard genuinely original in his theorisation is that the sign — complete with its structural law of value, and its 'simulated models' — does not stand in fateful opposition to Marx's *Capital*, but rather represents its perfect completion. Baudrillard is the last and best of all the Marxists because he has broken the code of the commodity-form in postmodern culture. And he has accomplished this task, not by recuperating the referential signifiers of the commodity-form (there is *no* privileging of needs or labour here) but by undertaking a radically deconstructive strategy of thought. Anti-romantic and anti-subjectivist, Baudrillard brings out the "referential illusion" at the heart of the purely *structuralist* logic of the system of advanced capitalism. In his estimation, modern culture has this *implosive* characteristic: use-value and exchange-value are stripped of their antinomic (and thus autonomous) status, and are transformed into endlessly refracted (and random) points in an aimless cycle of exchange which, being semiurgical and mirror-like, traces the path of disintegration and regression in contemporary experience.

The theoretical implication is clear. After Baudrillard, *Capital* can only be read as a brilliant exploration of Nietzschean nihilistic culture. Baudrillard remembers Marx by resituating *Capital* as an historically specific study of the postmodern (capitalist) phase of the genealogy of Western nihilism.

Marx/Nietzsche

> Le tourniquet de la représentation y devient fou, mais d'une folie implosive, qui, loin d'être excentrique, louche vers le centre, vers sa propre répétition en abyme.
>
> *L'Échange symbolique et la mort*

> A born leveller, and a cynic . . .
>
> *Capital*

Thus just when we thought that the 'object' of *Capital* was about to disappear through the vanishing-point of the now obsolescent mercantilist law of value, Baudrillard has done the impossible. In a lightning reversal of effects, he has managed to radicalise *Capital* and make Marx dangerous once more. And he has done this by the simple strategy of finding Nietzsche in Marx's "circuit of capital," by bringing together Marx's famous "fetishism of the commodity-form" with Nietzsche's "will to power." After Baudrillard, it is impossible not to confront the political and theoretical conclusion that *Capital* is the reverse, but parallel, image of *The Will to Power*. This is not the will to power on its *historical* side (the psychology of sacrifice). The old and boring nihilism of Christian expression with its 'sickliness' (Nietzsche) sublimated in favour of the theological norms of 'virtue, goodliness, and beauty' is finally finished. No one cares anymore either about sanctity, and for the same reason, accumulation. On the downside of the will to power, the side of a cynical, infinite regress into disaccumulation, disintegration, and darkness, *Capital* can make its reappearance as the master text of the will to power on the side of power/seduction without limit. *Capital* is an exploration in depth of the purely *structuralist* phase of the will to power, in which a general psychology of seduction combines with this new "emotional combinatorial" — *conscience-liquidation and the narcissistic ego.*

Baudrillard's hard lesson is to read *Capital* as a brilliant recitative of the perfect nihilism at work in *The Will to Power*. Now this is a type of nihilism which functions under the language of the 'sign', which works to transform all of the 'big numbers of the real' (Baudrillard) — capital, labour, utility, use-value — into 'perspectival appearances' (Nietzsche) which, even at the moment of their inception, are already on a downward, implosive spiral. *Capital* is thus a tragic reflection on the nihilism in the Western mind, because the 'commodity-form' with its "double metamorphosis into signs," with its "howling circuit of capital," with its constant "pumping out" of the sphere of living, concrete labour into *abstract labour*, (with Marx's theorisation of dead money, dead labour, dead society) become images which race past one another and then explode like reality-flashes on their way to a final, convulsive moment of exhaustion): the detritus of the postmodern age.

The nihilism in Western culture which reached its (saintly) apex in the sickly psychology of sacrifice in Christian metaphysics, with its fetishism of conscience-recuperation and self-crucifixion, and then (supposedly) vanished as the psychological locus of the modern mind, did not, in fact, go away. Marx's *Capital* has an almost geographical importance in tracing the genealogy of nihilism in the postmodern project: an infinitesimal, dark spot on the furthest horizon of the Western mind, a distant nova which, in a sudden fantastic explosion of energy, expanded as the exchange-principle spread out. *Capital* becomes *the* text of the postmodern century when the imperfect nihilism of the psychology of sacrifice passes over into the perfect (cynical) nihilism of the psychology of seduction. What makes *Capital* such a compelling account of the 'value-form' of postmodern nihilism is that Marx stumbled upon the basic formula (in structural and not historical terms) for the functioning of nihilism in postmodern experience. When Marx, in his classic essay, "The Fetishism of Commodities and the Secret Thereof," [24] said that the commodity abounds in "metaphysical subtleties and theological niceties," that it is "magical" and "alchemical," and that "to find an analogy, we must have recourse to the mist-enveloped regions of the religious world," we should take him seriously. For the commodity-form is, in fact, only a modern (material) formulation of a more ancient (metaphysical) principle. The commodity-form, this nucleus of the capitalist cycle of exchange,[25] is *morphologically identical* (though driven on by the charisma of a different reality-effect: accumulation, not grace) to the old Christian doctrine of the trinity. Not the doctrine of the trinity as an expression of theology, for the trinity is no more the "reflex" of God than the "circuit of capital" is the reflex of economy, but, instead, the trinity as the *fundamental metaphysical code* for the operation of the "will to will" as the nucleus of Western (and now postmodern) experience. Long before the commodity disappeared into the void of its own simulacra, the doctrine of the trinity expressed perfectly the 'structural law of value' at the centre of power and truth. The precursor of the sign, the trinitarian formulation, with its "semantic cancellation" to a language of no nation, with its presentation of its antinomic terms (father and son) as contingent effects, and its reduction of living, embodied experience to an empty cycle of exchange, is the *degree-zero* in Western consciousness. To the same extent that the Christian expression of the will to power deployed 'God' as a reality-effect, disguising the inner, surrealistic slide in the circuit of grace, the "circuit of capital" with its commodity-form undergoing an endless "double metamorphosis" also deploys *accumulation* (consumption/production) as our incarceration in the discourse of a fully abstract (disembodied) power.

Nietzsche knew that nihilism would be forced to operate in the language of value: indeed, 'value-form' was his expression for the purely fictitious, cynical power at the centre of Western experience. This was why Nietzsche[26] always insisted that nihilism is about the "projection of the conditions of (our) preservation into predicates of existence." And Marx too recognized that the commodity-form (expressed in the purely antinomic terms of use-value/exchange value; labour for consumption/labour for production) produced a fully *abstract and random power*. In "Machinery and Modern Industry," Marx was, in fact, a precursor of McLuhan's (*The Medium is the Massage*) description of the processing of workers in the industrial simulacrum. McLuhan noted that (our) relation to the technostructure was that of the "sex organs of the machine world," [27] but Marx preceded him in speaking of the *dead power* at work in the factory system of production:

> Every kind of capitalist production, in so far as it is
> not only a labour process, but also a process of

> creating surplus-value, has this in common, that it
> is not the workman that employs the instruments
> of labour, but the instruments of labour that
> employ the workman. But it is only in the factory
> system that this inversion acquires technical and
> palpable reality. By means of its conversion into an
> automaton, the instrument labour confronts the
> labourer, during the labour-process, in the shape
> of capital, of dead labour, that dominates, and
> pumps dry living, labour-power.[28]

But what Marx missed in his demonic portrayal of 'dead labour'
— and what Nietzsche and today Baudrillard discovered — is that
the commodity-form is not antinomic but trinitarian. The silent *third-term*
in the production of dead labour, dead capital, and cynical power,
is that the presence of the 'will to will' as the *abstract unity* which
coordinates the antinomies of *living* labour does not exist outside
of exchange, and the dynamic principle of the capitalist exchange-
process is that it traces and retraces the same cycle of accumulation
and disintegration which Nietzsche described as the "eternal
recurrence."

> Value therefore now becomes value in process,
> money in process, and, as such, capital. It comes
> out of circulation, enters into it again, preserves
> and multiplies itself within its circuit, comes back
> out of it with expanded bulk, and begins the same
> round ever afresh.[29]

This fantastic "inversion" of the order of experience; this
"satellisation of the real"; the "semantic reduction" of living
labour-power through a "semiological cancellation" to the general
universal equivalent of dead money; this fetishism of the sign is
what drives *Capital* and makes of it a bitter description of the
contemporary, 'fictitious' form of the will to power.

Marx was a romantic in the tragic tradition. Against the
demonic thrust of *Capital*, against our obliteration in the abstract
medium of the 'instruments of production', he wished to preserve
a privileged space of freedom in concrete, living labour, in use-
value with a vertical axis, in something *real*. But Nietzsche[30] was
more grimly realistic. He said of the "slandered instincts" that
they could not be preserved in our plunge downwards into the

simulation of the social. Marx's 'living labour' is the economic analogue of Nietzsche's 'slandered instincts'. But against Nietzsche's conclusions concerning the cancellation of the *real* at work in the cycle of an *abstract power* that was always only a perspectival simulation, Marx wished to preserve the ontological autonomy of labour. Everything in *Capital* is perfectly down-beat on the abstract disembodiment of labour: its exhaustion in its present 'pumped out' form; its decadence as only another instance of a 'condition of survival projected into a predicate of being'; its location as the (utopian) criticism which volatilises the scheme of production. But Marx fatefully compromised: against the theoretical momentum of *Capital* as a brilliant vivisection of nihilism (now operating in the perfectly *relational* language of seduction), Marx turned, instead, to a *naturalistic* interpretation of labour. Marx's 'compromise', his blindness to the existence of the commodity-form only as an "*abstract unity*" giving a certain coherence to experience, makes of him, like Kant, a 'great delayer'. At the very last moment, *Capital* transforms itself into its opposite: a dogmatic, because antinomic, defence of the deep categories of the capitalist *episteme* which, in any event, can only save itself from (our) knowledge of the darkness within by legitimating representational logic, and the 'referential illusion'. In making of labour a referential finality, Marx was the brilliant perpetrator, and then victim, of a sign-crime.

We are deep into Nietzsche's cycle of the 'in vain', the downside of the cycle of cynical power, a time of the most intense disenchantment with the psychology of sacrifice, that, in medieval times, went under the sign of *acedia*. *Acedia* meant a sudden loss of the will to go on, a mutiny of the living body against a cynical power. Baudrillard tells us we're deep in the cycle of *acedia* again and the certain sign of its presence is what Barthes described in *The Empire of Signs* as the contagion of "panic boredom" which spreads out everywhere. It's panic boredom, not fear, which is after all the psychological fuel for the 'howling spirit of revenge' that operates as the emotional combinatorial of the postmodern system. Consequently, while Marx may have analysed capitalism in its bullish phase, Baudrillard's thought begins with the instant inversion of the 'circuit of capital' into the cycle of disintegration, exhaustion, decadence, and 'viciousness for fun'. Now there is a desperate search for a revival of the real (*real people, real values, real sex*). But as Baudrillard tells us, if there is today such desperate fascination with the *real*, it is because we live with the terrible knowledge that the real does not exist anymore, or, more precisely, that the *real* appears to us only as a vast and seductive simulation.

Indeed, between Marx and Baudrillard, there are two types of nihilism. Marx's circuit of capital produced as its psychological fall-out Nietzsche's last men. In *Time as History*, the Canadian philosopher George Grant observed that, everywhere today in Europe and North America, 'last men' have become the inhabitants (Baudrillard's 'silent majorities') of the postmodern order who "want their comforts in pleasure and entertainment" but who can never intensely experience the agony of Nietzsche's abyss, because "they have never learned to despise themselves." [31] The psychology of the 'last men' alternates between the poles of a 'howling spirit of revenge' and the happy consciousness of consumer culture: they have learned to love deeply, and so need deeply, as their very principle of programmation, the seductive strategies of consumer culture. However, beyond the 'silent majorities' of last men, Baudrillard points to the existence of the other, more advanced, version of modern nihilism: the 'perfect nihilist'. From the command posts of advanced capitalist society, perfect nihilists ride, as their principle of being, the hurricane of the downward spiral of the 'circuit of capital'. They are the bionic beings (part sign/part body) who act — and perhaps only can act — in the full knowledge of cynical power and cynical history. Indeed, the political method of the 'perfect nihilists' is to embrace cynicism itself as a strategy of command. More aware than the 'last men' of consumer culture of Nietzsche's legacy to us of "freedom in a universe indifferent to our purposes," the perfect nihilists would always prefer to will cynically than not to will at all.[30] Baudrillard's world of the *simulacrum* is the perfect freedom of remaking the world in a universe which provides no purpose to our willing.

Which is just to say that Baudrillard has succeeded, where many others have failed, in deciphering the 'social hieroglyphics' of the commodity-form. He has done so in two ways. First, he has discovered the 'pure sign' to be the essence and secret destiny of the commodity-form. Second, he has disclosed that if the 'fetishism of the sign' indicates the spreading out of the exchange-process in Western experience (one that is semiurgical, random, abstract, and tautological), this is because at the (analogical) centre of the sign is the 'structural law of value', and at the nucleus of the structural formulation of value-exchange (hidden under the refuse of price, abstract labour, and surplus-value) is Nietzsche's 'will to will'. What else could Baudrillard have meant in *The Mirror of Production* by the co-referentiality of signifier/signified but that the very centre of the cycle of capital accumulation was a fantastic, surrealistic reversal? Baudrillard has revealed the existence of the 'will to will' as the third term, the abstract unity, which makes the mirror of production a totality, and lends to the fiction of *Capital*, the 'double-metamorphosis' of the commodity-form, a certain abstract coherency.

Marx and Nietzsche shared a deep and common affinity in meditating upon historical (Christian) and materialistic (capitalist) expressions of the will to power. Both Nietzsche and Marx always focussed on the main event: the unreal inversion of modern experience into an abstract postmodern unity, a unity which depended for its very (non)existence on the preservation of the 'referential illusion' at the heart of Western experience. What is still puzzling, though, is why the exponents of Western Marxism and critical sociology in particular, are so repulsed by Nietzsche's pessimism? Surely it cannot be a problem of political practice: even Sartre said that political practice in the postmodern century must begin, and perhaps can *only* begin, with unrelieved pessimism; to think without illusions and develop a realism of concepts on the basis of understanding cynical power. If Baudrillard's deconstructive image of the simulacrum, and his great refusals of the referential categories of history, society, and normalising power, accurately indicate a fundamental rupture in the objective constitution of advanced capitalism, then Nietzsche's 'pessimism' (which is really the method of 'perspectival' understanding) becomes an entirely *realistic* strategy for exploring postmodern experience. And this event, the interpretation of advanced capitalist society under the sign of nihilism is the basic condition for human emancipation as well as for the recovery of the tragic sense of critical theory.

But if it is not a question of the realism of political practice, then might it not be that the hostility of Marxist sociology for Nietzsche has its origins in Nietzsche's position as the stalking-horse of Marx's great compromise? Marx insisted that concrete labour, the historical side of use-value and an emancipatory production, be taken out of play, and preserved as a privileged ontology against the ablation of Capital. But Nietzsche's 'accusation' and his intimation of 'doom' for Marxist sociology was that in the postmodern (and so post-Marxist) century, there are no longer *any* privileged finalities. The "horizon has been wiped clean," not just of the finality of god (the *metaphysical* side of the will to power), but also of capital, labour, democracy, and utility, all the 'referents' of the real (the *productivist* side of the will to power).

Nietzsche's accusation of a cynical history and his poetic of an embodied power are the fateful forms of critique of the 'referential illusion'. In the postmodern century, the spectre/sign of Nietzsche haunts *Capital* now, and promises to return us, beyond Marx and Nietzsche, to the question of myth and enlightenment.

A.K.

9

THE FLIGHT OF HERMES

It is pleasant following the path of Michel Serres' *Hermes*. [1] The journey is to deliver a message surely enough, although the destination and the message seem a touch random. Yet the countryside appears to be well-known in that there are frequent stops to guide travellers, and to straighten up the boundaries along the way. Perhaps this is an old sense of justice. Commerce is transacted as well along the way, or at least the weights and measures are with us, and Hermes, from time to time, adds to his collection by what can only be called theft. Certainly we are paid by his string of stories, often called myths, and there is a musical accompaniment which he claims to have invented, and the occasional strange alchemy that transforms things. He seems warm to orators, and is very zealous in the protection of heroes — especially if they are French. And to top it all off, there is a promised trip to the underworld for those who are 'dead souls'. Hermes guides us there, although he seems a little hard on the others like Zeus, Mars, Sisyphus, Prometheus, but with a soft word for Pan, Orpheus and, of course, Penelope. He is especially cool to Ulysses and Socrates. Mind you, as I said at the beginning, it is a pleasant journey, one might even say seductive.

Serres' return to the mythological is to effect reversals of the understandings that we hold of the major elements of post-modern thought. In turn, Serres rewrites and rethinks our understanding of philosophy and the social. His work touches on a wide panoply of subjects from literature and the arts to the scientific disciplines of parasitology, information theory, mathematical

Gustave Doré, *The Wolf and the Lamb,*
based on the LaFontaine fable

topology, quantum physics, microbiology and thermodynamics.
But all are under the mythological structure of the Hermes myth;
a myth that understands the postmodern condition in terms of a
parasitical sense that defines the culture as entropic, wasteful and
excremental. Entering the sensorium of the postmodern world,
Serres' voyage is a seduction that casually rips open postmodernity, exposing the field of modern power and wastage.

The assault on the senses in postmodernism goes beyond that
of the excesses of the society of the spectacular. The spectacular
society moves from destruction to seduction of vision, hearing,
smell, touch and taste. The seductive as aesthetic and as anaes-
thetic underlies the dominant forms of late capitalism. This
society also pursues its seductiveness in the philosophy, language
and science that contribute to the culture. While Serres' attack on
late capitalism is a frontal one for having chosen false gods, and
for having murdered the messenger who brought them the news
of an imminent and continuing defeat, his thought signals the last
post of the postmodern journey.

Serres writes within the system that has given rise to the
postmodern world, and shares with this world its successive
nihilistic tendencies. Nevertheless, Serres wishes to present the
reversal of this world in a new understanding of the "senses". At
once in the middle of the postmodern condition, Serres, like

Hermes, attempts to give direction (sens) to where we might find our senses (sens). The senses will become something quite different following Serres' *Les cinq sens*.[2] The senses become "veils, boxes, tables, visits, and joy". Serres calls this a "resurrection" or a "renaissance", and, of course, it is to that extent a mythological return of Hermes.

But in another way, the return signals the end-point of post-modernity. Serres' world slips away. It merely slips away for those who have reached the end of the postmodern experience in the same way in which the traveller merely moves on. It is simply, for Serres, forgotten. To use Serres' analogy, this is a philosophy, which, is no, longer central to the exercise of power and is in fact the very product of the waste and entropic system which generates "turbulence and eddies" under which Serres takes comfort. What Serres' writings constitute is the highest form of post-modernity: cultured, intelligent, seductive, refined, civilized, successful, cutting, soothing, alogical, logical, nonsensible, sensible; to use Serres' style of writing. It is, as they say, a very pleasant journey.

Black Boxes: Thermodynamics and Parasitology

For Serres, the Hermes myth unlocks the key to Western mythology marking the "progress" in society towards the post-modern world. Hermes always "passes before", in Serres' vocabulary. He is the angel that passes like the wind, to continue the theological reference. Hermes is the laic spirit that has gone before in the topography of our social and political lives. Like the Borges' myth of the cartographer, Hermes has covered every nodal point in the field of experience only to disappear again when seen by us. Hermes sets out the structural nature of the mapping that overlies all possible experiences upon which the good work of postmodernity has erected its culture. This culture, for Serres, is always mythology, but the mythology is what we know as science. Thus, the text of postmodernity can only be read as that of science and technology, but it is a text that is constantly preceded by its mythological antecedents.

As Serres demonstrates in the early series of works under the Hermes' title, the field is contested between Mars and Venus. Mars is the victor of classical science, and of the topology of power and force that underlies the development of capitalism. But within this dominance appears, under late capitalism, the science of Venus which is sketched for us with Serres playing the role of Maxwell's demon. The demon transforms the landscape of Mars towards that of the sea of Venus. It is this transformation which underlies Serres' concern, in particular, for the science that moves from the mechanical towards the thermodynamic, and finally to the paramouncy of the "parasite" as the operator of the postmodern world. The 'field' of this engagement of the two sciences is sketched below in the analogy of the black boxes.

In the beginning, for Serres, there are black boxes. It is these black boxes that reveal the structure of scientific mythology. They tell us of the world we inhabit, or what Serres calls later our cosmology and our cosmetics. The world in the first instance is a black box which 'contains' our senses. The 'escape' from the box of these senses describes the passage from life to death. Inside the big box are boxes that come in many sizes, but each contains energy locked in a formless, dark, randomized space. This is the Eden myth, for Serres, not one of paradise, but rather one of pure potentiality. Each of us is a box charged with potential energy of the natural world. The primal black box is a reservoir, an encyclopedia, a library, a book or, in the vocabulary of the modern world, its Bataille's solar anus. In the end, there are also black boxes: that of the coffins, bones, skeletons and ruins of the civilizations that are sedimented in the archeological structure of the topological field. The return to mythology signals also that the final black boxes may, themselves, be the return to the natural world of the original darkness. This world is all powerful, but it is a world in which there is nothing there.

Serres' subject-matter, then, is the flow between black boxes. This flow he characterizes as the basis of human civilization. The science of this flow he identifies with thermodynamics. The operator which starts the flow is that of the parasite. The unlocking of energy by the operator creates civilization and its discontents.

In the classical age, the model of science was predicated on a direct laminar flow between the black boxes. This describes the "ideal" model of all knowledge and science in a system that predicts a perfectly equilibrated state. This is Mars. One enters a world where the concept and the object are identical, where all communications are perfect, where theory and practice meet: it is a world governed by the law of homeostasis. Or to express this according to the first law of thermodynamics, we enter a world of the conservation of all energies signified by the absence of turbulence, the absence of noise, the absence of rectifiers, the absence of social discontent and the absence of disease. The perfectly equilibrated state does nothing, says nothing, is perfectly predictable, perfectly reproducible, perfectly, in Serres' vocabulary, scientific, powerful and mastering. This is as true, in his world, for politics as it is for economics, and as it is for physics, medicine or philosophy. It is the world of the ontologically perfect, or the Hegelian end of history.

This perfect end to all things, to echo Immanual Kant, is also a world that, for Serres, speaks of the absence of life. It is the world of exploitation and servitude that is behind the ordering of capitalist systems as much as behind the ordering of the perfect reproducible age of reason. It is also a world that does not work. It is rejected by Serres for a world that bleeds: a world that is homeorretic and cannot maintain a homeostasis. This is Venus. This is a world that we also live in. Life begins with the cuts, the disturbances, the static, the noise representing the loss of perfect transmission of the energy flow between the black boxes. This is the world of the second law of thermodynamics, the world of entropy, the world of parasitical systems.

The movement towards postmodernity from modernity is the move towards this world of the second law of thermodynamics. This is the Hermes' myth reappearing again in a topology that maps the networks of channels and nodes used for the transformation of power into productivity, information and the discourse of language which dominates the ideology of late capitalism. But it is a world that is constantly losing its sense of completeness for it depends on the activities of the operator which stands against its very desire for a closed system. At the centre of this world is the parasite standing as the operator. Serres makes great use of the ambiguity of the word *parasite* in French which extends out into a number of meanings. From biology, he takes the notion of the parasite as both a harmful and destructive operator when, in its appearance as a destructive agent in the immune system, we are brought to disease and death, and yet on the other side, all health depends upon the activities of other parasitical bodies which bring back to balance the flow of power in the biological system. In the world of information theory, the parasite, again, is responsible for the transmission of messages between points, and yet it is, itself, the static in the line which impedes the communication. In the social realm, as we shall see, the parasite in late modernity in its guise of the aesthetic operator equilibrates late capitalism by its very critique which feeds upon the waste products of the system. Indeed, in each of the redefined five senses captured in the commentary and artwork below, we find the existence of the parasite as the exchanger which turns travel into tourist visits, tables into meals, boxes into nightclubs, veils into cosmetics, and *jouissance* into joy, and Hermes into a fashion label. This is a map of the ruined landscape of the postmodernist world, but from whose ruins Serres sees not the Hegelian owl of Minerva, but rather the flight, once again, of Hermes.

Power Dynamics

For Serres, power may be mapped on the axis described by the laminar flow of complete power captured in the claims to classical knowledge and science on the one hand, and on the other hand by the flow to the point of no power, or the depowered site, occupied periodically by the victim, citizen or, in the saturnalia of revolutionary thought, the site of the universal class. The claims of this system are as invariant from the beginning of time to the end. It also makes little difference as to whether the site of power is found in a conception of an absolute or powerful being, whether that be a god or a king or queen, or whether, following the model of decentralized power of Michel Foucault, power is found at the sites of the institutional interstices of society. For within the dominant mode of Foucault's power structure, one still finds the laminar flow exercised under the guise of a relationship of disciplining and punishing.

The reversal that Serres makes of this model is not one of turning it upside down, but rather to look towards the shifts in the historical understanding of power effected by the existence of the parasite. These shifts in the viewing of power are always presaged by their being recounted in the mythological or literary works immediately preceding the incorporation into the prevailing paradigm of a new science. To illustrate this, we return to Serres' comments on the paintings of William Turner, and his retelling of a La Fontaine fable.

Serres depicts Turner as the first genius of thermodynamics ahead of the articulation of the theory of thermodynamics by Lazare Carnot. His analysis turns on the interpretation of the painting, *The Fighting Temeraire*, as showing the shift from the mechanical age, represented in the painting by the wooden vessel, a ship of the wind and sail vintage, and by a barge representing the

J.M. William Turner, *The Eruption of Vesuvius,*
Yale Center for British Art,
Paul Mellon Collection

new world of post-mechanical power. The barge tows the wooden
ship presaging the passage into the new world of Turner's "fire,
wind and speed". Again, a similar but more direct translation of
the laws of thermodynamics is captured in the painting of the
erupting Vesuvius. As Serres points out, Turner is not a pre-
impressionist so much as a realist of the senses. Vesuvius is a heat
engine built upon the reservoir of molten lava at the earth's core
which results in the spewing of the lava in the fireworks giving the
painting its spectacular quality. We assume, then, after the lava
has been spewed out that it makes its way in a circular flow back to
the original reservoir to be reheated, leading again to a series of
further eruptions. This is also an example of the second law of
thermodynamics in that the inefficiency, or the entropy, of the
exploding mountain creates an energy field which is dissipated
throughout the social landscape.

There are a number of conclusions that can be drawn from
this. The first is clearly that the path of science has been to
harness the thermodynamic power so that the transfer of energy
from one state to the other is as efficient as possible in creating
the work-labour relationship. This is a similar principle to the
harnessing of rivers, or to the heat exchangers that have invaded
everyday life in our refrigerators, air conditioners or furnaces.
We can see the overall reversibility of this mode of power is quite
different from that of mechanical process with an on-and-off

capability. The laminar power of thermodynamics is unidirectional, although circular.

The Turner painting may also stand as a postmodernist work
to the extent that it depicts the social diffusion of power in late
capitalism under the sign of the spectacular. Here power is
mapped over the field in a wasteful and an entropic manner, but,
nevertheless, with the spectacular effects of the society of
images. A similar form of carnival-like paintings can be found in
the works of Joseph Wright in his series of the eruption of Vesuvius
which preceded Turner's, or in the series of fireworks displays.
Wright, like Turner, can balance these pictures with depicitons
of scientific experiments. In Wright's case, this is captured most
vividly in the picture *Experiment on a Bird in the Air Pump*. Both
painters draw the path from the mechanical age to the new age of
thermodynamics which, for Serres, underlies a new understanding of power.

The dynamics of power relations are also mapped in the fables
of La Fontaine, which Serres uses as the basis of his conception of
political power. In particular, Serres analyzes the fable concerning the wolf and the lamb. Picture, if you will, a wolf upstream
from a lamb. The wolf accuses the lamb of spoiling the water. The
lamb offers a number of defenses, such as that it is downstream
from the wolf and, therefore, could not spoil the water, to which
the wolf responds that it must have been one of the lamb's siblings,
to which the lamb counters that it has no siblings, to which the
wolf proceeds to accuse the lamb's parents, to which the lamb
indicates its parents are dead, and so it goes until the wolf tiring of
the argument eats the lamb up ("sans procès"). In Serres sense,
the wolf is in the position of classical power as the majorant
against the lamb, or minorant. The lamb is given the role of the
powerless. The analogy can easily be drawn between a king and a
political system, and that of a citizen. The dynamics between the
wolf and the lamb always indicate that laminar power is severed
from knowledge. The lamb is right in each of the assertions
against the wolf, but it is to no avail. Power develops its algorithm
in a closed system of thought for which, by definition, there is no
majorant definition above it. The wolf has an answer to everything, precisely because the system, to function as a system,
always answers with a view to re-establishing hemeostasis or
equilibrium. To continue the classical version of the myth, the
lamb ends up in the position of the powerless who is to be
sacrificed to the system of the power structure. Serres draws a

number of conclusions from this.

The futile attempts of the lamb to avoid the slaughter signifies the identification of power and violence that is rooted in all communities. That is, the wolf and the lamb are part of a community, but, in this case, the community is that of a classical system of knowledge. In this Serres has added very little to the debate on the nature of power since Hobbes. Serres also draws the conclusion that the lamb's disturbance of the flow of power and politics is precisely where one may find knowledge and productivity. The entry of the lamb into the stream is the disturbance that yields the dynamic of conversation, or the dialectic which exposes both the wolf and the lamb. The intervention of the lamb allows one to read the knowledge at the base of a system whose information content is that wolves eat lambs. If there is no disturbance or turbulence in the laminar flow, there is no knowledge of the true relationship of the laminar field. Again in the postmodern context, this drives Serres' thought towards looking to the turbulence in the system as the source of knowledge set against the modern trend to information theory which sustains the classical notion of power. Once the model is made more complex by placing other lambs and wolves along the river's edge, there is the possibility that the turbulence of one lamb may not necessarily lead to the extinction of all lambs, and that the system may, indeed, function on the basis of periodic lambs to the slaughter, but not of all lambs to the slaughter.

What the story of the wolf and the lamb demonstrates is that the understanding of politics that stems from the social contract theory must undertake a reversal to enter into the postmodernist discourse. The paradigm of the wolf-lamb model is the Hobbesian model of Leviathan and the individual which structures the authoritarian claims of the social contract of liberalism. The common energy of this system is represented by the Leviathan and, in particular, in the Hobbesian world, by the fear that has accompanied the exercise of power on a masterservant or king-citizen basis. The laminar flow of the "unknown", or to express it in terms of the fable, the lack of the majorant above the wolf to channel the power away from violence, always creates fear. Thus the classical authoritarian Hobbesian model generates, from its conception of power, the politics of fear.

Politics as Paranoia

This dynamic leads Serres to retranslate Rousseau's social contract from the unity of all wills to a contract of all against one. Serres defends what has often been seen as Rousseau's personal paranoia as a true capturing of the actual social order. In *Rousseau: Judge of Jean-Jacques*, Rousseau captures radically, for Serres, the nature of the political order. This work, for Serres, displaces *The Social Contract* as Rousseau's contribution to political thought. Rousseau is correct precisely in fearing that he will be the lamb to be gobbled up by the wolf. The Hobbesian war of all against all will, in fact, turn out to be the war against each one separately. It is precisely this logic which underlines Jean Baudrillard's sense in which the nuclear age, with its threat of the extermination of all, has no longer any political force against the fear one has as an individual facing the terrorist threat to airline travel. The nuclear threat is relevant only to the classical age of power whereas the terrorist threat, following Umberto Eco's *Travels in Hyperreality*, [3] is a logical extension of late capitalism's ability to structure the cultural order on the basis of turbulence and the wastage of a limited number of lives.

Serres' reversal of the understanding of the traditional social contract cascades down throughout the theory to change other fundamental principles of liberalism as it enters the postmodern age. For example, the description at the beginning of the second part of Rousseau's *The Discourse on the Origins of Inequality*, that property was established when an individual first enclosed a piece of ground, is retranslated by Serres into the discourse of the entropic or waste system. Property is founded precisely when the first excrement appeared on the land, thereby driving off all other individuals, and establishing the claim to property. Power systems, then, are redefined by their abusive nature, in the first instance, as opposed to the traditional liberal theory of the precedence of use. Again, following the sense of Serres' redefinition of classical power, this abusiveness will appear in the waste products of the exercise of power. The proximity in French between *propre* and *propriété* leads Serres to identify the two as the network of modern capitalist society, which establishes its boundaries or laws on the basis of waste. We will meet this dynamic again when we sit down to table with Serres.

The reversal of the property relationship from one of use to abuse follows the direction of Georges Bataille's critique of political economy. Use values in his reformulation of a "general economy" must be based upon excess. Following Baudrillard's *The Mirror of Production*, [4] Serres accepts the fact that the product-producer relationship must in the postmodern world give way to the excessive abuses of the consumer. But Serres' reversal of this system is found in the movement to the parasite that encourages circulation. It is the "clinaman" in the form of the universal exchangeability of money that is critical. And it is precisely the fact that money contributes nothing to the productive process other than its value as an operator to change the state which focuses Serres' attention. In the postmodern context, money is part of the sign system which captures the advertising promotional aspects of late capitalism. In this culture, one is beyond both the producer and the consumer who remained entrapped in the classical notion of power that is driven by its own wastage.

The Founding of Rome

The classical law of power that underlies the capitalist model and, in particular, the liberal-authoritarian elements, whether they come from Rousseau or Hobbes, is set in the identification of power and violence that is the founding act of all communities. This is signified both in the La Fontaine fable of the failure of the lamb against the wolf, but also in the general model of liberal society captured in Bentham's panopticon. Foucault has also captured this dynamic in his various studies of the nexus of surveillance and punishment as the basic structure of power relations in capitalism. But as we have seen earlier, this model, for Serres, proves inadequate as a description of the origins and the contemporary aspects of late capitalist society. The eye must give away to the ear, or, as Serres often expresses it, Hermes will kill the panopticon.

The attack on the surveillance punishment model of power by Serres extends back, on the one hand, to the founding acts of western culture in the establishment of Rome, and forward to his understanding of the rebirth of power as a tattooing or mapping on the landscape or the body. We turn, first, to the anthropology.

Serres' work has been influenced strongly by the writings of Réné Girard, and, in particular, the thesis held by Girard in *Violence and the Sacred*. [5] Girard traces the history of western society from what he sees as the necessary victimization of one member of the social community in order to channel the violence implicit in the aboriginal disorder of nature. The violence is channelled onto one individual rather than onto the collective as a way of preserving a community. In essence, this is a primal form of Rousseau's paranoia that the world is all against one. In early societies, this violence was enacted in the rituals of sacrifice with the victim standing in for the king. Killing the victim rather than the king preserved the integrity of the social order, although allowing for the necessary release of violence or rebellion. This permitted the king not only to preserve his person, but to reinforce the power of his office against direct usurpation. Again, Girard will interpret events such as saturnalia as similar forms of displacement giving rise to symbolic sacrifice as means of preserving the social order.

In the development of liberal society, the rule of law has taken the place of the king. Law becomes the emanation of the king which serves to limit violence by holding the passions and desires in check through displacement onto an outside abstraction, rather than a direct ritual sacrifice. Law, then, serves the role as the necessary outlet for the desires, but in a form that limits the interaction in a community, and thereby removes the threat of civil war. This is a logic that is very close to the Hobbesian Leviathan who was "asked" to restrain all in the politics of fear.

According to Girard, at the base of this dynamic is the fear of the "same" which is manifested in the hostility which twins feel for each other. It is the loss of one's sense of self by being recognized in one's identical twin that leads to the original violence of the founding act of Rome. Fraternal conflict is inevitable wherever there is an ontology of identity, in which case the attempt at differentiation will always lead to violence. Hence the importance of the sacrificial victim which gives a way of eliminating the confusion between self and other through a re-establishment of difference as the basis of a sense of being.

In Serres' work entitled *Rome*,[6] he retraces the fraternal conflict between Romulus and Remus which is captured analogically by the bones found at the base of archeological excavations. Thus the social history of Rome is left in the sediments, carrion, and skeletal remains. The wolf twins stand for the very beginning of Western culture steeped in the violence of the classical model of power, yet whose anatomical remains draw Serres to the reformulation of power. Serres will attempt to capture both the highest point of Rome, the capital dome, and the birds that give the auguries for the Roman political system, and its lowest point captured by the archeology of violence under the founding of the city.

The shift in the understanding of power is, again, exemplified by Serres' interpretation of the Vittore Carpaccio picture of *St. George and the Dragon*.[7] St. George is on his horse engaged in combat with the dragon. They form an arch. Below the arch, we can see the bodies that have been torn apart. The limbs which have been strewn about represent the remains of Adam and Eve. This picture will capture both the biological field and the field of Christian topology. The picture emphasizes the image of the parasitical function as abuse and use which comes to supplant the moral categories of good and evil. This is a reformulation of the equilibrium in society founded on the violence continuously present beneath an ontology of the identity of being.

St. George and the dragon, in the Carpaccio picture, are clearly mutually dependent on each other in a relationship (that we will explore later) which is similar to that of the host and the guest. In this case, rather than in the La Fontaine fable of the wolf and the lamb, the outcome of the contest is not in the destruction of either party, that of St. George and the dragon, but rather in the third party to the relationship captured by the hacked up bodies below the arch formed by the dragon and St. George. The tale of society then becomes, for Serres, not the triumph of the hero over evil, a triumph that at best could only be momentary, but rather the triadic relationship that is present in all theories of equilibrium. On a social stage, this gives rise to the nihilistic violence under the arch of the sacred.

The unity of this picture is not founded on a field of knowledge based on an aesthetic or ethical ideal, but rather through the actions of a parasitical operator which has generated the cultural values that stand steeped in the violence of the social. Just as Orpheus, in passing beyond Cerebus' eye in his travel to the underworld, is finally hacked to bits by those individuals driven to destruction by Orpheus' lyre.

Serres, in reversing the lineaments of power which establishes the violence underneath all founding communities, has recourse again to Hermes and, in particular, to Hermes' theft of Apollo's herd. Again it's not the panopticon here, but the noise of the cows attracting Hermes' attention which is Serres' message. Noise is what Hermes hears from the cavernous black box, undetectable visually, but which penetrates through the boundaries into

Vittore Carpaccio, *St. George and the Dragon*

the social setting, just as it penetrates into the underworld. Similarly, Serres looks to the role of the geese and augury as representing the political art of the Roman empire. For Serres, noise as much as anything else will found the social. Precisely because noise stands against the politics of social science in favour of a politics that is random, topographical, undesired and wasteful. This is a politics which is not one of speech and the sustaining of the writing of difference, but rather the noise of the nonsense or the parasitical operator.

The silence of the hacked-up bodies underneath St. George and the dragon signals the silent third of all social relationships. This is not Sartre's formulation in his *Critique of Dialectical Reason*, [8] of a third whose presence orders the other either by terror or by the oath. Rather the third, in Serres' case, is always the excluded third who may not always be present, but who is always necessary to any relationship. This is a presence that is not unlike that of the randomized squawking of the geese in the capital dome, signalling an opportunity which may appear to transform the actions of individuals in a way in which Italy may yet be freed from the Barbarians.

Nouvelle Cuisine

Social relationships in the postmodern age have come to be epitomized by the dinner party, and if you are on the upper side of the mean income, on what sort of new and exotic delights from former peasants' menu you can serve to your guests under the label of 'nouvelle cuisine'. The dinner table also stands as a primary example, for Serres, of the theory of the excluded third. The dinner table is the inheritor of the Western tradition's concern for logic and speech, and hence sends Serres back to the original founding sense of the Socratic dialogue and, in particular, of the symposium.

This mythology might be characterized in the following fashion. In the beginning, there was a dinner party to which not everybody was invited. Neither, on the other hand, were all the guests who attended invited. Everyone was expected to bring something, which may be called a gift. Although, again, many people had very little to bring other than, as Serres points out in references to fables throughout history, such things as smoke following Molière's "Don Juan", or the more common gift of the twentieth-century intellectual — that of speech. It also appears that from the beginning, the meal had as its purpose in the minds of many of the participants an end-point in sexual relations, although, as we know from the history of meals, very few consummations of this desire ever could take place. The meals usually start out in a friendly and hospitable circumstance, and move, by the operator of the food and liquor, towards a situation characteristic of the saturnalia of role reversals and speeches. In Serres' reenactment of the symposium, Socrates moves from the lover of knowledge and speech, to the lover, and, then, to the silence of the "addicted".

The dynamic of this process may be traced in Serres' playing with the various ways in which language describes the gift or *le don*. Serres is attempting here to reverse the sociology of Marcel Mauss. The gifts brought to the feast are predominantly that of things that signify nothing. Speech and smoke become the signs of the modern gift precisely because of their importance for the understanding of the development of western philosophy. To what is given, the *ad-done*, one moves, to what may be translated as, what is said, the *ad-dire*, or more forcibly in the sense of the English "ad-diction", or what happens to you when you engage in the use of drugs: addiction. Thus the history of meals begins with the sense that it is a process under the sign of a drug. The drug that addicts one to the meal is, from the first instance, that of speech. Speech then becomes dependent upon the pharmakon whose drugs can alter the states of the participants, again following the general sense of the table as festival or saturnalia. In Western philosophy, speech has come to dominate the tradition stemming as it does from the Socratic dialogues. For Serres, the dialogues, however, are formally fixed in the tradition with the events of the last days of Socrates. In the sacrifice at the end to Asclepius, Socrates signifies the failure of his speech which ends by the taking of the hemlock.

The progress of speech as the sign of Western philosophy leads to the death and closure of being in the acceptance of the drug, the ad-diction, the 'adire' of the platonic dialogue. But as a dialogue, it forever remains unconsummated as the revellers at the end of the party have transformed the original hospitality towards that of the hostility of those attempting to seduce and parasite the guests. The seductions have been resisted; and even if they are not, the state of the revellers is such as to preclude any consummation in their drugged state.

There is here a modern analogy to the problem of having invited the guests who then eat your food, drink your wine and refuse to leave. In this case, the party is transformed from the welcoming community of brotherhood of the initial invitation, or 'social contract', to the war against the guest, or the hostility implicit upon those whose gifts have turned out to be nothing but that intellectual babble characteristic of discourse.

This underscores the prominence of speech, or the "verb", as the central operator in the power system of modern societies. This is found, for Serres, in the use in administrative structures where the communique has come to replace the "five senses" transforming us into speaking machines which have been fabricated along the lines of robots who in the end neither drink, nor have any taste for the food that has been put before them. A similar domination of language will reappear in the mediascape that is composed under the norm of seduction which can never be fulfilled, or in science which translates the "verb" into information theory, and the closure of classical knowledge. We, then, produce a world dominated by abstractions and codes that become moral, legal, rigorous and informative for all while turning a hospitable environment towards that of hostilities. The movement in deconstructionist theory by such thinkers as Jacques Derrida is but the last gasp of this structure which is on the brink of its own meaninglessness as the codes are layered one on top of the other, yet signifying less and less. It is the world of Roland Barthes' fashion system painting an overdetermined, but structurally lifeless, body whose meaning has been parasited in the very process of the fabrication of the codes that support it.

One's social reality is caught up in this shifting to and fro of the various aspects of the conversation at the dinner table. One's sense of self is captured by the fleeting relationship that one has in the go-around of criticisms at the table. These relationships are depended upon the exchanges, or transformations, in the power discourse made by the invisible operator encoded in the gift relationship that is moving progressively towards violence. Being is only being to the extent that it is enmeshed in these transformations. Implicit in this is a general nihilism that invades the parasitical social network when it is acted out under the signs of violence. The post-Nietzschean will languishes in this backwater, or turbulence, of the parasitical profession *par excellence* — those who take for talk; the world of 'nouvelle cuisine'. Nothing, or speech, is given for something, or power, but it is only marginal, and fleeting — it is only entropic. Being is set forth on these communication lines as static bouncing around in network of books, lectures, telephone calls and meals. But always there is too much static, or noise, and always the line is eventually broken. The host wants the guests to go home, and the guests, themselves, exhausted by the process, are left in Socrates' position of having their last words as that of the taking of the hemlock.

The Last Supper

The diet of hospitality turning to hostility has, in Serres' work, a natural completion in the movement of the hostile towards the hospital. The other way of expressing this, in Serres' philosophy, is that the laminar flow of power released by a parasite will return to a status of equilibrium within an enclosed system of dominance. Thus the natural flow of events in a topographical field will follow the logic of the Rousseauean version of property given by Serre's ending, as we have seen, in the enclosure based upon waste. This is brought about precisely by the fact that the parasite is always the third at any table, as we have seen. There are two examples of this phenomenon: one, following on the obvious similarity in Serres' vocabulary to the religious, and secondly, a reference in the political sphere which Serres does not make, but which highlights the movement, in Serres' thought, as it progresses backwards into the French tradition to recover the notion of 'sens'.

The paradigm case of last suppers is, of course, the one attended by Jesus Christ and his followers. It takes little, for

Serres, to draw the analogy between the betrayal of Christ, and his sense that the movement in the field of good and evil can only occur through the transforming of one to the other. This requires the betrayer, or the operator. There is also, no doubt, a similarity in the structure of the language which Serres uses to describe the parasite, and the sense of the third, as a "holy ghost". Serres will refer often to "the angel that passes" as a way of describing the invisible yet, nevertheless, felt presence of what rather aptly could be called in this case Maxwell's demon.

Serres also sees in the structure of meals an important shift in the operators of the social from a dependency on speech towards an original priority to taste and touch. The betrayal of Christ is depicted in many of the last supper scenes by the movement of Peter's hand knocking over the shaker which, for Serres, unveils the basic "honesty" of the sense of touch, especially as contrasted with that of a dissembling look. Nevertheless, the operators, in Serres' world, are always 'beyond good and evil' to the extent that the passing of the angels reverts in the final analysis, to the flight of Hermes that precedes the holy ghost or wind.

The second example is drawn from the geographical space within which Serres has worked, and about which he remains curiously silent. There are very few local examples of the dynamic of the parasite played out in French society given by Serres. This example inserts him into the midst of a form of "turbulence", that of the situation that was gripping France during the period of the conflict in Algeria. Serres' position stands in contrast with the overlapping topology of the existential, ethical perspective of Albert Camus. This is a contrast of the "fuzzy" set, to use Serres' language drawn from mathematics, to the binary choices given by politics. The comparison shows again the shift that predominates in Serres' network from the ethical towards the biological, and raises the issue of the nihilistic core of Serres' commitment to postmodernism.

In the mid-fifties, before the Algerian conflict yielded its most violent moments, Albert Camus sketched out a story entitled *L'Hôte*. [9] The title captures precisely the ambiguity of the parasitical relationship found in all social relations according to Serres. In Camus' case, we have an important political setting which establishes an interplay between the mythological and social. The French word "l'hôte" can be translated in English either as guest or host, and it retains its ambiguity not only in Camus' story, but within Serres' system in mapping the topography of power systems as we have seen.

Camus' story is a simple one focussed on an incident that occurs in a remote Algerian setting. Here, a French-speaking school teacher, who has been born in Algeria, is asked by the local prefect to take an Arab who has committed the domestic crime of murder to a police station in an adjoining town. The fact that it is a domestic crime is an important in linking Serres' analysis to Camus. Both return to depictions of everyday life as the structural ground for a theory that attempts to found the senses. Camus' story turns on the interaction between the "silent Arab" and the school teacher. Again the movement away from speech by Camus precedes the similar attack on the primacy of the "verb" in Serres' work. The Arab and the school teacher spend the night in the school room after having taken a meal in preparation for the next day's departure, this being a form of the interrupted meals that Serres describes in his work *The Parasite*. [10] The next morning, they both set off. The school teacher then leaves the Arab halfway to the police station, thus indicating that the choice is open to the Arab as to whether he proceeds along to the station or not. Again we have the conception of a voyage into a field that is not determined, but rather contains within it the random elements of choice given both by Serres in an ontological physics, and by Camus at the moral and ethical level. Camus' story ends when the teacher returns to the school where he finds written on the blackboard "You have handed over our brother. You will pay for this."

Camus was attempting with the story to pose the ethical dilemma facing one in a political situation where the homeland, or the "kingdom", was being torn apart by a political intrusion creating an "exile" — to refer to the title of the collection of short stories that contains *L'Hôte*. Here, it is unclear (and, as Serres points out, this is similar in all political systems) as to who is the host and who is the guest. Which of the two was parasited? Or were both of them parasited, or was the real parasite the "third" excluded from the interaction of the two individuals but, nevertheless, who is always present as the political community of the majorant? The excluded third stands for the parasitical operator that 'makes' the drama of the story. The exclusion is, however, an exacting one. From Serres' perspective, the story illustrates a dynamic that leads away from the existential considerations of being towards the nodal mapping of quasi-subjects over the field of relationships. His theory is most directly set against the expressed reaction of the "hero" of Camus' story who attempts to establish a human ground outside the political conflict. For Camus, the "ancient community of dream and fatigue" links the Arab and the school teacher. It is precisely this community which is shattered in Serres' analysis by the reversibility of the guest-host relationship. Neither one can establish itself against the presence of the excluded third, to whom the drama is always intended for, but to whom it is never directed. The power structure is never converted by claims of community outside the laminar flow.

One is left uncertain about the fate of both the Arab and the school teacher and, for that matter, the fate of Peter's denial. For Serres, as much as for Camus, the fate of the human condition may be more entangled with what happens to these interrupted journeys than with following the path of the powerful and the righteous. There is less uncertainty about the fate of Serres' politics. Either he is pushed to the holy spirit where one finds one's reward in heaven, or he travels down the road of the politics as paranoia. This road can only lead to the nihilism of the ambivalent parasitical operator. This, at least, seems to be what happens when one extends Serres' analysis on the journey through the northwest passage to the Americas.

The Pestilential Society

To the extent that Serres' analysis can be worked out in literary form, one could find no better example than the writings of Thomas Pynchon, and, in particular, the comparisons to Pynchon's *V.* [11] and *The Crying of Lot 49.* [12] Turning to *V.*, there is in the text a description of the effects consequent on the inhabitants of New York placing their pet alligators in the sanitation system. This could be described as a way of ridding themselves of parasites. We know that the path in the sanitation system leads to the sewers which, in Serres' analysis, is a perfect replication of the structure of a network that holds the city together. The fate of the friendly little alligator, who is sent to what is deemed to be perdition, is, of course, that they grow up to be rather large ferocious beasts that inhabit the sewer system. This establishes part of the plot in Pynchon's novel; the shooting of alligators as a modern form of sport.

The waste system also forms the core image of *The Crying of Lot 49* captured in the communication network that is established by the secret postal society. Pynchon's concern, like Serres', centers on the second law of thermodynamics stating that all systems are entropic. All systems generate, in the transformation from one state to another, energy that is dissipated into a waste function. This energy is then recaptured in the postal network as an underground culture. This follows Serres' analysis of the development of the social as the distortion in the exercise of equilibrated social control. In *Crying of Lot 49*, the creation of Oedipa Maas' being is precisely the tracking of the underground communication system as she embarks upon the search for the source of the thermodynamics, or motivator, at the core of this sanity/insanity network. The search is for the energy that comes from the dual sense of entropy as a physical conversion of thermo-quantities, and as a converter of thoughts or concepts in a mail system. This is characterized as a system of transformations in the social structure based upon a set of silent operators or "demons". These operators, Maxwell's demon or clinamen, provide nothing of lasting value to the system, but rather are the transformers between ready-states. They are parasites.

Thus, the flow that establishes the direction in North American societies is similarly to the move from hospitality, that is of the reception of the guest-host, to the hospitality, that is of the reception of the guest-host, to the hospital, which is the clearing of the house of pests after the meal into a sanitized space, which leads then, of course, to the establishment of hostilities amongst individuals who have been excluded by the hospitality process. These exclusions appear as the waste system. Power then may flow unimpeded to the holders of property. By this, the "culture" of the society becomes dirty, excremental, dissipated, yet this culture is the only recourse against the sterility of the sanitized environment. For life to be lived, these parasites, according to Serres, must be invited back.

Instead of use values in a system like this, one has abuse values, where the parasites enter only to abuse the host, and yet in such a fashion that the host will survive the abuse. This is Pynchon's America: sick, abusive, wasteful but not yet dead.

It is precisely this waste system which characterizes the later stages of the postmodern phenomenon where large segments of the society can be both peripheral, and yet integral to the survival of the overall organism. The very dependency of the system on the parasites that provided it with use and abuse values allows postmodernism to welcome both critical and apologetic views at the same time. The society works quite well, thank you, on layers from the sewers to the skyscrapers — well as long as one considers the wastage in human and natural resources as a concomitant to the sustaining of the overall edifice. This edifice could be compared to a retro-virus which changes its coded structure in reaction to the attempts of the system to drive out the unwanted parasitical functions. Unlike Jean Baudrillard's characterization of this system in his *Simulations*, [13] the genes become quite malleable over the longer term under Serres' biological system. It is a system that feeds on the "noise" or "virus" generated by itself which, in turn, creates further noise yet again. It is the reversal of Durkheim's organic whole, yet, it is value-free precisely because all values can exist simulataneously at one stage of the system or the other. Thus the highest form of late capitalism is characterized as that of a cultural converter which creates an entropic system of waste which, by its very nature, re-energizes a power of dominance in exploitation, or by giving those who have been "wasted" the opportunity, if they survive at all, of a "pleasurable" existence.

Cosmetic Culture

The most prevalent depiction of the postmodern world is that it has become a simulacrum in which the nature of the real is severed from the natural and becomes solely what has been reproduced. It is this world that has exploded the self over a technological field, and made the individual susceptible to the attack on the body by the promotional and advertising culture. The simulacrum has appropriated the sensorium, and freed from the restraint of the real creates *virtual products*, both individuals and images, in a steady stream of fashions. It is the world whose very seductiveness places it under the sign of the beautiful.

For Serres, the simulacrum has its origins in the beginning of Western thought in the writings of Lucretius. Lucretius is the originator of the simulacrum as it is presented in his poem *On the Nature of the Universe*. Lucretius founds a conception of science which is different from the one that we have seen underlying the classical theory of knowledge. Lucretius begins his work with the dedication to Venus which stands in contrast to the god Mars who presides over our current scientific enterprise. Thus, Lucretius presents the senses under the guise of the god of beauty. On the nature of things becomes the model of the physical universe; it becomes its simulacrum.

In one way, it may be said that Serres' recent work is an attempt to rewrite Lucretian physics. The simulacrum created by Lucretius is a reading of the text of the natural world, just as Serres believes his own work, *Les cinq sens*, is a similar reading of our contemporary world. This is especially true when one examines Serres' comments on the French impressionist Pierre Bonnard.

Serres calls Bonnard's paintings simulacrums precisely because they capture the senses. Again Serres, playing on the double significance of words, points out that cosmetics and cosmology occupy the same terrain. Bonnard's paintings become, as cosmetics, a description of the cosmos that we live in.

The Bonnard painting entitled *Nude Before a Mirror*, completed in 1933, provides an example of what Serres intends. The painting is discussed under a subheading entitled *Voile* or veils. The woman is seen as veiled by her bathrobe which "appears" to form part of her skin. Serres will call this "tattooing" which he believes captures the way in which the skin or the flesh is marked by its experience in the world.

This forms the basis of a defence of empiricism by Serres, but an empiricism that takes reality in itself as the veiling that experience has mapped on the body. Thus the Bonnard painting stands in a double sense for Serres to represent the original condition of humanity captured by the woman's nudity. On the other hand, the civilizing influence is not far off, and may be seen in the cosmetics table to her right. All skin is tattooed, that is to say all skin has cosmetics on it, and all individuals may be likened to artists in their chambers when applying 'makeup'. Thus the application of cosmetics leads Serres to his conception of the aesthetic which underlies the cosmological dimension of impressionism.

Serres' analysis of Bonnard fits under the sign of his analysis of Lucretius. They both have as a direction, or 'sens', that of the beautiful. This is a "soft" beauty to be contrasted with the "hardness" of the marble statues that form part of the classical civilization, and its dedication to "hard" science. It is a beauty that has turned impressionism into the impressing on the quasi-subject/quasi-object of the environment within which one lives. The existence of the mirror in the Bonnard painting, which reflects the self as the self is reflected back, signals, for Serres, the superiority of this simulacrum to that of the reproducibility of virtual bodies under the sign of postmodernism. The pheno-

Pierre Bonnard, *Nude Before a Mirror*

menology of the hard sell of the advertising industry is contrasted to the soft seduction of the Bonnard painting.

It is precisely this topology of the skin which leads Serres to redefine the nature of the social in terms of the geometry of the tactile. The skin becomes the multisensorial receptor upon which the sense of the common is inscribed. The skin takes on the mark of its locality, yet by participating in the expanded sensorium that Serres believes is the product of the voyaging of life, the skin comes to be marked by the several voices, by the noises of the social. The transcendental, then, presents itself as that part of the world where the abstractions that mark the skin manifest themselves in the form of a reality that is touchable, tastable, and hence understandable. Cosmology as cosmetics is Serres at his postmodern best.

Ode to Joy

Serres has remarked that the 'best' definition of a parasite is a thermal exciter. This is to be contrasted with the 'worst' defini-

tion of the parasite captured by the homecoming of Ulysses.
Ulysses entering his house where the guests have been revelling
ends their revel with the "unidirectional sens" of the arrow that
kills them. Each model is a reenactment of the common sense
(sens) and of the common direction (sens) of the voyage of Hermes
on the one hand, and the voyage of Ulysses on the other.

In many ways, this is a drama that has been reenacted earlier in
French letters by Albert Camus. Sisyphus stealing away from the
underworld enters the realm of sensuality captured so lyrically by
Camus in his essays on Tipasa. Sisyphus' fate at the hands of the
gods is to be reconfined to Hades giving rise, in Camus' thought,
to Prometheus' rebellion. And, indeed, at the end of *The Rebel*, [14]
we have the homecoming of Ulysses, not as the slaughtering of
the revellers, but of the finding by Western culture of its Ithica. If
one wants an ode to joy, the politics and art of Camus' rebel must
be contrasted to the science and philosophy of Serres' Hermes.

It is with this in mind that one approaches the last chapter of
Les cinq sens entitled "joie". Like Camus, Serres tracks back to the
Nietzschean world by stating that the body itself only comes into
existence with the dance. Here the post-Nietzschean dance of
the five senses takes solar energy and converts it into the joy of
life. The body becomes the thermal exciter. The dancer *par
excellence* clearly is Hermes.

Hermes' joyful wisdom shares the lightness of Nietzsche's
Dionysus, but his wisdom is not that of the will to power. Hermes
has become a creator of the postmodern age whose will is determined by the mythology of science in the will-to-will. Hermes'
return is not that of a homecoming, but that of the traveller who,
wearied of travels, cannot remember which tourists' sight he has
seen and whether he has been there before.

For the flight of Hermes is precisely predicated on the
fundamental forgetting that inhabits the postmodern condition.
Hermes forgets in the same way in which we forget how we walk,
talk, eat or swim, to use examples given by Serres. Hermes is
completely post-Nietzschean.

The postmodern culture is a forgetting, a forgetting of origins
and destinations, and it is very much the flight of Hermes from
trend to trend, from ad to ad. It is at this point that the postmodern discourse becomes identical with the discourse of science.
Science requires this forgetting, and so does postmodernity. We
live in a world that is only scientific. It may be that Serres' exit
from the postmodern debate frees him from the classical notion

of power, or a reality governed by the seductions of the media culture, or the grip of the performance principle in administrative and bureaucratic systems. It may be that Hermes' role as Hermes *trismegistus* can overcome these chains on his feet, and that as the god of science, commerce and the arts that his message will be received. However, the trip seems far too easy, far too seducing and far too forgetful of the very postmodernity that has given rise to its flight to end in joy.

D.C.

10

PARSONS' FOUCAULT

At the deepest level of Western knowledge,
Marxism introduced no real discontinuity; it found
its place without difficulty, as a full, comfortable
and, goodness knows, satisfying form for a time
(its own), within an epistemological arrangement
that welcomed it gladly (since it was this arrangement that in fact was making room for it) and that
it, in return, had no intention of disturbing and,
above all, no power to modify even one jot, since it
rested entirely upon it.

Michel Foucault, *The Order of Things*

The Splitting of the Atom

In *The Order of Things*, Foucault writes that "Marxism exists in
nineteenth-century thought like a fish in water,"[1] precisely
because bourgeois and revolutionary theories of economics, while
displaying a surface opposition, share a common condition of
possibility in the appearance of a "new arrangement of power."
Now, however, on the question of power as opposed to capital,
and in the midst of the radical anxiety of twentieth-century
experience, it might fairly be said that Foucault's meditation on
power, a meditation which by his own account ranges through
the entire corpus of his work, takes its place quietly and without a
fundamental note of discordance in the *episteme* of bourgeois
sociology. I would say further, without criticism, that Foucault's

understanding of the surface play of power, what Jean Baudrillard has described elsewhere as a "mythic discourse" on the filiation *en abîme* of power,[2] is perhaps nothing more than the completion, and certainly not less than the mirror-image, of another disembodied discourse on power, presented by that most grimly realistic of bourgeois sociologists, Talcott Parsons.

The event that, taking place at the beginning of the twentieth-century, clearly and decisively divides the modern bourgeois sociology of power from its neneteenth-century counterparts, and from which Parsons' theorizations and Foucault's thought follow, is nothing less than the movement from classical physics to modern biology, and particularly to the "new" genetic biology. For in the change from physics to biology as the mode of theoretical knowledge that constitutes power, there swiftly emerged a bourgeois discourse on power, its origins and methods of operation, which claimed, for the first time, that power was not after all to be reduced to an innocent (and why would we not say, in nostalgic remembrance, sentimental?) struggle between entities (interests, classes, groups) separated at a distance and causally interconnected, but was, in fact beyond all specific contents (phenomenal existence), the form or transparent medium, through which the life of the social species was to be prolonged and, to further that "natural purpose," improved.

Bourgeois sociology has by now completed the great shift to the biological conception of power, which announces a grand reversal of the "order" or "structure" of control, between culture and economy, between the categories of power and capital. Even when presented in the crudest of Darwinian terms by Herbert Spencer, this conception already contained the essential bourgeois discovery that political economy would now take its place within a "regulatory" order of dominations and powers. Who could have suspected that of the two thinkers, Marx and Spencer, it would have been Marx's fate to bring the classical discourse to a close (in the release of a dynamic vision of human freedom), and Spencer's fate to initiate a postmodern, structuralist discourse on power? And, ironically, in the same tired way in which new cultural forms are often energized by the content of preceding historical periods, Marxism is now a main content of the neo-Spencerian age. That this is a Spencerian age is attested to in the articulation, at first by Parsons and then by Foucault, of the principles of the new structuralist discourse. This discourse is the outcome of three strategic lines of thought, all of which meet in the creation of a radically new, and thus radically structuralist, conception of power, truth, and life. The new genetic biology of combinants and recombinants contributes (analogically, it is true, but in the specific sense of structural similitude) to an interpretation of power as a "site of battle" between genetic heritage (the categorical imperative?) and the empirical "range of variations" (the phenomenal world).[3] Cybernetic theory undermines, with one contemptuous blow, the theoretical justifications of the old materialism by establishing the new epistemological premise that information is *regulatory* of energy in much the same way that culture is *constitutive* of economy. And linguistic theory (which is only the most visible "sign" of a postmodern discourse that also involves molecular biology and cybernetics) displaces the "commodity conception" of power by emphasizing that power, understood as a specialized language, is a "medium" of exchange precisely in the sense that the grammar of power (the "code" of authority and its political significations) is the discursive form (the "silent language") within which the adaptation, or shall we be honest and say the "disciplining," of the social species takes place.[4]

With a proper, and perhaps even prim, sense of Victorian innocence, contemporary traditions of political economy insist on the right to be the last defender of Newtonian politics. With all the theoretical naiveté of a tradition that has managed (against a political history that declares its falsity) to miss not only the point but also the century, the political economy of power rushes past the actual ways by which the power apparatus now constitutes itself to take on in battle the representational "ghosts" of the past: class struggle, capitalist hegemony, power as possession. But Foucault is not a political economist, nor does he aspire to energize the radical structuralism of postmodern century with the ideological content of the Newtonian regime. Whatever the origin of Foucault's turn to biology, it is within the deep logic of the trajectory of thought traced out by political biologists, ranging from Spencer to Parsons, that his thought is to be located. This is not to say, of course, that Foucault's thought is party to "evolutionism," nor is it to maintain that his project is the advocacy of a simple organic metaphor. But then, need it be said, Parsons' political biology always claims that there is an order of difference between natural and social management of the species and that, in justifying itself (by way of analogy to natural evolution), power, understood as a social strategy, finds in the need to work on behalf of the *life* of the human species a discursive validation for the extension of its order of normalizing practices.

It is, perhaps, of little importance that Parsons and Foucault do not participate in a common political practice or that they reach different conclusions with regard to the political practices that follow from the constitution of power in the image of the biological metaphor. Was it not, in fact, precisely because those other curious intellectual peers — Augustine and Faustus, Marx and Smith — did *not* repeat one another but, in their grand reversal of categories, opposed one another, that each represented the completion of the trajectory of thought initiated by his opponent? Foucault is entangled with the Parsonian discourse. For between Parsons and Foucault, there is not the emptiness of non-identity, but, it might be said, the comforting similitude of the identity of opposites. With the happy sigh of one who has finally come home, Parsons confessed that he had ended up as a Kantian. And Foucault is, perhaps, the primal scream of a theory that, having renounced the possibility of knowledge of the *Ding an sich* (all in the name of the critique of ontology), is forced into a nominalism that is bleak with despair. Both theorizations of "bio-power" rush to a common fate: that of Parsons, the revelation of the totalitarianism at the center of the metaphysics of Western knowledge; and that of Foucault, to be the truth-sayer of the political practices that follow when "history has no meaning." [5]

Bad Infinity

> Discourse is not life: its time is not your time; in it, you will not be reconciled to death; you may have killed God beneath the weight of all that you have said; but don't imagine that, with all that you are saying, you will make a man that will live longer than he.
>
> Michel Foucault, *The Archaeolgy of Knowledge*

Why be unfair to Foucault? From "The Discourse on Language" to *The History of Sexuality*, he never tires of trying to free himself from being named a structuralist — from, that is, developing a thematic on power that makes reference ". . . to the great model of signs and language," or from the invocation of a theory of language which is situated only within the sociology of signs and symbols. And yet, for all of his protestations, and precisely because of the fact that Foucault does not trade in the semiology of power, I consider his meditation on power a classical example of hyperstructuralism. What has been called structuralism, at least in its literary representations from Bataille to Barthes and Derrida, is but the surface sign at the level of sociolinguistics (or perhaps psycholinguistics) of the symbol of a more pervasive "deep structuralism" that is now the horizon, the limit and possibility, of the production of Western knowledge. It is not to the barren world of semiology nor to the sociology of signifiers and significations that Foucault's thematic on power makes reference. Foucault is a structuralist, not in the linguistic, but in the profoundly philosophical sense that his discourse on power reflects a radical transformation of the form and content of Western experience in the direction of structuralist principles. Thus, Foucault's thought is structuralist in a mimetic sense: its categories — discursive knowledge, not intuition; relation, not sense; conditions of possibility, not ontology — reflect a social reality which, at the level of categorical knowledge and categorical politics, has been transformed in a structuralist direction.

It is to the philosopher of Königsberg that Foucault's structuralism may be traced. For is it not Kant who, in his radical scission of sensuous experience from the categories of understanding and in his intimations of a world invested and controlled by a power that would be radically relational, was the precursor of "deep structuralism?" And is it not Kant's "relational" understanding, his silencing of the "maundering fanaticism" [6] of the sensible world in favor of a "pure consciousness of form," which is the siren that calls forth the new world-hypothesis of structuralism? The thesis of bio-power is profoundly structuralist because it is radically Kantian; and it is Kantian to the extent that the new genetics, language theory, and cybernetics are strategies — nothing but political mechanisms — for suppressing the "maundering fanaticism" of sensuous experience. It is at this more intensive philosophical level, and *not* at the conventional, narrow empirical site of semiology, that Foucault's thought is, almost constitutively, structuralist. And it is in this unnoticed region of metaphysical assumptions, a domain that is far from the surface conflicts of the sciences of signs and symbols, that Parsons and Foucault reach agreement on what Karl Jaspers said of Kant: that understanding in the postmodern age (and, hence, the relation of truth and power) is discursive ". . . because it produces objects in respect to its form, not in respect to its existence." [7]

The "Kantian subordination" is not only the vital principle but the actual epistemological context within which Foucault's reflections on power, and also Parsons', take shape. Parsons' famous dualism — phenomenal "exigencies" and noumenal "normativity" — represent in the language of sociology what Kant previously termed the struggle of existence and the "understanding." And, for Foucault, the connection is all the more transparent. He says, without recrimination, that in every society ". . . the production of discourse is at once controlled, selected, organized and redistributed according to a certain number of procedures, whose role is to avert its powers and its dangers, to cope with chance events, to evade its ponderous, awesome materiality." [8] And speaking of the investiture of sex by the will to knowledge, Foucault writes of himself: "You, on the other hand, are in a symmetrical and inverse position: for you, there remain only groundless effects, ramifications without roots, a sexuality without a sex. What is this if not castration once again?" [9] Foucault's analytic of power," his meditation on the "will to truth," derive from the implications of the Kantian investiture, or should we say *siege*, of sensuous experience by the categories of "discourse." Foucault is not incorrect, or in bad faith, in claiming against conventional formalisms, whether linguistic, sociological, or psychological, that he should not be victimized by a misplaced nominalism (i.e. one that places his writing in the camp of the new monism of language). No, Foucault is after something more fundamental, something that escapes the vision of the linguistic monad: his project is to discover, after Parsons, the discursive implications of Kant's will to knowledge. And, to this end, Parsons and Foucault stand now as positive and negative polarities, the environment and antienvironment, of the spread of the will to truth across twentieth-century experience. The conjunction of truth, life and power as the axes of the discourse of "bio-power" makes of the postmodern age that of Kant.

All of which to say simply that the discourse of political biology is the "mother lode" of structuralism. In the meeting of Kant and Spencer, the will to truth finds its embodiment in the (admittedly rarified) claim that knowledge now will combine with "governance" for the perpetuation of the "cultural heritage" of the society. Thus, what appear in the writings of Parsons and Foucault are monochromatic images of a power made inevitable by its presuppositions, and that operates by transforming its conditions of possibility (a "normalized" society) into a methodology of political practice (rules of inclusion, exclusion, and prohibition). The discourse of political biology claims not only that power speaks for life, but insists also that the management of the life-functions of society (the regulation of health, intelligence, affect, body, and population) is "limitless." As Hegel foresaw, the form-alism of power would only lead to "bad infinity"; that is, to a dynamic of instrumental activism in which everything is reduced to the nihilism of "means in search of means." [10] Durkheim was the first to seize on the significance of a regime of bio-power driven forward by the principle of the "bad infinity." He said, in the fateful language of *normativity*, that suicide now becomes a deviation from the norm specifically because the struggle of contemporary politics is carried on at the fundamental threshold of life and death.[11] Death was less a private tragedy than a public threat to the order of permissions and prohibitions represented by the normative (life-managing) order. And is it not so un-remarked, because it is so unremarkable in its self-transparency, that within the apparatus of death rituals there has been imposed a normalization of death? The mourning ritual is thus to death what psychiatry is to madness and art criticism to artistic creation: a normalization, and thus incarceration, of an absence made less menacing by being confined to the silent region of non-reason.

The "bad infinity" wagers its struggle on the methodological possibility of substituting social life for biological death, on behalf of a power apparatus which to the extent that it manages to substitute *its* survival for my death finally overcomes the tragedy of finality. Jean Baudrillard, of course, sensed something of this truth in noting that the power-play in the form of the "bad infinity" is fascist in character. It presents itself in the aesthetic ritual of death" as a power that is not the signification of a sovereignty, a people's will, a trust. And power can do this because it has *no* representational function: the secret of power's existence is, quite simply, that "power does not exist." [12] Limit-lessness means that power is the name given to a certain coherency of relations: the terms of the relation (existence, ontology, corpo-reality) disappear and the "radical relationalism" that is the language, the medium, of power transcends sensuous experience. Then, in a reversal too bitter for acknowledgment, it returns to the source of its energy — sensuous existence — but in the form of that which is most positive and benign: it returns, that is, under the guise of the "ideolect" of life management and in the garb of truth. But this so surprising? Kant, who sensed the terrorism (he insisted that this was freedom) of truth, spoke of the "trans-cendental deduction," and Spencer thought of power in terms of the regulation of life. Spencer embodies Kant, and what is put in play by both is a power that is a matter of "groundless effects" and "ramifications without roots." [13] A limitless power that is also a fascist power, but could it not be that this fascist power is only a prolegomenon to the play of power to come?

Foucault's theorization of power delivers us only to the ascending spiral of the "bad infinity." A procedural image of power appears which, being groundless — a matter, that is, of relations rather than representations — reproduces itself in an endless spiral of exchanges, which, at once, plays the finite against the abstract, desire against order, as in a house of mirrors. Parsons, of course, never promised more than unhappy consciousness. His is the easy consciousness of the bourgeois personality who finds in the "relational" conception of power nothing more stirring than the search for a permanent and immutable basis for politics. But Foucault reaches the limit of the critical attitude, for he finally delivers on the relentless determinism which is at the center of Nietzsche's "will to power" and of Goya's "sleep of reason." Just as he saw clearly that Marx, because of his radical affirmation of history, was destined to be the last citizen of the nineteenth-century, so too Foucault, because of his radical assent to a power that "does not exist," is the first theorist of power of the postmodern century. And, to the extent that Marx could not complete the truth of Capital, so, equally, Foucault is only able to bring to the surface of language, without the hope of an exit, the strategies of this new mode of power: the "disciplinary society," "technologies of power," and an endless play of interventions upon the population and within the body.

Beyond the "Marxian Subordination"

> At the heart of power is a war-like relation and not that of an appropriation.
> Michel Foucault, *Power and Norm*

> We consider a generalized medium (like power) to be contentless.
> Talcott Parsons, *Action Theory and the Human Condition*

In the fateful convergence of Parsons' and Foucault's images of a "relational power" there is to be found a truth-saying about the actual operations and circumlocutions of the postmodern "power apparatus" that is so transformative in its logic, so comprehensive in its critical implications, that its very statement threatens to jeopardize the way in which power is "thought" within the Western tradition. Almost clumsily, with arguments that reveal traces of their deep embeddedness in the classical economy of power, Parsons, and then Foucault, stumbled upon a new terrain, a new constitutive dimension of twentieth-century politics. Martin Heidegger once said that the fate of the modern age was coeval with the transformation of Neitzsche's will to power into the more symbolic relationship of the "will to will." [14] What is at stake in a politics mediated by the "will to will" is the possibility that the *noumenal forms* of the life-order (which might be called, in their various symbolic representations, "discourse," "structural logic," "scientific-technical rationality," "the family of the generalized symbolic media") have broken free of their anchorage in sensuous existence, moved now by the dynamic impulse of an autonomous life-will. The "mirror" of politics is the appellation given to a political discourse in which nothing "in-itself" is at stake, only the symbolic play of a "power" that can never be appropriated, or for that matter, grounded, once and for all, in any of the *terms* to the power relation.

The silent, theoretical compact, the new Magna Carta of power, struck by Foucault and Parsons on the "relational" character of postmodern power, is as explicit, and terrifying, a political description as could be provided of the truth carried forward by the eruption of the will to will. Parsons continued to think in the mental framework of the old world of Newtonian politics when he insisted that the category of "freedom" still had some representational bearing on a "power" that recedes now like the shadow form of abstract realism into the invisible grammar of social discipline.[15] But Foucault, perhaps not even yet aware of the magnitude of the "discovery" of relational power, nonetheless has the sense to be alert to the opening of a new continent of the will, as we can see when he reflects, almost naively like a thinker pushed ahead by events, on the existence now of a "diabolical" will.

The threshold conflict in Foucault's discourse on power has to do with the struggle that he provoked against the "Marxian subordination" of power to some final, reassuring originary: class, commodity-form, instrumental state, historical dialectics.

But, what is less noticed, but undoubtedly of greater theoretical, and hence practical, significance, is that Foucault's famous refusal of the Marxian subordination takes its place in a queue that forms behind Parsons' quiet refusal of the "liberal subordination" of power. Like Foucault, Parsons also renounces the task of searching for a monistic ground (a class, a state, an individual's magical "capacities") to which power may be referred for its explanation. Thus, we have not one but two "post-Marxists," who declare against Marxism for precisely the same reasons that they were motivated, perhaps even compelled, to declare against the liberal regime of power.

Parsons and Foucault are conspirators of a common kind: whether their thought moves against classical Marxism (the search for the "headquarters" [16] that presides over rationality) or against classical liberalism (the nostalgia for the "individual" [17] who is the exerter of his capacities), an entirely common, and specific, series of theoretical renunciations appears. It is as if, although entering the discourse on power against radically different manifestations of the classical *episteme* (as different, I imagine, as that curious dissimilitude, but also filiation of identity, between Hobbes's "possessive" conception of power and Marx's "appropriation" of the power-relation on behalf of Capital), Parsons and Foucault turn out to be mining the very same historical vein. Consequently, the ultimate similarity of these two grand "refusals," originating as they do in quite opposite, incompatible, and independent, lines of theoretical analysis is like a laboratory experiment which, in its independent duplication of findings, verifies an emergent truth. And that truth is simply that the "relational" power of which Foucault and Prsons speak undermines the *whole* foundation, both liberal and Marxist, of the classical representation of power. This at least, is the implication of the "four refusals" of the Marxian and liberal, subordinations of power.[18] To these I now turn, *seriatim*.

The Refusal of a "Representational" Power: The theorizations of Parsons and Foucault converge, at first, in a common refusal to grant "regulatory" priority (here I do not mention *critical* or *ontological* priority because these have also been refused as the categories of the classical discourse on power) to the mode of economic production in the relationship of power and capital. Foucault said of the Marxian conception of power that it is premised on an "economic functionality of power." This economic functionality presents as the condition of possibility of power that it serve simultaneously to maintain "relations of production and . . . class domination which the development and precise forms of the forces of production have rendered possible" [19] Or, as Foucault says in "Power and Norm: Notes," power is to be freed "from the notion of subordination . . . from the idea that power is a definite type of maintenance, continuation or reproduction of a mode of production . . . which is always prior, if not historically, then analytically." [20] Parsons, of course, long precedes Foucault in the refusal to make power representational of an economic mode of production and, behind that, of an originary class of founding act of individual self-interest. For Parsons, power is to be liberated from its dependency on an economic *logique* precisely because the constitution of postmodern society around a silent "order of cybernetic control" (relations govern content, information regulates energy) situates the "power system," not as a subordinate of economy, but as *constitutive* of labor and capital. [21]

The Refusal of a "Distributive" Power: Foucault severs his perspective from the traditional viewpoint that power is a finite commodity — an "appropriation" or a "possession" — that can be taken out of circulation with the intention of reducing the total amount of power available to be distributed. Power is to be freed from the prison-house of the commodity form, that is, from ". . . the theoretical scheme of appropriation . . . the idea that power is something that is possessed — something that definite people possess — something that others do not possess." [22] Against the "commodity conception" of power, Foucault insists that power is the name (we will return to his nominalism) that one ". . . attributes to a complex strategical situation in a particular society." [23] And against the viewpoint that power is something that is "acquired, seized, or shared, something that one holds onto or allows to slip away," [24] Foucault speaks of power as a multiplicity of force relations and of their struggles and confrontations which, sometimes forming a "chain or a system," find embodiment in the "state apparatus, in the formulation of the law, in the various social hegemonies." [25]

In much the same way as Foucault, but with a theoretical rigor that is "technical and positive," Parsons also refuses to ground the play of power in a discourse that insists power be envisaged as something hierarchical, fixed, and determinate in its quantity, an object finally of appropriation and possession. To Foucault's image of the "complex strategical situation" of power, we might counterpose Parsons' refusal of a "zero-sum conception of power." [26] Over and against the classical liberal conception of power as the "capacities of a man," Parsons insists that the condition of possibility of power is that it be de-individuated (having a "collective," not "individual" reference) and that it produce "bindingness" (he sometimes says "diffuse social solidarities") across the "social community." In what catastrophe theorists would describe as a perspectival drama, Parsons refuses a distributive conception of power (". . . who has power and what sectoral interests he is serving with his power") [27] in order to speak of power as a "generalized, symbolic medium of exchange:" in short, to say of power that it is a *language* and not a possession. [28] In his reflections on the secret that was to be disclosed by the disciplinary power of Bentham's *Panopticon*, Foucault mused, in "The Eye of Power," that the ascendant quality of power today is that "it is a machinery which no one owns."

The Refusal of a "Sovereign" Power: Parsons and Foucault have not transgressed the limits of representation and distribution, these nodal points of the classical discourse on power, only to fall back into the comforting explanandum of the juridical model of power. The fateful "chopping off of the head of the king" also meant that power was freed of its exclusive relation to law, to the juridical discourse, in order to enter society (to act, in fact, as a condition of possibility in the creation of the "disciplinary society") under the mythic, and almost benign, form of the "normalizing discourse" of the human sciences. This negation of the classical association of power and sovereignty is really the decisive line of demarcation between a "relational" and "combinatorial" conception of power (the threshold of modernity") and the now obsolete interpretation in which power could finally be localized in a fixed, almost reassuring, model of stratification and hierarchies. [29] Sovereignty, the actual person of the monarch or the State, was taken to be the limit, even at the elemental level of life and death, of power-relations: sovereignty was thus considered to be constitutive of, rather than constituted *by*, the relations of power. For Foucault, the juridical model of a sovereign power is relative to the classical age of the West: a history in which power was exercised "mainly as a means of deduction, a subtraction mechanism, a right to appropriate a portion of the wealth, a tax of products, goods and services, labor and blood, levied on the subjects." [30] And what follows, of course, is that the juridical existence of sovereignty puts into play as its condition of possibility power as a fundamental "right of seizure." The great model of sovereignty does not place in question the "biological existence of a population"; it insists only on the right of the State to appropriate life as a way of "suppressing" it.[31]

Equally, for Parsons, the juridical limitation on power is refused because it does not reflect the transformation of the basis of power away from its prior "localization" and "externalization" in the State apparatus, and toward its new presentation as a transparent "symbolic medium of exchange." In awful, but fully faithful, *technical* language, Parsons speaks of power as the "circulatory process" of any "collective system"; and he means by the collective system, not a fixed institution or structure, but a mobile, disciplinary coherency — an imposed normativity — that is given to any of the relations of society.[32] Foucault says that power has escaped its localization in the institutions of the state, and is put into play now as a fluctuating series of discursive procedures in the regions of sexuality, the family, asylum, prison, hospital, and school. Parsons is probably the more radical in insisting that power does not now only take on the disguise of the norm, but conceals itself in the form of the *normativity* of health, knowledge, public morality, and even eroticism. Perhaps it is for this reason that Parsons claims that "theoretical knowledge" is the storm-center of the contemporary age; and that theoretical knowledge is exercised now within a domain of clinical practices: medicine, penology, the "helping professions." But, ironically, the sequel to this conjunction of truth and power is that when the glorious day finally comes that Marxism manages to overcome its cranky bias against the "relative autonomy" of the State and liberalism succeeds in transcending a constitutional interpretation of power, the locus of power will have already taken flight from its juridical basis; and from the sites of the languages of sexuality, of health, of technology, it will glance back, laughing, at nostalgic mentalities which insist that what is itself constituted by power (the state) be mistaken as a site for the constitution of power.

The Refusal of Power as an Order of Prohibitions and Transgressions: Following in the tragic sense of Nietzsche, rather than in the *laicisme* of Marx, Foucault has reflected that power is tolerable "only on the condition that it mask a considerable part of itself."[33] For Foucault, and for Parsons, the paradox of the way in which power comes into play is simply that the great order of prohibitions and transgressions, the eternal "no" that stands in front of and outside of human discourse, represents, not the essence, but the necessary failure of power. Parsons states this new "truth" of relational power most clearly when he writes that "force, rather than being the characteristic feature" [34] is, in fact, a special limiting case of the deployment of power. Coercion, this most manifest of the order of prohibitions and transgressions, represents the regression of power to a lower domain of generalization: the prohibition, backed up by even the most magisterial "show of force," is the emblematic sign of the failure of the *symbolic* currency of power. Do we need to recall that for Parsons the "freedom" that is put into play as a result of the transformation of the "nature" of power (from a bureaucratic to a cybernetic power) is not our liberty, but this strange and terrible freedom of *power to power* (or, as Heidegger said, the "will to will")? Little wonder that Parsons can say with such equanimity that the language of power appears now not only in the form of "compulsory suppressions" but also of "permissive order."

And Foucault follows this register of truth by noting paradoxically that power as "negation," as a "pure limit set on freedom" is, perhaps, the "general form of its acceptability." The existence of prohibition makes power bearable by setting a limit on the incarceration of desire. To establish the limits of transgression is also to suggest that there is a tiny space left for the play of human freedom. And, of course, Foucault with resigned melancholy and Parsons with melancholy resignation theorize that the great, almost sacred, order of negations and compulsions operates now only as a deflection, a path around the empirical functionings of the power apparatus. Foucault maintains that power "that counts" is typified by positivity and helpfulness; and Parsons says that the "sanctions" that matter are not those of the open "refusals" but the strategies of inducement and persuasion that are the signs of ideology, but also of a whole range of "normalized discourse." In the midnight sun of domination, power is no longer limited to the drawing of the blood of appropriated *and* exteriorized subjects. There is no elegant simplicity of "binary opposition," of the struggle between master and bondsman, which, after all, always had the easy merit of preserving *both* terms of the relation. The postmodern discourse of power absolves the old, comforting dualisms ("activity-passivity," "rulers-ruled," "center-margin") [35] in favor of a power experience that situates symbol and effect as mirrored images of one another. Power can appear in the disguise of seduction, because it is first a discipline; and it maintains a surface disguise of punishment because *its* freedom depended on the overcoming of its disciplinary threshold.

A Fascist Power

The classical discourse of power has been undermined by that most insidious and irreproachable of opponents: a profound, sudden, and irreversible transformation of the historical mode of constitution of power. The "analytical realism" of Parsons and the "analytics of power" of Foucault respond to a common truth: it was not, in the end, the ideological recriminations leveled against one another by socialism and liberalism, these political expressions of the classical economy of power, that brought to its conclusion the representational theory of power,[36] it was something more fundamental and sinister. And this was, simply stated, that unnoticed in the clash of perspectives between the great, worldly "power systems" (which loudly took up as their justificatory ideologies and as their energizing contents the political economy of a class that was absolutized as the "universal class" and, on the other side, the liberation of an "individual" constituted through a system of property rights), there was taking place the ascendancy and universalization of the *medium* of power itself. That the developing, real autonomy of power (in opposition to the historical regime of ideology — the historical nucleus of classical discourse) as the new capital of twentieth-century experience went relatively unnoticed may have been because its presence was first apparent, not in the surface play of warring contents, but at the level of structure; not in its empirical effects, but in the form of symbolic exchanges; and not in the struggle of ideology, but in the language of procedure and mediation. Not without some embarrassment did the advocates of the classical ideologies of the age of capital (organized socialism and institutionalized liberalism) realize one fine day that beyond the false appearances of ideological discord, they were bound together in a common discourse — a discourse of a power that operated now in the life-form of relationality and symbolic exchanges. And these same gangsters, realizing that skepticism could only be hidden by the administration of universal terrorism, also did not acknowledge that by a trick of fate they were the shifting, provisional "content" (I would say "controllers," but who is really in control of the "mirror of politics?") of a power that needed to have its functions, its conditions of possibility, embodied in human speech.

The language of power, transparent, mediational and content-less, stands at the end, not at the beginning, of civilization. For to the *history*, and thus to the substance, of civilization, the post-modern discourse on power reveals only a void, a "dead power" (Baudrillard). Because on the dark side of power, the side on which power has no existence as a representation, there remains only a power that is put into play as symbols without founding referents — a fascist power, the *void* that is Baudrillard's "dead" power, a pure instrumentality without signification. The loss forever of a founding subject, of signification, also means that fascist power must commit its fate to the amnesic language of formalism (and, quite appropriately, semiotics makes its appearance as the Gregorian Chant of a *structuralist* power).

Foucault and Parsons are explorers of the new topography of fascist power: a power that displays its symbolic effect in a discourse that ranges from the language of "macropower" (the sociology of cultural functionality) to that of the "micropowers" (the "verification" of sexuality, penology, health norms). It is not at all from the same perspective that Parsons and Foucault witness the birth of fascism as the secret of postmodern power. Indeed, their images of power are *reverse images* of one another; and to shift from the "macropower" of Parsons to the "micropower" of Foucault is to move, as if in a tiny catastrophe of perspective, from the background to the foreground, from white to black topography, as in an Escher painting. But in this swift, silent change of perspective, from the foreground of Foucault to the background of Parsons, there remains a continuity of vision, a common morphology, in which the play of fascist power is traced back and forth from its deep assumptions to its practical manifest-ations. And it might be said that the perspectival reversal of Foucault and Parsons in these reverse but mirrored images of the same continent of power intensifies the resulting description of the power apparatus.

Thus, Parsons approaches the "problem" of power from the viewpoint of "institutionalized liberalism," [40] a new ideological formation that shifts the center of power from the "possessive individual" to the "freedom" that is to be found within "positive social organization." By contrast, but still in an almost morpho-logical relation of similitude, Foucault addresses the play of micropowers within the dark underside of these very same "positive social organizations." And Foucault reveals that Parsons' "institutional freedom" is the unrelenting domination of a society that seeks to install a normalizing discourse across human experience. Foucault is the interlocutor of the actual strategies and tactics by which the "technical and positive" power of institutionalized liberalism is put into play as a "circulating medium:" one which resists localization in the name of "generalization" and which, finally, circulates through the social body, not as an end, but as a "symbolic effector." [41]

To read Parsons and Foucault *against* one another (but also on the basis that we are in the company of *the* polarities of the same discourse on power) is to travel simultaneously down both sides, to oscillate from foreground to background, of a common discursive understanding of power. What, after all, could be a greater clash of perspectives, yet more entangled in a common truth, than the convergence of Parsons' image of the "societal community" [42] as the outcome of the new biology of power and Foucault's haunting description of the "disciplinary" society? Parsons always defended the societal community as the locus of "diffuse enduring solidarity," [43] and he maintained that the societal community (a new type of collective formation that superseded class, individual, nation) was a product of an "institutionalizing" discourse that wedded politics and the biological canon. Foucault writes of the conjunction of power and truth (the truth, that is, of power's claim to speak on behalf of the social species) that it would be more accurate now to consider society, not as a penal system, but as a disciplinary system: "that is . . . a society equipped with an apparatus whose form is sequestration, whose aim is the constitution of labour-power and whose instrument is the acquisition of discipline and customs or habits." [44] Foucault's "sequestration" is the parallel, but reverse, image of Parsons' "diffuse enduring solidarity"; and to the "institutionalization" of the societal community, he provides the mirror of the "normalizing" society. ". . . (T)he apparatus of sequestration fixes individuals to the production apparatus by producing habits by means of a play of compulsions, teachings, and punishments. This apparatus must manufacture a behaviour that characterizes individuals, it must create a nexus of habits through which the social 'belongingness' of individuals to a society is defined, that is, it manufactures something like the norm." [45]

From an appreciation of the "societal community" (benign and monotonous, almost a fantasy of the managerial ethos, in its technical and positive play of power) as the foreground of the "disciplinary power," everything follows. The circulation of power which, being "contentless," poses continuously, and almost teasingly, the challenge of "simulated recoveries" that can be resurrected at the level of a "macrophysics" of power (Parsons) or in the language of "microphysics" (Foucault). The circulatory medium of power can be explored in its interiority (what is actually said about sexuality, about the medicalization of madness) or in its exteriority (Parsons was, after all, an *analytical*, not an empirical, realist). Or the mirror of power can be reflected in its production of discursive knowledge. Foucault says, with anguish, that what gives power its vitality, "what makes it accepted, is quite simply the fact that it does not simply weigh like a force which says no, but that it runs through, and it produces, yet induces, pleasure; it forms knowledge (*savoir*), it produces discourse; it must be considered as a productive network which runs through the entire body much more than a negative instrument whose function is repression." [46] And Parsons might respond that power is a "specialized language," but it is also a language that is *regulatory* of that matrix of exchanges that takes place (everywhere) between normativity and the play of empirical variations.

The Power System

That Parsons and Foucault represent complementary, although opposite, phases in the "strange loop" of postmodern power is of more than suggestive importance. Over and beyond their shared and explicit "refusals" of the Marxian subordination, they have also "discovered" four secrets about the ways in which fascist (normalizing) power now constitutes itself. We should not be surprised to learn that the "will to will," this emblematic sign of a power that is "limitless" precisely because it no longer has the responsibility of representing real existence (ontology), presents itself now in the discursive form of the "power system." Foucault reminds us that the "power system" is not to be thought of as an institution or a structure, but rather as a complex strategical intervention by which power is set in sway across as "multiplicity of sites." [47] And Parsons notes that the power system is a "fluctuating medium" which is not only capable of inflating and deflating its extensiveness, but is also the disenchanted currency that mediates the relations of *all* parties to the human discourse.

This is, after all, a power that resembles in its operation more the model of the computer (with its programming, relays, transmissions, and encoding of language) than the classical symbol of the machine; a power, that is no longer a matter of fluid mechanics but of the "field" of electronics. While the classical conception of power coincided perfectly with the birth of bureaucracy (*distributive* power being the power that could be doled out, controlled, or even saved within the great schemata of a hierarchical administrative rationality), the postmodern discourse of power complements the development of "technocracy." For in substituting managerialism based on professional knowledge for "line authority," and in setting in play a conception of power that has its limit and possibility the "management of life," technocracy carries forward the modern discourse of power. But this is only to say that the "power" that circulates as the life-force (and why not be frank and simply say, as the blood of the social body?) is *not* the same power as that which was always held in bondage by the classical discourse. For the classical discourse, from Hobbes to Marx, could never escape the representational theorization of power.

The representational image of power always insisted on taking power out of play (or, perhaps, on removing the threat of power) by displacing its mediational qualities into the surface play of its effects. At work was an eternal reduction that limited the power of power to manifestations of interest, ideology, psychological "drives." This may have simply been the classical rumblings of ontology, or perhaps of history, at work; in any event, we know that everyone present at the feast of classicism had a strong, almost proprietary, interest in maintaining the illusion that power could be localized, perhaps in the state, but at all costs could, most certainly, be safely incarcerated. This is such an apparent characteristic of the classical discourse (a "world-hypothesis" shared by all ideologies) that we might say now that the great struggle over capital (which everyone took to be the sign of materialism) was really a last defense of history and, thus, of ontology against the coming liberation of an (ahistorical and de-ontologized) power.

If it is strange to think of Adam Smith as the last of the ontologists, then it is at least as peculiar to consider Kant (most certainly not Marx) as the precursor of the postmodern discourse. This, at least, is the radical implication summed up in the image of the "power system." There is now only the silence of non-recognition between classical and postmodern power. The classical interpretation of power, because it was representational, always held open the promise of freedom *in* ontology, and sometimes *against* history. But the postmodern presentation of power, because it *begins* with the abandonment of representationalism (which was also the space of "otherness"), speaks of a New World of power that is unrelentingly deterministic. This is a power that is *transparent and mediational* rather than representative, *normalizing* as opposed to prohibitional, and *regulatory* rather than critical. Or, to put this another way, the power system is a confluence of four secrets: power now justifies itself through appeals to a biological metaphor; it combines with theoretical knowledge in producing a normalizing discourse; the "field" of power relations is experienced as a "circulating medium" of symbolic exchanges; and power has as its political effect the creation of a technocracy that makes "authority" prescriptive.

The Discovery of Power and Life (the Biological Metaphor): The primary line of theoretical convergence between Parsons' and Foucault's images of the power system lies in their mutual recognition that power now justifies itself on the basis of an appeal to a biological ethos. Of this radically new realignment of power and biology, Parsons says: "My own present view is that the theoretical logic of social science theory should be closer to the Mendelian than to the Newtonian model." [48] Of course, for Parsons there was in the sound of this new combination of politics and biology ("with its endless reshuffling of qualitatively distinct units") [49] only the comforting sign of a final "coming home" to his first discipline, the study of biology. And while he is careful to say that the relationship between *gene* and *symbol* (between the "system of cultural symbolic meaning" and "genes in biological heredity") is only an *analogous* relationship (and this in the "structural sense"), he also notes that the regulative function of power is to mediate the genetic constitution of the species (that grey region of "normative culture") and the "phenotypical organization of organisms" (history).[50] The appeal to the biological ethos thus makes the "management of life" both the condition of possibility of power and the categorical imperative of politics. It is, indeed, a change of profound magnitude when power invests life, for this indicates that just as nothing escapes life, without being a threat to life, so also nothing may evade power without representing a menace to the claim of power to speak on behalf of the species. The "therapeutic" investiture of medicine, education, labor, and sexuality is, consequently, central to the task of the power system in making the biological norm of a "healthy society" prescriptive.

Parsons is explicit about the theoretical impossibility of separating power from life, or of discussing the "regulatory" functions of power outside of the biological discourse. Thus, for example, he follows the geneticist Alfred Emerson in remarking on the similarities between the genetic reproduction of the species and the social "requirements" for the reproduction of the societal community. And he says with Ernst Mayr (in *Population, Species and Evolution*) that there is an explicit analogy between the properties of biological communities and those of the societal community: the "reproductive community" is like the "population" of the societal community; "territorial community" is analogous to a "politically organized society;" and the "genetic community" is structurally similar to "common culture." [51] Thus, on the basis of analogy (though Parsons always replaced concrete action with *analytical* action), the genetic canon of the natural species is transcribed onto the level of the human species. In a theoretical rupture that is surely equal to the naming of a "possessive" power in Hobbes's *Leviathan*, Parsons equates the relationship of gene and phenotype (the biological canon) with the order of relationships between normative culture and its environment (the social canon). In both instances, it is a matter of producing a discourse that will mediate, or should we say *regulate*, the relationship between the genetic heritage of the social species and the limitless play of practical existence. And the discourse that will produce this active mediation of symbol and effect will be that of a normalized (institutionalized) society.[52]

Foucault has done nothing else than to account, after the fact and in tragic and elegiac prose, for the consequences that follow the alignment of power and life into a common discourse. "The mechanisms of power are addressed to the body, to life, to what causes it to proliferate, to what reinforces the species, its stamina, its ability to dominate . . . ?" [53] Foucault follows the "Copernican Revolution" of Parsons by noting that when the "technologies of power" invest life, then power itself speaks to "both sides" of the discourse. For this is an age in which the strategies of "adaptation to the species" and the practice of "social eugenics" upon the "body" and the "population" have replaced the warring dualities (always safely externalized) of the classical discourse. For when Foucault says that sex now becomes "a crucial target of a power organized around the management of life rather than to the menace of death," [54] then he has also recognized that power now wagers itself on the possibility of overcoming finality.

The Discovery of Power and Normalization: The biological canon makes culture constitutive of economy by reversing the order of control between the realm of symbolization and material signification. Parsons and Foucault achieve a second ground of "consent" to a relational power when both can say that conjunction of power/life releases in its wake a dense matrix of "micro-powers"; a presentation of power not under the awesome sign of the state or of economy, but under the more banal sign of the lowly *norm*. Thus, Foucault describes the discourse "that will accompany the disciplinary power [as] that which grounds, analyzes, and specifies the norm in order to make it prescriptive." [55] And Parsons replies, always from the side of the technical and positive play of the power system, that "institutionalization [Foucault's "normalization"] is like natural selection." [56]

The secret that is revealed by the association of power with the production of normalized discourse is that "truth" itself is drawn within the discourse of postmodern power, and that a precise and dramatic line of convergence is established, not only between power and truth, but really among the triumvirate of life/power/truth. The constitution of truth (the establishment of normativity in health, education, labor) becomes both a condition of possibility for and an object of the (biological) ethos of life-management. The epistemological region of truth-falsity is thus drawn into a fateful parallelism with health/disease, life/death, knowledge/ignorance, labor/unemployment, and realism/utopia. Who might have known that the lowly norm, this small play of micropower, would constitute itself as an epistemological division between truth and error that, in an endless *mirrored* effect, would rebound and amplify into a series of exclusions, prohibitions, and divisions at the levels of axiology, esthetics, necessity, and politics? Small wonder that the policing of the Gulag and of the "positive social organizations" of the West is done in the name of "verifi-cation." For what is verified is political loyalty itself; and thus, in a small but momentous step, the epistemological norm (truth/error) is made convergent with the political norm (loyalty/disloyalty). Foucault says of the political strategy effected by the conjunction of power and the will to truth that:

> Modern humanism is . . . mistaken in drawing the

line between knowledge and power. Knowledge
and power are integrated with one another, and
there is no point in dreaming of a time when
knowledge will cease to depend on power . . . it is
not possible for power to be exercised without
knowledge. It is impossible for knowledge not to
engender power.[57]

In the silent "shuffling and reshuffling" of possibilities for
normativity, the truthful becomes the real, the real becomes the
desired, and the desired, the manageable *for life*.

Parsons is explicit on the significance of normalization as the
procedural logic by which a line of convergence is established
between the mirrored images of cultural heritage (symbol =
gene) and the phenotypical (the *Ding an sich*) level of organisms.
Following in the therapeutic mode, Parsons notes that "living
systems" require a code or a program ". . . and another set of
symbols which implant the genetically given pattern at the
phenotypical levels in organisms." [58] For Parsons, power serves
now as the "language" that mediates the sphere of cultural
practices (the genetic code of authority) and the multiplicity of
sites (exigencies) that are to be invested by the will to truth. It is
surely a sign of an Orwellian "vaporization" of sensuous experience
that Parsons, in words that are dull and chilling in the revelation
of a fascist power, says that institutions are ". . . complexes of
normative rules and procedures which, either through law or
mechanisms of social control, serve to regulate social action and
relationships."[59] The sounds of history recede, the struggles of
warring ideologies abate, and what is left is the quiet "shuffling
and reshuffling" of all contents through the regulatory procedures
of institutions. In the Mendelian politics of normalization, a
radical structuralism is installed in which all "events are evacuated
of their contents." And the radical structuralism of the normalizing
discourse, this center of fascist power, Foucault describes wearily
as the "apparatus of sequestration," creating only the "social
belongingness of individuals to a society . . .?" [60]

The Discovery of Power/Language (a Limitless "Circulating Medium"):
But what is the center (the degree of ontology) of this power
system which, in a mimicry of natural life, produces its disciplinary
effects through a set of discursive practices that are, to be sure,
always rooted in the will to truth? To the insistent demand for an
ontological grounding for power, Foucault replies, almost

laconically, that the secret of power is its transparency: "power in the substantive sense *'le' pouvoir*, doesn't exist. What I mean is this. The idea that there is either located at or emanating from a given point something which is a 'power' . . ." [61] Beyond the great binary divisions of society and beyond even the "locus of a great Refusal," there exists a "network of power relations" that ends by "forming a dense web that passes through apparatuses and institutions, without being exactly localized in them . . ." [62] It might be said that Foucault consents to the exclusively "relational" character of power relationships, and thus theorizes a power that is not exterior to other relationships ("economic processes, knowledge relationships, sexual relationships") but, rather, *immanent* in the interplay of "nonegalitarian and mobile relations." Thus, much as in the tradition of radical empiricism (one end of pragmatism), Foucault postulates a "power experience" that, in its condition of possibility and in its practice, both encircles the "subjects" who are drawn into the power network and, moreover, as a certain "field of force relations," always manages to evade localization in the terms (caste, class, group, individuals) that it mediates.

And, as might be expected, the power experience is intimately linked with the production of discourse; for it is "discourse which transmits and produces power" and it is the analysis of the specific productions of discourse that reveals the exact relationship that holds between power and knowledge (the shifting curvature of normativity). A microphysics engenders a field of micropowers; and this play of micropowers cannot be located in the search for "general unities" but is discernible only in the interstices, the fissures, of the power network. And between the actual experience of micropower (at the level of sexuality, penology, the family) and "macroscopic" institutions, there is not a relationship of causality or simple dependency, but "analogical" relationships that draw together the center of "authority" and its range of prescriptive practices.

It would not be inaccurate to state that Foucault's opaque way of circling around and around this decentered power is an almost crude description (and a nonspecific one) of what Parsons already described as a "generalized, symbolic medium of exchange." What Foucault alludes to, sometimes under the rubric of "the rule of double conditioning" or of "the rule of the tactical polyvalence of discourses," Parsons describes as the constitution of power in the postmodern regime as a "circulating medium" without limit. For Parsons, the secret of the "power network" is that power circulates now (always immanent to but never localized in) through the societal community (or, inversely, the "disciplinary society") like a language, and much like those other languages that are disenchanted symbols — money, intelligence, health, influence, and value-commitments. Power has its own grammatical-syntactical structure, its own specific codes (authority), and its own "symbols of effectiveness." Thus, those who would search for the historical originary of power will be disappointed; for power operates now, not in the name of representation, but always as a *symbol of effectiveness*.[63] In a description that is remarkably convergent with Foucault's insight into the relational character of power relationships, Parsons also posits that the power network is a circulatory medium, and one that is relational and combinatorial in character. The power system is combinatorial to the extent that the magnitude of the power network can be expanded or contracted, inflated or deflated from the sites of power itself. And power is relational because it is "dead" in itself; and has now value only in exchange: the production of social "belongingness"; the "authoritative" legitimation of rules governing contractual agreements in the economy; the translation of health norms into prescriptive practices.

The Discovery of Power/Technocracy (The "Transcendental Deduction" and the New Class): There is a final moment of theoretical convergence between Parsons' and Foucault's interpretations of power as a circulating medium. And this is simply that the "regulatory" functions of the power network (the production of rules governing the use of power; that is to say, how the norm is to be made prescriptive) are embodied finally in a *professional* ethos that is carried forward by a new class that acts as the verifiers of the norm. Parsons always insisted that "professionalization was at the center of modern societies"[64]; and for the same reason he noted that the swift emergence of "theoretical knowledge" also meant that the *cognitive complex* was becoming a central aspect of the societal community. For Parsons, power could safely pass from its ground in "individualistic liberalism" to the domain of a "circulating medium," specifically because the conversion of power into a symbolic language opened up possibilities for a full normalization of society. When power is conceived as a "specialized language," it reveals a new possibility for the social species to be "governed" within the invisible and formal "regulator" of cybernetics itself.

This entails, of course, that in the new power system, "information controls energy" in much the same way that the "code of authority" governs the actual mode of operation of political practice. Cybernetics in conjunction with language theory discloses the real methodology by which a normalized society will be produced. Cybernetics introduces the division between "rules of use" and "empirical situations," between, that is, procedures (programs) high in information and practices (deployments) high in energy — this old division between reason and existence — as the radically new condition of possibility of the power system. And language theory (in the sense of a grammatical-syntactical structure that contains codes and symbolic effectors) provides for the "embodiment" of cybernetics in the actual play of the power network. For power to be a language that is limitless (because it is always deployed in exchange, not in use), it must first have as its condition of constitution a structure of grammatical-syntactical rules (authority) that may be wagered at the practical level in a struggle that is no less serious for being always symbolic.

It is, finally, the discourse of *professionalism* that embodies the discursive logic of the power network. In the professional ethos, there is to be found the governing idea that power should speak now, not in terms of transgressions and prohibitions, but on behalf of life. Carrying forward into practice the biological metaphor, the professional complex serves to define, to administer, and to verify the implantation of the discursive practices of normativity. Thus, Parsons can say that after the industrial and democratic revolutions there was another, and this time less visibly turbulent, revolution: a "cognitive" revolution that centered on education itself.[65] And Foucault can say: "The discourse of the king can disappear and be replaced by the discourse of him who sets forth the norm, of him who engages in surveillance, who undertakes to distinguish the normal from the abnormal; that is, through the discourse of the teacher, the judge, the doctor, the psychiatrist, and finally and above all, the discourse of the psychoanalyst." [66]

The deployment of the normalizing discourse as the center of the power network is, in its practice, dull and prosaic. At work is a power that does not gambol with mythical discourse, but simply a power that expresses itself in the normalizations of the human sciences. And, of course, what is at stake in the normalizing strategies of the human sciences and, by extension, in a developing technocracy that also prides itself on being a major site for the deployment of "theoretical knowledge," is the management of the technical, procedural logic of the societal community itself. The logic of the human sciences has also become the discursive practice of the power system — because the power system ultimately need its programmers and decoders; because it, too, requires that power take on the appearance of the norm and that the norm be presented as nothing more sinister than managerialism itself. What this indicates, perhaps, is that the new class of "technocrats" — the famous membership of the "helping professions" and of the technical intelligentsia — may be the practical embodiment of a power that finally works by abolishing the *Ding an sich* and by instituting in its place the "bad infinity'" of a shifting normativity. The question that remains, however, is whether the Gulag and the disciplinary society are exceptions to the *positive* discourse of normalization or emblematic of a power system that, based on the logic of the "bad infinity," is also condemned to the bad destiny of a fascist power.

The Image of Prison and the Prison of the Image

It is likely, I would conclude, that the reverse, but parallel, visual imaginations of René Magritte ("Black Magic," "The Lovers," "Discovery," "La Clef des champs," "La Mémoire," "Ceci n'est pas une pipe") and Edward Hopper ("The Secret") provide an intense expression of the relationship of Parsons and Foucault on the question of power. To migrate from Hopper's melancholy realism to Magritte's lament on a nameless power is an almost identical movement of thought to that other migration: the shift in perspective, but not essential identity, from the positive domination of Parsons' societal community to the negative truth of Foucault's disciplinary society. In his wonderful commentary on the secret of Bentham's *Panopticon*, Foucault remarked that the modern prison, understood as the centering-point of the epistemology of discipline, has radically reversed the principle of incarceration.[67] In contrast to the traditional (or should we say *classical*) order, where transgression (in the symbolic form of the prisoner) is excluded into the darkness of the cell, the modern *Panopticon* reverses the order of imagery. The jailer, in his central citadel, watches in darkness; and what he observes across the circular courtyard of the carceral are prisoners who are brought, not fully into light, but into the light that makes of the prisoner a silhouette. The absurdity, and yet transparency, of this new form of domination (the prisoner who is reduced to the universal form of the "silhouette" and the jailer who is also incarcerated in darkness) symbolizes the nameless, relational power that has been meditated upon, in reverse but identical ways, by Parsons and Foucault. And I might wager that it is possible, just possible, that in the almost serpentine twisting of Parsons and Foucault as they confront one another across the space of a common, but reverse, image of power, they, too, are locked together like jailer and prisoner in the modern *Panopticon*.

Perhaps in the next century another poet may have the insight to say of Foucault what Octavio Paz remarked, in our time, of Sade:[68]

> Prisoner in your castle of crystal of rock
> you pass through dungeons, chambers and galleries,
> enormous courts whose vines twist on sunny pillars,
> seductive graveyards where the still black poplars dance.
> Walls, things, bodies, reflecting you.
> All is mirror !
> Your image persecutes you.
>
> A.K.

1
The Body in Ruins

FRANCESCA WOODMAN'S
SUICIDED VISION

In the same way that Susan Sontag once described Antonin Artaud as a writer "suicided by society", the photography of Francesca Woodman is that of an artist suicided by her body.

To meditate on Woodman's photographic practices is to be in the presence of a suicided vision of the postmodern kind, literally and semiologically, and one which is all the more courageous and profoundly original because in a media scene in which power speaks in the disembodied language of body invaders, Woodman's photography is that of a performance artist of the blood. [1] In her photographic productions, it is the *body* itself, her body and sometimes that of a friend, which is invested across the camera's visual field: sometimes as a *transgression* (the *Space* sequence); sometimes as a parodic play on the pornographer's art (*New York*); at other times as a Kafkaesque reflection, like Gregor Samsa in *The Metamorphosis*, on the transmutations of the flesh (*Eel Series*); but, most often, as an exact and tragic recitative of the inscription of power on the text of the body (*House #4, Then at one point I did not need to translate the notes; they went directly to my hands, Space, House #3*). Indeed, one might say of Woodman's photography that, more than most, she made of her body a mirror of domination, a fleshly inscription and transgression of a power which functions as Artaud hinted, and then Deleuze and Guattari after him in *Anti-Oedipus* insisted, as a "body without organs": perfectly rhetorically and topologically, all a matter of the play of a delocalized, dematerialized, and dehistoricized investiture of the poli-

Francesca Woodman, *no.25*, from *Space²* Providence, 1975-76

tical economy of signs on the text of the flesh. Woodman made of her body a receptacle for the violence of signs at the (disappearing) centre of dead image-systems.

However, unlike Ortega's philosopher whose *consciousness* is at "the height of his times", Woodman's photographic practice is all the more privileged because as a woman's vision of the taking possession of the flesh by the signs of dead power, it is not just her consciousness (though that too), but her *body* which is at the height of her times. Her flesh in all of its mutations — a labyrinth of dependency, a rhapsodic break in the relational field of power, a theatre of parody, a space traveller in sign-metamorphosis — reflects all of the tensions, paradoxes, and contradictions in the postmodern scene. Against the privileging of the romance of the body now taking place (from the psychoanalytical recuperation of pre-oedipalized experience and Kristeva's theorisation of somatic experience to the desperate recycling of Rabelaisian 'laughter' in art theory), Woodman's final instruction, before her suicide, is all the more bleak. She is the artist who actually re-produced in photography Foucault's grim pronouncements in *Discipline and Punish* on the fate of the body in postmodernity:

> The body is the inscribed surface of events, traced by language and dissolved by ideas, the locus of a dissociated self, adopting the illusion of a sub-stantial unity — a volume in disintegration. [2]

Francesca Woodman, *no. 26 House #3*, Providence, 1975-76

Francesca Woodman, *no. 5*, New York, 1979-80

THE AESTHETICS OF SEDUCTION:
EDWARD HOPPER'S BLACK SUN

Edward Hopper is the American painter of technicisme. If by technicisme is means an urgent belief in the historical inevitability of the fully realized technological society and, if further, technicisme is understood to be the guiding impulse of the American Republic, at least since the inception of the United States as a society with no history before the age of progress, then Hopper is that curiosity, an American artist who, breaking decisively with the equation of technology and freedom in the American mind, went over instead to the alternative vision of *technology as deprivation*.

Quantum Physics as Decline

One painting by Hopper reveals fully the price exacted for admission to the fully realized technological society, and speaks directly to the key issue of technology and power in the postmodern condition. Titled *Rooms by the Sea*, the painting consists simply of two rooms which are linked only by an aesthetic symmetry of form (the perfectly parallel rays of sunlight): emptiness (there are no human presences) and perfect stillness (the vacancy of the sea without is a mirror-image of the deadness within). Everything in the painting is transparent, nameless, relational and seductive; and, for that reason, the cumulative emotional effect of the painting is one of anxiety and dread.

Edward Hopper, *Rooms by the Sea*
Yale University Art Gallery

Rooms by the Sea is an emblematic image of technology and culture as degeneration: nature (the sea) and culture (the rooms) are linked only accidentally in a field of purely spatial contiguity; all human presences have been expelled and, consequently, the question of the entanglement of identity and technique never arises; a menacing mood of aesthetic symmetry is the keynote feature. Indeed, *Rooms by the Sea* is a precise, visual depiction of the postmodern world in the disintegrative vision of quantum physics, a world in which science is the language of power. Edward Hopper can paint technology as deprivation so well, because he was the American artist who first stumbled upon the new continent of quantum physics as an exact, social description of American culture in radical decline. And, since American culture, as the dynamic centre of advanced modernity, is world culture, Hopper's artistic vision of the black sun, the emblematic sign of technological society, takes on a larger historical significance.

Rooms by the Sea gives us an early warning of the great paradigm-shift prefigured by the new cosmology of quantum physics. Quantum physics, the cutting-edge of the technological system of hypermodernity, holds to a purely relational (and hyper-Derridean) world-view: *aesthetic symmetry* (charm, truth, strangeness, beauty) is its key regulatory feature; random and unpredictable *quarks* from one energy level to another are its principle of action; purely contiguous relations of a spatial order across bounded energy fields are its horizon; structural relationships of similitude and difference are its basic geometry; an infinite regress of all matter, from the hyper-density of black holes to the purely disintegrative world of sub-molecular particles (the high-energy physics of bosons, leptons, and quarks) in the *creatio ex nibilo* of unified field theory is its central canon. But it now contains a fifth force — the *hyper-charge* — which is the postmodern contribution to the old physical world of gravity, electromagnetism, weak and strong forces. Quantum physics gives us a world which is a matter of probability, paradox and irony; where singular *events* (with their representational logic) dissolve into relations across unbounded energy fields; and in which the dualisms of classical physics are rejected in favour of structural and, thus, morphological relations of identity and similitude. And the world of quantum physics is what the French theoretician, Jean-François Lyotard, has described in *La Condition postmoderne* as the age of the death of the grand récits; and what, before him, Michel Foucault said would be the spreading outwards of the discourse of a "cynical power:" a power which speaking in the name of life itself would remain a matter of pure relationalism — "groundless effects" and "ramifications without root."

Rooms by the Sea shows us that in the hyper new world of technology power no longer speaks in the forbidding tones of oppression and juridical exclusion, it no longer appeals for its legitimacy to the "grand récits" of classical physics, whether in the form of Newtonian politics, Hobbesian science, or Spencerian society. Power, a "cynical power," reveals itself now in the language of an *aesthetics of seduction. Rooms by the Sea* is an emblematic sign of the relational power of technological society as the language of an aesthetics of seduction. Its design-logic is relational *not* representational (the sea and the sunlight exist only to show the absence of any references to nature); its figurations are sharply geometrical as if to remind us of the privileged position of mathematics in the new universe of science and technology; and its language is purely structural (there is no referential "event," only the empty ideolect of the image itself). What is particularly striking about *Rooms by the Sea* is the mood of anxiety, dismay and menace it establishes as the emotional counterpart of the aesthetics of seduction. The door opens directly onto the sea; the sun is brilliant, but austere and cold; and the rooms are perfectly empty. This painting is not, of course, about "rooms by the sea"; it is about *us*: an exact clinical description of what we have become in the age of cynical power, of excremental culture, the

Edward Hopper, *High Noon*

death of the social, and the triumph of the language of signification. *Rooms by the Sea* is, in a word, the truthsayer of a postmodern condition in which power speaks in the language of the aesthetics of seduction.

The American Landscape

Edward Hopper could paint the dark side of postmodernism so well because his was that authentic American artistic vision which understood exactly, and with no reservations, the intimations of deprival in the midst of the technological dynamo. It was Hopper's fate to understand that the will to technique — the coming to be of a society founded on the technical mastery of social and non-social nature — was the essence of the American polis. Hopper's paintings begin, in fact, at that point when technique is no longer an object which we can hold in front of ourselves as a site of contemplation, but when technique is us: that is, when technology invests the realms of psychology, political economy, and social relationships. Indeed, what is most fascinating about Hopper's artistic works is that they represent a recitative of American "being" in the postmodern condition: *waiting* with no expectation of real relief from the detritus of the simulacrum; communication as radical isolation; *endless motion* as the nervous system of the culture of style; *radical dislocation* as the inevitable end-product of shifts in neo-technical capitalism; and profound *solitude* as the highly paradoxical result of a culture in which power reduces itself to an aleatory mechanism, and where even sexuality is fascinating now only when it is the scene of an "imaginary catastrophe".

An earlier sketch of Hopper's classic painting, *House by the Railroad*, called "An American Landscape" suggests that all of Hopper's artistic productions represent an interrogation of the "psychological" American landscape, one charged by the driving spirit of technicisme, and typified by a growing radical improverishment of American existence. And, just as the original sketch for *House by the Railroad* moved from an unfocussed naturalism to the geometrical lines and angular deprivations of the final painting, so too Hopper's vision as it moved from the externals of technological domination (the political economy of *House by the Railroad* and *Gas*) to the psychology of technological society (*New York Office*, *Western Motel*, *Approaching a City*) and, thereupon, to the aesthetic symmetries of *High Noon* and *Rooms by the Sea*, traced the landscape of "technique as us" from its surface manifestations to its investiture of the interstices of American being. Thus, Hopper's artistic rendering of the deep deprivations of technological society move from the plane of physical dislocation (*Four Lane Highway*) to psychological displacement (the radical solitude of *Excursion into Philosophy* and *Western Motel*) and, thence, to social displacement (*Early Sunday Morning* is a grisly example of Sartre's culture of "alterity") and culminating in the perfectly aesthetic (because so well harmonized and symmetrical) and perfectly impoverished visions of *High Noon, People in the Sun,* and *Rooms by the Sea.*

Hopper's artistic vision is unrelenting. The figures in *People in the Sun, Excursion into Philosophy*, and *Western Motel* are not waiting for the coming of a radical crisis. On the contrary, they are so inert and so overcome with a sense of melancholy resignation *because the catastrophe has already taken place, and they are its victims and not so happy survivors.*

Excremental Culture

Hopper's artistic vision might be studied then as a brilliant, visual history of the disaster triumphant which has overwhelmed American public and private life in the late twentieth-century. In his works, we are in the privileged position of being present on the dark side, the side of the excremental vision of technological society. Hopper situates us as voyeurs (*Office in a Small Town, Night Windows, Morning Sun*) observing victims of a catastrophe.

Edward Hopper, *Office in a Small City*
Metropolitian Museum of Art

The reduction of the observer to the position of voyeur and of the human figures in the paintings to melancholy victims is accompanied by another great reduction. It is often said that Hopper, in the best of the romantic tradition, uses the artistic device of "windows" to disclose the tension between nature and culture or, at least, to introduce some sense of electric tension to otherwise dead landscapes. This is profoundly mistaken. The windows in his paintings are, in fact, *trompe l'oeil*, diverting our attention away from the fact (and thus emphasizing) that there is no "inside" and "outside" in these artistic productions. Like the simulated (and post-classical) world of power which they so brilliantly, and painstakingly, portray, what we see on the *outside* of the windows is actually what is happening to us on the inside as we are processed through the designed world of the technological system. And, as if to give a hint that the woman in *Western Motel* is coded by the perpetual motion of the automobile, that the worker in *Office in a Small City* is coded by the logic of bureaucratic industrialism, or that the male figure in *Excursion into Philosophy* is coded by Sartre's logic of the "vacant look," the windows are perfectly transparent, perfectly mediational, and perfectly empty. In Hopper's world, a circular logic of sign and event is at work. Culture is coded by the signs of nature; nature is processed by technique; and *we are coded* by the false appearance of antinomic reciprocities between nature and culture. This means, of course, that Hopper's American landscape understands technique to be much more than machine objects, but a whole system of cultural preparation, a theory of labour as estrangement, and, most of all, a relational power system designed to exclude the human presence.

Two paintings are particularly emblematic of Hopper's searing vision of postmodernism as excremental culture. *High Noon* and *People in the Sun* are grisly and overwhelmingly sad portraits of the deadness of the spirit and radical impoverishment of human vision which has been the achievement of contemporary culture. Here, even nature is menacing (the austere and cold sunlight of *High Noon*), the poses are grotesque (the "people in the sun" of leisure society in their business suits), and there is an overwhelming sense of psychosis within the vacant acts of waiting (for nothing) and looking (to nowhere) of the woman in *High Noon* and the leisured Americans (as victims) of *People in the Sun*. In these two paintings, what is presented in all of its pathos and in all of its "intimations of deprival" is a brilliant vision of technology as degeneration. And, as Jean-Paul Sartre predicted that the contemporary century would culminate in the detritus of the culture of "alterity," Hopper has given us a vision of excremental culture in all of its hysteria. Perhaps what is most unsettling is that Hopper's artistic vision can be so authentically American because, in these scenes of technology as deprivation, we can also recognize that it is *we* who suffer most deeply the "intimations of deprival" of the fully realized technical system. *Real* cultural degeneration, *real* excremental culture for Hopper at least, is the coming to be of a society founded on the equation of technology and freedom. Hopper is the artist of the chilling vision of the *black sun*, in the prophetic sense, the truthsayer of the deadness within American, and thus world, culture which reduces itself to the Nietzschean vision of "a little voluptuousness and a little cynicism."

Theory in Ruins

HABERMAS' COMPROMISE

We present here two theses on the intellectual and political legacy of Jürgen Habermas, each of which alludes to a determinate limitation in his theoretical project, and each of which indicates exactly why Habermas' unhappy turn to the pragmatism of rationalist language philosophy prevents his thought from achieving an adequate understanding of postmodern society which operates now, no longer just under the dark sign of Nietzsche, but, more to the point, under the sign of Bataille's general economy of excess.

1. The first thesis — Habermas' *pragmatic compromise* — has to do with his much-publicized break with the tragic (and, as yet, philosophically unassimilated) tradition of critical theory which received its most eloquent expression in Adorno and Horkheimer's *Dialectic of Enlightenment*. Against the main theses of *Dialectic of Enlightenment* — that the "fully enlightened world radiates disaster triumphant", [1] that "humanity instead of entering a truly human condition is sinking into a new type of barbarism" [2] (the concentration camp on the side of power and oppression; the mediascape on the side of power and seduction); and that (as Horkheimer stated, with resignation, in *Dawn and Decline*) the *petitio principii* of culture today is the movement from lightness to darkness and that "in periods of decline such as the present, the higher truth lies in madness" [3] — Habermas broke ranks and ran for the shelter of the pragmatic compromise culminating in that politically moribund, because theoretically eclipsed, ode to scientific rationality (in linguistics, in politics, in psychology, in

ethics) — *The Theory of Communicative Action*.

In *Dialectic of Enlightenment*, a text which begins by under-mining the authority of scientific rationality by insisting that the "meaning of science has become problematical" — not just because of the convergence of a purely formalist and mathe-maticized science with the "ticket thinking" of technological society, but because positive science is still "mythic fear turned radical" and, as such, operates under the grip of the mythic curse of fatal necessity — Adorno and Horkheimer set out to reflect deeply on the worst that can be thought or imagined: injustice for the powerless as the juridical sign of Western civilization, and the tortured screams of the innocent as the political outcome of positive science's epistemology. [4] The opening words of *Dialectic of Enlightenment* reflect the urgency of Adorno and Horkheimer's genealogy of the entwinement of myth and enlightenment:

> The dilemma that faced us in our work proved to be the first phenomena for investigation: the self-destruction of the Enlightenment. We are wholly convinced — and therein lies our *petitio principii* — that social freedom is inseparable from enlightened thought. Nevertheless, we believe that we have just as clearly recognized that the notion in this very way of thinking. no less than the actual historic forms — the social institutions — with which it is interwoven, already contain the seed of the reversal universally apparent today. If enlightenment does not accomodate reflection on this recidivist ele-ment, then it seals its own fate. If consideration of the destructive aspect of progress is left to its enemies, blindly pragmatized thought loses its transcending quality, and, its relation to truth. In the enigmatic readiness of the technologically educated masses to fall under the sway of any despotism, in its self-destructive affinity to pop-ular paranoia, and in all uncomprehended absurdity, the weakness of the modern theoretical faculty is apparent. [5]

It is our thesis that the lasting legacy of Jürgen Habermas is repre-sentative of the "blindly pragmatized thought" alluded to in this passage. His political legacy has been to work a great reversal and cancellation of the radical insights into the "recidivist elements" in Enlightenment named so accurately in *Dialectic of Enlightenment* — namely, "noontide panic fear" as the popular psychology of the postmodern bourgeoisie; "ticket thinking" as the locus of the conservative mood; "the disembodied yes-men of today as the direct descendants of the irritable apothecaries, the passionate rose-growers, and the political cripples of yesteryear"; communication as "radical isolation"; and identitarianism and equivalence as the cold light of Reason which breaks out in the fascist dawn. [6] In the same way that Peter Sloterdijk traced out in *Kritik der zynischen vernunft* the suppression and reversal of classical *Kynicism* (that radical and popular philosophy from below which refused *all* the symbolic totalities of the Greeks) into its opposite, *cynicism* (truth-telling by contemporary elites accompanied by their denial of the ability to do anything about it), [7] Habermas is the contemporary cynic to the kynicism of *Dialectic of Enlightenment*. While Habermas' philosophical importance has been that of a firebreak, transforming the radical critique of the self-liquidating tendencies of Enlightenment into its opposite — the Kantian-inspired theory of communicative rationality so ridiculed and as a hermeneutics so decisively abandoned in *Dialectic of Enlightenment* — this is not to deny Habermas' lasting legacy as a purely *literary* one. Habermas' pragmatic refusal of the dark lessons of *Dialectic of Enlightenment* is a brilliant, yet grisly, example of the traumatized German mind after the Second World War which, because it could not bear to think directly about the entwinement of reason and irrationalism, (good as parodic of evil, self-destruction and self-preservation as the twin reflexes of the bourgeois mind, or the deep relationship, as reflected upon by Benjamin and Jünger, between technology and fascism) screened out from theory the *irrational* (the problem of evil as diathonic and parodic with the good). As the leading exponent in social theory of the traumatized German mind, Habermas wrote a trauma-theory: a social theorisation which took shelter in the rationalist citadel of the "freely communicating self," in the "ideal speech situation" of rationalized ethics, in the world as a parsed sentence, because it could not bear to stare directly into the dark abyss of enlightenment's dialectic. [8] As Nietzsche anticipated in *The Gay Science*, this tradition of post-catastrophe thought sacrificed truth-telling in the name of self-preservation; it substituted for a genealogy of evil the dead philosophical act of a genealogy of validity-and truth-claims; and, for better or for worse, it blindsided itself to science as a technical practice which, if it does not have any substantive goals, also has no capacity to reflect on its own nihilism.

Now let us be more specific as to the main lines of Habermas' challenge to *Dialectic of Enlightenment* and why we think he is so remarkably silent on the book's key chapter, "The Elements of Anti-Semitism", that haunting analysis of the conflation of reason and fascism where Adorno and Horkheimer locate the decisive moment of reversal and self-liquidation in contemporary culture, and where enlightenment reverses itself and arcs back to it origins in mythic fear. We argue that Habermas has nothing to say about "The Elements of Anti-Semitism" because his thought operates within the limits of a deep compromise-formation which screens out irrationalism in human experience and, by blindsiding itself to the parodic character of the economy of excess, makes it constitutively impossible for him to reflect on fascism as the second nature of enlightenment discourse, and compels him, in the end, to privilege a hyper-rationalist linguistic paradigm and defend technology as species being. All this without any sense of irony, contradiction, or parody whatsoever.

In a major article, "The Entwinement of Myth and Enlightenment: Re-Reading *Dialectic of Enlightenment*", [9] Habermas challenged the movement in the critical theory of society from Marx to Nietzsche, and warned of a possible conjuncture between a "Nietzsche restored by some post-structuralist writers", [10] namely Derrida and Foucault, and the charter members of critical theory, notably Adorno and Horkheimer (though we would also include Benjamin for his reflections on technology and fascism, and Franz Neumann for writing an ideology-critique [11] which paralleled the main lines of "The Culture Industry" in *Dialectic of Enlightenment*). Habermas' challenge is direct. It contests a vision of historical emancipation based on ideology-critique and a defense of the emancipatory potential of Reason against a nihilistic interpretation of culture that works both to undermine all the categories of the Real and to demonstrate the purely parodic quality of the " *grand récits*" in the general economy of excess. Habermas thus raises the decisive question haunting the postmodernism project. Under the sign of Nietzsche, Bataille, Derrida and Foucault, does post-structuralism represent the direct continuation of the tradition of the critical theory of society? Is nihilism, not as a portent of political quietism, but as the only

possible basis of historical emancipation; and the nihilistic interpretation of the parodic quality of contemporary culture, with its
insistence on thinking progress/regression as diathonic to the
contemporary situation, siding with Nietzsche and de Sade as
theorists of decline, the only existent critique of the fate of
modernity?

Habermas' world is that of the old hermeneutic-modernist
theory and aesthetics. The world of the *Either/Or*: either system
or lifeworld; either knowledge *or* human interests; either ideology-
critique of the Marxian kind *or* "totalizing self-referential critique" [12] of the Nietzschean model; either communicative rationality *or* strategic action; either the affirmation of truth and
validity claims, the affirmation of scientific rationality and the
defense of technology as species being *or* "de-differentiation," [13]
Habermas' real nemesis. Like Kant before him, Habermas wants
a legislative (procedural and juridical) model of reason, with *real*
truth and validity claims, which would resist the relational play of
a dead power that fills in all the cracks. In fact, Habermas wants
what *Dialectic of Enlightenment* — with its searing insights into
enlightenment as "mythic fear turned radical", its political
analysis of the anti-semites moved by the drive to project their
own terror onto victims without, its deconstruction of bourgeois
elites trying desperately to escape the myth of fatal necessity by
sacrificing *you and me*, and its underming of the "polarities" of the
Western mind as nothing but the epistemology of incipient
fascism — cannot give him. From Habermas' rationalist perspective, *Dialectic of Enlightenment* falls into a "performative
contradiction."

> If they do not want to give up the goal of an ultimate
> unmasking and carry on their critique, they must
> preserve at least one standard for their explanation
> of the corruption of all reasonable standards. At
> the level of reflexion achieved by Horkheimer and
> Adorno, every attempt to set up a theory was
> bound to lead into an abyss: as a result, they
> abandoned any theoretical approach and practice
> *ad hoc* determinate negation, thereby opposing that
> fusion of reason and power which fills in all the
> cracks. The praxis of negation is what remains of
> the "spirit of. . . unrelenting theory." and this
> praxis is like a vow to turn [14] back even. . . as it

reaches its goals, the demon of merciless progress.

What is really bothering Habermas is what Nietzsche said in *Beyond Good and Evil* about the fallacyof the "either/or":

> Indeed, what forces us to suppose that there is an essential opposition of true and false. Is it not sufficient to assume degrees of apparentness, and, as it were, lighter and darker shadows and shades of appearance — *indifferent values* to use the language of the painters? Why couldn't the world that concerns us be a *fiction*? And if somebody asks, but to a fiction there surely belongs an author? Couldn't one answer be simply: why doesn't this *belongs* perhaps belong to the ficiton too? By now is one not permitted to be a bit ironic about the subject no less than about the predicate and object? Shouldn't the philosopher be permitted to rise above faith in grammar? [15]

Or, as Adorno and Horkheimer argue in one of the concluding theses of *Dialectic of Enlightenment*:

> What seems intolerable is any attempt to break away from the Either/Or, to overcome mistrust for the abstract principle and infallibility without doctrine. [16]

After Nietzsche, *Dialectic of Enlightenment* rises above "faith in grammar" and does so as a general discourse on the nihilism within the logic of Western civilization. This is one intellectual meditation which is *against forgetting* and *for remembrance*. Adorno and Horkeimer refuse to close the wound of Western consciousness by imposing the hyper-rationalist logic of the either/or as a way of suppressing historical remembrance; they insist on "discarding the last vestiges of innocence in regard to the tendencies and habits of the age." If, in the end, they privilege the play of *indifferent values*, this is philosophy that is at the height of its times because the authors of *Dialectic of Enlightenment* refuse to "blink" before the dark abyss within and without. More than an academic text intent on dissolving the world of "communicating subjects" into the monadology of parsing sentences, *Dialectic of Enlightenment* is a poem written in the shadows of the concentration camp. And if this book assumes an importance for the postmodern condition, it is for its refusal of Nietzsche's retreat into the silence of madness or the consolation of false hope. Adorno and Horkheimer wrote a text for the next generation, for the "imaginary witness":

> It is not the portrayal of reality as hell on earth but the slick challenge to break out of it that is suspect. If there is anyone today to whom we can pass the responsibilities for this message, we bequeath it not to the "masses", and not to the individual (who is powerless), but to an imaginary witness — lest it perish with us. [17]

2. The second thesis — *Habermas outflanked* — has to do with a major theoretical limitation, indeed fatal flaw, in Habermas' resolutely sociological interpretation of the ultramodern world of communicative action. It is our position that because of Habermas' ethical compromise on the question of the grammatical attitude of the "either/or", denial of the self-liquidation of the foundational polarities of Western culture into an indifferent play of floating signifiers, his pragmatism blindsides him to the self-destructive tendencies, the mythic necessity of excess, in the postmodern scene. Habermas has managed to miss *the big event* in late bourgeois society.

He blinked at the flipping over of the old hermeneutical (and dualistic) world of System and Lifeworld (the aesthetic antinomies of modernism) into the postmodern irreality of a *structural paradigm*: a structural paradigm driven from within by the conflation of the language of genetic biology and cybernetic technology; structured by the public (and nihilistic) morality of instrumental activism; coded by the patterning of "institutionalized individuals" as vacant nodes on a relational (and indifferent) power grid in which power speaks in the structural languages of exteriorization, not rationalization; signification, not normalization; sign, not norm; simulation, not institutionalization; and semiurgy, not socialization. Habermas' famous 'blink' at the name of Nietzsche and the hyperreality of a decentered culture unified only by the media massaging the missing matter of the social dooms his thought to an intellectual trajectory which misses in its entirety the *key* tendency of postmodern existence: the death of the social and the triumph of an empty (signifying) culture. In the twilight time of the twentieth century, Habermas clings, as he does in *The Theory of Communicative Action,* [18] to the modernist antinomies of system *and* lifeworld, reason *and* rationalization, but only to confirm the accuracy of Nietzsche's prophecy that pragmatism is the "compromise which confirms." Outside the "infallibility" of theoretical doctrines, the postmodern scene is marked by *the violent transformation of system into lifeworld; and the implosion of reason into rationalization.* For the "structural paradigm" [19] as the locus of the postmodern condition implies the end of the panoptic space of difference and the creation of an hallucinogenic network of delocalized, dehistoricized, and deterritorialized power. The 'lifeworld' has been broken into by the space invaders of the relational power-system, and, to the same extent, 'reason' has been coded (tattooed) from within by the body invaders of cosmetic culture.

Ironically, it is both Nietzsche's insistence on thinking through the impossible tension between the "revenge-seeking will" and "time's it was" and Adorno and Horkheimer's tragic meditation on the entwinement of myth and enlightenment (as the locus of the general economy of excess and self-liquidation) that makes their theoretical project fully relevant to an understanding of late twentieth-century experience. These may be theorists who are (in Habermas' terms) the "dark writers of the bourgeoisie" but, if so, this only means that Nietzsche, Adorno, and Horkheimer including also Bataille, Artaud, and Foucault, belong to a longer tradition of thought, which, breaking with "faith in grammar", insists on meditating anew on the 'tremendous event' which *is* contemporary experience. And that is nothing less than Nietzsche's 'vertigo':

> What did we do when we unchained this earth
> from its sun? Whither is it moving now? Whither
> are we moving now? Away from all suns? Are we
> not plunging continually? Backward, sideward,
> foreward, in all directions? Is there any up or down
> left? Are we not straying as through an infinite
> nothing? Do we not feel the breath of empty
> space? [20]

But, against Nietzsche's concept of the will or against Bataille's concept of sovereignty, there is always Habermas' reflection (with and against Foucault) that shows exactly how, in forgetting the vertigo of the 'tremendous event', Habermas has outflanked himself:

> The other economy of bodies and pleasures of which we can in the meantime only dream — with Bataille — would not again be an economy of power but a postmodern theory which could render account of the standards of critique which implicitly have always been used. Until then the resistance can take its motive but not its justification from the signals of body language, from the non-verbalized language of the tortured body that refuses to be sublimated into discourse. [21]

In the background, there is only the sound of Foucault murmuring that in the age of 'vertigo', plunging in empty space, the transgression of the body is not in the order of a rationalist cut or of a "standard of critique", but the throwing of the dice across a universe of indifferent values. It is because of the terrible knowledge of "time's it was" that there appears the 'tortured body'; in fact, the incarceration of the tortured body within the will to power of "standards of critique" is the sure and certain sign of Nietzsche's vertigo. Habermas' peaceable kingdom of reason is just another reenactment of the "noise of the gravediggers", but, this time, working in reverse form, to block out the smell of decompositon.

ADORNO'S HUSSERL

There is no escaping the Nietzschean pronouncements of Adorno's *Against Epistemology*, a text written just after Adorno's flight from the fascists and which, while specifically focussed on a series of theoretical refusals of Husserl and phenomenological antinomies, has a more urgent historical importance as a precursor of the postmodernist critique of representation. *Against Epistemology* is particularly appropriate now, when under the pressure of a poststructuralist theorisation which is revealed to be an exact description of the internal logic of advanced capitalist society as it operates under the structural law of value, philosophy everywhere — and nowhere more desperately so than in contemporary French thought in the post-Foucauldian era — runs for the conservative cover of the transcendental subjectivity of the phenomenological antinomies once again. The injunction to reread Adorno is, therefore, also a recommendation to meditate anew the political regression implicit to the phenomenological antinomies, and follow through the opening made by *Against Epistemology* to the other side of Nietzsche's *The Will to Power*. This is not just the nihilistic side of the critique of the will to power as a "perspectival appearance", but the dark side of *The Will to Power*, the often unread, last half of a text where the *thinking subject* is disclosed as an ideological expression of the convergence of power and knowledge. And here artistic consciousness of the body as a "solar system" *and* a torture chamber is theorised as one possibility beyond the stasis of the postmodern moment.

Adorno's refusals of the phenomenological antinomies

(eloquently developed in Husserl's *Cartesian Meditations, Logical Investigations,* and *Formal and Transcendental Logic*) are explicit, and identifiable as:

• a *political* refusal of the philosophy of origins which, taking place under the sign of epistemology, reduces existence to the "aporias of transcendental subjectivity." For Adorno, epistemology — which always runs to the polarities of "replica realism" and "dogmatic idealism" — represents an *ideological* regression to the logic of absolute finality (where fascism itself is only a nostalgic execution of the lordship of the spirit), and an *ontological* reduction to Nietzsche's museum of "concept mummies." Here, the *Cartesian Meditations* is itself symptomatic of the sense of dread which pervades the bourgeois sensibility because, in its "identity of the spirit with itself and the subsequent synthetic unity of apperception," it projects itself compulsively and dogmatically. As Adorno argues, epistemology runs to the "fetishism of knowledge," since in its quest for the "pure realization of the principle of identity through seamless reduction to subjective immanence, (epistemology) turns, despite itself, into the medium of non-identity."

• an *ethical* refusal of the immanently ideological reduction inherent in the scienticization of philosophy. Before Foucault's theorisation of the entwinenment of power and knowledge, Adorno grasped the central political compromise inherent in the project of phenomenology that takes as its immediate categories the conservative and regressive ideals of science. Against the phenomenological reduction of knowledge to the reifying processes of science, Adorno insisted that *reification* ("One more step and the metaphysics of absolute spirit could be called the inconsistent spirit") and *irrationalism* ("irrationalism clings inalienably to European rationalism") are the dark aporias of logical absolutism.

• a *civilizational* critique of phenomenology as nothing more than bourgeois thought in its last "dissociated, fragmentary determinations posited one after the other and (resigned) to the mere reproduction of what is" and Husserl's doctrine of ideas as emblematic of the "system in ruins."

> The exhibition spaces of Husserlian demonstrations are always removed from the praxis of society. As a melancholy memorial, their inventory takes on a *paltry* aura of significance which Husserl interprets

as essential. The obsolete expression 'inventory' belongs to the Secessionistic inventory of visions, streams of lived experience, and fulfillment, just as the upright piano belongs to the Isle of the Dead. Optical illusion and movable scenery meet in Husserl's texts.

Long before Lacan's insight concerning *misrecognition* as the basis of the fictive unity of the bourgeois ego, Adorno came to the same conclusion, at the level of epistemology whereby the phenomenological antinomies are the "mirror-stage" of the equally fictional unity of the bourgeois mind. Lancan's *misrecognition* is Husserl's *bracketing* of experience:

> Like the photographer of old, the phenomenologist wraps himself with the black veil of his 'attitude,' implores the object to hold still and unchanging and ultimately realizes passively and without spontaneity of the knowing subject, family portraits of the sort that mother 'who glances lovingly at her little flock.' Just as in photography the *camera obscura* and the recorded pictorial object belong together so in phenomenology do the immanence of consciousness and naive realism.

This is to theorise, then, that "phenomenology revolves itself": "Husserlian over-subjectivity also means under-subjectivity"; Eliatic Metaphysics is "identical with the nothingness which Eliatics disavow"; the thinking subject is colonized from within and without by the play of a disembodied power; and the progressive features of Husserl's philosophy (thought 'moving beyond itself') turns regressive and programmatic as soon as Husserl "presents the aporias as positive determinations and hypostatizes the subjective phase as immanence to consciousness as well as the essentiality of the fact-free concept." And so epistemology is the will to power masquerading as knowledge in the world as a "peep show stage", a "Panopticum Waxworks", holding still for the phenomenologist as a "sparkling collection of well-founded noematic 'senses', aloof and odd, like pictures in a gallery." Phenomenology is fictitious because it does not know whether to take "the internal as the external or vice-versa."

In *Against Epistemology*, Adorno might insist anew that "all reification is a forgetting", but then he could already anticipate the eventual recycling of Husserl and the phenomenological antinomies as the key epistemological tendency for bourgeois thought at the most radical moment of the contemporary crisis. In its privileging of the fictional unity of the thinking subject, in its re-presentation of actual social antinomies as logically ante-cedent, in its aporias of transcendental experience, phenome-nology is an ideology of resignation, of *misrecognition* as the central epistemological formulation of late bourgeois thought. For Adorno, phenomenology is not untruth, but something much worse. *It is truth in untruth.* But like Marx's double return of history (once as tragedy and then as burlesque), signs of the regeneration of phenomenology as a constitutive response to the unbearable pressures of the postmodernist negation of the found-ational *récits* have this comic quality:

> Dread stamps the ideal of Husserlian philosophy as one of absolute security, on the model of private property. Its reductions aim at the secure: viz. the immanence to consciousness of lived experiences whose title deeds the philosophical self-conscious-ness to which they 'belong' should possess securely from the grasp of any force; and essences which, free from all factical existence, defy vexation from factical existence.... Security is left as an ultimate and lonely fetish like the number one million on a long deflated bank note. More overtly than any-where else the late bourgeois quality of pheno-menology becomes evident.

In the fin-de-millenium the reappearance of phenomenology as the newest alternative to the poststructuralist legacy of Foucault, Barthes, Irigaray, and Derrida has a real political significance. It is an early warning system that the bourgeois mind, under the double impact of the crisis without (of political economy) and of the crisis within (of liquidated identity) is in flight once more to the fictional security of the 'bracketed' world of the pheno-menological antinomies. Like Italo Calvino's *CosmicComics*, the bourgeois mind reconfirms its own revocation in the 'distorted figure of dread' which goes by the name of the 'absolute security' of phenomenology. The 'thinking subject' and the concept museum of the 'lifeworld' are last outbursts of modernist nostalgia before the relational play of disembodied power and sliding bodies in hyperspace. Epistemology has become the 'blink' of Nietzsche's last man.

TELEVISION AND
THE TRIUMPH OF CULTURE

Mediascape

This essay is about what the West German film director, Wim Wenders, has described in *Chambre 666* as the "anti-matter of cinema" — television. We will present, and defend, a theoretical strategy for interpreting television as the Real World — the excremental vision *par excellence* — of a postmodern culture, society and economy in radical decline. In much the same way that video art teases to the surface the inner semiurgical laws of motion of television as simulacrum, this essay examines television for what it really is — a mediascape! It's TV then, not just as a technical object which we can hold apart from ourselves, but as a full technical ensemble, a social apparatus, which implodes into society as the emblematic cultural form of a relational power, which works as a simulacrum of electronic images recomposing everything into the semiurgical world of advertising and power, which links a processed world based on the exteriorisation of the senses with the interiorisation of simulated desire in the form of programmed need-dispositions, and which is just that point where Nietzsche's prophetic vision of twentieth-century experience as a "hospital room" finds its moment of truth in the fact that when technique *is* us, when TV is the real world of postmodernism, then the horizon finally closes and freedom becomes synonymous with the deepest deprivals of the fully realized technological society.

But, of course, if we can speak now of power and TV, this just might mean, as Foucault has intimated, that the disappearing locus of power has probably already slipped away from TV as the real world, and taken up residence now in that digital paradise, that perfectly postmodern world, of the computer.

TV or Not TV

We would like, then, to examine three theses concerning television, the death of society, and the triuimph of an empty, signifying culture. Specifically, we begin with two great refusals of conventional interpretations of television: a refusal of the *positivist subordination* of television to a representational logic (to TV as a mirror of society); and a refusal of the *Marxian subordination* of television to a cultural reflex of the commodity-form (to TV as an electronic reproduction of ideological interests). Against this double-subordination of TV to a reflex of society or ideology (against what amounts to a *modernist* reduction of television to a xerox copy of culture, society and economy), we want to argue just the opposite.

TV is, in a very literal sense, the real world, not of modern but of *postmodern* culture, society and economy — of society typified by the dynamic momentum of the spirit of technicisme triumphant and of real popular culture driven onwards by the ecstacy and decay of the obscene spectacle — and that everything which escapes the real world of TV, everything which is not videated as its identity-principle, everything which is not processed through TV as the technical apparatus of relational power *par excellence*, is peripheral to the main tendencies of the contemporary century.

In postmodernist culture, it's not TV as a mirror of society, but just the reverse: *it's society as a mirror of television*. And it's not TV as a reflex of the commodity-form, but the commodity-form in its most advanced, and exhausted, expression living finally (as Marx prophecied) as a pure image-system, as a spectral television image. As the wall posters everywhere around Montréal these days tell us, the major philosophical question is: *TV or Not TV*. Or, if you prefer a small variation, it's TV or the Museum.

Indeed, there was a report recently released by the *West German Ministry of Internal Affairs* on the subject of the "effects of new information and communication techniques on the arts and culture" [11] which said without any sense of irony:

According to experts, museums and galleries will not be threatened by any proliferation of television programs and the increasing spread of new information and communication techniques. They may even profit from this, because the museum, with its "still" pictures and exhibits, will become even more attractive as a relief from television. Museums have a so-called escape-function because they offer a refuge from an increasingly technical world. Television and the museums will not compete with each other in the future; on the contrary, they complement each other. [2]

Television now is the real world of a postmodern culture whose *ideology* is entertainment and the society of the obscene spectacle; [4] whose *culture* is driven onwards by the universalization of the commodity-form; whose politics gravitate around the *life-style issues* of the new middle class; whose major form of *social cohesion* is provided by the pseudo-solidarities (pseudo-mediations) of electronic television images (not Durkheim's "collective representations", but Sartre's "serial culture"); whose *public* is the dark, silent mass of viewers who, as Jean Baudrillard says, are never permitted to speak and a media elite which is allowed to speak "but which has nothing to say"; [5] and where that which is bought and sold in a society where class has disappeared into mass and mass has dissolved into the new black hole of the "blip" is something purely psychological: *empty, abstract quanta of audience attention*, the rise and fall of which is measured incessantly by overnight statistical polling.

But why go to the theorists? TV advertisers and programmers are much better. Speaking about *Miami Vice*, the head of series programming at NBC said recently in an interview in the *New York Times*: "There's a buzz out there about the show" ('out there' is the dense, black shadow of that missing social matter — the audience). "In the way it's shot, where it's shot, the kind of people it has, *Miami Vice* conveys a certain dreamlike quality, yet a certain humanity." Michael Mann, the producer of the show, is much more direct: "The secret of its success. No earth tones. We want to feel electric, and whenever we can we use pastels that vibrate."

A recent ad in *Variety* magazine, the bible of TV advertisers, said it all. It's an ad for TV Brazil and it shows a picture of the world with dots everywhere on it, from India to Australia to Eastern Europe and North America, everywhere, in fact, where TV Brazil productions are shown. The caption is about McLuhan and it says simply: "Maybe *this* is what he meant by the global village?"

Three Theses

Our general theorisation is, therefore, that TV is the real world of postmodern culture which has *entertainment* as its ideology, the *spectacle* as the emblematic sign of the commodity-form, *lifestyle advertising* as its popular psychology, pure, empty *seriality* as the bond which unites the simulacrum of the audience, *electronic images* as its most dynamic, and only, form of social cohesion, *elite media politics* as its ideological formula, the buying and selling of *abstracted attention* as the locus of its marketplace rationale, *cynicism* as its dominant cultural sign, and the diffusion of a *network of relational power* as its real product.

Our *specific* theorisations about TV as the real world of postmodernism take the form of three key theses:

Thesis 1: TV as Serial Culture

Television is the emblematic cultural expression of what Jean-Paul Sartre has described as "serial culture". The specific context for Sartre's description of "serial culture" is an extended passage in *The Critique of Dialectical Reason* in which he reflects on the philosophical implications of mass media generally, and on radio broadcasting specifically. [6] Sartre's media analysis is crucial because it represents the beginning of a serious existential critique of the media, from radio to television, and because in his highly nuanced discussion of radio broadcasting Sartre provides some entirely insightful, although grisly, clues as to the fate of society under the sign of the mediascape. For Sartre, the pervasive effect of mass media, and of radio broadcasting specifically, was to impose *serial structures* on the population. Sartre can say that the voice is "vertiginous" for everyone just because the mass media produce "seriality" as their cultural form. [7] And what's "serial culture" for Sartre? It's a "mode of being", Sartre says, "beings outside themselves in the passive unity of the object" — [8] which has:

- "absence" as the mode of connection between

audience members
- "alterity" or "exterior separation" as its negative principle of unity
- "impotence" as the political bond of the (media) market
- the destruction of "reciprocity" as its aim
- the reduction of the audience to the passive unity of the "practico-inert" (inertia) as its result
- and the "three moment" dialectic: triumph (when you know that you're smarter than the media elite); "impotent indignation" (When you realize that the audience is never permitted to speak, while the media elite are allowed to speak but have nothing to say); and fascination (as you study your entrapment as Other in the serial unity of the TV audience, which is the "pure, abstract formula" of the mass media today). [9]

The TV audience is Sartre's serial culture *par excellence*. The audience is constituted on the basis of "its relation to the object and its reaction to it"; the audience is nothing more than a "serial unity" ("beings outside themselves in the passive unity of the object"); membership in the TV audience is always only on the basis of "alterity" or "exterior separation"; impotence of the "three moment" dialectic is the iron law of the hierarchical power of television; "abstract sociality" is the false sociality of a TV audience which as an empty, serial unity is experienced as a negative totality; the image is "vertiginous" for everyone; and the overall cultural effect of television is to do exactly what Sartre prophecied:

> The practico-inert object (that's TV) not only produces a unity of individuals outside themselves in inorganic matter, but it also determines their isolation and, insofar as they're separate, assures communication through alterity. [10]

In just the same way that the gigantic red star of the supernova burns most brilliantly when it is already most exhausted and imploding towards that dark density of a new black hole, TV today can be so hyper-spectacular and so desperate in its visual effects because, as Sartre has hinted, its real existence is "inertia" and it is always already on the decline towards the realm of the "practico-inert". What's TV then? It's Sartre's "serial culture" in electronic form, from the "viewer as absence" and "alterity" as TV's basic principle (McLuhan's "exteriorisation" of the central nervous system) to the TV audience as that "serial unity" or "negative totality", the truth of whose existence as *pure inertia* (Sartre's being in the *mud* of the practico-inert) can be caught if you glance between the laser canons of colour TV as they blast you and catch the black patches, the dead darkness to infinity, which is the pure inertial state which television struggles so desperately to hide. And that darkness to infinity between the hysterical explosions of the laser beam? That's Sartre's "serial culture" as the sign of contemporary society: just when the image becomes "vertiginous" for everyone; when the viewer is reduced to "absence"; and when vacant and grisly "alterity" is the only bond that unites that negative totality — the "audience".

Thesis 2: Television as a Postmodern Technology

Television, just because it's an emblematic expression of Sartre's "serial culture" in electronic form, is also a perfect model of the processed world of postmodern technology. And why not? TV exists, in fact, just at that rupture-point in human history between the decline of the now-passé age of sociology and the upsurge of the new world of communications (just between the eclipse of normalized society and the emergence of radical semiurgy as the language of the "structural" society). TV is at the border-line of a great paradigm-shift between the "death of society" (modernism with its representational logic) and the "triumph of an empty, signifying culture" (the "structural paradigm" of postmodernism). In the Real World of television, it's:

- Sign *not* Norm
- Signification *not* Socialisation [11]
- Exteriorisation of the Mind (McLuhan's processed world) *not* (Weber's) Reification
- (Baudrillard's) "simulacrum" *not* institutional discourse
- Radical semiurgy *not* (Foucault's) Normalization
- Simulation *not* Rationalisation
- An empire of voyeurs held together by up-scale titillation effects (from the valorisation of corpses to the crisis jolts of bad news and more bad news)

and blasted by the explosions of the laser beam
into the pulverized state of Sartre's "serial beings"
and *not* the old and boring "structure of roles" held
together by the "internalization of need-dispositions".

- Power as seduction *not* (primarly) power as coercion
- Videation not institutionalisation
- Not society (that's disappeared and who cares) but
  the triumph of the culture of signification

If TV is the processed world triumphant, this just means that it
functions to transform the old world of society under the sign of
the *ideology of technicisme*. By technicisme we mean that ideology,
dominant in contemporary consumer culture, which holds (as
William Leiss has noted) to the historical inevitability and ethical
desirability of the technical mastery of social and non-social
nature. The outstanding fact about the TV "network", viewed as
one dynamic expression of the spreading outwards of the fully
realized technological society, is that it screens off any sense of
technology as *deprival*. Like a *trompe l'oeil*, television functions as
"spectacle" to divert the eye from the radical impoverishment of
life in technological society. Indeed, television screens off any
sense of technology as deprival by means of three strategic
colonizations, or subversions, of the old world of society.

1. The Subversion of Sociality: TV functions by substituting the
negative totality of the audience with its pseudo-mediations by
electronic images for genuine sociality,and for the possibility of
authentic human solidarities. It's electronic communication as
the anti-matter of the social! Indeed, who can escape now being
constituted by the coercive rhetoric of TV and by its nomination
of fictional audiences. We are either rhetorically defined North
Americans as we are *technocratically* composed as an audience by
the self-announced "electronic bridge" of the TV networks; or
we are the electronically constituted audience of Nietzsche's
"last men" who just want their consumer comforts and blink as
we celebrate the breakdown of American institutions. In *St.
Elsewhere*, everything is held together by hi-tech and the joke:
nurses kill doctors; the medical staff resent their patients for
dying; and patients are forced to console doctors and nurses alike
in their distress over the inability of medical technology to

overcome mortality. In *Dynasty*, it is the object-consciousness and dream-like state of the cynical culture of advanced capitalism itself which is celebrated. And, in *Family Feud*, we celebrate normativity or statistical polling ("survey says"): the very instruments for the measurement of that missing social matter in the new universe of electronic communications — the audience — which exists anyway in the TV universe as a dark and unknown nebula.

The TV audience may be, today, the most pervasive type of social community, but if this is so then it is a very special type of community: an *anti-community* or a *social anti-matter* — electronically composed, rhetorically constituted, an electronic mall which privileges the psychological position of the voyeur (a society of the disembodied eye) and the cultural position of *us* as a tourists in the society of the spectacle.

2. The Psychological Subversion: In the real world of television, technology is perfectly interiorized: it comes *within* the self. There is now such a phenomenon as the TV *self*, and it builds directly on Sartre's sense of "serial being". The TV self is not just a pair of flashing eyeballs existing in Andy Warhol's languid and hypercynical state of "bored but hyper." The TV self is the electronic individual *par excellence* who gets everything there is to get from the simulacrum of the media: a market-identity as a consumer in the society of the spectacle; a galaxy of hyperfibrillated moods (the poles of ressentiment and manic buoyancy are the psychological horizon of the TV family); traumatized serial being (television blasts away everything which cannot be reduced to the technological limitations of "good visuals" or, as Sartre has said, to "otherness"). Just like in David Cronenberg's classic film, *Videodrone*, television functions by implanting a simulated, electronically monitored, and technocratically controlled identity in the flesh. Television technology makes the decisive connection between the simulacrum and biology by creating a social nerve connection between spectacular visuals, the news as crisis interventions (image-fibrillation) and the psychological mood of its rhetorically constituted audience. TV colonizes individual psychology best by being a "mood setter".

3. The Technological Colonization: The outstanding fact about TV as the real world is that it is a perfect, even privileged, model of how human experience in the twentieth-century is actually transformed to fit the instrumental imperatives of technological society. Marx might have had his "factory" as a social laboratory for studying the exploitation of "abstract labour"; Hobbes might have written with the ping-pong universe of classical, Newtonian physics in mind (in the old world of modernist physics it's all action-reaction with things only causally related at a distance); but we have television as a privileged model of how we are reworked by the technological sensorium as it implodes the space and time of lived human experience to the electronic poles of the "screen and the network" (Baudrillard). Television is the real experience of the ideology and culture of *technicisme*.

1. The dominant *cultural formation* is the psychological voyeur and the audience linked together by images created by media elites, but this only in the form of electronic stimuli formulated in response to the incessant polling of the dark nebula of that missing social matter — the TV audience.

2. *Hyper-simulation* is the (disappearing) essence of technically-mediated experience: staged communications, fabricated events, packaged audiences held hostage to the big trend line of *crisis moods* induced by media elites for an audience which does not exist in any *social* form, but only in the abstract form of digital blips on overnight rating simulacrums.

3. The *language of signification* and its surrealistic reversals is the basic codex of the real world of television culture. Cars *are* horses; computers *are* galaxies, tombstones or heartbeats; beer *is* friendship. This is just to say though that Barthes' theorisation of the *crossing* of the syntagm of metaphor and metonymy as the grammatical attitude of postmodern culture is now the standard language of television

4. TV is *information society* to the hyper, just though where information means the liquidation of the social, the exterminism of memory (in the sense of human remembrance as aesthetic judgement), and the substitution of the simulacrum of a deterritorialized and dehistoricized image-system for actual historical contexts.

What is the perfect example of television's technological colonisation of the space of the social imaginary? It is that wonderful channel on Montréal television which consists of a screen split among 17 images, constantly flickering with dialogue fading in and out, and with the only thematic mediation consisting of a voice-over across the galaxy of disappearing images. That split-screen with its disembodied voice and its pulsating, flickering images *is* the emblematic sign of contemporary (signifying) culture. It is also the social space of serial being in a perfectly serialized culture: background radiation the presence of which only indicates the disappearance of the old world of (normative and representational) society into the new universe of (semi-urgical and relational) communications.

Thesis 3: Entertainment as the Dominant Ideology of TV Culture

Television is the *consumption* machine of late capitalism in the twentieth-century which parallels the *production* machine of primitive capitalism in the seventeenth-century. Television functions as *the* simulacrum of consumption in three major ways:

1. In *The Society of the Spectacle*, Guy Debord remarked that the "spectacle is capital to such a degree of accumulation that it becomes an image." [12]   That's TV: it is the break-point where capital in its final and most advanced form as a spectral image begins to disappear into itself and becomes that which it always was: an empty and nihilistic sign-system of pure mediation and pure exchange which, having no energy of its own, adopts a scorched earth policy towards the missing social matter of society. Like a gigantic funeral pyre, capital, in its present and most exhausted expression as an image, can shine so brilliantly because it sucks in like oxygen any living element in culture, society or economy: from the ingression of the primitive energy of early rock n' roll' into Japanese car commercials, and the psychological detritus of anal titillation in jean advertisements to Diana Ross' simulated orgasm in a field of muscle (which is anyway just the American version of Carol Pope's (*Rough Trade*) simulated crotch-play in *High School Confidential* that, in the proper Canadian way, plays at the edge of exhibitionism and seduction).

2. Entertainment is the *ideolect* of television as a consumption

machine. What is the essence of entertainment or promotional culture? It is just this: the "serial unity" of vicarious otherness which, Sartre predicted, would be the essential cultural text of society in radical decline.

In a recent debate on the state of television, published by *Harper's* magazine, (and which begins with the wonderful lines: "Disparaging television has long been a favorite national pastime — second only in popularity to watching it"), [13] Rick Du Brow, television editor of the *Los Angeles Herald Examiner*, said that TV, which has always been more of a "social force" than an art form, is "part of the natural flow of life." [14]

> When you go to the theater, or to a movie, something is presented *to* you by the creator. But in television there's a very important creator who isn't critical to the other forms — the viewer. . . With the vast number of buttons he can press at home, the TV viewer (Sartre's "absence") creates his own program schedule — a spectacle that reflects his private tastes and personal history. . . Today, each viewer can create his own TV life. [15]

Du Brow's "creator" — the "viewer creating his own TV life" — is something like Marshall McLuhan's wired heads as the circuit egos of the processed world of electronic technology. In McLuhan's terms, life in the simulacrum of the mediascape consists of a big reversal: the simulacrum of the image-system goes inside; consciousness is ablated. In the sightscape of television, just like before it in the soundscape of radio, the media function as a gigantic (and exteriorised) electronic nervous system, amplifying technologically our every sense, and playing sensory functions back to us in the processed form of *mutant* images and sounds. TV life? That's television as a mutant society: the mediascape playing back to us our *own* distress as a simulated and hyperreal sign of life.

And why not? At the end of his life, Michel Foucault finally admitted that power functions today, not under the obsolescent signs of death, transgression, confessionality and the *saeculum* of blood, but under the sign of life. For Foucault, power could be most seductive just when it spoke in the name of life, just when it was most therapeutic and not confessional. Following Foucault, we would just add that power in the new age of the mediascape is most seductive, and thus most dangerous, when it speaks in the name of life to the hyper — TV life. And television is most grisly in its colonisation of individual consciousness, most untheorised as a vast system of relational power, and most fascinating as the emblematic form of the death of society and the triumph of signifying culture just when it is most *entertaining*. And it is most entertaining when it is a vast electronic simulation, a sensory play-back organon, of *mood*: mood politics, mood news, mood drama, and even, if we take seriously the "happy-time announcers" of Los Angeles TV, *mood weather*. But, then, why be surprised? Heidegger always said that "mood" would be the locus of culture at the end of history, tracing a great ellipsis of decline, disintegration, and disaccumulation *par excellence*. TV life? That's the ideolect of entertainment as a great simulacrum of "mood": sometimes of the radically oscillating moods of that great *absence*, the viewer, which is programmed now to move between the poles of "panic anxiety" and "manic optimisim"; and always of the herd moods of that equally great electronic *fiction*, the audience.

3. *TV functions as a consumption machine (most of all) because it is a lifestyle medium*. In a superb article in a recent issue of *The Atlantic*, James Atlas argued the case that TV advertisers are no longer so concerned with the now-passé world of demographics (that's the ideolect of the social), but are instead intent on shaping advertising to fit the size of target VAL's. [16] And what are VAL's but the identification of target audiences by "values and lifestyles": the "super-achievers" (call them "yuppies" now, but Talcott Parsons described them long ago as "institutional liberals" — upscale technocrats with a minimal social self and a maximal consumer self who define freedom within the limits of mass organizations); the "belongers": the old class of middle North Americans who value, most of all in nostalgic form, the social qualities of friendship and community and at whom the fellowship hype of beer commercials is directed; and the new, rising class of middle Americans who value the friendship of the herd most of all, and at whom are targeted the belongingness hype of commercials for the *Pepsi Generation* or the promotional hype, under the sign of altruism, of *Live Aid* or *We are the World*; or, finally, the "emulators": what David Riesmann used to call "other-directed personalities": bewildered and in the absence of their own sense of self-identity, hyper-sensitive to the big trend lines of contemporary culture as defined by media elites.

The conclusion which might be derived from VAL's research, or from Arnold Mitchell's book, *The Nine American Lifestyles*, is that class society has now dissappeared into mass society, and that mass society has dissolved into the TV blip. The notion of the serial self in electronic society as a TV blip, a digital neuron floating somewhere in the bigger circuitry of the screen and the network may appear vacuous, but that is only because that's exactly what the TV blip with a lifestyle is, and has to be, in the new relationship between television and the economic system. The political economy of TV has such a perfect circularity about it that its serial movement could not sustain anything more substantive, and anything less instrumentalist in the consumerist sense, than the '80s self as a blip with a lifestyle. From the viewpoint of an image-hungry audience, the product of television is, and obviously so, the spectacle of TV as a simulacrum of lifestyles. But from the perspective of TV advertisers and media programmers, the *real* product of television is the audience. So, what is TV? Is it the manipulation of society by a media elite using the spectacle as a "free lunch" to expand the depth and pace of universal commodity-exchange in the market place? Or is it the manipulation of the media elite by the audience, that electronic congerie of TV blips with nine lifestyles, using the bait of their own consumer gullibility as a lure to get what they want most: free and unfettered access to the open skies of serial culture? What's TV: *The Will to Power* or *Capital*? The high commodity society of neo-technical capitalism or Nietzsche's culture of nihilism? *Or is TV both?* "The spectacle to such a degree that it becomes an image" *and* a perfectly cynical exchange between media programmers operating under the economic imperative to generate the biggest possible audience of TV blips at the lowest possible price for sale to advertisers at the highest possible rate of profit; and an electronically composed public of serial beings which, smelling the funeral pyre of excremental culture all around it, decides of its own unfettered volition to celebrate its own exterminism by throwing its energies, where attention is the oxygen of TV life, to the black hole of television?

TV or Not TV? Well, you just have to listen to the stampeding of feet and the rustling of the flashing eyeballs as the TV blips, who constitute the growing majority of world culture, are worked over by the exploding laser beams to know the answer. And TV life? Well, that's technology now as a simulacrum of disease.

Postmodern America in Ruins

ARE WE HAVING FUN YET?

Eric Fischl's paintings perfectly capture the fun mood of America in ruins. If Fischl's artistic productions have attracted such widespread media attention (*Vogue* magazine's "artist to watch"; major features in *Vanity Fair* and *German Playboy*; even a philosophical essay by Arthur Danto in the *New Republic*), it's because he so brilliantly works the terrain of high emotional realism for a cynical culture. In *Dialectic of Enlightenment*, Adorno and Horkheimer argued that the "triumph of advertising in the culture industry is that consumers feel compelled to buy and use its products even though they see through them." [1] In the same way, the artistic imagination of Eric Fischl has been absorbed so quickly because he "sees through" the ruined surfaces and shattered psychology of the American Republic in its postmodern moment of exhaustion.

It is, however, the particular triumph of the American Republic that this excessive vision of self-liquidation is also a fun advertisement for the power and seduction of that culture. Fischl's vision of excess matches perfectly the popular mood of an American (and thus world) culture on its downside, where the privileged psychological position is that of voyeur (*Birthday Boy*); the dominant social sensibility is 'viciousness for fun' (*A Woman Possessed*); where the religion of America is America (*Christian Retreat*); where there's sex without the passage of bodily fluids (*Bad Boy*); and where, if the ruins within are without expectation of relief (*The Visitor*), the ruins without is television, the dominant social code of a 'solar anus' culture (*Inside Out*). Fischl's artistic

Eric Fischl, *Bad Boy*

production is the narcissistic nihilism of Nietzsche's society of the "last man": a mouth (*Barbecue*); a masturbating hand (*Sleepwalker*); a distended ear (*The Power of Rock n' Roll* which consists of a nude child clothed only with a Sony Walkman in a suburban living-room); and a sex organ (from the bored sodomy of *Inside Out* to the panic sex of *Bad Boy*). These are deep mythological paintings at the dark side of mythic fear turned radical, where it's no longer fascism with its nostalgic and ritualistic invocation of power and terror but, perhaps much worse, a whole society of dead souls who confuse leisure with freedom.

In a Swiss art magazine, Fischl said this about the subjective transgression which is the visual language of all his paintings:

> This other aspect of life, symbolic or whatever, is not allowed to exist because it can't be verified except subjectively and subjectivity is not allowed. There are things that are no longer allowed to be thought about because they are bad. So that's what we have. I will not be subjective. I will not think bad thoughts. [2]

If Fischl is the quintessential artist of postmodern America, it's because he actually paints the inner subjective terrain of television culture, disclosing what happens to us as we are processed through the mediascape. Fischl's world is the exact visual analogue of the spinning society in the quantum age theorised by Jean Baudrillard:

> But today the scene and the mirror no longer exist; instead, there is a screen and network. In place of the reflexive transcendence of mirror and scene, there is a nonreflexive surface, an immanent surface where operations unfold — the smooth operational surface of communication.
> . . . the schizo is bereft of every scene, open to everything in spite of himself, living in the greatest confusion. . . He is only a pure screen, a switching center for all the networks of influence. [3]

In Fischl's paintings, everyone lives with the knowledge that the end of history has already happened, and that we are arcing back towards a great and fatal implosion, whose form Don Dellilo in *White Noise* called a "slow brain fade" as we are blasted apart by the violence of the mediascape, or the Shuttle's "major" system malfunction. If Baudrillard makes of the schizoid self the emblematic sign of the death of the social, Fischl does him one better. He actually paints the faces and bodies of the ascendant middle class and the key sites (suburbia as Kant's peaceable Kingdom) of the parasitical culture of postmodern America: between dread over the transmission of bodily secretions and fear about the immanent breakdown of the technical system. In Fischl's world, we live on the psychological edge of being voyeurs with flashing eyeballs and parasites who feed on (*demand*) disaster scenes as ways of enticing us back from 'slow brain fade.' In Fischl's world, sex (most of all) is fun only to the extent that it is excremental: seduction without love (*Inside Out*); desire without a referent (*Bad Boy*); the "body without organs" (*The Visitor*). Fischl paints nihilism in its purely seductive, and thus purely excremental, phase. Like an American Bataille of the art world, Fischl teases out the excesses of a middle-class gone cynical.

Thus, for example, *Daddy's Girl* works the psychological edge of what Fischl calls "pure equivocation" that runs the line between ecstacy and decay as key cultural codes. This painting, is a chilling reminder of 'viciousness for fun' as the dark sign of Christian voluptuousness and the (disappeared) American family.

Eric Fischl, *Daddy's Girl*

Here Daddy is a potential sexual transgressor (the drink by his side), and also Daddy as the sometimes source of paternal affection. In *Daddy's Girl*, a sign-crime in the highly coded terrain of the familyscape takes place: children are simultaneously potential victims of adult sexual congress and loved dependencies. In *Anti-Oedipus*, Deleuze and Guattari talked about the disintegration of the old oedipal triangle of Mommy-Daddy-Me, but Fischl shows that violence and seduction are now the psychological terminal-points of the power relation of Daddy and Me. Mommy has disappeared, and who cares. This is the patriarchal power field of leisure society, where sexual desire is a throw of the dice between incest and fatherly love.

   A Woman Possessed teases out parasitism and violence as the psychological signs of leisure society. In *Habits of the Heart*, Robert Bellah — America's leading theorist of civil religion — found traces in the ruins of contemporary American culture for a new (and nostalgic) recycling of the political myth of liberty and justice (the founding compact of bourgeois society). [4] Yet Fischl's *A Woman Possessed* is more convincing as a political reflection on the civil polity of postmodern America. This is a painting, not under the sign of de Toqueville's *Democracy in America* restored by the theorists of liberal burnout desperate for the recuperation

Eric Fischl, *A Woman Possessed*

of community, but of America as the triumph of parasitical culture. The death of community and the immolation of substantive social relationships are the keynote features of *A Woman Possessed*; scavenging dogs its dominant moral force; and the woman possessed is simultaneously the object of a counterfeit ethics of charity and of idle curiosity with her coming death. In *A Woman Possessed* the politics of charity disappears into its opposite: a cynical fascination with bad luck (always that of others).

The hypercoldness of cynical culture American-style achieves its most bleak (and deeply parodic) expression in *Bad Boy*, a painting where even sex is parasited just for the fun of it. In Fischl's world, sexuality is interesting only when it disappears (as desire) into the tedium of gender-lack. This is sex as the privileged sign of the cracked surfaces and ruined interiority of what Michel Foucault, in "Preface to Transgression", said would be the postmodern fate: a twilight time between exhaustion and excess, between the limit and transgression. [5] If Fischl's artistic vision represents an implicit refusal of natural sex and discursive sexuality, it's to privilege an image of sex as hyper-parasitism. The woman is sexually incited by the voyeuristic gaze of the boy, but there is no reciprocity of desire. Here, voyeurism as sexual transgression is only *trompe l'oeil* distracting attention from the real event of this scene. The (transgressionary) gaze of the boy

Eric Fischl, *Inside Out*

may be an object of sexual fascination for the woman, but he acknowledges only the languid irrealism of dead sex by going for the big signifier of money (his hand reaches for the open purse). Like the television world of *Birthday Boy* which explores sex as (bored) entertainment for a leisure culture that oscillates between exhaustion and excess, *Bad Boy* is a painting about cultural residue in Bataille's economy of excess.

Fischl can protest that all of his artistic productions work the edge of a "lost innocence," but in postmodern America even true confessions are lies. In *Bad Boy* and *Birthday Boy* there is no innocence at all: their emotional effect is of the hypercoldness within; their psychological line is about sex as fascinating only if it exceeds the limits of transgression; their context is the highly segmented space of suburbia (where Father disappears, and its Mommy and the children this time who are (doubly) parasitical); their method is collage (Fischl says that he moves things to different positions to see what will happen); and their common object is leisure society as a Sadean filling up of all the orifices, the vagina (*Bad Boy*), the eyes (*Birthday Boy*), the anus (*Inside Out*), the ears (*The Power of Rock n'Roll*), and the mouth (*Barbecue*). Fischl's world is that of the cusp between seduction and excrement, exhaustion and excess, transgression and the limit, after it has overflowed.

UNTITLED

Put yourself in the place of Alex Colville's man. Not any-where, but rather on the Western coast of California looking out over the blue expanse of the Pacific Ocean. Below the ocean gently rolls broken only by the foam as it hits the beach. Behind, the Browning .35 lies on the table. The table has evidently been used to make clothes. The man, headless and naked from the waist, leans against the window frame, his pose captured in the portrayal of the buttocks.

The brilliance of the Colville painting — completed in 1967 — is precisely to have seized the transformation to postmodernity: the American empire passing the severed parts of the American self signalling the destruction of the social. Society, by its implosion, exposes the self that abandons the struggle for free-dom, and rests content in the landscape of the Pacific. This landscape is at once seductive in its tranquillity, and assured in its violence. Colville's gun and Colville's ocean capture the American psyche.

And the picture is a reading of the self because the social no longer exists. It is a reading of the self that has reached contentment with nihilism: the table is swept clean. Yet the very sterility of the expanse of water, juxtaposed with the sterility of the table, is almost of no consequence for the relaxed pose of the man threatens no one, and for this very reason is the most threatening of all postures.

Colville's man has donned the most modern of fashions, that of seduction and violence. He no longer has need of clothes, gun, or scale — only the very light breeze coming from the ocean. Fashion, war, and nature all are painted in the light of a society that can take them for granted, and has. The very forgetting of these basic constituents of the struggle in the capitalist world signals the advent of postcapitalism in its aesthetic form. It is also as a signal of the movement beyond the politics of engagement, or a politics beyond the fashion industry, that Colville's painting becomes one of the most modern paintings of the twentieth century.

Alex Colville, *Pacific*, 1967

Colville's hyperrealism allows him to paint the internal dynamic of relationships. He has moved beyond the voyeurism of an art that wishes to see into the assumed hidden recesses of the individual or the social. His art is a constant reversal of perspective — by means of binoculars, sunglasses, or the stare of the individual. Faces have no deep meaning precisely because there is no deep meaning to find. Individuals are frozen into relationships that are both sterile and sterilizing, and yet have beneath them the tenderness of being authentically modern, relationships founded upon hyperrealism.

Alex Colville, *Morning*, 1981

In 1981, Colville returned to a familiar theme, depicting a couple in the painting *Morning*. The woman is holding in front of her face a mirror, which Colville had found in a museum in Berlin, dating from the Egyptian eighteenth century.[6] The mirror is bronze. Behind the woman a man is in the act of shaving, and behind him is a familiar symbol in Colville's work, a cat shown only partially in the picture on the wall. This as Colville often will point out of his pictures, is intimacy, yet an intimacy that is thoroughly modern.

The intimacy of the individuals is that of a simulacrum designed by the codes of a society that dedicates the morning ritual to cleansing and beautification of the body. In this case, the concern for the cosmetic world obliterates both the face of the man and the woman. Even elements of the past, such as the Egyptian mirror, have little relevance other than as decimated symbols. The mirror, the symbol of life, becomes no longer a reflecting surface for either the individual or life. Its very antiquity has obliterated its ability to reflect images. It stands only as a symbol of the image of a self that has been shattered. Reflective consciousness no longer works in the simulacrum. Indeed, it doesn't really matter whether the woman sees herself, or whether the man shaves, because the body has become the site of the impregnations of the postmodern text. Both individuals automatically will wear the latest fashions; they need not see themselves to know this.

Yet, for Colville, these individuals have an intimacy that is captured by his own autobiographical sense that he is the defender of the family and its structure. It is precisely because the codes in postmodernity may be passively used as seductive that the body can still remain the site of a pleasurable sensuality. But there is nothing more than this at stake in the painting. Sex, if there is any, will take place in a quiet and peaceful manner without even touching or physical exertion. The juxtaposition of the bodies is sufficient to engage in symbolic exchange for the creation of new images and new individuals. This is aesthetic sex.

The obliteration of the mythology of time in North American culture is a sign of the liquidation of the American empire, and its warrior values. As time loses its place in a culture that cannot produce the 'high' values of the European past, the sense of the social begins to flee towards a spatial domain governed by movement. Power, which had been concentrated in stationary

Alex Colville, *Western Star*, 1985

reservoirs of capital, land, or knowledge becomes diffused over an environment constantly on the move. Opening up the spatial dimensions of existence blows the concentration of power out into the small towns and cities, as centres of micropower replicating the cosmology of postmodernity.

Thus the communications industry becomes linked with the transportation industry as purveyors of the latest fashions throughout the main streets of America, the very sign of postmodernity that can be read anywhere on any main street or in any gas station in the United States. This gives rise to some of the most penetrating American art, captured, for example, in Edward Hopper's 1940 work entitled *Gas*. And similarly we find in Colville a whole series of paintings that depict main street life (such as his 1979 painting by that title). These establish the sense of communication and flight as the essence of the postmodern experience.

In Colville paintings, trains, canoes, bicycles, or trucks often appear alongside animals. Many works such as *Cyclist and Crow*, 1981, *Sign and Harrier*, 1970, *Dog and Bridge*, 1976, *Swimming Dog and Canoe*, 1979, and perhaps Colville's most well-known painting *Horse and Train*, 1954, show the profound relationship in Colville of the symbiosis between technological creations (man and woman) and the natural world (animals) in the development of postmodern America. On the one hand, Colville has subordinated his genius to a belief the natural world may still hold a balance that is disrupted by the intrusion of the hardness of technological realism. Many of these paintings foretell of the impending collision of the bounded and constrained world of humanity against the fundamental freedom found in the flight of birds. On the other hand, this naturalism itself is bent back in the seductive power of the fleeing social as it meets itself in everyday life on main street.

Colville's 1985 work entitled *Western Star* brilliantly depicts the seductive destructiveness of postmodernity. The painting is situated in a familiar truck stop. In front of the truck, the driver is poised with a camera taking the picture of a 'fashion model'. The truck stands in the same relationship to the gun in Colville's earlier painting *Pacific* as the encoding of the power of modern society. This time, however, the gun has been translated into the force of communication, a presentation of power through the technology of everyday life. The woman in the picture has similarly been transformed into the concomitant of the communication industry, the fashion industry. The woman is a mirror image of the beauty of the truck, each wearing the seductive powers of sex and technology. Colville's natural world has been decimated, but again the decimation is that of postmodernity, where animals become coats whose chief function is beyond use — for display purposes only.

In this setting the brilliance of Colville's vision may be appreciated. Here he depicts the attendant with the camera taking the picture of the fashion model. For in the postmodern world it is the camera which displaces the work of art, in the form of the hyperrealistic aesthetic associated with a studied, but dead existence. Colville's man with the camera enters Barthes' studio, not as a 'camera lucida', but rather within the enclosure of a structure of power and seduction. Beyond the panic of a 'camera negrida', Colville's camera is the true incarceral capturing not the image of the fashion model so much as the image of the spectator of cosmetic reality. Colville's world comes truly 'in camera': an imaging system that is used for the seductiveness of the advertising industry, as Colville himself was used as a camera for the experience of North America in the Second World War.

Western Star is the triumph of culture. It renders our society like the ruins of antiquity: a beautiful and pleasing place to visit. Like the ruins, we have forgotten its origin and authorship, recalling only that this is an untitled site.

Notes

I. Sunshine Reports: Theses on the Postmodern Scene

1.

1. Michel Foucault, *Language, Counter-Memory, Practice*, edited by Donald F. Bouchard, Ithaca, New York: Cornell University Press, 1977, p. 35.

2. F. Nietzsche, *Thus Spoke Zarathustra*, New York: Gordon Press, 1974, p. 169.

3. G. Bataille, *Visions of Excess: Selected Writings, 1927-1939*, Minneapolis: University of Minnesota Press, 1985, p. 5.

4. J. Baudrillard, "Forgetting Foucault", *Humanities in Society*, Vol. 3, No. 1, Winter, 1980, p. 103.

5. *Op. cit., Visions of Excess*, p. 84.

6. F. Nietzsche, *The Gay Science*, translated by Walter Kaufmann, New York: Random House, 1974, p. 181.

7. *Vogue*, February, 1986.

8. Gilles Deleuze and Félix Guattari, *Anti-Oedipus: Capitalism and Schizophrenia*, New York: Viking, 1977, pp. 292-301.

9. M. McLuhan, *Understanding Media: The Extensions of Man*, Toronto: McGraw-Hill, 1964, p. 26.

10. Michel Serres, *Les cinq sens*, Paris: Grasset, 1985, p. 310.

11. Sam Schoenbaum, "The Challenge of Loss", *Art and Text*, 17, pp. 91-92.

12. *Ibid.*, p. 92.

13. Jean-François Lyotard, "Answering the Question: What is the Post-Modern", *Origins, Originality and Beyond*, Sydney, Australia: Art Gallery of New South Wales, 1986, p. 19.

14. Jean-François Lyotard, *La condition postmoderne: rapport sur le savoir*, Paris: Les éditions de minuit, 1979, pp. 31-35.

15. J. Baudrillard, *Simulations*, New York: Semiotext(e), 1983, pp. 54-58.

16. F. Nietzsche, "What is the Meaning of Ascetic Ideals", in *Toward A Genealogy of Morals*, New York: Random House, 1967, aphorism 28.

17. Peter Burger, *The Theory of the Avante-Garde*, Minneapolis: University of Minnesota Press, 1984.

18. *Ibid*.

19. Guy Debord, *La société du spectacle*, Paris: Éditions champ libre, pp. 20-21.

20. C. Offe, "Theses on the Theory of the State", in *The Contradictions of the Welfare State*, London: Hutchison, 1984, pp. 119-129.

21. *Ibid*.

22. Marilouise Kroker et. al; (editor), *Feminism Now: Theory and Practice*, Montréal: New World Perspectives, 1985, pp. 5-6.

23. Luce Irigaray, *Ce sexe qui n'en est pas un*, Paris: Les éditions de minuit, 1977, p. 205.

24. See particularly, Alice A. Jardine, "Theories of the Feminine: Kristeva", *enclitic*, 4,2 (Fall, 1980), pp. 5-15.

25. Michel Foucault, *The History of Sexuality: Volume 1, An Introduction*, New York: Pantheon, 1978, pp. 135-159.

26. Gilles Deleuze and Félix Guattari, "What is a Minor Literature", Mississippi Review 31 (Winter/Spring 1983), pp. 16-27.

27. For a brilliant account of Lacan's theorisation of the "fictive unity" of the bourgeois ego, see Jon R. Schiller, "With Such Privacies Can a Man Feel Well", in the special issue, *Psychoanalyis, Ideology and Language, Canadian Journal of Political and Social Theory*, Volume 4, Number 2, 1980, pp. 9-22.

28. *Ibid.*, pp. 28-31.

29. *Ibid*.

30. For a representative statement of Serres' position on science and power, see Michel Serres, *Hermes: Literature, Science, Philosophy*, Baltimore: The John Hopkins University Press, 1982.

II. Sign Crimes

2.

1. Michel Foucault, *The History of Sexuality, Volume 1: An Introduction,* (New York: Pantheon, 1978), p. 151.

3.

1. Charles Norris Cochrane, *Thucydides and the Science of History*, Oxford: Oxford University Press, 1929.

2. Charles Norris Cochrane, "The Latin Spirit in Literature," *University of Toronto Quarterly*, Vol. 2, No. 3, 1932-33, pp. 315-338.

3. Charles Norris Cochrane, *Christianity and Classical Culture: A Study of Thought and Action from Augustus to Augustine*, Oxford: Oxford University Press, 1940.

4. Charles Norris Cochrane, "The Mind of Edward Gibbon I," *University of Toronto Quarterly*, Vol. 12, No. 1, 1942-43, pp. 1-17; and "The Mind of

Edward Gibbon II," *University of Toronto Quarterly*, Vol. 12, No. 2, 1942-43, pp. 146-166.

5. Charles Norris Cochrane, *David Thompson: The Explorer*, Toronto: MacMillan, 1924.

6. Cochrane, *Christianity and Classical Culture*, p. 468.

7. Cochrane, "The Latin Spirit in Literature," p. 338.

8. This, at least, was Cochrane's position in *Christianity and Classical Culture*.

9. Cochrane described Plotinus and Porphyry as mediational movements in philosophical discourse; a trembling mid-point between the birth of Christian metaphysics and the death of the disembodied *logos* of Plato. Plotinus followed a programme of *ascesis* (the 'evacuation' of the soul of all elements of complexity) and Porphyry had recourse to *theurgy*, (an early example of psychoanalysis.) *Christianity and Classical Culture*, pp. 429-430.

10. And, of course, all of Cochrane's thought stands as a response to precisely this possibility.

11. Cochrane never suspected though that in Augustinian realism there is, above all, the first stirrings of the birth of nihilism. Augustine stands on the dark side of Nietzsche as much as Foucault is the future of Nietzsche's 'will to will.'

12. *The Confessions of St. Augustine*, translated by E.B. Pusey, London: Collins Books, 1961. See, for example, chapter 8.

13. It is my thesis, after Heidegger, that Augustine's discourse on the "flame of the will" installed a transparent, contentless and mediational 'power' 'a dead power' at the epicentre of Western experience.

14. Stephen B. Pepper, *World-Hypotheses: A Study in Evidence*, Berkeley and Los Angeles: University of California, 1942.

15. Cochrane, The Mind of Edward Gibbon I."

16. Cochrane, "The Latin Spirit in Literature."

17. Christopher Dawson, *The Judgement of the Nations*, London: Sheed, 1943, p. 5.

18. Eric Havelock, *Prometheus*, Seattle: University of Washington Press, 1968, p. 16.

19. Cochrane, *Christianity and Classical Culture*, p. 241.

20. *Ibid.*, pp. 399-455.

21. Cochrane's search for a solution to the problem of *identity through change* is the common feature which grounds his historical realism and his turn to Augustinian vitalism.

22. Because dialectics oscillates between pragmatic naturalism and hyper-rationalism, neither of which exhausts the heterogeneity of human experience.

23. See specifically Cochrane's critique of Lockean epistemology in "The Mind of Edward Gibbon."

24. Cochrane understood, in fact, that Augustine's doctrine of the trinity (a doctrine which located in the mirror of the trinity an indeterminate recession towards that which never was, but which could only be known in its absence,) was also a significant act of metaphysical closure. In the mirror of the trinity a reversal of the order of experience occurs: a reversal in which the region of non-being nihilates facticity. It was the arc of a dead power represented by the movement of the will to will between two signs that were reverse images of one another. This leads directly to the writings of Nietzsche, de Sade and Camus.

25. Cochrane's tragic sensibility paralleled the cultural pessimism of Herodotus; the third term from which he always sought escape was mythic consciousness.

26. Cochrane, *Christianity and Classical Culture*, p. 445.

27. The search for a mode of scientific history which in establishing the foundation of creative politics rendered possible an escape from the poetic consciousness of Herodotus was a theme of *Thucydides and the Science of History*.

28. Cochrane, *Christianity and Classical Culture*, p. 468.

29. *Ibid*.

30. *Ibid*.

31. *Ibid*.

32. *Ibid*.

33. *Ibid*.

34. For an excellent description of the working out of *ricorso* in language and myth, see Northrop Frye, *The Great Code: The Bible and Literature*, New York: Harcourt, Brace, Jovanovich, 1981.

35. Cochrane, *David Thompson: The Explorer*, p. 170.

36. *Ibid*., p. 169.

37. For an account of how Thucydides applied the principles and methods of Hippocratic medicine to the interpretation of political history, see *Thucydides and the Science of History*, pp. 14-34.

38. Cochrane, "The Latin Spirit in Literature," p. 331.

39. Cochrane, "The Mind of Edward Gibbon," p. 166. This article represents Cochrane's most mature account of the historical imagination and, indeed, is the moment at which his thought is its most metaphysical.

40. For a full account of the early Christian attitude to the 'apotheosis' of promethean consciousness, see *Christianity and Classical Culture*, pp. 359-398.

41. *Thucydides and the Science of History* represents a synthesis of an empirically informed history (Thucydides) and a theory of creative politics based on the model of the Athenian polis.

42. *Ibid*., pp. 26-34.

43. It was Cochrane's thesis, of course, that the genealogy of this failure of the

Graeco-Roman mind begins and ends with the metaphysical impossibility of naturalism, with, that is, the impossibility of maintaining a creative politics on the basis of a rationally divided experience. Augustine's contribution was to repudiate a dialectical conception of power in favour of a relational one.

44. For a brilliant account of the psychological differences which established the Greeks and Romans as mirror images of one another, see "The Latin Spirit in Literature."

45. Cochrane, "The Latin Spirit in Literature," p. 330.

46. *Ibid.*, pp. 321-322.

47. *Ibid.*, p. 322.

48. "It was not John Locke but Cicero who (in a little-noticed passage) first asserted that the state exists to protect property," "The Latin Spirit in Literature," p. 323.

49. *Ibid.*, p. 322.

50. *Ibid.*, p. 331.

51. *Ibid.*, p. 325.

52. *Ibid.*, p. 334.

53. *Ibid.*, p. 337.

54. *Ibid.*, p. 333.

55. *Ibid.*, p. 335.

56. *Ibid.*, pp. 337-338.

57. *Ibid.*, p. 338.

58. See George Grant, *Technology and Empire*, Toronto, Anansi: 1969, and Dennis Lee, *Savage Fields: An Essay in Literature and Cosmology*, Toronto: Anansi, 1977.

59. Cochrane, "The Latin Spirit," p. 338.

60. After Jean Baudrillard's description of power as dead "in-itself" moving between signifier and signified as symbolic effects of one another, I take Augustine to be the first theoretician who radicalized the infinite possibilities which would be opened to the disciplinary method if the void of the 'flame of the will' were to overcome the facticity of the flesh. I understand Nietzsche's will to power, Heidegger's critical account of the will which moves restlessly to impose value, and Foucault's nightmarish vision of the 'eye of power' as the first awakening of thought to the transparent and mediational quality of modern power. See, in particular, F. Nietzsche, *The Will To Power*, New York: Random House; 1968, M. Heidegger, *The End of Philosophy*, New York: Harper and Row, 1973; and Michel Foucault, *Folie et déraison, Histoire de la Folie à l'âge classique*, translated as *Madness and Civilisation*, New York: Pantheon Books, 1965.

61. Cochrane, "The Latin Spirit in Literature," p. 338.

62. Martin Heidegger, *The Question Concerning Technology and Other Essays*, New York: Harper and Row, 1977, p. 79.

63. Cochrane, *Christianity and Classical Culture*, "Nostra Philosophia: The Discovery of Personality," pp. 399-455 and "Divine Necessity and Human History," pp. 456-516.

64. Jean Baudrillard, "Forgetting Foucault," *Humanities in Society*, Vol. 3, No. 1, Winter, 1980, p. 108.

65. Cochrane, *Christianity and Classical Culture*, p. 360.

66. *Ibid.*, p. 431.

67. *Ibid.*

68. *Ibid.*, p. 422.

69. *Ibid.*, pp. 424-425.

70. *Ibid.*, p. 425.

71. *Ibid.*, p. 428.

72. *Ibid.*, p. 403.

73. *Ibid.*

74. *Ibid.*, p. 403.

75. *Ibid.*, p. 407.

76. *Ibid.*, p. 439.

77. *Ibid.*, pp. 433-434.

78. *Ibid.*, p. 438.

79. *Ibid.*, p. 446.

80. *Ibid.*, p. 444.

81. The "desubstantialisation of nature" is accomplished by transforming the world of factual experience (yes, sensuous experience,) into a "privation," an "absence," a "lack." Augustine's revolutionary conception of the will as the vital force of the modern personality was shadowed by that other sign: "to nill." Thus, what is instituted by Augustine is simultaneously the sovereignty of the void as the centre of Western experience and an order of transgressions. The theory of human action which is revealed by trinitarianism is nothing less than what we later witness as "institutionalization" (Talcott Parsons) or "normalization" (Michel Foucault).

82. But the God to which the self is referred is in Augustine's terms immutable, indivisible, omnipotent and sexless: yes, at the beginning and always a dead God.

83. Cochrane, *Christianity and Classical Culture*, p. 396.

84. *Ibid.*, p. 415.

85. *Ibid.*, p. 403.

86. *Ibid.*

87. *Ibid.*

88. *Ibid.*, p. 404.

89. *Ibid.*, p. 412.

90. *Ibid.*, p. 400.

91. *Ibid.*, p. 402.

92. *Ibid.*, p. 414.

93. *Ibid.*, p. 415.

94. *Ibid.*, pp. 471-516.

95. Or, as Cochrane says: "History in terms of embodied *logos* means history in terms of personality." *Christianity and Classical Culture*, p. 480.

96. *Ibid.*

97. *Ibid.*, p. 513.

98. *Ibid.*, p. 506.

99. *Ibid.*, p. 506.

100. *Ibid.*, p. 513.

4.

1. F. Nietzsche, *The Will to Power*, trans. Walter Kaufman and R.J. Hollingdale, New York: Vintage, 1968, pp. 14-15.

2. William Leiss has described this process as the reduction of culture and society (as mediated by subjective consciousness) to the technology of "machine-processed information."

3. It was Augustine in *De Trinitate* who first established the epistemological grounds for the "closing of the eye of the flesh" and for the "direct deliverance" of consciousness to the undivided will of the trinitarian formulation. Augustine was the first of the structuralists because his doctrine of the "mirror of the trinity" breaks with a representational theory of power and with the classical economy of reason. In his classic metaphysical text, *De Trinitate*, Augustine developed a fully modern theory of *personality* and *history*. I interpret Augustine's "direct deliverance" to the purely symbolic sphere of the "flame of the will" to be the precursor of Foucault's nightmarish vision of the eye of power, of Nietzsche's power as a circular, "spherical space," of Heidegger's critical account of the nihilating will, and of Baudrillard's "dead power." This is only to say that Augustine developed the fundamental, theoretical foundations for a structuralist description of a *tautological exchange-process*. Within this tautological cycle of symbolic exchange, ideology functions not merely as truth-value, but as *desire. Ideology is metonymic to the metaphor of power*. See Augustine's *The Trinity*, Washington: The Catholic University of America Press, 1962.

4. This is the world of Barthes' "power as an *atopic* text," Althusser's "synarchy," Baudrillard's "simulacrum," Grant's "technological dynamo," and Adorno's "open-air prison." See particularly: Ronald Barthes, *The Pleasure of the Text*, trans. Richard Miller, New York: Hill and Wang, 1975; J. Baudrillard, *L'Échange symbolique et la mort*; G. Grant, *Technology and Empire*, Toronto: House of Anansi, 1969; and T.W. Adorno, *Prisms*, London.

5. Marshall McLuhan. *Understanding Media: The Extensions of Man*, New York: McGraw-Hill, 1965, p. 57.

6. J. Baudrillard, "Forgetting Foucault," trans. Nicole Dufresne, *Humanities in Society*, 3, 1, 1980, p. 103.

7. Martin Heidegger in his essay, "The World of Nietzsche" elaborates the meaning of Nietzsche's "the will to will" as developed in *The Will to Power*.

8. J. Baudrillard, "Forgetting Foucault," p. 103.

9. *Ibid.*, p. 104.

10. F. Nietzsche, *The Will to Power*, p. 35.

11. *Ibid.*

12. Foucault's sociological description of the society of surveillance fails to capture what Nietzsche has said is the cycle of disintegration and reversibility in the will to power. Foucault's later works, *The History of Sexuality* and *Discipline & Punish* privilege the norm as the discursive foundation of the "power apparatus." Of the two, Baudrillard is the more insightful concerning the fascination, the seduction, of disintegration as the charismatic force of modern power. In his earlier philosophical essays in *Language, Counter-Memory and Practice*, Foucault's thought hovered around Nietzsche's understanding of nihilation as the genesis of Western experience. In its movement from philosophy to sociology as the entry-point to the discourse on power, Foucault's analysis has become trapped in the object of its critique: the nameless, decentered power of the Panopticon.

13. R. Barthes, *The Pleasure of the Text*, p. 7.

14. R. Barthes, *Critical Essays*, Evanston: Northwestern University Press, 1972, p. 242.

15. R. Barthes, *The Pleasure of the Text*, p. 7.

16. *Ibid.*, p. 6.

17. Baudrillard's theorization of the "radical semiurgy" at work in the imposition of an "image-system" as the structure of social exchange is very similar to McLuhan's conception of the "massaging" of the ratio of the senses in a cybernetic society. For a superb account of the semiurgical process in McLuhan's thought, see: John Fekete, "Massage in the Mass Age: Remembering the McLuhan Matrix," *Canadian Journal of Political and Social Theory*, 6, 3 (1982) pp. 50-67. For Baudrillard's account of the "radical semiurgy" in relation to the process of consumption, see *Le système des objets*, Paris: Gallimard, 1968.

18. Habermas' project of "universal pragmatics" is a continuation, in critical form, of Kant's nominalism. Habermas cannot ground the rationality-principle in the realm of facticity. To do that, he would have to err on the side of Sartre's absorption with the body; and the other side of this variant of existentialism is Nietzsche's unsparing pessimism. And Habermas cannot go forward into a relational theory of "truth," for on that side waits Althusser's relativism. In a word, Habermas' "emancipatory" project is trapped between Nietzsche and Althusser, between relativism in scientific

garb and the *regressus in infinitum*. While the "Kantian No" that *is* Habermas' discourse opens up a path between madness and suicide, it only means that he may not yet have mediated upon Nietzsche's aphorism: "The criterion of truth resides in the enhancement of the feeling of power." *The Will to Power*, (534).

19. Augustine's central epistemological doctrine of the *"Crede ut intellegas"* is based on a purely rhetorical theory of power. In fact, Augustine invented the exact grammatical rules by which a "tautological power" operates. Augustine's theory of a "spherical space" of the will is best outlined in *De Trinitate*, Book 11. The central metaphor of this text is that of the "eye of the mind."

20. Nietzsche's "perspectival appearance" of the will to power is the equivalent of Augustine's simulation of the "flame of the will" and, for that matter, of Baudrillard's theorization of power as a "perspectival simulation."

21. J. Baudrillard, *L'Échange symbolique et la mort*, pp. 89-95.

22. Alain Robbe-Grillet, *Le voyeur*, Paris: Les éditions de minuit, 1955, p. 7.

23. J. Baudrillard, "Forgetting Foucault," p. 109.

24. F. Nietzsche, *The Will to Power*, p. 549.

25. J. Baudrillard. *L'Échange symbolique et la mort*, pp. 89-95. Of *le code structurel*, Baudrillard argues: "A la limite d'une extermination toujours plus poussée des références et des finalités, d'une perte des ressemblances et des désignations, on trouve ce signe digital et programmatique, dont la 'valeur' est purement *tactique*, à l'intersection d'autres signaux et dont la structure est celle d'un code micromoléculaire de commande et de contrôle." p. 89.

26. Augustine, *The Trinity*, p. 488.

27. *Ibid.*, p. 483.

28. J. Baudrillard, *Op. cit.*, The "semiological reduction" of the exchange processes characteristic of advanced capitalism to the algorithmic and binary logic of the 1/0 is the fundamental ground of "la loi structurale de la valeur."

29. F. Nietzsche. *The Will to Power*, pp. 549-550.

30. M. Foucault. *The History of Sexuality*, p. 95. Foucault says of the "relational character of power relationships. Their existence depends on a multiplicity of points of resistance... These points of resistance are present everywhere in the power network. Hence there is no single locus of great Refusal, no soul of revolt, source of all rebellions, or pure law of the revolutionary." pp. 95-96.

31. The critical beginnings of Parsons' theoretical development of a *relational* description of power is to be found in his essay, "On the Concept of Political Power" in *Politics and Social Structure*, New York: The Free Press, 1969, pp. 352-404. The concluding technical note to the essay on political power represents the theoretical ground for Parsons' later development of a complete theory of the "family of generalized, symbolic media of exchange" as the central mediations of advanced industrial societies. While

the "family of symbolic media" was limited at first to the exchange-processes of power, money, influence, and value-commitments, Parsons extended this theorization into an analysis of other mediations, including health, personality, intelligence, and affect, as central media of exchange. In my reading, Parsons' image of a "relational" power represents the end of Kant's rebellion against representationalism; and for that matter, the "power" around which Parsons' thought hovers is the positive face of Foucault's "disciplinary society." That Foucault and Parsons move along a common trajectory of thought (one which draws together knowledge/power/life) is illustrated by their common preoccupation with the *clinical* applications of knowledge. Thus, I would compare Foucault's *The Birth of the Clinic: An Archeology of Medical Perception* with Parsons' studies of the investiture of health by the "normalizations" of the human sciences. See, for example, "Health and Disease: A Sociological and Action Perspective," in *Action Theory and the Human Condition*, New York: The Free Press, 1978. Baudrillard's theorization of the "pure sign" and Barthes' description of an "image-system" represent precisely the same theoretical trajectory (as that of Parsons/Foucault), but at the level of a *communicative* as opposed to *sociological* description of a "cybernetic" exchange-process. In precisely the same way that Foucault/Parsons represent parallel but reverse images of a sociological conception of a relational power-system, I also view Baudrillard/Barthes as convergent but reverse images of a communicative theory of relational power.

32. M. Foucault, *Op. cit.*, p. 151.

33. Kant's nominalism was intended to provide a regulatory and procedural structure of experience which, operating at the level of epistemology, would suppress the "dark side" of the cycle of disintegration. For Nietzsche, the Kantian project was a "desert."

34. J. Baudrillard, "Forgetting Foucault," p. 103.

35. John Berger, *Ways of Seeing*, New York: Viking Press, 1972.

36. Baudrillard's "*jouissance*" is the same concept as Barthes' "bliss": both are typified by a swift contraction between exterminism and progression (Nietzsche's "iron ring" of experience). See Barthes' *The Pleasure of the Text*, p. 19; and Baudrillard's *De la séduction*, pp. 44-54.

37. Nietzsche (*The Will to Power*) and Grant (*Technology and Empire*) say the same thing about technology and power: Grant's claim that "technique is ourselves" parallels Nietzsche's aphorism: "We are its commandment" (p. 356).

38. M. Foucault, *Language, Counter-Memory, Practice*, Ithaca: Cornell University Press, 1977, pp. 29-52.

39. G. Bataille, "L'expérience intérieure," in *Oeuvres*, quoted in M. Foucault, *Language, Counter-Memory, Practice*, p. 44.

40. M. Foucault, *Language, Counter-Memory, Practice*, p. 43.

41. R. Barthes, *Critical Essays*, p. 245.

42. T. Parsons, *Social Systems and the Evolution of Action Theory*, p. 134.

43. M. Foucault, *Op. cit.*, p. 35.

44. Ivan Eyre, *Visions* interview for TV Ontario series on Contemporary Canadian Artists, 1982, p. 5.

45. M. Foucault, *The History of Sexuality*, p. 86.

46. *Ibid*.

47. *Op. cit.*

48. J. Baudrillard, *Pour une critique de l'économie politique du signe*, pp. 95-109.

49. R. Barthes, *Critical Essays*, pp. 239-247.

50. R. Barthes, *Image-Music-Text*, trans. Stephen Heath, Glasgow: Fontana/Collins, 1977, see particularly, "Rhetoric of the Image," pp. 32-51.

51. R. Barthes, *Critical Essays*, p. 240.

52. *Ibid*.

53. *Ibid.*, p. 242.

54. *Ibid.*, p. 244.

55. *Ibid*.

56. Michel Foucault, *Power/Knowledge*, edited by Colin Gordon, New York: Pantheon, 1980, p. 133.

57. In the *Empire of Signs*, Barthes speaks of "panic boredom."

58. R. Barthes, *The Pleasure of the Text*, p. 35.

59. *Ibid.*, p. 44.

60. G. Grant, *Technology and Empire*, p. 143.

61. *Ibid.*, p. 40.

62. Sartre, "Language," in J. Streller, *To Freedom Condemned*, p. 49.

63. *Ibid*.

64. Sartre, "The Body," in J. Streller, *To Freedom Condemned*, p. 76.

65. *Ibid*.

66. An excellent account of the significance of Goya's "sleep of reason" for an understanding of the Enlightenment (Nietzsche's "sickliness") is given by David Cook, "The Dark Side of Enlightenment," *Canadian Journal of Political and Social Theory*, 5, 3 (1981), pp. 3-14.

67. F. Nietzsche, *The Will to Power*, Aph. 28, pp. 19-20.

68. Martin Heidegger, "The Word of Nietzsche: God is Dead," in *The Question Concerning Technology and Other Essays*, New York: Harper Colophon, 1977, p. 69.

69. *Ibid.*, p. 68.

70. This is the stock phrase used by Talcott Parsons to describe the incarceration of the "subject" in the "system of modern society. I view the epistemological strategy involved in the "internalization of need-dispositions" as the break-point between a utilitarian conception of personality and the "anachronic subject" of the programmed society of advanced capitalism. The system of "need-internalization" sets up a mirroring-effect between

desire (the psychological site of the body) and the consumer society. Baudrillard's analysis of the "mirror of production" might well be viewed as a political recitative of the sociology of Parsons' *The Social System.*

71. Of the "semiological wash," McLuhan says: "Man becomes, as it were, the sex organs of the machine world, as the bee of the plant world, enabling it to fecundate and to evolve ever new forms. The machine world reciprocates man's love by expediting his wishes and desires, namely in providing him with wealth." *Understanding Media: The Extensions of Man*, p. 46.

72. Marshall McLuhan, *The Medium is the Massage.*

73. J. Baudrillard. *L'Échange symbolique et la mort*, p. 77.

74. J. Baudrillard, "Forgetting Foucault," p. 102.

75. R. Barthes, *The Pleasure of the Text*, p. 67.

76. Jean-Paul Sartre, *To Freedom Condemned*, p. 78.

77. F. Nietzsche, *The Will to Power*, p. 715.

78. *Ibid.*, p. 46, (Aph. 46) *"Weakness of the will*: that is a metaphor that proves misleading. For there is no will, and consequently neither a stronger nor a weaker will."

79. R. Barthes, *Critical Essays*, p. 242.

80. J. Baudrillard, "Forgetting Foucault," p. 109. Nietzsche also discussed the metamorphosis of the sign as "perspectival appearance. *To Freedom Condemned*, p. 15.

81. Of the "plenitude of the void," Heidegger says: "The principle can no longer be the world of the suprasensory become lifeless. Therefore nihilism, aiming at a revaluing understood in this way, *will seek out what is most alive"* (my italics), "The World of Nietzsche," p. 70. It's the "seeking out of what is most alive" by a nihilating power which I understand to be the basis of the *charismatic flight of power from one denotative sign-system to another.* If we were to read Nietzsche and Augustine against one another, it might be said that "grace" is charisma because it is the "brilliance" (Nietzsche) of nothingness. But "nothingness" always seeks out that which is dynamic in existence; nihilism operates in the tongue of the seduction-appeal of progress, speed-up, and high acceleration.

82. I am referring to the primal distinction between Heidegger and Sartre. Sartre said that nihilation is *not*, but Heidegger's Nietzsche is wiser: "Nothing is befalling being," M. Heidegger, "The World of Nietzsche," p. 79. And in the background there is Nietzsche who, I believe, would give the nod of assent to Heidegger: "Nihilism stands at the door: whence comes this uncanniest of all guests?" *The Will to Power*, (Aph. 1), p. 7.

83. F. Nietzsche, *The Will to Power*, p. 326.

84. M. Heidegger, "The Word of Nietzsche," p. 68.

85. J. Baudrillard, "Forgetting Foucault," p. 102.

86. *Ibid.*, p. 110.

87. *Ibid.*

88. M. Heidegger, "The Word of Nietzsche," p. 69.

89. For Baudrillard, "the frenzied semiurgy that has taken hold of the simul-acrum" is carried out within a "lightning-quick contraction in which an entire cycle of accumulation, of power, or of truth comes to a close." "Forgetting Foucault," pp. 90 and 111. Baudrillard's deficiency is that in this writing he comes as close as any contemporary thinker to the secret of the "plenitude of the void"; but then, he veers away from radical meta-physics, collapsing all the while into a creative, but vacuous, sociology of the "frenzied semiurgy." His later works, *De la séduction, L'Échange symbolique et la mort* are limited by their lack of philosophy. Like Barthes, Baudrillard's analysis is trapped in the mirroring-effect of the pure image-system.

90. M. Heidegger, *Op. cit.*, p. 69.

91. Max Weber, *Theory of Social and Economic Organization*, edited by Talcott Parsons, p. 359.

92. M. Heidegger, "The Word of Nietzsche," p. 70.

93. The method of radical metaphysics is intended to disclose the genealogical traces of nihilism as the "inner logic" (Nietzsche) of Western experience. What is at stake in this project is the uncovering of the basic genetic code of the "exchange-processes" which have mediated European, and world, history. Thus, my theoretical supposition is that Heidegger's critical statement "Nothing is befalling being" (the *lack* at the centre of exchange) is a bridge between Nietzsche's description of the "psychology of Paul" (the original *sickliness* in Christian theology), and the nihilism of the political economy of advanced capitalist societies. Mass consumpsion, organized within Baudrillard's "simulacrum" and fueled by the *vide* from which all sign-systems are an attempted escape, is still based on the most primitive principles of Christianity as the first nihilism. Nihilism works its deepest effects in the *most materialistic* deployments of the exchange-system. That which made the "psychology of Paul" a condition of possibility of Western experience has now been transformed into the popular ideology of advanced capitalism.

94. J. Baudrillard, *Le système des objets*, pp. 89-90.

95. F. Nietzsche, *The Will to Power*, p. 346.

96. J. Baudrillard, "Forgetting Foucault," p. 103.

97. F. Nietzsche, *The Will to Power*, "The most extreme form of nihilism would be to view that *every* belief, every considering-something-true, is necessarily false because there is simply no *true world*. Thus: a *perspectival appearance* whose origin lies in us (in so far as we continually *need* a narrower, abbreviated, simplified world), pp. 14-15.

98. *Ibid.*, p. 13.

99. J. Baudrillard, *Op. cit.*, p. 103.

100. Jacques Lacan, *The Language of the Self*, translated by A. Wilden, Baltimore: John Hopkins Press, 1968.

101. The creation of "opthalmia" as an artistic strategy has been pioneered by

Donny Proche, a contemporary Canadian artist.

102. R. Barthes, *Critical Essays*, p. 243.

103. R. Barthes, *The Pleasure of the Text*, p. 49.

104. A critical account of the limitations of French rationalism, new and old, is provided in Andrew Wernick's "Structuralism and the Dislocation of the French Rationalist Project," J. Fekete, ed., *The Structuralist Allegory: Reconstructive Encounters with The New French Thought*, Minneapolis: University of Minnesota Press, 1984.

105. J. Baudrillard, "Forgetting Foucault," p. 105.

106. J. Baudrillard, *Le système des objets*, p. 283. "C'est finalement parce que la consommation se fonde sur un *manque* qu'elle est irrépressible."

107. Baudrillard's convergence of Kafka and the *optics* of structural linguistics is brought to completion in two texts: *De la séduction* and *L'Échange symbolique et la mort*.

108. "La production théorique, comme la production matérielle, perd ses déterminations et commence à tourner sur elle-même, décrochant 'en abyme' vers une réalité introuvable. Nous en sommes là aujourd'hui: dans l'indécidabilité, à l'ère des théories flottantes comme des monnaies flottantes," J. Baudrillard, *L'Échange symbolique et la mort*, p. 21.

109. "Autonimiser l'économique est une stratégie idéologique." J. Baudrillard, *Le miroir de la production*, p. 126. Barthes' "anaclictic topos" is a central theme of *The Pleasure of the Text* as much as the images of the "satellisation of the real" and the "aesthetics of hyper-realism" are deployed in Baudrillard's *L'Échange symbolique et la mort*.

110. R. Barthes, *The Pleasure of the Text*, p. 38.

111. *Ibid.*, p. 14.

112. *Ibid.*, p. 16.

113. J. Baudrillard, *Pour une critique de l'économie politique du signe*, p. 100.

114. R. Barthes, *Op. cit.*, p. 16.

115. R. Barthes, *Op. cit.*, p. 21.

116. J. Baudrillard, "L'Hyperréalisme de la simulation," in *L'Échange symbolique et la mort*, pp. 110-117.

5.

1. Jean Baudrillard, "Forgetting Foucault," *Humanities in Society*, Vol. 3, No. 1, Winter, 1980, p. 110.

2. *Ibid.*

3. *Ibid.*, p. 105.

4. *Ibid.*, p. 110.

5. *Ibid.*

6. Jean Baudrillard, *L'Échange symbolique et la mort*, Paris: Éditions Gallimard, 1976, p. 14.

7. *Ibid.*, p. 115.

8. *Ibid.*, pp. 114-115.

9 *Ibid.*, p. 115.

10. *Ibid.*, p. 76.

11. F. Nietzsche, *The Will to Power*, trans. W. Kaufmann and R.J. Hollingdale, New York: Vintage Books, 1968, p. 7.

12. For Baudrillard's most comprehensive description of the critique of the political economy of the commodity-form, see his text, *Pour une critique de l'économie politique du signe*, Paris: Gallimard, 1972. In this text, Baudrillard explores the significance of "la réduction semiologique" for a critique of the referent of production. Baudrillard discusses the "satellisation of the real" in two important essays, "L'économie politique comme modèle de simulation" and "L'hyperéalisme de la simulation," both of which appear in *L'Échange symbolique et la mort*.

13. *The Confessions of Saint-Augustine*, translated by E.B. Pusey, New York: Collier Books, 1961, p. 129.

14. *Ibid.*, pp. 129-130.

15. *Ibid.*, p. 131.

16. *Ibid.*, p. 128.

17. Charles Norris Cochrane, *Christianity and Classical Culture: A Study of Thought and Action from Augustus to Augustine*, Oxford: Oxford University Press, 1940. It was Cochrane's thesis that Augustine's development of the "trinitarian formulation" provides the "creative principle" for the imminent unification of Western experience that classical discourse had always sought for in vain.

18. St. Augustine, *The Trinity*, Washington: The Catholic University of America Press, 1963. Augustine's "trinity" fuses the abstract referents of knowing/willing/knowledge as co-relational predicates of each other. It's not that becoming is its own ground, as much as the opposite: the abstract referents of experience simulate the ground of unification to which concrete experience will be delivered. Augustine says, for example, "But in these three, when the mind knows itself and loves itself, a trinity remains: the mind, love, and knowledge; and there is no confusion through any comingling, although each is a substance in itself, and all are found mutually in all, whether each one in each two, or each two in each one. Consequently, all are in all." This is the metaphysical genesis of the simulacrum because the three *relations* in the trinity are *abstractions* from embodied experience. *The Trinity*, p. 227.

19. In *The Confessions*, Augustine emphasized the possibility of the "direct deliverance" of consciousness. "For I AM, and KNOW, and WILL; I AM KNOWING AND WILLING: and I KNOW myself to Be, and to WILL; and I WILL to BE, and to KNOW," p. 234.

20. St. Augustine, *The Trinity*, p. 483.

21.   The trinity provides an abstract unity for Western experience, a simulated coherency which is carried forward, on the side of sacrificial power, by the referents of beauty, truth, and goodness. This is also Nietzsche's combination of the will to virtue, the will to truth, and the will to judgement as the abstract coherency of the will to power.

22.   The abstract unity of Western experience traces an internal curvature in which the categories of existence refract one another: Augustine remarks that "the mind should know itself as it were in a mirror," *The Trinity*, p. 298.

23.   R. Barthes, *Critical Essays*, Evanston: Northwestern University Press, 1972, p. 242.

III. Sliding Signifiers

6.

1.   *A Lover's Discourse*, p. 31. All references to Barthes' work are from the English translations published by Hill & Wang.

2.   Critics such as Philip Thody in his *Roland Barthes: A Conservative Estimate*, Macmillan Press, London, 1977 stresses the importance in Barthes' work of the mask, of what Barthes refers to as *Larvatus prodeo*. (I advance pointing to my mask). To the extent that this reflects Barthes' concern the body itself disappears, yet we have Barthes' insistence that the critic treat the mask as the route to the body, not its end.

3.   Barthes takes over the concept of bliss(*Jouissance*) from Jacques Lacan though the sense being advanced here focuses on the metaphysical rather than psychological and marks Barthes' later separation from Lacan's thought.

4.   See Maurice Blanchot, *The Space of Literature,* translated by Ann Smock, University of Nebrask Press, 1982.

5. In an article on the Enlightenment I have tried to set out the suffocation of the imagination in the liberal tradition through a study of de Sade. See David Cook, "The Dark Side of Enlightenment", *CJPST*, Vol. V, No. 3.

6. *The Pleasure of the Text*, p. 57.

7. Annette Lavers begins her interesting and helpful study of Barthes with the profound misunderstanding of what is at issue philosophically by seeing the 'key' to Barthes in the 'tension' between the collective and the individual. Barthes' project is more ambitious in claiming to reconstitute the understanding of the individual and society. See *Roland Barthes: Structuralism and After*, Methuen, N.Y., 1982, p. 3.

8. One example among many being the prominence of *steak frite* to French life beyond its putative value as food.

9. *Mythologies*, p. 9.

10. While Barthes uses almost exclusively French examples, one can see a similar structure in, for example, English literature. To take one novel, Thackery's *Vanity Fair*, the author is conscious of the need to create the artifice of the conflict creation and resolution and openly says so in the novel. Miss Sharp's sudden marriage is announced as much for keeping the plot moving as anything else. The stated awareness of this technique ultimately will end this form of novel, or rather reduce it to our current 'soaps'.

11. Maxwell Smith among others in his *Roland Barthes*, TWAS no 614, 1981 has pointed out Barthes' late introduction to Saussure and his later movement away from semiology. This is consistent with the claim made here that Barthes' preoccupation was more fundamentally with the relation of power and meaning.

12. See Pamela McCallum, "Desire and History in Roland Barthes," *Canadian Journal of Political and Social Theory*, Vol. VI, No. 3, 1982.

13. Philip Thody remarks that Barthes took little or no active political involvement in the major political events in France from IndoChina right through to the Algerian crisis. See *Op. Cit.*, p. 48. See also Barthes's comments in *Le grain de la voix*, Paris: Editions du Seuil, 1981, p. 336.

14. Cf. J.P. Sartre, *What is Literature*.

15. The fascination of Barthes for this aspect of Sartre's thought expressed in Sartre's *The Psychology of Imagination* remains as witnessed by Barthes' dedication of *Camera Lucida* his last work to Sartre's *L'Imaginaire*.

16. *Writing Degree Zero*, pp. 93-94.

17. *Ibid.*, p. 45.

18. *Ibid.*, p. 46.

19. *Ibid.*, p. 35.

20. Albert Camus, *The Stranger*, Vintage Books, New York, 1946.

21. *Writing Degree Zero*, p. 83.

22. See Connor Cruise O'Brien, *Albert Camus*, Fontana, 1970.

23. See for example the collection of *Lyrical and Critical Essays* edited by Philip Thody, Vintage Books, New York, 1970.

24. "The Tour de France as Epic" in *The Eiffel Tower*, pp. 79-90.

25. I am, however, in agreement with Jonathan Culler's statement in his *Barthes*, Fontana Modern Masters, 1983, that Nature returns in Barthes' work in the concept of the body. (p. 120) Barthes failure to appreciate this leaves myths themselves always entrapped in doxa.

26. A similar turning away from the problem of economics is conspicuous in Barthes' treatment of Japan in *The Empire of Signs.*

27. *The Eiffel Tower*, p. 818. *Writing Degree Zero*, p. 26.

28. *Writing Degree Zero*, p. 26.

29. The form of Barthes' later writing also approaches the axiological. The text takes the form of 'definitions' which overdetermine the subject or provide the reader with the plenitude of meaning in the text. There is a parallel between this format and the desire to strike a new 'science' reminiscent of Hobbes' style.

30. *Roland Barthes*, p. 77.

31. *S/Z*, p. 88.

32. *Ibid.*, p. 88.

33. *Ibid.*, p. 90.

34. The will-to-power or possession finds its opposite in the non-will-to-possess described later. But even at this point the problem of 'possessive individualism' has been shifted from the realm of political economy described by C.B. Macpherson to a critique of political economy from the outside.

35. *S/Z*, p. 76.

36. See again the argument in "The Dark Side of Enlightenment" *Op. Cit.*, where the logic of deisres is traced to the social contract as a repressive institution and Barthes' comments in *Image, Music, Text*, pp. 76-77.

37. *Pleasure of the Text*, pp. 57-58. The remarks in parenthesis are Barthes'.

38. *Ibid.*, p. 61.

39. *Roland Barthes*, p. 112.

40. Julia Kristeva, "How Does One Speak to Literature" in *Desire in Language: A Semiotic Approach to Literature and Art*, p. 111.

41. *Pleasure of the Text*, p. 4.

42. *Ibid.*, p. 10.

43. *Ibid.*

44. *Ibid.*, p. 47.

45. *Roland Barthes*, p. 71.

46. *A Lover's Discourse*, p. 11.

47. *The Pleasure of the Text*, p. 13.

48. *Ibid.*, p. 3.

49. *Ibid.*, p. 14.

50. *Ibid.*, p. 30.

51. *Ibid.*, p. 16.

52. *Roland Barthes*, p. 147.

53. *The Pleasure of the Text*, p. 53.

54. *Roland Barthes*, pp. 132-33.

55. *The Pleasure of the Text*, p. 15.

56. See the final section of *A Lover's Discourse* entitled "Sobria Ebrietas" pp. 232-234.

57. The movement in Barthes' thought towards the Orient is marked most explicitly by his 1970 publication of *The Empire of Signs* translated into English in 1982. The work is striking in the repeated theme of silence and emptiness which opens up a space for the appearance of the individual. One example amongst many is the following taken from the section "Exemption from Meaning": 'All of Zen, of which the haiku is merely the literary branch, thus appears as an enormous praxis destined to halt language, to join that kind of internal radiophony continually sending in us, even in our sleep (perhaps this is the reason the apprentices are kept from falling asleep), to empty out, stupefy, to dry up the souls' incoercible babble; and perhaps what Zen calls satori, which Westerners can translate only be certain vaguely Christain words (illumination, relation, intuition), is no more than a panic suspension of language, the blank which erases in us the reign of the Codes, the breach of that internal recitation which constitutes our person, . . .' pp. 74-75.

58. *The Pleasure of the Text*, p. 48.

59. *Ibid.*

60. Barthes leaves the quote in the original without translation which has been followed by the translator Richard Miller. The quotation has been translated for me by Kenneth R. Bartlett of the Department of History, University of Toronto, as follows. "Then my mother conceived so much fear that she brought forth twins — both me and (my) fear at the same time". Annette Lavers speculates that this may also be reference to the theme of the erotic novel *Emmanuelle, Op. Cit.*

61. *Roland Barthes*, p. 188.

62. *Ibid.*, p. 131.

63. *Ibid.*

64. See J.P. Sarte, "Reply to Albert Camus", *Situations*, Fawcett Books, New York, 1966, p. 76.

65. *Camera Lucida*, pp. 106 and 107.

66. *Ibid.*, p. 78.

67. *Ibid.*, pp. 87-88.

68. *Ibid.*, p. 49.

7.

1. Immanuel Kant, *The Critique of Judgement*, translated by J.C. Meredith, London: Oxford University Press, 1952.

2. Martin Heidegger, *Kant and the Problem of Metaphysics*, Bloomington: Indiana University Press, 1962.

3. Immanuel Kant, *Kant's Political Writings*, edited H. Reiss, Cambridge: Cambridge University Press, 1977, p. 46.

4. *Ibid.*, p. 45.

5. Hans-Georg Gadamer, *Truth and Method*, New York: The Seabury Press, 1975. For a very interesting study of Gadamer, Arendt and Kant, see Ronald Beiner, *Political Judgement*, Chicago: University of Chicago Press, 1983.

6. Martin Heidegger, *The Basic Problems of Phenomenology*, Bloomington: Indiana University Press, 1982, pp. 131-132.

7. Immanuel Kant, *Groundwork for the Metaphysics of Morals,* New York: Harper Torch, 1964, p. 68.

8. Reiss, *op. cit.*, p. 42.

9. *Ibid.*, p. 54.

10. Hannah Arendt, *Lectures on Kant's Political Philosophy,* edited by Ronald Beiner, Chicago: University of Chicago Press, 1982, p. 54.

11. Hans Saner, *Kant's Political Philosophy,* Chicago: University of Chicago Press, 1978, p. 298.

12. Immanuel Kant, *On History*, Indianapolis: Bobbs-Merril, 1963, pp. 74-86.

IV. Postmodernism and the Death of the Social

8.

1. Jean Baudrillard, *In the Shadow of the Silent Majorities*, New York: Jean Baudrillard and Semiotext(e), 1983, pp. 3-4.

2. *Ibid.*, p. 6.

3. For Baudrillard's most explicit discussion of the simulacrum, see "L'hyperréalisme de la simulation," *L'Échange symbolique et la mort*, Paris: Editions Gallimard, 1976, pp. 110-117.

4. *Ibid.*, p. 68.

5. *Ibid.*, pp. 70-71

6. *Ibid.*, p. 71.

7. *Ibid.*, p. 73.

8. *Ibid.*, p. 77.

9. *Ibid.*, pp. 72-73.

10. *Ibid.*, pp. 82-83.

11. *Ibid.*, p. 83.

12. Baudrillard's refusal of the "perspectival space of the social" is aimed directly at Foucault's theorisation of the closed space of the "panoptic." Baudrillard's closing of the ring of signifier/signified or, what is the same, his theorisation of simulacra in conjunction with the structural law of value breaks directly with Habermas' hermeneutical interpretation of ideology. Against Habermas *and* Foucault, Baudrillard theorizes a non-representational and non-figurative *spatialized* universe. See particularly J. Baudrillard, "The Implosion of Meaning in the Media," as translated in *In the Shadow of the Silent Majorities*, pp. 95-110.

13. *Ibid.*, pp. 105-106.

14. *Ibid.*, p. 96.

15. *Ibid.*p. 107.

16. *Ibid.*, p. 108.

17. *Ibid.*

18. *Ibid.*, pp. 108-109.

19. *Ibid.*

20. *Ibid.*, p. 109.

21. *Ibid.*

22. For Baudrillard's most careful theorisation of the three orders of value, see particularly Chapter II, "L'Ordre des Simulacres" (pp. 75-128) and Chapter III, "La Mode ou la Féerie du Code" in *L'Echange symbolique et la mort*, pp. 129-151.

23. For an *excellent* account of the purely abstract character of the logic of signification, see Charles Levin, "Baudrillard, Critical Theory and Psychoanalysis," *Canadian Journal of Political and Social Theory*, Vol. 8, Nos. 1-2, (Winter, 1984).

24. As Marx says of the purely *cynical* existence of the commodity-form: "In this sense every commodity is a symbol, since, in so far as it has value, it is only the material envelope of the human labour spent upon it." Karl Marx, *Capital: A Critique of Political Economy (Volume I)*, Moscow: Progress Publishers, p. 92.

25. *Ibid.*, p. 92. "In proportion as exchange bursts its local bonds, and the value of commodities more and more expands into an embodiment of human labour in the abstract, in the same proportion the character of money attaches itself to commodities that are by Nature fitted to perform the social function of a universal equivalent."

26. F. Nietzsche, *The Will to Power*, translated by W. Kaufmann and R.J. Hollingdale, New York: Vintage Books, 1968, p. 276.

27. M. McLuhan, *Understanding Media: The Extensions of Man*, Toronto: McGraw-Hill, 1964, p. 56.

28. K. Marx, *Capital: A Critique of Political Economy*, Vol. 1, Book 1, translated by S. Moore and E. Aveling and edited by F. Engels, Moscow: Progress, 1954, p. 399.

29. F. Nietzsche. *The Will to Power*, p. 546.

30. *Ibid.*, p. 415.

31. G. Grant, *Time as History*, Toronto: Canadian Broadcasting Corporation, 1969, p. 47.

32. *Ibid.*, p. 35.

9.

1. Michel Serres, *Hermes:Literature, Science, Philosophy*, edited by J. Harari and D. Bell, Baltimore and London: The John Hopkins University Press, 1979.

2. Michel Serres, *Les cinq sens*, Paris: Grasset, 1985.

3. Umberto Eco, *Travels in Hyperreality*, New York: Harcourt Brace Jovanovich, 1986.

4. Jean Baudrillard, *The Mirror of Production*, St. Louis: Telos Press, 1975.

5. Rene Girard, *Violence and the Sacred*, Baltimore and London: The John Hopkins University Press, 1979.

6. Michel Serres, *Rome: le livre des fondations*, Paris: Grasset, 1983.

7. See Michel Serres, *Esthétiques sur Carpaccio*, Paris: Hermann, 1975.

8. J.P. Sartre, *Critique of Dialectical Reason*, London: New Left Books, 1979.

9. Albert Camus, "The Guest" in *The Fall and Exile and the Kingdom*, New York: The Modern Library, 1957.

10. Michel Serres, *The Parasite*, Baltimore and London: The John Hopkins University Press, 1982.

11. Thomas Pynchon, *V.*, New York: Bantam Books, 1963.

12. Thomas Pynchon, *The Crying of Lot 49*, New York, Bantam Books, 1966.

13. Jean Baudrillard, *Simulations*, New York: Semiotext(e), 1983.

14. Albert Camus, *The Rebel*, New York: Vintage Books, 1956.

10.

1. Michel Foucault, *The Order of Things* (London: Tavistock, 1966), p. 274. p. 274.

2. Jean Baudrillard, "Forgetting Foucault," *Humanities in Society*, 3:1 (Winter 1980), 87. Baudrillard begins with the important insight that Foucault's discourse, representing as it does a "mirror of the powers it describes," constitutes not a discourse of truth, "but a mythic discourse in the strong sense of the word."

3. Talcott Parsons, "Some Problems of General Theory in Sociology," in *Social Systems and the Evolution of Action Theory* (New York: The Free Press, 1977), pp. 229-69.

4. Talcott Parsons, "Social Structure and the Symbolic Media of Exchange," in *Social Systems and the Evolution of Action Theory*, pp. 204-28.

5. Michel Foucault, "Truth and Power," in Colin Gordon, ed., *Power/Knowledge* (New York: Pantheon, 1980), p. 114.

6. Karl Jaspers, *Kant* (New York: Harvest, 1962), p. 96.

7. *Ibid.*, p. 98.

8. Michel Foucault, "The Discourse on Language," in *The Archaeology of Knowledge* (New York: Harper Colophon, 1972), p. 217.

9. Michel Foucault, *The History of Sexuality. Volume I: An Introduction* (New York: Pantheon, 1978). p. 151.

10. See, in particular, G.W.F. Hegel, *The Phenomenology of Mind* (New York: Harper Colophon, 1967), pp. 207-13.

11. Emile Durkheim is perhaps the first modern theoretician of "normalization" and, for this reason, Parsons and Foucault commonly locate the "regulative" conception of power in his analysis of normativity.

12. Baudrillard, "Forgetting Foucault," p. 108.

13. Foucault, *The History of Sexuality*, p. 217.

14. An excellent description of the "will to will" is to be found in Michael A. Weinstein, "Lament and Utopia: Responses to American Empire in George Grant and Leopoldo Zea," *Canadian Journal of Political and Social Theory*, 5:3 (1981), 44-55.

15. For Parsons, freedom is a correlate of "institutionalized individualism." Advanced liberalism differs from the classical doctrine of liberalism by severing the question of freedom from its basis in "individual capacities" and, in turn, transforming freedom into a matter of "choices" within positive social organizations. A "relational" power also is aligned with a freedom that is dead.

16. Foucault, *The History of Sexuality*, p. 95.

17. Talcott Parsons "On the Concept of Political Power," in *Politics and Social Structure* (New York: The Free Press, 1969), p. 353. Parsons' theorization of a relational mode of power begins with this essay, which provides the basis for his later development of a complete theory of the "family of generalized, symbolic media" as the mediational points of advanced industrial societies.

18. An insightful, although overly sociological, collection of readings by and about Foucault's theorization of power is provided in Meaghan Morris and Paul Patton, eds., *Michel Foucault: Power, Truth, Strategy* (Sydney: Feral Publications, 1979). For an explicit discussion of Foucault's four refusals, see "Power and Norm: Notes."

19. Foucault, "Two Lectures," in *Power/Knowledge*, pp. 88-89.

20. *Michel Foucault: Power, Truth, Strategy*, p. 59.

21. Parsons, "The Relations between Biological and Socio-Cultural Theory," in *Social Systems and the Evolution of Action Theory*, p. 120.

22. Foucault, "Power and Norm: Notes," in *Michel Foucault: Power, Truth, Strategy*, p. 59.

23. Foucault, *The History of Sexuality*, p. 93.

24. *Ibid.*, p. 94.

25. Foucault writes in *The History of Sexuality*, p. 93: "The analysis, made in

terms of power, must not assume that the sovereignty of the state, the fear of the law, or the over-all unity of a domination are given at the outset: rather, these are only the terminal forms power takes." Foucault's meditation on a "relational" power is strikingly similar to William James's theorization of a "relational" consciousness. At a moment far earlier than Foucault or Parsons, James anticipated the decline of the "entitative" (Newtonian) model of the social universe and the emergence of a radical relationalism as the basis of epistemology, politics, and ontology.

26. Parsons, "On the Concept of Political Power," p. 353.

27. *Ibid.*

28. Parsons, *Social Systems and the Evolution of Action Theory*, pp. 204-28.

29. Parsons, *Politics and Social Structure*, pp. 356-59.

30. Foucault, *The History of Sexuality*, p. 137.

31. *Ibid.*

32. Parsons, *Politics and Social Structure*, pp. 387-95.

33. Foucault, *The History of Sexuality*, p. 86.

34. Parsons, *Politics and Social Structure*, pp. 365-66.

35. *Michel Foucault: Power, Truth, Strategy,* p. 60.

36. The "analytics" of Foucault and Parsons reflect their common deployment of a discursive rather than intuitive logic. Parsons says, in fact, that the logic of teleonomy is *nomic* rather than nomological. Nomic propositions imply a "putative necessity" in the domain of social relationships and are the epistemological sign of a "deductive-propositional" system of human action. Foucault also says that the power system appears in the form of a deductive-propositional system, and that we might best proceed nominal-istically, by naming the concrete expressions of power. Thus, while nomological thought is the analogue of the Newtonian sciences, nomic thought is the epistemological epicenter of the biological model.

37. Baudrillard, "Forgetting Foucault," p. 110.

38. *Ibid.*

39. *Ibid.*

40. For Parsons, the central element of institutionalized liberalism is that it is typified by the public morality of "instrumental activism." The public ethic of instrumental activism makes the maximization of the generalized symbolic media of exchange — money, power, influence, value-commitments — the "regulatory idea" of advanced liberal societies. This entails, of course, that the standards by which normalization is governed and its immanent value-principles are linked together as complementary aspects of the maximization of the transparent and relational media of exchange, these conditions of possibility, of modern society. In the discourse released by the "morality" of instrumental activism, there is now only an absence, a void, that seeks to be filled by any energizing content. I do not think that Foucault is mistaken when he says of structuralism that it evacuates the concept of its content, but he might also have remarked that the turn to this empty region of sign and signification is a reminder of the

death that inhabits, that pulsates from, the decentered surface of modern life.

41.   Or, as Foucault states:
Now, the study of this micro-physics presupposes that the power exercised on the body is conceived not as a property, but as a strategy, that its effects of nomination are attributed not to "appropriation," but to dispositions, manoeuvres, tactics, techniques, functionings; that one should decipher in it a network of relations, constantly in tension, in activity, rather than a privilege that one might possess. *Discipline and Punish: The Birth of a Prison*, trans. Alan Sheridan (New York: Pantheon, 1977), p. 26.

42.   Parsons, *Politics and Social Structure*, pp. 41-55.

43.   Parsons, *Social Systems and the Evolution of Action Theory*, pp. 366-88.

44.   *Michel Foucault: Power, Truth, Strategy*, p. 64. Foucault's basic essay on the unity of power/knowledge in a society of normalization is to be found in "The Carceral," in *Discipline and Punish*, pp. 293-8.

45.   *Michel Foucault: Power, Truth, Strategy*, p. 65.

46.   *Ibid.*, p. 36.

47.   Foucault, *The History of Sexuality*, p. 93.

48.   Parsons, *Social Systems and the Evolution of Action Theory*, p. 134.

49.   *Ibid.*, p. 133.

50.   For a full description, see Parsons, "The Relations between Biological and Socio-Cultural Theory," pp. 118-21.

51.   Parsons, *Social Systems and the Evolution of Action Theory*, pp. 110-11.

52.   For Parsons' most complete statement of this process, see "A Paradigm of the Human Condition" in *Action Theory and the Human Condition* (New York: The Free Press, 1978), pp. 352-433.

53.   Foucault, *The History of Sexuality*, p. 147.

54.   *Ibid.*

55.   *Michel Foucault: Power, Truth, Strategy*, p. 66.

56.   Parsons, *Social Systems and the Evolution of Action Theory*, p. 220

57.   *Power/Knowledge*, p. 52.

58.   Parsons, *Social Systems and the Evolution of Action Theory*, p. 120.

59.   Parsons, "Social Structure and the Symbolic Media of Interchange," in *Social Systems and the Evolution of Action Theory*, p. 207.

60.   Foucault and Parsons converge on the claim that "something like belongingness" is produced by the play of power. Parsons views belongingness as the attribute of "diffuse collective solidarities," while Foucault envisions it as the positive side, the reverse image, of the code of punishments typical of disciplinary power.

61.   Foucault, "The Confession of the Flesh," in *Power/Knowledge*, p. 198.

62.   Foucault, *The History of Sexuality*, p. 96.

63. Parsons' most significant, but also least noticed, theorization of a "relational" society is found in *Action Theory and the Human Condition*. In this collection of essays, Parsons traces out fully the implications of the theory of the symbolic media of interchange for such newly appropriated regions as health, disease, intelligence, and affect. Always, the movement is against a representational logic and toward a "symbolic" understanding of the play of modern power. In *Discipline and Punish*, Foucault also notes this extension of the *nomos* of a symbolic power saying that now punishment is not of a different order from education and health.

64. Parsons, "The Professional Complex," in *Action Theory and the Human Condition*, pp. 40-45. Parsons' analysis of the "professional complex" is convergent with many of the assumptions behind Alvin Gouldner's reflections on the "new class." Parsons views the professional class as the ascendant class in advanced industrial societies. This is a new social class that is drawn together by its common foundations in theoretical knowledge, fiduciary responsibility, specialized competence, technical solidarity, and the use of symbolic capital. The development of the "professional complex" is the organizational expression of Foucault's normalizing society.

65. Parsons, "The University Bundle," in Action *Theory and the Human Condition*, p. 136.

66. *Michel Foucault: Power, Truth, Strategy*, p. 66.

67. Michel Foucault, "Panopticism," in *Discipline and Punish*, pp. 195-228; and "The Eye of Power," in *Power/Knowledge*, pp. 147-65.

68. Octavio Paz, "The Prisoner (Homage to D.A.F. DeSade)," *Early Poems 1935-1955* (Bloomington: Indiana University Press, 1973).

V. Ultramodernism

11.1.

1. For an excellent photographic reproduction and commentary on Francesca Woodman's vision, see *Francesca Woodman: photographic work*, Wellseley College Museum and Hunter College Art Gallery, 1986; and Abigail Solomon-Godeau, "Photography: Our Bodies/Our Icons", *Vogue*, February, 1986, p. 98.

2. Michel Foucault, *Discipline and Punish: The Birth of the Prison*, New York: Pantheon, 1977, p. 138.

11.3.

1. Max Horkheimer and Theodor W. Adorno, *Dialectic of Enlightenment*, New York: Herder and Herder, 1972, p. 3.

2. *Ibid.*, p. xi.

3. Max Horkheimer, *Dawn and Decline: Notes 1926-1931 and 1950-1969*, New York: The Seabury Press, 1978, p. 181.

4. *Dialectic of Enlightenment*, p. 16.

5. *Ibid.*, p. xiii.

6. Thus, for example: "With the extension of the bourgeois commodity economy, the dark horizon of myth is illumined by the sun of calculating reason, beneath whose cold rays the seed of the new barbarism grows to fruition. Under the pressure of domination human labour has always led away from myth — but under domination always returns to the jurisdiction of myth." *Dialectic of Enlightenment*, p. 32.

7. Peter Sloterdijk, *Kritik der zynischen Vernunft*, Frankfurt/Main Suhrkamp Verlag, Neue Folge, Band 99, 1983.

8. It's the very same with Habermas' rationalist subordination of Foucault's theory of power. See particularly, Jurgen Habermas, "The Genealogical Writing of History: On Some Aporias in Foucault's Theory of Power", *Canadian Journal of Political and Social Theory*, Vol. X, Nos. 1-2, 1986, pp. 1-9.

9. Jurgen Habermas, "The Entwinement of Myth and Enlightenment: Re-Reading *Dialectic of Enlightenment*", *New German Critique*, No. 26, Spring/Summer 1982, pp. 13-30.

10. *Ibid.*, p. 3.

11. Franz Neumann, *The Democratic and Authoritarian State: Essays in Political and Legal Theory*, Glencoe: Free Press, 1957, pp. 270-300.

12. Jurgen Habermas, "The Entwinement of Myth and Enlightenment: Re-Reading *Dialectic of Enlightenment*", pp. 27-30.

13. *Ibid.*, p. 29.

14. *Ibid.*

15. F. Nietzsche, *Beyond Good and Evil, Basic Writings of Nietzsche*, translated and edited by Walter Kaufmann, New York: Modern Library, 1968, p. 236.

16. The chapter on "Juliette or Enlightenment and Morality" ends with these words: " 'Where do your greatest dangers lie?' was the question Nietzsche once posed himself, and answered thus: 'In compassion.' With this denial he redeemed the unshakable confidence in man that is constantly betrayed by every form of assurance that seeks only to console." *Dialect of Enlightenement*, p. 119.

17. *Ibid.*, p. 256.

18. Jürgen Habermas, *The Theory of Communicative Action: Reason and the Rationalization of Society*, Boston: Beacon Press, 1984.

19. Ironically, the most complete social theory of the "structural paradigm" as the locus of advanced modern societies has been provided by Talcott Parsons. Just because he had no commitment to preserving 'reason', Parsons was freed to theorize the purely structural language at the basis of the relational power-system of late modern societies. This is to indicate, of course, that Parsons, not Habermas, is the theorist *par excellence* of post-

modern society.

20. F. Nietzsche, *The Gay Science*, aphorism 125, *Basic Writings of Nietzsche*, New York: Modern Library, 1968.

21. Jürgen Habermas, "The Genealogical Writing of History: On Some Aporias in Foucault's Theory of Power", p. 8.

11.4.

1. Theodor W. Adorno, *Against Epistemology: A Metacritique (Studies in Husserl and the Phenomenological Antinomies)*, Cambridge: The MIT Press, 1984. Unless otherwise indicated, all quotations are from this text.

11.5.

1. In May 1985, *Exposition Vidéo*, a presentation and interpretative analysis of video in relation to television (and society) was held under the auspices of Vidéographe/G.R.A.A.V (conservateur: Jean Gagnon) in Montréal.

2. Werner B. Korte, *ABT-EMPIRICA*, research summary of a report prepared for the West German Federal Ministry of Internal Affairs on the "effects of new information and communication techniques on the arts and culture".

3. *Ibid.*, p. 19.

4. Guy Debord, *Society of the Spectacle*, Detroit: Black and Red, 1983, theses 29 and 30.

5. Jean Baudrillard, "The Ecstacy of Communication" in *The Anti-Aesthetic: Essays on Postmodern Culture*, edited by Hal Foster, Port Townsend: Bay Press Books, 1983.

6. Jean-Paul Sartre, *Critique of Dialectical Reason: Theory of Pracial Ensembles* (1) London: Verso/NLB, 1982, pp. 271-276.

7. *Ibid.*, pp. 275-295.

8. *Ibid.*, p. 271.

9. *Ibid.*, p. 274.

10. *Ibid.*, p. 271.

11. For a brilliant account of the culture of signification, see Jean Baudrillard, *In the Shadow of the Silent Majorities*, trans. by Paul Foss, Paul Patton and John Johnston, *Semiotexte*, New York: Foreign Agents Series, 1983.

12. Debord, thesis 34.

13. "Television Looks at Itself: Proprietary Thoughts on the Future of Prime Time", *Harper's*, March 1985, pp. 39-49.

14. *Ibid.*, p. 47.

15. *Ibid.*

16. James Atlas, "Beyond Demographics", *The Atlantic*, vol. 254, no. 4, pp. 49-58.

11.6.

1. Max Horkheimer and Theodor Adorno, *Dialectic of Enlightenment,* New York: Herder and Herder, 1972, p. 167.

2. Eric Fischl, "I will not be subjective. I will not think bad thoughts", *Parkett*, no. 5, 1985, pp. 31-45.

3. Jean Baudrillard, "The Ecstacy of Communication", in H. Foster (editor), *The Anti-Aesthetic: Essays on Postmodern Culture*, Port Townsend, Washington: Bay Press, 1983, pp. 126-127.

4. Robert Bellah, *et. al., Habits of the Heart,* New York: Harper and Row, 1986.

5. Michel Foucault, "Preface to Transgression," in Donald F. Bouchard, *Language, Counter-Memory, Practice: Selected Essays and Interviews,* Ithaca, New York: Cornell University Press, 1977, pp. 29-52.

6. See David Burnett, *Colville*, Toronto: McClelland and Steward, 1983, p. 219.